THE WARS OF THE BRUCES

For Dorothy

THE WARS OF THE BRUCES

Scotland, England and Ireland 1306–1328

Colm McNamee

TUCKWELL PRESS

First published in 1997 by
Tuckwell Press Ltd
The Mill House
Phantassie
East Linton
East Lothian EH40 3DG
Scotland

ISBN 1 898410 92 5

British Library Cataloguing-in-Publication Data
A Catalogue record for this book
is available on request from the
British Library

Typeset by Hewer Text Composition Services, Edinburgh
Printed and bound by Cromwell Press, Melksham, Wiltshire

Contents

Preface

This is a study of war and society in the British Isles. It began life as an Oxford D.Phil on the effects of Scottish raids on northern England, but since its completion in 1989 the following changes have been incorporated: a synthesis of recent research on the war in Scotland; additional sections on other theatres of war, namely Ireland, and the war in the North and Irish seas; and some consideration of the wider implications of the Wars of the Bruces, for England and Ireland as well as Scotland, as a phase in the political development of the British Isles. The emphasis on the wider implications of the war is justified by the fact that the vast bulk of the archive material relating to the war emanates from the English royal government which was unable to operate in Scotland from 1311.

My approach is to examine the Wars of the Bruces as a whole, to consider relationships between the various theatres of war and to take into account economic, social and geographical constraints and motivation. The effects of the Wars outside Scotland have never been systematically examined; but an excellent start was made in the transcending of national histories in Dr. Sean Duffy's 1991 article 'The Bruce Brothers and the Irish Sea World, 1306–29', in *Cambridge Medieval Celtic Studies* xxi (1991), 55–86. Endeavouring, however, to maintain a strong narrative thread and to keep the text comprehensible to the non-specialist, I have found it necessary to devote separate chapters to various theatres of war. I have striven to maintain a balance between integration and clarity. There is one theatre of conflict which I have not covered, namely the diplomatic wrangles at the French and papal courts. Lacking familiarity with the sources and finding it adequately covered in existing works, I have left the further elucidation of this aspect to other writers. I would venture to say that as a study of war and society in the British Isles, the present work has not suffered markedly from the omission.

The Anglo-Scottish wars of 1306 to 1328 have tended to be written of principally in terms of biographies of the major characters. Robert I, Edward I and the English earls of Pembroke and Lancaster have all been the subject of great biographies, and a biography of Edward II is forthcoming. To these the present work is heavily indebted; and as the title suggests, I have found it undesirable to suppress the role of the personalities. This book is a drawing together of the work of many scholars: Duncan and Barrow, Phillips and Maddicott, Prestwich and Fryde, Lydon and Duffy, to name only the main authorities. My debt to them will be readily apparent to the reader.

Furthermore, the writing of this book has been greatly facilitated by the appearance in recent years of several major contributions to the history of the period; these include the supplementary volume to Bain's *Calendar of Documents Relating to Scotland*; Duncan's edition of the *actae* of Robert I, published as the fifth volume of the *Regesta Regum Scottorum*; Prestwich's biography of Edward I and Barrow's revised edition of *Robert Bruce and the Community of the Realm of Scotland*; and finally, the new edition of Barbour's *Bruce*.

I have tried to make the history as comprehensible to as many readers as possible by reducing technical terms to a bare minimum, referring to translations of the narrative sources where possible, and using the more familiar forms of place and personal names (hence MacDowell rather than MacDoual, Harclay rather than de Harcla, and Larne rather than Ulfreksfiord). I strayed from this general rule in the case of Gaelic Irish forms, where I have abided by the usage of the *New History of Ireland*.

Manuscript references are to documents held in the Public Record Office, London, unless some other record repository is specified.

Acknowledgements

Professor A.A.M. Duncan of the University of Glasgow was the prime mover behind this present work. He wrote to me in September 1995 encouraging me to publish my doctoral thesis. He has read draft chapters and has made many invaluable suggestions and comments. I think Professor Duncan had in mind a book very different to this when he first wrote to me, and I hope he finds no cause to regret his encouragement. Dr. David Ditchburn of the University of Aberdeen has been extremely helpful. He very kindly obtained material to which I would not otherwise have had access, and read and commented on a draft chapter. Dr. John Maddicott of Exeter College, Oxford, supervised the original thesis, and Mr. James Campbell advised and commented on the same. I am very grateful to both.

At the Queen's University of Belfast, Professor Bruce Campbell made available to me information from *Inquisitiones Post Mortem* contained in his Pre-Black Death Database; Dr Kay Muir and her team at the Ulster Placenames Project advised on problems relating to Irish placenames and personal names; Dr. Judith Green and Dr. Marie Thérèse Flanagan provided advice and encouragement. In a very real way Anthony Sheehan made it possible for me to write this book by providing access to wordprocessing facilities and by finding solutions to innumerable technical problems. Dr. Janette Lee provided similar assistance in the production of maps. Anthony and Estelle Sheehan very kindly assisted with translation of several awkward passages of Latin.

I acknowledge the assistance of the Department of Education for Northern Ireland who awarded a Major State Studentship (1982–1985); and the Institute of Irish Studies at Queen's University Belfast, where I was Junior Research Fellow (1990–1991).

I am also very grateful to the following who helped in various ways: Professor David Harkness, Dr. Mary O'Dowd, Paula Gibson and John and Gerard McNamee. Above all I thank my wife, who has supported me during the writing of the present work and to whom this book is dedicated.

For any mistakes which this book may contain the responsibility is entirely my own.

List of Maps and Charts

Abbreviations

AA	*Archaeologia Aeliana*
BAR	Bursar's Account Rolls
Barbour, *The Bruce*	*Barbour's Bruce*, ed. M.P. McDiarmid and J.A.C. Stevenson (3 vols.) (Scottish Text Society, 4th series, 1980–85)
Barrow, *Robert Bruce*	G.W.S. Barrow, *Robert Bruce and the Community of the Realm of Scotland* (Third Edition, London, 1988)
Bower	*Scotichronicon by Walter Bower*, ed. D.E.R. Watt (1989–91) (Vol. 6) (Books XI and XII)
BL	British Library
Bridlington	*Chronicles of the Reigns of Edward I and Edward II*, ed. W. Stubbs, ii, Gesta Edwardi de Carnarvon Auctore Canonico Bridlingtoniensi (R.S., 1882–3)
CChR	*Calendar of Charter Rolls*
CCR	*Calendar of Close Rolls*
CCW	*Calendar of Chancery Warrants*
CDI	*Calendar of Documents Relating to Ireland*, ed. H.S. Sweetman (5 vols.) (London, 1875)
CDS	*Calendar of Documents Relating to Scotland* (5 vols.), vols. i–iv ed. J. Bain, 1881–88; vol. v (Supplementary) ed. G.C. Simpson and J.D. Galbraith (Scottish Record Office, 1988)
Chart. St. Mary's Dublin	*Chartulary of St. Mary's, Dublin*, ed. J.T. Gilbert (2 vols.) (R.S., 1884)
CIM	*Calendar of Inquisitions Miscellaneous*
Clyn	*The Annals of Ireland by Friar John Clyn and Thady Dowling*, ed. R. Butler (Dublin, 1849).
CPR	*Calendar of Patent Rolls*
CWAAS	*Cumberland and Westmorland Archaeological and Antiquarian Society*
DCD	Muniments of the Dean and Chapter, Durham
Duffy, 'Bruce Brothers'	S. Duffy, 'The Bruce Brothers and The Irish Sea World, 1306–29', Cambridge Medieval Celtic Studies xxi (1991), 55–86
EcHR	*Economic History Review*
EHR	*English Historical Review*
Farrer, *Lancashire Inquests*	*Lancashire Inquests, Extents and Feudal Aids, Part II* 1310–1323, ed. W. Farrer (Lancashire and Cheshire Record Society LIV, 1907)
Flores Hist.	*Flores Historiarum*, ed. H.R. Luard, iii (R.S., 1890)
Foedera	*Rymer's Foedera* (Record Commission, 1816)

Fordun	*John of Fordun's Chronicle of the Scottish Nation*, ed. W.F. Skene (The Historians of Scotland Vol. IV, Edinburgh, 1872)
Fraser, *Ancient Petitions*	*Ancient Petitions Relating to Northumberland*, ed. C.M. Fraser (Surtees Society clxxvi, 1966)
Fraser, *Northern Petitions*	*Northern Petitions*, ed. C.M. Fraser (Surtees Society cxciv, 1981)
Fryde, *Tyranny and Fall*	N.Fryde, *The Tyranny and Fall of Edward II* (Cambridge, 1979).
Guisborough	*The Chronicle of Walter of Guisborough*, ed. H. Rothwell (Camden 3rd series lxxxix, 1957)
Hist. Mun. Docs.	*Historical and Municipal Documents of Ireland, 1172–1320*, ed. J.T. Gilbert (R.S., 1870)
IHS	*Irish Historical Studies*
Lanercost	*The Chronicle of Lanercost*, ed. and translated H. Maxwell (Glasgow, 1913)
Le Bel	*Jehan le Bel: Les Vrayes Chroniques*, ed. M.L. Polain, i (Brussels, 1863)
Liber Quot.	*Liber Quotidianus Contrarotulatoris Garderobae*, ed. J. Nichols (Society of Antiquaries, 1787)
Maddicott, *Lancaster*	J.R. Maddicott, *Thomas of Lancaster* (Oxford, 1970)
Melsa	*Chronica Monasteria de Melsa*, ed. E.A. Bond, ii (R.S., 1867)
MC	Miscellaneous Charters
NHI	*A New History of Ireland*, Vol. ii *Medieval Ireland, 1169–1534*, ed. A. Cosgrove (Oxford, 1987)
NAI	National Archives of Ireland
NCH	*A History of Northumberland* (15 vols.) (Northumberland County History Committee, Newcastle upon Tyne, 1893–1940)
NH	*Northern History*
P&P	*Past and Present*
Parl. Writs	*Parliamentary Writs and Writs of Military Summons*, ed. F. Palgrave (Record Commission, London, 1827)
Phillips, *Aymer de Valence*	J.R.S. Phillips, *Aymer de Valence, Earl of Pembroke, 1307–1324* (Oxford, 1972)
Phillips, *'Documents'*	J.R.S. Phillips, 'Documents on the Early Stages of the Bruce Invasion of Ireland, 1315–1316' *PRIA*, lxxix, c (1979), 247–70
Pluscarden	*The Book of Pluscarden*, ed. F.J.H. Skene (The Historians of Scotland, Vol. X, Edinburgh, 1880)
Powicke, *Military Obligation*	Powicke, M., *Military Obligation in Medieval England* (Oxford, 1962)
PRIA	*Proceedings of the Royal Irish Academy*
PRO	Public Record Office (Chancery Lane, London)
PRONI	Public Record Office of Northern Ireland
Prestwich, *Edward I*	M. Prestwich, *Edward I* (London, 1988)
Raine, *Scriptores Tres*	*Historiae Dunelmensis Scriptores Tres*, ed. J. Raine (Surtees Society ix, 1839)

Reg. Halton	*The Register of John de Halton, Bishop of Carlisle, 1292–1324,* ed. W.N. Thompson (2 vols.) (Canterbury and York Society, 1913)
Reg. Greenfield	*The Register of William Greenfield, Lord Archbishop of York, 1306–1315,* ed. A.H. Hamilton Thompson and W. Brown (5 vols.) (Surtees Society, 1931–40)
Reg. Melton	*The Register of William Melton 1317–40,* ed. R.M. T. Hill and D. Robinson (3 vols.) (Canterbury and York Society, 1977–88)
Rot. Scot.	*Rotuli Scotiae* (2 vols.) (Record Commission, 1841)
Rot. Parl.	*Rotuli Parliamentorum, 1272–1326,* ed. J. Strachey *et al* (London, 1767)
RPD	*Registrum Palatinum Dunelmense; the Register of Richard de Kellawe,* ed. T.D. Hardy (4 vols.) (R.S., 1873–78)
RRS	*Regesta Regum Scottorum*
R.S.	Rolls Series
Sayles, *Affairs of Ireland*	*Documents on the Affairs of Ireland before the King's Council,* ed. G.O. Sayles (Irish Manuscripts Commission, Dublin, 1979)
Scalacronica	*Scalacronica,* ed. and transl. H. Maxwell (Glasgow, 1907)
Scammell, 'Robert I'	J. Scammell, 'Robert I and the North of England', *EHR* lxxiii (1958), 385–403
SHR	*Scottish Historical Review*
Summerson, *Medieval Carlisle*	H. Summerson, *Medieval Carlisle: the city and the borders from the late eleventh to the mid sixteenth century,* i (CWAAS Extra series xxv, 1993)
TDGNHAS	*Transactions of the Dumfriesshire and Galloway Natural History and Antiquarian Society*
TRHS	*Transactions of the Royal Historical Scoiety*
Trokelowe	*Johannis de Trokelowe et Henrici de Blaneforde Chronica et Annales,* ed. H.T. Riley (R.S., 1866)
VCH	*Victoria County History*
Vita Edwardi II	*Vita Edwardi Secundi,* ed. N. Denholm Young (London, 1957)
Walsingham	*Thomas Walsingham, Historia Anglicana,* ed. H.T. Riley, i (R.S. *1863)*

Illustrations

Lordship and Nationality in the British Isles in the Early Fourteenth Century

L ate in the summer of 1306 the English King's vassals smashed their way with siege engines into Dunaverty Castle on the west coast of Scotland,[1] only to find that their quarry, Robert Bruce, self-proclaimed King of Scots, had taken flight for Ireland over the perilous western sea. But though he had escaped with his life, it seemed he had lost all else. Within months of a makeshift enthronement he had been routed in battle; his leading supporters hanged or imprisoned; his wife and sisters sent as captives to Edward I of England. His bid to revive the kingship of Scotland lay in ruins; and with it the prospects for a Scottish kingdom independent of England. But only the man who loses everything is free to make a new beginning, and therein lay the saving grace of his situation.

Robert's flight from the clutches of Edward I makes a poignant vignette, for which his verse biographer borrows a selection of epithets from Virgil: the strong swell, the swift current, the high waves. Another source describes Robert as 'another Aeneas, fleeing alone from the captivity of Troy'; and a third sets his solitude starkly against the great emptiness:

> . . . the aforesaid king was cut off from his men and underwent endless woes, and was tossed in dangers untold, being attended at times by three followers, at times by two; and more often he was left utterly alone without help. Now passing a whole fortnight without food of any kind to live upon but raw herbs and water; now walking barefoot; when his shoes became old and worn out; now left alone in the islands; now alone fleeing before his enemies; now slighted by his servants, he abode in loneliness.[2]

Robert's island odyssey has excited curiosity out of all proportion to its historical importance. Rathlin, Orkney, Norway and the Hebrides have all been suggested as his possible places of refuge.[3] The passionate interest in the fugitive king 'going on foot through the mountains and from isle to isle'[4] endures because Robert in that moment has seemed to embody the identity of the Scottish nation, as Aeneas was thought to embody that of Rome. In abandoning his homeland, Robert becomes free to abandon dependence upon conventional sources of strength. Henceforth the success of his cause appears to depend not upon the usual sinews of war: gold and iron; but upon intangible qualities and resources: time and space; tradition and patriotism; loyalty, revenge, and his own inspired leadership. In some versions of the story the direction of his flight has an added significance, in that Robert carries in his own person the identity of the Scottish nation from danger of extinction at home to safety in the legendary Irish homeland of the Scots. In the imagination of generations his escape to the west has appeared as an appeal from a brutal feudal present to an heroic, archaic past in an uneven struggle against the most powerful of medieval kingdoms. The voyage mends Robert's personal fortune, and also redeems the Scottish nation. It is a nadir which marked the beginning of a personal and national recovery unparalleled in the history of these islands.

APPROACHING THE WARS OF THE BRUCES

The wars of Robert and Edward Bruce have an obvious importance in historical terms. They embrace much more than seizure of kingship by Robert Bruce – Robert I as he is properly known to history. They constitute a unique episode in the history of the British Isles, during which England's hegemony, so vigorously established by Edward I, was dramatically overturned. Robert returned to Scotland, drove out the English and succeeded in winning the support of the Scottish aristocracy and in identifying his own cause with that of Scottish independence. The war thus unleashed spilled far beyond the borders of Scotland. Robert mounted successive and devastating raids on the north of England; and at Bannockburn he inflicted on the English their greatest defeat since Hastings. His depredations in northern England are well documented (much more so than the ravages of civil and patriotic war in Scotland). For the best part of a decade he held one fifth of the kingdom of England in tribute. And while Robert conspired with disaffected English aristocrats, and sought overseas alliances to isolate England, Edward his equally ambitious brother invaded Ireland, was acclaimed king of that country and occupied Ulster for three years. Even in Wales the Bruces threatened the hitherto unchallenged ascendancy of the English, raiding Anglesey and threatening to stir up general revolt. As never before, and seldom since, the political development of these islands was 'in the melting pot'.

This is of course Scotland's heroic age; and from earliest times it has never wanted for storytellers. From the later fourteenth century there survives the most remarkable narrative of these events, an alliterative poem of 13,000 lines of rhyming couplets written in 1375 by John Barbour and entitled *The Bruce*.[5] Barbour celebrates the life of the hero king, the epic quality of events, the high deeds of great men. He revels in the telling of dramatic episodes: the 'Great Cause', an international tribunal as to who was the rightful King of Scots; the terrorising of Scotland by the garrisons of Edward I, England's brilliant and aggressive king; the murder by Bruce of 'the Red Comyn', his leading rival; and the grand *dénouement* of the battle of Bannockburn. It is courtroom drama, historical romance and murder mystery combined, and with battle sequences on the scale of a Hollywood epic. Like present-day screenwriters and authors of historical fiction, Barbour gloried in the romance and pageantry, the noble and chivalric aspects of the conflict. The social and economic effects of the conflict did not of course concern him; and even down to the present, historians have tended to neglect these dimensions, in favour of biographies of the principal characters involved in the conflict. Excellent biographies of Robert Bruce and Edward I dominate the recent historiography.[6] This book is intended to focus upon the relationship between war and society; yet it is impossible to ignore the roles of personalities, for the whole period derives its identity from the ambitions and designs of Robert and Edward Bruce and their opponents. It seems only just to call these years of the Scottish Wars of Independence the *Wars of the Bruces*; for they were inflicted on the British Isles by the consuming ambitions of the Bruce brothers, in reaction to the aggressive expansionism of English kings.

Nevertheless the jealous documentation of the English king's revenues places in context the actions of individuals; and, in England at least, allows us some grasp of the material and human costs of war, in terms of harvests ruined, barns destroyed and cattle driven off. Financial accounts of manors 'in the king's hand' afford occasional glimpses of tides of refugees; of banditry flourishing in the wake of war; and of the activities of scavengers, speculators and opportunists for whom war to the death provided a way of life. Administrative records also reveal many details of how military science was developing. Despite the central importance of a few setpiece battles, this was not on the whole a war of contests between serried ranks of armoured knights, but a barbarous affair of mounted raids on civilian populations.

Since they were so much wider than other Anglo-Scottish conflicts, the Wars of the Bruces belong properly to the history of the whole of the British Isles.[7] To writers of 'national' history an overall understanding of the conflict will remain elusive; it demands rather an integrated approach, spanning the whole of the archipelago. Reliance on the archive of the English monarchy for documentary sources is unavoidable; but an Anglocentric interpretation of documents and events will distort any understanding of relationships. The war in Scotland has been the subject of intensive study.[8] But the narrative of war from 1314 is dominated by spectacular devastating raids into England by Robert's lieutenants, Thomas Randolph and James Douglas; and historians of England have abandoned the north of England at this period, much as the English government of the time abandoned it.[9] To historians of Ireland the Bruce invasion provides an unusual distraction from the long-term decline of the Anglo-Norman colony.[10] But until recently events in Ireland had been studied largely in isolation from the war in Britain and this cannot be right. Robert I intervened personally in Ireland on at least four separate occasions, and apparently considered Irish affairs integral to the success of his struggle. Other theatres of war too require to be integrated into an overall picture: bitter struggles took place in the Isle of Man and on the Irish Sea; on the North Sea the Scots found allies in the Flemish and German traders; and an equally furious battle for influence was waged in diplomatic terms at papal and French courts.

LOCAL AND EUROPEAN CONTEXTS

The need for a cross-national approach is evident from the family background of the Bruces and from their position in local society. The *de Brus* lords of Annandale were an Anglo-Norman aristocratic dynasty, one of many encouraged to settle in Scotland by the Scottish kings of the twelfth century in order that they might provide knights in support of the monarchy.[11] Robert the first of the name came from Brix in the Cotentin peninsula. For services to King Henry I of England this Robert was granted Cleveland in Yorkshire; and he also received a grant of Annandale from King David I of Scotland. The Bruces had therefore been established in Scotland for two hundred years before Robert Bruce, the seventh of the name, seized the throne.[12] Annandale was adjacent to Gaelic-speaking Galloway, and the grant of Annandale to the Bruce lords had been intended to strengthen that march against incursion by Gaelic lords. But as often happens on a frontier between warring cultures, each side began to adopt some of the customs and traditions of the other. Over time the Bruces developed associations with the native Gaelic aristocracy.[13] Robert Bruce the sixth, the father of the future king, married the daughter of the last Gaelic earl of Carrick. Marjory, the mother of Robert I, was therefore a scion of Gaelic rather than Anglo-Norman aristocracy. The family may have adopted some Gaelic social customs. In particular, the children may have been fostered in the households of Gaelic aristocrats for training in social graces. Barbour mentions Robert's foster brother; another source suggests that Edward Bruce was also fostered with a Gaelic lord.[14] Associations with their peers of 'Anglo-Norman' origin were probably of greater importance to the Bruces. Among their traditional allies were their neighbours on the western seaboard, the hereditary Stewarts of Scotland, and their neighbours across the North Channel, the de Burgh Earls of Ulster.[15] The Bruces also continued to hold lands in England to a rather greater extent than any of their Scottish peers, namely the manors of Tottenham near London, Writtle in Essex and Hart in what was then the Bishopric (now the county) of Durham.[16]

In cultural terms the Bruce Lords of Annandale remained very much a part of the chivalric, aristocratic and largely francophone *milieu* of medieval Christendom that was in many respects enjoying its heyday in the late thirteenth century. The great enterprise of Christendom, crusade against the infidel, was only just beginning to flag. Robert Bruce the fifth had accompanied Edmund, brother of Edward I, on his expedition to the Holy Land.[17] Philip the Fair, the autocratic King of France, was able to arrange for the dissolution of the Knights Templar at the Council of Vienne in 1311. Popes, broadly recognised as the leaders of Christendom, still strove to assert the supremacy of their spiritual authority over that of kings. Edward I clashed repeatedly with Boniface VIII on issues touching his authority; but the removal of the papal court into the shadow of the French king at Avignon by 1316 indicates that the emphasis was now on accommodation rather than confrontation with secular powers. Knighthood remained the aspiration of *gentil* classes, even if they now occasionally deferred the honour to avoid costly and irksome social duties with which it was associated.[18] Pride was taken in the display of armorial devices. The 'Song of Caerlaverock' describes the colourful heraldic devices borne by knights and squires who followed Edward I on campaign in 1300; the drinking cup known as the Bannatyne mazer preserves the armorial bearings of Scottish aristocrats.[19] Tournaments were much in vogue, providing opportunities for displays of martial valour, pretexts for factional fighting and frequently some looting of the surrounding countryside.[20] Arthurian literature and pageant were in fashion; Edward I was a great enthusiast, and twice held 'Round Tables' to entertain his court.[21] Right across Europe Latin prevailed as the language of 'official' documents, while French was the language which nobles had in common, even if it was not spoken in everyday life in Scotland or Ireland. This francophone aristocratic culture is generally labelled 'Anglo-Norman', in recognition of its eleventh-century origin in the Norman conquests. By the fourteenth century, this aristocracy had almost nothing to do with Normandy; but the anachronistic term is tolerated as it serves to distinguish the broadly similar English, Anglo-Scottish and Anglo-Irish culture from the distinctive aristocratic cultures of Gaelic Scotland and Ireland and Wales.

LORDSHIP, KINGSHIP AND GOVERNMENT AT THE END OF THE THIRTEENTH CENTURY

Whether in the Hebrides or the midland shires of England, early fourteenth-century lords competed bitterly with neighbours and peers for prestige and territory, in courts of law or in combat, and often in both simultaneously. They also sought alliance with families of similar standing in an effort to gain security for themselves and advantage over rivals. Marriage was one of the chief means of cementing such alliances. The family connections of one lord deeply involved in the Bruce Wars may be used to illustrate the web of aristocratic relationships which bound together lordly interests far distant in geographic terms. Richard de Burgh, Red Earl of Ulster, married his eldest daughter Elizabeth in 1304 to Robert Bruce, the future king, then Earl of Carrick and already a widower and father of a daughter. Earl Richard's sister Gelis was married to James the hereditary Stewart of Scotland, Bruce's traditional ally and neighbour. The Red Earl's second daughter, Matilda, was married to Gilbert de Clare, Earl of Gloucester and lord of Kilkenny; and his second son was married to Gilbert's sister. Other children of the Red Earl were married into important Anglo-Irish families: Catherine married Maurice fitz Thomas (later Earl of Desmond); Joan married Thomas fitz John (later Earl of Kildare); and Aveline married John de Bermingham, later to become Earl of Louth. Richard's fourth son Edmund married a daughter of Turlough Ó Briain, Gaelic Irish king of Thomond; while his youngest daughter Alicia married a lord of the English west march, Sir Thomas de Multon. Thus the children of the Red Earl brought him allies right across the British Isles.[22] While it was quite rare for one lord to build such a variety of wide-ranging connections, transmarine and cross-cultural marriages were not uncommon. These alliances could bear fruit of a material kind. In 1286 the Red Earl and another Irish magnate, Thomas de Clare, both campaigning in Connacht, were promised the support of four powerful Scottish magnate groups: the Bruces, the Stewarts, the Dunbars, and the MacDonald lords of Islay.[23]

Personal relationships among the 'Anglo-Norman' aristocracy were often framed within concepts of lordship and hierarchy. Lordship was expressed in many forms, but some generalisations may usefully be made. Rents were paid by tenants for use of the lord's land, mills and other facilities; and aids or subventions were paid to a lord by his vassals, either in coin or in kind, on set occasions. A lord frequently required vassals to attend at his court in practical acknowledgement of his jurisdiction. Frequently too, he required from them military service. This often took the form of 'knight service', provision of mounted armed warriors for so many days in the lord's army; but it could also involve provision of contingents of lesser warriors such as archers. In the western isles, provision of galleys ('ship service') was common. Lesser lords in pursuit of patronage and security tended to associate themselves with a greater lord and to attend him personally, and so a 'retinue' (or 'meinye' in Scotland) would form about the figure of a great magnate. In England terms of service could be specified in a written indenture; in Ireland the retinue of Anglo-Irish lords often included a Gaelic following or 'kern'. In terms of social and geographic influence lordships overlapped, the lord of the manor or locality acknowledging a hierarchy of superior lordships. Whereas modern society is occasionally characterised as stratified in terms of social class, the different strands of medieval aristocratic society were woven together by personal bonds of lordship and landholding, and by the economic and social influence which these relationships could command.

Over and above all other lordships in the British Isles was the kingdom of England, under the firm rule of Edward I.[24] Its strength lay in its size and consequent wealth of landed resources, in its central position with respect to the lordships which surrounded it, and above all in its unity. In England over three centuries Anglo-Saxon and Norman institutions had blended to produce a lordship peculiarly centralised and powerful. An Anglo-Saxon concept of monarchy lifted kingship far above and beyond ordinary lordship; the need for taxation advanced the development of administrative institutions; and the Norman institution of knight service required the aristocracy to furnish the king with heavy cavalry, regarded still in 1300 as the ultimate weapon of war. The King of England dispensed justice from an itinerant household, which was the principal source of royal patronage and access to high office. In time of war the royal household increased in size to provide the king with a powerful retinue of paid knights, the nucleus of the royal army. It also included both the king's closest councillors and his administrators. Formal institutions of government were overshadowed, controlled and staffed by household personnel: these formal institutions included the king's privy council, the Great Council, the exchequer (or accounting office), the chancery (or writing office) and parliament. This last-mentioned body had arisen largely in response to royal demands for taxation from his subjects, essential to pay for the king's wars. Parliament was a formal occasion, a concentration of all aspects of royal power in a single court, in which the most important laws and royal pronouncements were made. Through the presence of all the main lords of the land, spiritual and temporal, and also from time to time of elements representing knights, townspeople and lower clergy, parliament mustered assent to the king's government. It sanctioned (and occasionally withheld) financial subsidies from the laity. A 'lay subsidy' took the form of a grant of a stated proportion – a fifteenth for example – of the moveable wealth of the laity. Subsidies were also granted to the king by the clergy of the realm, assembled in convocation.

Within England there were many lordships or 'liberties', which enjoyed varying degrees of autonomy and privilege. Among the greatest territorial liberties was the Bishopric of Durham, within which the bishop had a very high degree of autonomy, even to the extent of minting his own coins. But on the death of a lord holding directly from the king, his lands and liberties would pass into the king's hands, and revenues would be collected for the king's use until the payment of a 'relief' by the heir. If the heir was a minor, his inheritance stayed in the hands of the king, exploited by royal officials or *escheators* until he came of age. Similarly on the death of a bishop, episcopal estates and revenues were managed by royal officials until a new bishop was consecrated. These windfalls, known as *escheats*, are important. While the royal archive has largely survived, we possess only chance survivals from the records of other great lords. For the duration of seigneurial minority or episcopal vacancy, therefore, accounts of escheats preserved in royal archive provide a window on the condition of estates about which we would otherwise know nothing.

Ten earls dominated the English aristocracy, and in their hands most of the landed wealth of the kingdom was concentrated. Below them in the social hierarchy were lesser lords, bannerets and barons; and below them the gentry, composed of knights, squires and substantial landowners. All the above-mentioned classes – the *gentil* classes – had the right to bear armorial devices on their personal seals and on shields, a badge of 'gentility'; but it was upon the gentry that the king depended to fill public office as sheriffs, coroners and justices. The whole edifice of lordship rested upon an English-speaking peasantry, whose produce, rents and services sustained the *gentil* classes.

It was upon the mobilisation of this wealth that England's ascendancy in the British Isles depended. Cash, as distinct from landed wealth, was generated by the towns, and especially by the export of wool for which England was famous. The early fourteenth century saw English wool exports at an all-time high of 36,000 sacks of wool; and although this had fallen somewhat by 1324, it was estimated that in that year the royal customs duties payable on wool and hides would bring in £13,000.[25] Customs revenue amounted to some 40 per cent of the English king's normal, regular income in that year. On top of this, the king could call for taxation, in the form of either lay or clerical subsidies. Yields from subsidies varied enormously, depending upon how they were collected. On top of this, the king could rely on revenues from his other territories. Gascon revenues were important, almost equal to those of the customs; revenues from Ireland, however, had declined to almost negligible proportions. But warfare was such an enormous drain upon the resources of the monarchy that, except towards the end of Edward II's reign, the king was always in financial difficulties, and he relied heavily upon Italian bankers.

Edward I was refining an already sophisticated legal system, and was continuing a process whereby the kings progressively arrogated to themselves the jurisdictions of lesser lords. For the purposes of royal taxation and administration England was divided into counties;

yet lordships, which often transcended county boundaries, remained fundamental to the exercise of political power in the localities. Earls, though they bore a title associated with a particular county or district, often held lands in many parts of the kingdom; and when the county court was summoned to discuss local issues, its business was dominated by the stewards of the great lords' estates, who would protect their lords' interests. The area of England of special significance for the Wars of the Bruces was of course the north. Although the area had long been fully absorbed into the kingdom of England, a number of regional peculiarities persisted.[26] It was a very distinct region of the kingdom. Still referred to as Northumbria in memory of the Anglo-Saxon kingdom, it was poorer than the south, at a distance from the centres of royal power and regarded by southerners as mountainous, windswept, cold and rainy. In ecclesiastical terms it possessed its own metropolitan, the Archbishop of York; in legal terms, a separate escheator was appointed for the north. A northern consciousness was reinforced by a sense of inferiority to the wealthy and privileged south.

Separate kingdoms they may have been, but Scotland and England were nonetheless bound together in that 'aristocratic web that was broken neither by the Irish Sea nor the Anglo-Scottish border'.[27] Aristocracies of both countries intermarried and were bound to one another by common culture and common interests. In terms of aristocratic and governmental institutions, the Scottish kingdom greatly resembled its southern neighbour in miniature.[28] The 'Anglo-Norman' aristocracy had been transplanted into Scotland, as Norman, English, French and Flemish knights and ecclesiastics settled there by royal invitation in the twelfth century. Though the facility to speak French endured among the Scottish nobility, their predominant language in 1300 was probably a Scots form of northern English. Scotland too had earls, who attended a parliament on great occasions; lords (or lairds) who supplied heavily armed mounted knights in time of war; and a king. But whereas in England the Anglo-Saxon language and customs had in most respects been long banished from aristocratic life, Scotland had still a powerful Gaelic aristocracy. Consequently Scotland was rather less of a unity than England, and western lordships tended to enjoy considerable independence from the monarchy. Two cultures were present in the Scottish kingdom: the mainly English-speaking lords, peasants and townsmen of the eastern coastal plains; and the Gaelic-speaking lords and peasants of the Highlands, the Western Isles and Galloway. Although there is no evidence at this stage that there was any significant tension between these cultures, they must to some extent have been in competition, and the Gaelic culture and language were probably in slow retreat. Many social institutions in Scotland, though outwardly 'Anglo-Norman', had a Gaelic origin. The Scottish earls were successors to the *mormaers*, or sea-stewards, the great

Map 1: The British Isles
Circa 1306

Dominant kin *MacRuairidh*
groups

Welsh Castles of
Edward I

Land over 600ft
(approximately)

Scale 0   50   100   150
                       miles

Orkney
(to Norway)

THE GAELTACHT

MacRuairidh

The Mounth

Aberdeen

MacDougall

Stirling

MacDonald

Scotland

Berwick

Kintyre

Carrick

Newcastle

Earldom

O Néill

of

Galloway

Carlisle

Bishopric of
Durham

Ulster

Vale of
York

Ó Conchobair

Man

Lordship

York

Meath

of

Dublin

Lincolnshire

Anglesey

Caernarfon

Ireland

Norfolk

England

Ó Briain

Wales

Suffolk

Carmarthen

London

officers of the Gaelic kingdom. Scottish kingship too was an indigenous development rather than an 'Anglo-Norman' import. The rites of royal inauguration contained elements unchanged from remote antiquity. Coronation was not the custom in Scotland or among Gaelic rulers in Ireland or Scotland; instead the Scottish enkinging ceremony involved the placing of the new king on a sacred stone, the Stone of Destiny at the Abbey of Scone. A period of English overlordship had existed in the late twelfth century, and in the 1160s a Scottish king had given military service in person in the army of Henry II of England. But there had been no recurrence of this; and Scotland had by 1296 enjoyed independence for over a century. The Anglo-Scottish border had been precisely defined by the early thirteenth century; there was as yet no Debateable Land where England merged or shaded into Scotland.[29]

Gaelic Scotland, in addition to being a part of the Scottish kingdom, was also a part of a wider Gaelic world, the Gaeltacht. This Gaelic-speaking area lay to the west of the English and Scottish kingdoms, and to the west of England's colony in Ireland, a great crescent of cultural homogeneity which spanned the northern seas, ruled by a multiplicity of unstable lordships.[30] Here successions to titles and lordships were unpredictable and warfare endemic; the Irish Gaeltacht was characterised by English settlers as a 'land of war'. After the Norwegian kingdom withdrew from the Western Isles in the 1260s the Scottish monarchy had enjoyed some success in drawing Gaelic lords into the sphere of its court. At this time too the de Burgh earldom of Ulster, by expanding into Donegal, threatened to sever the Scottish Gaeltacht from the Irish. Elsewhere in Ireland the 'Anglo-Norman' colony was in retreat and the 'land of war' spreading at the expense of the colony.[31] But since land in the Gaeltacht tended to be poor and the area an unpromising source of revenue generally, Gaelic lords – kings to their own people – were largely abandoned to their own devices by English and Scottish monarchies; until during the Wars of the Bruces it appeared to both protagonists, but especially to the Bruces, that advantage might be had from intervention. In open letters to Irish chiefs and Welsh magnates, Robert and Edward Bruce based appeals for support on what might be described as 'national' or 'racial' grounds[32] – common language and culture, and the common experience of oppression by the English. The Wars of the Bruces may then be interpreted as the violent reaction of the periphery against the imperialism of the centre, though to accept this view uncritically is to fall for the Bruces' propaganda hook, line and sinker.

AGRARIAN ECONOMY IN THE NORTHERN BRITISH ISLES, C. 1300

Alternatively, in economic terms the conflict may be interpreted broadly as one of highlands *versus* lowlands. The wars appear to have taken precisely this form, of hordes from the highlands and islands of Scotland swooping down on the plains of Lothian and Northumberland, Meath and York. There are strong indications that the Western Isles and the north of Scotland supplied the manpower for the Bruces' recovery of Scotland in 1307–14 and probably for the invasion of Ireland too; but in later years Scottish armies can only have been drawn from the most populous regions of the country, namely Lothian, the south-east and the eastern coastal strip. It is true, however, that the Wars of the Bruces originated in, and were at first contained in, parts of Britain that were relatively upland. They were by no means poor or bad lands; but on the whole arable farming in these areas survived under unpromising conditions.[33] Heavy annual rainfall and acidic soils necessitated a reliance on the cultivation of oats, which were tolerant of high rainfall, rather than on wheat. They were predominantly pastoral areas, and cattle husbandry tended to be commoner than the management of sheep flocks. Seasonal movement of cattle between summer and winter grazings appears to have been common to all of these regions.[34]

The fifty-year period leading up to the Black Death of 1347–50 has attracted great attention from economic historians.[35] At some point in the period c.1290 to c.1330, the population of medieval Britain reached its apogee, and thereafter began to decline. The great bulk of economic data derives from English estate and manorial records, and it is largely by extrapolation from the English evidence that educated guesses may be made as to conditions in Scotland, Wales and Ireland. Nevertheless what is broadly true of England seems to hold good for conditions over the whole of the British Isles.[36] For two and a half centuries the population of England had been expanding, and in response to the consequent land hunger, so too did the area under cultivation. Rises in both rents and food prices were largely symptoms of this land hunger; but other factors also contributed to the rise in prices, most notably the boom in the wool export trade which increased the amount of bullion in circulation and raised the prices of commodities.

Within a decade of 1300, however, the population of England began to decline. Trends are uneven and it is difficult to generalise, but it seems clear that 'wasteland' begins to figure more prominently in manorial accounts, indicating a reduction in the area under cultivation, and that rents and entry fines began to fall. Exactly what caused the change is still unclear. It used to be thought that soil exhaustion was chiefly responsible; the implication of which is that population was being forced down by long-term starvation. More recently it has been argued that weight must be given to the social context too; that lordship in particular was sufficiently powerful to influence economic and thus population trends. Diminishing rates of human fertility are likely to have resulted in a much more gradual alteration of population trends. Whatever the precise explanation, the corn-growing heartland of England was suffering from a crisis originating within the economy in the last decade of the thirteenth century and the opening decade of the fourteenth. Very soon afterwards, however, the whole of the British Isles and parts of Europe were reeling under the impact of a crisis inflicted by a wholly external factor: a series of crop failures which began in 1315 and lasted until the harvest of 1318, and in some places to 1321. This was caused by torrential rainfall in consecutive summers and it produced a widespread and prolonged food scarcity, causing food prices to soar.[37] It made the population more vulnerable to disease and, in places, caused actual starvation. It is known as the Great European Famine.

In the north of England (and possibly in Ireland and Scotland) the effects of crop failure may not have been quite so devastating as in midland and southern England. In these areas the evidence of land hunger is comparatively slight. Cultivation was on a much smaller scale than in the south; and there was an abundance of high grassland which could be used to supplement the cropping area for a year or two and then be abandoned. There was therefore more scope for grain production on poor-quality soils, and more land to offset the effects of soil exhaustion. Greater reliance upon pastoral farming rather than cultivation may also have cushioned the effects of crop failure. Yet northern Britain was far from immune to the economic crisis. Pastoral farming was as prone to natural disaster as arable. In 1315 chronicles report a disease affecting sheep; in 1319 a 'murrain' of cattle.

The economic background to the Wars of the Bruces is thus charac-terised by climatic change, crop failures, animal disease and growing misery for the mass of the population, certainly in the corn-growing heartlands of the British Isles; and perhaps to a slightly lesser extent in northern Britain and Ireland. The relationship between famine and war is intriguing. The Wars of the Bruces involved the desolation of much of Scotland, Ireland and northern England, and so greatly exacerbated the effects of natural disaster; Scotland may have been compensated to some extent by the influx of bullion, grain and livestock, the fruits of extortion and robbery during successful war in England and Ireland. Did harsh economic conditions in northern Britain engender war? It is not really possible to say. Superficially there is a correlation between what chroniclers record as 'bad years' and escalations in the war: this seems to occur in 1311 and again in 1315–18. But on closer examination the sources will not sustain any such sweeping generalisation. Where comparison can be drawn, chroniclers' reports of dire hardship often conflict with more reliable evidence of grain yields and bailiffs' accounts.[38] So while it may be tempting to represent the Bruce brothers as riding the whirlwind of economic distress, the picture

of starving Scots driven southwards by hunger to plunder the lowlands
of England and Ireland remains substantially unsupported.[39]

THE ENGLISH AND THE OTHER PEOPLES OF THE BRITISH ISLES

In the late thirteenth century, as today, the peoples of England, Scotland,
Ireland and Wales were self-consciously separate identities. Today we call
them nationalities; but the terminology of 'nationality' and 'nationalism'
is not entirely appropriate to the middle ages.[40] For one thing, these
identities were impaired by the much more pressing and immediate
demands for loyalty to the lord, to the kin-group; for another, they
were subordinated by the existence a universal church. It is safer to
speak of 'peoples', or 'solidarities' bound together by common customs
and law, common myths of origin and descent. But there was a fundamental difference between the peoples of Scotland and England, on the
one hand, and those of Ireland and Wales, on the other. The monarchies
which existed in Scotland and England, and the institutions upon which
monarchy depended, provided a focus, a definition and an affirmation
of the people's identity. They had achieved a match between people and
polity, 'regnal solidarity' as it is currently expressed; but in Ireland and
Wales, where society was divided between natives and settlers, no such
match existed.

Individual kings might aspire to govern several peoples; to do so was
testimony to their power and greatness. The English claim to suzerainty
over the whole of the British Isles has its roots in the aspiration of the
Anglo-Saxon kings of Wessex to the *bretwalda* or kingship of all Britain.
In the 990s Aethelred II called himself 'ruler of the English and governor
of the adjoining nations round about', and elsewhere 'emperor, by the
providence of God of all Albion'; while in a display of overlordship, King
Edgar in 973 was rowed on the River Dee by six or eight sub-kings of Wales
and Scotland.[41] Only after the Norman conquest did kings of England
apply themselves to making this claim a reality. Native principalities in
Wales came under pressure from Norman adventurers, who succeeded
directly in asserting their own lordship over the south of the country.
Norman military intervention in Ireland commenced in 1169; before
long virtually all the native rulers gave notice of submission. Norman
lords from England and Wales carved out great lordships; and a colony,
peopled predominantly by English-speaking farmers, developed on the
lowlands in the south and east.[42] In both Ireland and Wales, however, the
conquests were unco-ordinated, piecemeal, and driven by the opportunist
instinct of the Norman aristocracy. Because the territorial interests of
the Norman conquistadors were spread throughout Britain and other
lands, they were not given to concentrated or intensive interference in
any of their acquisitions. Norman conquests in Ireland and Wales were

therefore not subjected to intensive colonisation. Scotland, of course, was not conquered. But her rulers had been obliged to acknowledge for a time the overlordship of the King of England. From 1093 to 1124 the Kings of Scots were his vassals; and from 1174 to 1189 that subjection was formalised. After this time Scottish kings continued to do homage to each new king of England, though only for lands which the Scottish king held in England, the chief of these being the liberty of Tynedale and the Honour of Penrith.

As the thirteenth century progressed the relationship between the 'Anglo-Normans' and the subject (though hardly 'conquered') peoples of the celtic lands began to alter. Professor Davies offers a number of explanations as to why it became sharper and more confrontational.[43] The spirit of the early conquests, characterised by mutual recognition of interests, intermarriage, and 'a relatively easy-going tolerance of other peoples' norms', was replaced by a growing discrimination between English and subject peoples on grounds of race and language. English overlordship became more demanding and aggressive. One explanation advanced to account for this change is that after England lost Normandy to France in 1204 the celtic countries attracted the attention and interference which had previously been directed at the continental possessions of kings of England. A second factor was the growing power, self-assurance and belligerence of native polities. Partly as a result of copying the methods and approach of Anglo-Normans, native rulers became more belligerent. Briain Ó Néill attempted in 1259 to form a federation of native princes in Ireland and Scotland to resist the Anglo-Normans; and the power of Llywelyn ap Gruffydd threatened the stability of the English position in Wales until his death in 1282.[44] Simultaneous with these 'political' endeavours of the late thirteenth century there was a well-attested cultural renaissance in the celtic world, which in Ireland was tending to undermine the vigour and extent of the Anglo-Norman colony.[45] A third reason offered for the increasing conflict between English and celtic peoples is the expansion of English government and the administrative mentality which supported it.[46] An increase in the power of the kings of England was made possible by the growth of taxable wealth; and the growing competence of institutions of government (parliament, exchequer, chancery, courts and the institutions of local government) also contributed to their capacity to dominate. In Ireland and Wales Edwardian royal officials were on a mission to civilise, to regularise, to order and improve. English institutions and English law were perceived by settlers as civilising and productive of an ordered society. This perception encouraged intolerance of social institutions that were not English. By 1300 there were exchequers on the English model in Berwick, Dublin, Caernarfon and Carmarthen; in Dublin there was also a parliament, similar to that in England, but petitions from all over the English dependencies were heard at the English parliament. On the continent Gascony still remained to the King of England; and revenues from that duchy were accounted for at Westminster. In all the dependencies of England, justiciars, escheators, seneschals and other royal officers issued writs and collected revenues just as in England itself. The similarity between the system based largely at Westminster and the satellite administrations in the dependencies was often more superficial than real ('a thinnish coating over a very un-English set of political facts'[47]); nevertheless these bureaucracies gave Edwardian England the administrative capability to intensify English lordship in each of these countries.

By the late thirteenth century, the stage was set for this intensification of English lordship, driven not by fragmented aristocratic efforts, but by the centralising monarchy of Edward I. It was less tolerant of native institutions than its predecessors, and markedly more uniformist. It was less compromising with local law and custom, and more insistent upon the written record, particularly upon the system of financial accountability that was developing at Westminster. In Ireland this tightening of control took the form of an increased respect for the king's writ; a trend towards smaller administrative units; and a more regular supervision of the Dublin administration by Westminster. Irish laws were declared 'detestable to God and so contrary to all law that they ought not to be deemed law'.[48] Even so, Edward's interest in Ireland was confined to maximising revenues. Other aspects of the colony's well-being were ignored; and this intensification of royal lordship actually coincided with the diminution of the colony's geographical extent. In Wales the Edwardian reconquest took an altogether harsher form. Deploying manpower and money on a scale unparalleled, Edward achieved a thoroughgoing conquest of the north and west of the country in three great campaigns, 1277, 1282 and 1295.[49] He completed the encirclement of the country by building a spectacular series of stone castles along the northern and western coast. By the Statute of Wales, 1284, the laws and customs of Wales were overhauled and the country 'annexed and united' to the English crown. During the Welsh campaigns Edward perfected the bureaucratic and military machine which he was shortly to unleash upon Scotland.

NOTES

1 *CDS* ii, nos. 1833, 1834; *CDS* iv, p. 488; *CDS* v, nos. 457, 465.
2 Barbour, *The Bruce* III, 675–724; *Vita Edwardi II*, p. 13; *Fordun* ii, 335.
3 Barrow, *Robert Bruce*, pp. 166–70.
4 *Scalacronica*, p. 35.
5 *Barbour's Bruce*, ed. M.P. McDiarmid and J.A.C. Stevenson (3 vols.) (Scottish Text Society, 4th series, 1980–85).

6 Barrow, *Robert Bruce*; Duncan, *RRS*; Prestwich, *Edward I*; Maddicott, *Lancaster*; Phillips, *Aymer de Valence*; and also I.M. Davis, *The Black Douglas* (London, 1974).

7 For the purposes of this study the phrase 'British Isles' is taken to embrace Ireland and her associated islands.

8 Recent work on Scotland is usefully summarised in a review article by B. Webster, 'Anglo-Scottish Relations, 1296–1389: Some Recent Essays' *SHR* lxxiv (1995), 97–108.

9 Notable exceptions are: Scammell, 'Robert I'; E. Miller, *War in the North* (University of Hull Publications, 1960); and three articles by J.A. Tuck, 'Northumbrian Society in the Fourteenth Century', *NH* vi (1971), 22–39; 'War and Society in the Medieval North', *NH* xxi (1985), 33–52; 'The Emergence of a Northern Nobility', *NH* xxii (1986), 1–17.

10 O. Armstrong, *Edward Bruce's Invasion of Ireland* (London, 1923). Recent work is referred to on p. 199 below, n.1.

11 A.A.M. Duncan, *Scotland: The Making of the Kingdom* (Edinburgh, 1975), pp. 368–71.

12 A.A.M. Duncan, 'The Bruces of Annandale, 1100–1304', *TDGNHAS* lxix (1994), 89–102.

13 Duffy, 'Bruce Brothers', pp. 70–76.

14 Barbour, *The Bruce* VI, 579–82, 651; VII, 294–95; Duffy, 'Bruce Brothers', p. 72; Phillips, 'Documents', Appendix, pp. 269–70.

15 G. Barrow and A. Royan, 'James, Fifth Stewart of Scotland, 1260(?)–1309', *Essays on the Nobility of Medieval Scotland*, ed. K.J. Stringer (Edinburgh, 1985), pp. 166–94; T.E. McNeill, *Anglo-Norman Ulster: The History and Archaeology of an Irish Barony, 1177–1400* (Edinburgh, 1980).

16 *CDS* ii, nos. 1776, 1837.

17 Duncan, 'The Bruces of Annandale', p. 98.

18 P.R. Coss *The Knight in Medieval England, 1000–1400*, (Stroud, 1993), pp. 113–21.

19 *The Siege of Carlaverock*, ed. N.H. Nicholas (London, 1828); A.A.M. Duncan, *The Nation of the Scots and the Declaration of Arbroath (1320)* (Historical Association, 1970), p. 2.

20 M. Keen, *Chivalry* (London, 1984), pp. 203–12; Coss, *Knight in Medieval England*, pp. 53–56.

21 Prestwich, *Edward I*, pp. 120–21.

22 McNeill, *Anglo-Norman Ulster*, Appendix I; J.A. Watt, *NHI* ii, 353. It is not possible to say which Thomas de Multon (de Egremont or de Gilsland) Alicia married.

23 The document is known as the 'Turnberry Band', Stevenson, *Documents* i, 22–23.

24 The best short survey is Prestwich, *War, Politics and Finance*, especially pp. 41–66. It is described in greater detail in *The English Government at Work, 1327–1336*, eds. J.F. Willard, J.R. Strayer and W.H. Dunham (3 vols.) (Cambridge, Mass., 1940–50).

25 W. Childs, 'Finance and Trade under Edward II', *Politics and Crisis in Fourteenth Century England*, ed. J.Taylor and W. Childs (Gloucester, 1990), p. 27. The wool export boom of the early fourteenth century is evident from the graph of wool exports from Newcastle upon Tyne, Chart 7, p. 226 below.

26 H.M. Jewel, 'North and South: the Antiquity of the Great Divide', *NH* xxvii (1991), 1–25.

27 R. Frame, *The Political Development of the British Isles 1100–1400* (Oxford, 1990), p. 63.

28 Surveys of the medieval Scottish kingdom are available in Duncan, *Scotland: The Making of the Kingdom*, pp. 595–615; and R. Nicholson, *Scotland: The Later Middle Ages* (Edinburgh, 1974), Chapter 1 and especially pp. 21–23 on the institutions of government; M. Lynch, *Scotland: A New History* (London, 1991), Chapter 5, pp. 53–73.

29 G.W.S. Barrow, 'The Anglo-Scottish Border', *NH* i (1966), 21–42.

30 Frame, *Political Development*, Chapter 9. I will use the term *Gaelic* in Irish and Scottish contexts, reserving the term *Celtic* to include aspects which also relate to Wales.

31 Lydon, *NHI*, ii, Chapter IX, 'A Land of War', pp. 240–74.

32 For the pitfalls of applying this terminology to medieval politics, see S. Reynolds, *Kingdoms and Communities in Western Europe, 900–1300* (Oxford, 1984), esp. pp. 250–56.

33 E. Miller, 'Farming in Northern England During the Twelfth and Thirteenth Centuries', *NH* xi (1976 for 1975), especially pp. 3–7; and in *AHE* ii, 247–59.

34 J. McDonnell, 'The Role of Transhumance in Northern England', *NH* xxiv (1988), 1–17.

35 B. Harvey's introduction to *Before the Black Death: Studies in the Crisis of the Early Fourteenth Century*, ed. B.M. Campbell (Manchester, 1991), pp. 1–24. Also important is E. Miller's Chapter 7, 'Long Term Movements', in *AHE*, pp. 716–55.

36 Price evidence in Scotland has recently been subject to detailed investigation in E. Gemmill, and N. Mayhew, *Changing values in medieval Scotland: A study of prices, money and weights and measures* (Cambridge, 1995), pp. 11–16, where Scottish price fluctuations are shown to be closely related to well-documented trends in England.

37 Chart 1, p. 111 below incorporates a rough guide to changes in wheat prices over the period, and gives an indication of prices during the famine years of 1315, 1316 and 1322.

38 See Table 3 of E. Hallam, 'The Climate of Eastern England, 1250–1350', *Agricultural History Review* xxxii (1984), 130.

39 See p. 75 below.

40 Reynolds, *Kingdoms and Communities*, pp. 254–56; R.R. Davies, 'The Peoples of Britain and Ireland, 1100–1400, i Identities', *TRHS* 6th series iv (1994), 11, 16–20; R.R. Davies, 'The Peoples of Britain and Ireland, 1100–1400, ii Names, Boundaries and Regnal Solidarities' *TRHS* 6th series v (1995), 9–16.

41 Frame, *Political Development*, p. 16.

42 The conquests of Ireland and Wales are compared and contrasted in R.R. Davies, *Domination and Conquest: The Experience of Ireland, Scotland and Wales 1100–1300* (Cambridge, 1990).

43 Davies, *Domination and Conquest*, pp. 112–24.

44 Lydon, *NHI* ii, 244–46; D. Walker, *Medieval Wales* (Cambridge, 1990), pp. 111–33.

45 Lydon, *NHI* ii, 240–71.

46 Davies, *Domination and Conquest,* pp. 114–123.
47 R. Frame, 'Power and Society in the Lordship of Ireland 1272–1377', *P&P* No. lxxvi (1977), p. 5.
48 Lydon, *NHI* ii, 271; Frame, *Political Development*, pp. 144–51 and '"Les Engleys Neés en Irlande": The English Political Identity in Medieval Ireland', *TRHS* 6th series iii (1993), 90, 92–94.; *Foedera* i (II), 540.
49 J.E. Morris, *The Welsh Wars of Edward I* (Oxford, 1901).

CHAPTER ONE

The King of Summer: the Bruce Coup d'Etat in Scotland, 1306

I think you may be King of Summer;
King of Winter you will not be.

M edieval monarchy craved prestige, and prestige was bestowed above all by military adventurism. The situation of 'two kings on one poor island' therefore was not conducive to lasting harmony.[1] Wars between England and Scotland were then perhaps inevitable; yet the Edwardian imperialism experienced by Wales and Ireland did not necessarily presage any English attack on Scotland. Prior to 1296 the thirteenth century had been a period of unparalleled felicity in Anglo-Scottish relations. Peaceful co-existence was greatly assisted by the significant number of landholders who held territories in both kingdoms. At one stage in the thirteenth century nine out of 13 Scottish earldoms had property in England, and seven out of 22 English earldoms had Scottish landed interests.[2] War between the kingdoms, whatever the outcome, would cost these landowners dear. Co-existence was broken not by geo-political necessity but the rivalry between Bruce and Balliol for the kingship of Scotland and by the overweening ambition of Edward I. Before examining the chain of events that led to Robert Bruce's *coup d'état* in 1306, it is necessary to say something of how English involvement in Scotland began, and also something of the nature of warfare in the early fourteenth century.

THE ORIGINS OF THE SCOTTISH WAR OF INDEPENDENCE

The story of the rift between the kingdoms is too well known to bear repetition in any detail. Alexander III of Scotland died in 1286, leaving as his only heir a granddaughter, Margaret, the three-year-old 'Maid of Norway'. In accordance with the customs of the realm, aristocratic Guardians took temporary control of the Kingdom of Scotland during the interregnum, sent to Norway for the child and in 1290 arranged for her to marry Edward of Caernarfon, Prince of Wales, infant heir to Edward I and later to succeed as Edward II. But first they took steps to protect the liberties of the kingdom in the event of a union of the crowns. On 18th July the Treaty of Birgham-Northampton was agreed between the English and the Scots. Scotland was to continue 'separate, free in itself, without any subjection to the King of England'.[3]

In the autumn of 1290, before the marriage could take place, the Maid died. There now arose a danger of civil war in Scotland between two leading Scottish aristocratic factions, the Bruces and the Comyns. Violence threatened to erupt; but Edward I may have played up the danger of conflict in Scotland in order to intervene. He had an obvious interest in the stability of Scotland, all the more pressing because of the enmity of Philip the Fair, the powerful and hostile King of France. He may also have wished to exploit the situation by extracting recognition of the overlordship of Scotland, which he had claimed in 1278 and his father in 1251. Yet his intervention was invited, and at first it was not unwelcome. As a friendly neighbouring monarch he was to some extent a natural choice as arbiter in the issue of the Scottish succession.[4] He arrived at Norham on the River Tweed to preside as judge in the 'Great Cause' and set about claiming rights of jurisdiction. In a move calculated to extract that overlordship which he believed to be his right, Edward made it clear to the claimants or competitors that there would be no award unless acceptance of his overlordship was universally accepted. Then he demanded possession of the royal castles of Scotland, which put him in a position to enforce his decision. Although the Scottish parliament conceded nothing as regards Edward's claim to be overlord of Scotland, the competitors had no choice but to acknowledge it, since Edward would in any case be the adjudicator. Fourteen claimants appeared to protest titles to the throne; but the two leading contenders were Robert Bruce, grandfather of the future king and known to history as 'The Competitor'; and John Balliol, an ally of the powerful Comyn family. They were both descendants of David Earl of Huntingdon, grandson of David I of Scotland (1124–53). Balliol was the grandson of the eldest daughter of Earl David; whereas Bruce was son of his second daughter. After protracted deliberation Edward in 1292 awarded the kingdom to Balliol, and then received as overlord the homage and fealty of the new King of Scots.

The succession had been settled, but Edward continued to intervene in Scottish affairs, claiming an appellate jurisdiction in lawsuits on which King John had given judgement.[5] A man of his time, Edward I undoubtedly conceived it his duty to enforce his rights; but his insistence on them from 1292 created a wholly new situation. Scottish nobles despaired for the freedom of action of Scottish kings. In 1294 however the King of France, Philip the Fair, challenged Edward's control of Gascony by declaring it forfeit. This at once threatened the Scottish aristocracy with having to perform military service overseas for Edward, and the prospect of Edward's involvement in a continental war encouraged them to resist. In a palace revolution they forced the reluctant John to concede power to a council, which then made alliance with France. On 16th December 1295 Edward summoned the host of England to assemble at Newcastle on 1st March for war on the 'rebellious' Scottish king, and so he embarked upon the subjugation of Scotland by force. A brutal war of atrocity and reprisal followed. Scots who mistrusted the Balliol king and the Comyns who controlled him sided with the King of England. The chief of these was Robert Bruce of Annandale, father of the future king, who defended Carlisle against John Comyn, Earl of Buchan. All resistance was swept aside when the English army entered Scotland. Berwick was captured and the Scottish royal army routed in battle at Dunbar. King John resigned; and spinelessly Robert Bruce of Annandale asked Edward that he now be awarded the throne which Balliol had forfeited. Edward's scorn was withering: 'Have I nothing better to do than win kingdoms for you?' The English king was done with puppets, and was no longer prepared to settle for anything less than outright domination. The castles of Scotland were taken into his hands; and every substantial freeholder in Scotland was required to swear fealty to the king of England. A government was set up at Berwick through which Edward administered the country; and he removed the royal archive and sacred *regalia* of Scotland (including the Stone of Destiny) to Westminster. 'The conqueror was appropriating the past of the conquered people in order to replace it by his own emblems.'[6]

Resistance however grew in the north of Scotland and among the lower ranks of the Scottish gentry. The standard of rebellion was raised by Andrew Moray and William Wallace; and in 1297 while Edward I was in Flanders, they inflicted at Stirling Bridge a serious defeat upon an English army led by the Earl of Warenne. Moray was mortally wounded in the battle; but led by 'William the Conqueror' rebellion (in the name of King John) spread throughout Scotland. Wallace captured Berwick, driving the English out of Scotland altogether, and even led an invasion of Northumberland and Cumberland during which he tried to intimidate into surrender Carlisle and Newcastle.[7] On his return, however, Edward I defeated Wallace in battle at Falkirk in 1298. He reimposed his rule over most of southern Scotland; but Wallace, Sir John Soules and other 'Guardians of the Realm' established a rival authority to the north, and while Edward held the population centres and most of Scotland south of the Forth, these Scottish 'patriots' resisted from the forests and the north. In 1299 they succeeded in capturing the key fortress of Stirling Castle; but Edward responded by launching a series of *en masse* invasions, in 1300, 1301 and 1303–4. It is worth pausing to consider the nature of these armies and those of Edward II, which were awe-inspiring demonstrations of the power of the Edwardian state.

WARFARE IN THE AGE OF EDWARD I AND PHILIP THE FAIR

Details of royal expenditure on the invasions of Scotland are preserved in the Wardrobe Books, the royal wardrobe being a department of the household which was used by English kings in preference to the exchequer to fund their wars. These books contain a vast amount of information about the workings of the royal household, including details of payments to cavalry, infantry, craftsmen, labourers and others employed in each regnal year. The household however supplied only a part – albeit the largest part – of the fighting force; contingents brought and paid for by earls do not generally appear in the Wardrobe Accounts, because the earls considered it below their dignity to accept wages directly from the king.[8]

Warriors of knightly rank and above always fought as heavy cavalry, displaying banners and shields with splendidly colourful armorial devices and riding great *destriers* specially bred to take the weight of heavy armour. The standard heavy cavalry tactic had not changed for almost two hundred years.[9] Anchored firmly in the saddle by stirrups, the knights would charge at the enemy, lowering their lances while they gathered speed. Such was the momentum of armoured rider and armoured horse at the gallop, such the intimidating height of the ensemble that the opposing infantry rarely stayed to experience the impact, and so the cavalry charge could only be countered by a counter-charge. The armour worn by knights in the early fourteenth century was at this time the heaviest it would ever be during the middle ages, and could weigh in excess of 60 lbs (27 kg). The knight's head was protected by a *bascinet*, a helmet usually open at the face; the body by a coat of mail known as a *hauberk* and, increasingly, by the addition of strips of plate armour along the arms and legs. The portrayal of Andrew Harclay on the Carlisle charter of 1315 shows that by that time knights were already wearing plumes, and that a visor could be attached to the bascinet.[10] The horses, hugely expensive and well worth protecting, also bore some armour. One of the great logistical difficulties for the English in Scotland was how to keep their great horses in fodder. Oats and hay, peas and beans had to shipped north at great expense for the purpose. The Lanercost Chronicle remarks that 'the English do not willingly enter Scotland to wage war before summer, chiefly because earlier in the year they find no food for their horses'.[11] The Scots, who had fewer heavy cavalry, did not have such a problem.

Other cavalry – esquires, *soldarii* or men-at-arms – were mounted on unarmoured horses. The rider's body armour was often made of boiled leather, a cheaper and lighter alternative to metal armour. A particular type of mounted warrior came briefly into vogue during this period, known as the *hobelar*. They were introduced to the Scottish Wars from the marches of Ireland, and typically they wore leather armour and rode light horses or *hobins* rather than powerful *destriers*. As mounted raiders their mobility over rough terrain gave them a decided advantage over men-at-arms, and they were ideally suited to hit-and-run warfare. The tactics of these turbulent mercenaries were later adopted by the Scots in their raids on the north of England. While the Scottish raiders do not seem to have been referred to as 'hobelars' in the sources, it is certain that they operated in precisely this manner. The Scottish practice of fighting pitched battles on foot and with thrusting spear gave rise to the view that hobelars dismounted to confront an enemy, that they were in effect 'mounted infantry'. Certainly the Scottish raiders seem to have dismounted on the rare occasions when they took on an opposing army. But it was the devastating raid on rural communities of the countryside, the *chevauchée*, that was the essence of 'hobelar warfare'. Edward I employed Irish hobelars in significant numbers: almost 400 for the 1301 campaign and 500 for that of 1303.[12] They ceased to be employed on this scale for a time, but were reintroduced in 1315. Through bitter experience Edward II came to realise that the Scots could only be brought to battle by light cavalry.

Archers did not yet play a pivotal role on the battlefield. The term was often applied to general infantry; but specialised bowmen were only just beginning to be employed in large numbers, and keeping archers in arrows was already a major problem. London, Lincolnshire and Yorkshire sent bows and quivers of arrows to the siege of Stirling in 1304. Barbour seems to have been impressed by the density of volleys at Bannockburn.[13] Nevertheless, this was before the heyday of the longbow; and there is no evidence for the popular belief that Welsh contingents were mainly archers, or that effective use of the 'longbow' was introduced into England by Edward I from Wales. The crossbow was still the weapon of preference, and crossbowmen received a daily wage of 3d or 4d as opposed to the 2d paid to archers. Crossbowmen were often employed in castle garrisons, and Edward II employed Gascon crossbowmen as part of his bodyguard during the invasion of Scotland in 1310 and in large numbers in that of 1322.[14]

The military history of the period is commonly written in terms of common infantry overcoming the dominance of aristocratic heavy cavalry. At the battle of Courtrai in 1302 the weavers of the Flemish towns, fighting on foot, had defeated the flower of French chivalry; at Bannockburn the Scottish infantry were to inflict a similar discomfiture on the English heavy cavalry. In fact heavy cavalry continued to be the most highly valued form of military service throughout the middle ages; but there was at this time considerable experimentation with specialised varieties of infantry. At the battle of Falkirk William Wallace had resisted a heavy cavalry charge by deploying infantry spearmen in dense formations known as *schiltroms*. So far as we can tell, these were hollow squares or circles bristling with pikes, likened by Barbour to the spines of a hedgehog.[15] The English, for their part, experimented with heavily armoured infantry. In 1306 the *aketon*, a quilted surcoat padded with wool, was the commonest form of armour among infantrymen.[16] Throughout his reign, however, Edward II extracted from rural communities both an increasing period of military service and additional and more expensive armour. This emphasis on heavy armoured infantry was clearly a response to encounters with the Scottish schiltrom Edward II's efforts in this regard were given additional impetus by the experience of defeat by infantry spearmen at Bannockburn in 1314. In November 1314 London was requested to supply 300 crossbowmen with aketon, bascinet and *colerettos* (a broad collar of mail), besides crossbows and quarrels, to serve at the king's expense in the defence of Berwick. Thereafter successive levies of infantry were required to possess additional armour: in 1316 infantry were to have aketon, bascinet and lance, or at least aketon; in 1318 a levy on towns required aketon, *hauberk*, bascinet and iron gauntlets.[17] In 1319 Edward ordered that infantrymen possessing goods to the value of between 100s. and 10 marks should have aketon, hauberk, bascinet and iron gauntlets and a horse, 'fit for a hobelar'.[18] By these measures Edward might have wished to ensure that English levies had the equipment needed for garrison duty, sieges and other relatively static situations that might be encountered during invasions of Scotland. Countering the Scottish hobelars in their capacity as highly mobile raiders was much more difficult; and neglect of this aspect left the whole of northern England unprotected from their ravages.[19]

Hobelars and heavy infantry then passed in and out of fashion; but the common footmen, known as *pitaille* or *rebaldaill*, though despised and very poorly equipped, were a perennial feature of medieval hosts. Infantry contingents in Edward I's armies rarely exceeded 10,000 troops, and numbers always fell away rapidly after the start of the campaign both as a result of desertion and as contingents completed their periods of service. On the occasion of the Falkirk campaign Edward did however manage to raise 25,700 troops, the largest army of the period. In addition to the troops, the armies of the period were followed by a rabble of footmen, servants, carters and keepers of baggage. These were the *poveraill*, described by Barbour as 'worth nothing in battle', but who intervened with striking effect at Bannockburn.[20]

The present work confines its survey of the economic effects of war to the areas directly affected. However, it is important to recognise that the capacity to field even such small armies required a mobilisation of resources far beyond the war zone.[21] Wales, Ireland and Gascony all contributed foodstuffs and manpower towards Edward I's invasions of Scotland; but England herself bore the brunt of royal demand. Military service, though not perhaps the heaviest burden which war imposed on the peasantry, provoked vigorous and widespread resistance from 1315 to 1317. Commissariat arrangements placed an enormous strain on the resources of English counties far to the south of the war zone. Foodstuffs of every kind were requisitioned by purveyance, an arbitrary system of purchase on credit that was open to abuse by royal officials and always deeply resented by local and religious communities. Purveyances in England fell heaviest on the counties which produced most grain – Lincolnshire, Yorkshire, Norfolk and Suffolk, and also on Essex. From these counties grain could be easily shipped up the east coast to Scotland. An entirely arbitrary exaction that needed no consent, purveyance raised food prices, and violently disrupted both local economies and long-distance trade. Furthermore the frequency and rate of royal financial demands also increased to meet the colossal cost of the wars, and in 1315 and 1316 Edward II collected lay subsidies in two successive years. Dr. Maddicott points out that whereas the lord's exactions were mainly recurrent and predictable, royal demands in respect of purveyance, taxation and military service were arbitrary and irregular, and all the more damaging as a result. No corner of England, no segment of the population remained unaffected by the royal demands for victual and money.

THE 'KING OF SUMMER'

Like many other Scots, the Bruces adhered to Edward I on the outbreak of war in 1296. Their stance was determined largely by two facts: their bitter rivals, the Comyns, were leading the patriotic resistance to Edward; but first and foremost, the Bruces passionately believed in their own claim to the kingship and clung to Edward as the only hope of realising it. It is therefore surprising to encounter, during the rebellion of Wallace and Moray, Robert Bruce, Earl of Carrick and the future king, as one of the leaders of patriotic resistance. He is unlikely however to have been fighting purely for patriotic motives and against all self-interest. Rather, he may have given up hopes of receiving the kingship from Edward I, and concluded that, since a Balliol revival seemed unlikely, the patriots would be forced to recognise his own title to the throne.[22] By 1301, however, the tide had turned. Anglo-French *détente*, negotiated at Asnières, had profound consequences for Scotland. The cause of King John revived with diplomatic intervention by Philip the Fair and the Papacy. Edward I was prevailed upon to transfer John himself to papal custody in July 1299. From the Pope Balliol came into the custody of Philip the Fair, who was anxious to keep Edward occupied in Scotland. It was now even possible that Philip would intervene in Scotland with troops on John's behalf. Bruce's hopes of acquiring recognition from the patriots were dashed; and he returned 'to the peace of' Edward I in the winter of 1301 to 1302. The terms of his surrender have been preserved: his freedom, titles and claims were all guaranteed by the English king.[23] But it is not clear whether this guarantee extended to the Bruce's claim to the Scottish throne; the terms are tantalisingly vague. To encourage Bruce's defection, it is possible that Edward I dangled before him the prospect of a limited restoration of the Scottish kingship, in the person of Bruce himself. But there seem to have been other more immediate inducements. Bruce's second marriage, to Elizabeth de Burgh daughter of the Earl of Ulster, follows directly upon his change of sides, and the prospect of this too may have tempted him to abandon the patriotic cause. The de Burgh marriage promised a revival of the long-standing alliance between the Bruce, de Burgh and Stewart families.

Bruce's surrender to Edward I in 1301 or 1302 was part of a gradual but general collapse of patriotic resistance. To crush the remaining resistance Edward mobilised men and resources on a scale unparalleled in medieval history. Successive invasions *en masse* were launched: already in 1300 an army of 9,000 English and Welsh infantry had occupied southern Scotland; in 1301 and 1303 armies of similar size were deployed. All the resources of the Edwardian state were mustered against the Scots; all the technology of the age harnessed. Great siege engines, the *Warwolf* and the *Parson*, were applied to demolish the walls of Stirling Castle (the focus of remaining resistance); primitive explosives were also used in the work; and ingenious prefabricated bridges were floated up the North Sea to assist in projecting an army north of the Forth. In 1304 the Scots asked for terms and a general surrender ensued. Resistance at Stirling duly collapsed in 1304; in 1305 Wallace was captured, taken to London and tortured, humiliated and executed for the gratification of the mob.

In the service of Edward I Robert Bruce played 'an active though never a brilliant or conspicuous part'.[24] He served as Sheriff of Lanark and Ayr; Edward Bruce, Robert's younger brother, served in the entourage of Edward of Caernarfon Prince of Wales. What was it, then, that drove Robert Bruce into rebellion in 1306? And given the abject state of the country, what made him think he had the slightest chance of reviving and retaining the kingship of Scotland? Professor Barrow argues that as head of his family (since his father's death in 1304), Earl of Carrick, possessor of estates in England as well as in Scotland, he had never been more powerful than at this stage; and that he may have been biding his time until this point. Coupled with this, Professor Prestwich points out that a number of petty discontents (difficulty in reclaiming expenses, arguments over rights claimed in Annandale) may have rankled; and that he may have felt himself entitled to richer rewards than those Edward had bestowed.[25] As the fateful year 1306 opened, one fact must have been weighing heavily with all the magnates of Britain: that Edward I, now 67, could not be expected to last much longer.[26] Perhaps in preparation for the king's demise, and in an effort to guarantee some security in an uncertain future, Bruce began to exchange promises of solidarity with other magnates. In 1304 or 1305 he had made a pact with Bishop Lamberton of St. Andrews, promising mutual assistance in the event of future perils.[27] At about the same time he is said to have made a similar agreement with John Comyn who was effectively the head of the great Comyn connection, long the Bruces' main rivals for power in Scotland.[28] It seems that among the Scottish aristocracy a debate on the status of the realm was already taking place. Passions were stirred by an assembly in May 1305 at Scone (the place where Scottish kings were inaugurated in an age-old ritual, and a location with powerful associations). The formal purpose of this assembly was to select representatives for the next parliament in England, but it broke up without agreeing anything.[29] Then at Edward I's parliament at Westminster in September 1305, twenty of the king's councillors met with nine Scots as representatives of community to draw up an Ordinance for the governance of Scotland. This document made provision for formal offices of government, and for a revision of Scottish law; but it carefully avoided describing Scotland as a realm, and the implication was that Scotland had been relegated to the status of a kingless 'land', like Ireland, without a king and directly subservient to the English crown.

It is impossible to discern whether the Ordinance provoked any reaction – hostile or otherwise – among the Scottish aristocracy; all one can say is that, together with the advanced age of the English king, it may have fomented political speculation. Early in 1306 Bruce and John Comyn agreed to meet on 10th February in Greyfriars church at Dumfries. Both the principals brought along followers; on Comyn's side was his uncle, Sir Robert Comyn. The agenda is unknown, but the arguments reached sudden and violent climax when a fight broke out and Bruce struck Comyn with his sword. Bruce's followers later finished him off. Chroniclers colour the story according to their various prejudices; Scottish narratives allege that Comyn had betrayed to Edward I Bruce's plans to seize the throne, English writers invariably accuse Bruce of murder.[30] On the face of it, it seems unlikely that Bruce had arranged the meeting in order to assassinate a rival for the throne. Murder and sacrilege are not normally to be expected of any man set upon winning hearts and minds. A power-struggle between these leaders of aristocratic factions may have lain at the heart of the quarrel; but the earliest account relates only that Bruce accused Comyn of blackening his reputation with the English king. On balance it seems that the brawl had less to do with revival of the Scottish kingship than with Robert's standing at the English court. 'Bruce had blundered into being an accessory to a murder which had nothing to do with reviving the patriotic cause.'[31] To his family and followers, however, it may have seemed that Robert had brought ruin on them all. Retaliation by the Comyns and their allies would be swift and bloody.

Edward I had news of the murder by 23rd February.[32] According to one source, Bruce made an appeal of some sort to Edward, threatening to defend himself 'with the longest stick that he had' if this appeal were unsuccessful. Professor Duncan thinks it likely that Bruce demanded a comprehensive pardon to shield him from the fury of the Comyns.[33] There was no reply from court; and as a last resort Bruce was forced to assert in arms his claim to kingship. It was the only way he could raise an army. This rather desperate decision seems to have been taken during a fleeting visit to Robert Wishart, Bishop of Glasgow and veteran of patriotic resistance. Before rushing off to Scone, Bruce took care to secure a series of castles in the southwest: Dumfries, Dalswinton, Tibbers (held by John Seton), Ayr, Loch Doon (a Bruce castle, held by Christopher Seton), Caerlaverock, Dunaverty (held by Malcolm fitz Lengleys or MacCulian) and a half-finished castle at 'Tolibothvill'.[34] Probably they were taken with a view to keeping open the way for reinforcements from Ireland or the Western Isles, and they were provisioned by a nocturnal raid on the English stores. In April Robert was also believed to be in control of Ayr, Galloway and Dumbarton; but it seems that he had more castles than he could garrison, for his men later abandoned some of these strongholds after demolishing fortifications and ruining stores.[35]

Unable to await the end of the Lent, the enkinging ritual was planned for the first available feast day, and at a dignified but hasty ceremony at Scone on the feast of the Annunciation, 25th March 1306, Robert I was enthroned. Two days later, on Palm Sunday, high mass was celebrated.[36] The traditions of Scottish monarchy were honoured as far as circumstances would allow. The heir to the earldom of Fife was not present to lead the king to the throne as tradition demanded, but his aunt, Isabel Countess of Buchan, supplied his place. The Stone of Destiny had been removed to adorn the shrine of St. Edward at Westminster Abbey by Edward I; but Scone was itself powerful evocation of royal tradition. Robes and regalian insignia, mothballed since the monarchy had been in abeyance, were produced. Absolution for the slaying of Comyn had already been granted by the Bishop of Glasgow, and solemn oaths were now sworn. Even so the makeshift nature of the ceremonials may have been difficult to disguise; Robert's wife is said to have reproved her husband, mockingly addressing him as the 'king of Summer'.[37] This anecdote may be an accurate reflection of de Burgh scorn for Bruce pretensions. The turnout of aristocracy at his enthronement was nevertheless greater than might have been expected. No bishops were present; the senior ecclesiastic was the Abbot of Scone. The earls of Athol, Menteith and Lennox, and the bishops of Glasgow and Moray were his foremost allies. Robert may have

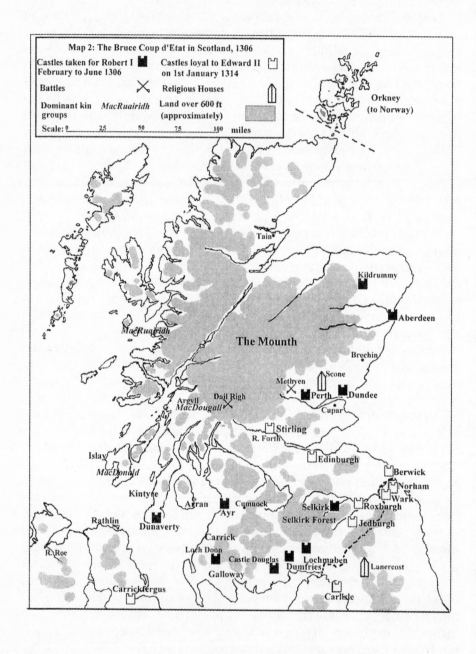

Map 2: The Bruce Coup d'Etat in Scotland, 1306

Castles taken for Robert I
February to June 1306

Castles loyal to Edward II
on 1st January 1314

Battles

Religious Houses

Dominant kin   *MacRuairidh*
groups

Land over 600 ft
(approximately)

Scale: 0   25   50   75   100   miles

Orkney
(to Norway)

Tain

Kildrummy

Aberdeen

MacRuairidh

The Mounth

Brechin

Methven   Scone

Dail Righ

Argyll
MacDougall

Perth   Dundee

Cupar

Stirling

R. Forth

Edinburgh

Islay

MacDonald

Berwick

Norham

Kintyre

Arran   Cumnock

Ayr

Selkirk   Wark
Roxburgh

Selkirk Forest   Jedburgh

Rathlin

Dunaverty

Carrick

Loch Doon

Castle Douglas   Lochmaben

Dumfries

Lanercost

R. Roe

Galloway

Carrickfergus

Carlisle

had the support of James, the hereditary Stewart of Scotland, if tenants and family adhered to the traditional alliance with the Bruces; but James himself was infirm and in no position to offer open allegiance.[38] Many lesser nobles supported Robert, among them James Douglas, Thomas Randolph, Reginald Crawford, Robert Boyd, Neil Campbell and Gilbert Hay who were to become his close companions. Simon Fraser, one of the most steadfast in resistance to Edward I, raised the men of Selkirk Forest independently of Bruce. Most others seem to have joined him out of fear or intimidation. Vital segments of the Scottish aristocracy would have nothing to do with the Bruce monarchy. The Comyns and their allies the MacDougalls of Argyll bayed for revenge against the murderer of John Comyn; other lords such as Patrick Earl of Dunbar and Malise Earl of Strathearn recognised Edward I as the only legally constituted king. Whatever sympathy Robert might have stirred, most Scots must have considered resistance to Edward I futile.

In the face of such divided loyalties the ignominious collapse of the Bruce *coup* was only a matter of time. Robert travelled to the northeast of the kingdom, to Aberdeen and possibly further north, demanding military service and money, promising favours in return for support and threatening dire vengeance on any who failed him. His allies secured the towns of Brechin, Cupar and Dundee.[39] East coast ports were bullied into providing cash; merchants of Dundee and Aberdeen were seized as hostages for payment. Bailiffs at Perth were thrown in prison and threatened with death until they paid up £54 which Robert claimed as rents due to him as king.[40] Homage and military service were exacted from often reluctant lairds; in the case of the earl of Strathearn, by threat of hanging. But now the English magnates Henry Percy and Robert Clifford were closing in on the southwest with over a hundred cavalry.[41] As early as 22nd February they had recovered Tibbers castle; on 3rd March they had possession of Dumfries, where Robert's garrisons had deliberately spoiled the provisions; Ayr too had been slighted and relinquished, probably for want of military service.[42] In June Aymer de Valence (later Earl of Pembroke) advanced from Berwick, with 300 cavalry and over 2,000 infantry. Valence recaptured Cupar and Perth, and Robert moved to confront him. In the twilight of 19th June, Valence caught Bruce's force by surprise at Methven. Hastily the knights accompanying Robert covered their heraldic devices with white cloth to preserve their anonymity, for Edward I had promised a terrible vengeance.[43] The Scottish infantry bore the brunt of the fighting, but were eventually forced to flee. Guerilla resistance continued for a short time, led by Simon Fraser, until he too was rounded up and executed.[44] Robert was lucky to escape with his cavalry; but they too were defeated a few days later at Loch Tay.[45]

By the end of July most of Robert's supporters in the east had been

captured; by August Valence was able to report that he had the situation
'well settled' north of the Mounth.[46] The Bishops of Glasgow and St.
Andrews were arrested. Menteith was imprisoned and stripped of his
lands; Strathearn was captured, and, to prove his willingness to cooperate
with the English, sent his son to assist in the pursuit of Robert and his
family. Badly mauled, the Bruces' army fled to the west, but at Dail Righ
they ran into the men of Lorn, followers of MacDougall. Another defeat
scattered what had remained of the army. Robert's sisters may have
been captured after Methven; his queen and daughter Marjory had been
taken to safety in Kildrummy Castle by the earl of Atholl. The keeper of
Kildrummy was Neil Bruce, the new king's brother, and as the English
approached, queen and daughter were taken from the castle to a place of
sanctuary at Tain, from where they may have hoped to reach Norway. But
there they were captured by the earl of Ross and delivered into the hands
of Edward I. Kildrummy fell to Edward of Caernarfon in September.[47]
Magnanimity could not be expected and it was not forthcoming. Neil
Bruce was drawn, hanged and beheaded at Berwick, the first of four
Bruce brothers to die in the war. Fraser, Atholl and others were taken to
London to be executed. In a punishment grotesque in its cruelty, Robert's
sister Mary and Isabel Countess of Buchan were imprisoned in cages on
the battlements of Roxburgh and Berwick castles.[48] Unusually lenient,
on the other hand, was the treatment of Elizabeth, Robert's queen. It
seems she was distancing herself from her husband's pretensions and
her stance was in keeping with that of her father, the earl of Ulster.

Two of the Bruce brothers, Thomas and Alexander, may already have
been mustering allies in Ireland since February. Robert and Edward now
fled to the southwest, seeking refuge in the lands of Lennox, Campbell
and MacDonald. Here too the Bruce position was collapsing. James the
Stewart had bowed to the prevailing wind and entered Edward I's service
on 1st July; and the ancestral Bruce castle of Lochmaben had surrendered
to Edward of Caernarfon on 11th July.[49] By the end of June the hunt was
on for the 'King of Summer', or 'King Hobbe' as the English satirists
called him:

> Now King Hobbe to the moors has gone,
> To come to town he has no desire.[50]

Throughout the summer the ailing Edward I travelled painfully
northwards to take charge.[51] Taking up residence at Lanercost Priory,
he took to his sickbed, but showed keen interest in the pursuit. Resistance
was now confined to a few castles on the west coast; Loch Doon castle was
under siege in August.[52] By the end of July the pursuit may have moved
to the coast, since boats for men-at-arms were ordered to be provided
from the waters around Carlisle and sent to Carrick.[53] Barbour relates
that unseasonal weather obliged Robert to make for shelter in Kintyre.

On the way, he was joined by his follower Malcolm Earl of Lennox. Crossing Loch Lomond, they are said to have been pursued by hostile galleys, but, rowing by way of Bute they made it safely to Kintyre, where, Barbour says, they were received by Angus Óg MacDonald of Islay. Robert chose to continue his flight because he feared treason.[54] The vigour with which Percy and Clifford applied themselves to the siege of Dunaverty in September suggests that they thought Bruce was within. This siege was carried on in tandem with the siege of Robert's relatives at Kildrummy.

Taking to the sea, Robert was not short of options. He could travel to Orkney, where he would be sure of refuge, for his sister Isabel was dowager queen of Norway; he could sail for the Western Isles, where he could be sure of support from Christina MacRuairidh, who had married into the family of Mar, the family of Robert's first wife. Probably he intended to return on or in time for the death of Edward I. It is unlikely that as yet he despaired of regaining the throne; but then, darker days lay ahead.

NOTES

1 The phrase comes from Sir Walter Scott, *The Talisman* (Centenary Edition, Edinburgh, 1887), p. 30.
2 Frame, *Political Development*, pp. 59–60.
3 Prestwich, *Edward I*, p. 361; Stevenson, *Documents* i, 162–73.
4 Prestwich, *Edward I*, Chapter 14; Barrow, *Robert Bruce*, pp. 28–30. Documents relating to the Great Cause are printed in *Edward I and the Throne of Scotland, 1290–1296*, ed. E.L.G. Stones and G.G. Simpson (2 vols.) (Oxford, 1978).
5 Prestwich, *Edward I*, pp. 371–73; Barrow, *Robert Bruce*, pp. 51–53, 57–62.
6 Davies, *Domination and Conquest*, p. 125. A similar fate had befallen the coronet of the Prince of Wales and the jewel or crown of King Arthur, and the fragment of the true cross which was the most potent relic of the Welsh, *Y Groes Naid*.
7 For the Wallace rebellion, see H. Gough, *Scotland in 1298* (Paisley, 1888) and C. McNamee, 'William Wallace's Invasion of Northern England, 1297', *NH* xxvi (1990), 40–58.
8 M. Prestwich, 'Cavalry Service in Early Fourteenth Century England', in *War and Government in the Middle Ages*, ed. J.B. Gillingham and J.C. Holt (Woodbridge, 1984), pp. 147–48.
9 R.H.C. Davis, *The Medieval Warhorse: Origin, Development and Redevelopment* (London, 1989), pp. 11–29; and, most recently, M.Prestwich, *Armies and Warfare in the Middle Ages: the English Experience* (Newhaven and London, 1996), pp. 18–30.
10 Plate 3.
11 *Lanercost*, p. 190. In the spring of 1311, the English were inactive and 'waiting for the grass', *CDS* iii no. 202, pp. 40–41.

12 J.F. Lydon, 'The Hobelar: An Irish Contribution to Mediaeval Warfare', *The Irish Sword* ii (1954–56), 12–16; 'Irish Levies in the Scottish Wars, 1296–1302', *Ibid.* v (1963), 214; and 'Edward I, Ireland and the War in Scotland, 1303–1304', *England and Ireland in the Later Middle Ages: Essays to Jocelyn Otway-Ruthven*, ed. J. Lydon (Dublin, 1981), p. 57.

13 J. Bradbury, *The Medieval Archer* (London, 1985), pp. 71–90; Prestwich, *Armies and Warfare*, p. 135.

14 Bodleian Library MS Tanner 197, ff. 46, 46d; BL MS Stowe 553, f. 83.

15 Barbour, *The Bruce* XII, 352–56.

16 The aketon is clearly depicted on the effigy of Bricius McKinnon, plate 1. *Late Medieval Monumental Sculpture in the West Highlands*, K.A. Steer and J.M.W. Bannerman (Royal Commission on the Ancient and Historical Monuments of Scotland, 1977), pp. 23–27 and plate 8.

17 Powicke, *Military Obligation*, pp. 141–60.

18 Powicke, *Military Obligation*, p. 148; *Rot. Scot.* i, 159–60, 163, 204.

19 J.O. Morris long ago highlighted the inconsistency in Edward's strategy, 'Mounted Infantry in Medieval Warfare', *TRHS* 3rd series viii (1914), 80–91.

20 Barbour, *The Bruce* VIII, 275–76, 368; XI, 242–46, 426–32.

21 J.R. Maddicott, *The English Peasantry and the Demands of the Crown, 1294–1341* (*P&P* Supplement 1, 1975).

22 Barrow, *Robert Bruce*, pp. 121–22.

23 Prestwich, *Edward I*, p. 496; the terms of surrender are printed in Barrow, *Robert Bruce*, pp. 122–23.

24 Barrow, *Robert Bruce*, pp. 141–43.

25 Prestwich, *Edward I*, pp. 505–6.

26 In September 1306 Edward at 67 years of age was reported to be convalescing from illness, 'hearty and strong enough, considering his age', *CDS* ii, no.1832, p. 491.

27 Barrow, *Robert Bruce*, p. 131; *CDS* ii no. 1818, pp. 487–88.

28 *Fordun* ii, 330–33 ; Barrow, *Robert Bruce*, pp. 139–40.

29 Prestwich, *Edward I*, pp. 503–4.

30 T.M. Smallwood, 'An unpublished early account of Bruce's murder of Comyn' *SHR* liv (1975), 1–10 examines a version of Peter Langtoft's chronicle. *Guisborough*, pp. 366–67 is the earliest source. Compare *Bower* vi, 309–13.

31 *Guisborough*, pp. 366–67; Duncan, 'War of the Scots', p. 135.

32 *CDS* v no. 472(r), p. 203.

33 Duncan, 'War of the Scots', p. 136.

34 *CDS* ii, no. 1811, pp. 485–86; *CDS* v, no. 472(d), p. 199; *CDS* v, no. 492(xii), pp. 211–13.

35 E101/369/11, f. 83d. On 5th April Edward I ordered that ships bearing provisions from Ireland were not to land at these destinations, *CDS* ii nos. 1753, 1763; Duncan, 'War of the Scots', pp. 136–37.

36 Barrow, *Robert Bruce*, pp. 148–53.

37 *Flores Hist.*, 130.

38 G.W.S.Barrow and A. Royan, 'James Fifth Stewart of Scotland', in *Essays on the Nobility of Medieval Scotland*, ed. K.J. Stringer (Edinburgh 1985), p. 180.

39 Duncan, 'War of the Scots', p. 137; *CDS* iii, no. 68, p. 13.

40 Duncan, 'War of the Scots', p. 137.
41 *CDS* v no. 420, p. 191.
42 *CDS* iv, Appendix no. 11, pp. 389, 390–91, 396–97; Duncan, 'War of the Scots', p. 137.
43 Prestwich, *Edward I*, pp. 506–7.
44 *CDS* ii no. 1811, pp. 485–86.
45 Duncan, 'War of the Scots', p. 138.
46 *CDS* ii no. 1820, p. 488.
47 *CDS* v nos. 444, 471.
48 This outrageous punishment is discussed in Prestwich *Edward I*, pp. 508–9 and references given in note 164 there. Similar treatment was meted out to the Welsh rebel, Owain son of Dafydd ap Gruffydd *CDS*, iii no. 16, p. 4.
49 *CDS* v no. 471, p. 197; *CDS* ii no. 1803, p. 485.
50 *CDS* ii Addenda no. 1979, p. 526; *The Political Songs of England*, ed. T. Wright (Camden 1st series vi, 1839), p. 216.
51 *Itinerary of Edward I Part II 1291–1307* (List and Index Society 132, 1976), pp. 273–80.
52 *CDS* ii no. 1819, p. 488.
53 *CDS* ii no. 1821, pp. 488–89.
54 Barbour, *The Bruce* III, 367–674.

CHAPTER TWO

Robert I, Edward II and the Kingdom of Scotland, 1307–1314

'After the death of le Roy Coveytous'

The activities of the Bruces in exile were far removed from appeal to an ancient celtic past, or retreat to a mystical source of the kingdom to recharge the batteries of Scottish nationhood. Rather they were concerned with present realities, the assembly of victual and cash, galleys and warriors. It was a time of arm-twisting, of calling in favours, of wrangling over payments and services due. The voyage into exile may have taken the well-known route, frequented for at least a generation past by MacSween and MacDonald galloglasses seeking employment as mercenaries in the endless wars of Ireland. Barbour states that Robert landed on Rathlin Island off the Antrim coast; Barrow suggests that he was making for the lands of his ally the Stewart in the Roe valley in Derry.[1] Yet there is no evidence that Robert set foot in mainland Ireland at this time. The greatest Ulster magnate, Richard de Burgh the 'Red Earl' of Ulster, was Robert's father-in-law. He had his differences with Edward I at this time over pay and conditions for service in Scotland; and chroniclers hint darkly that he was in league with Robert.[2] In fact he appears to have been consistently loyal to the English king under the most trying circumstances and to have had little time for his son-in-law's claim to the Scottish throne. There is no evidence that Hugh Bisset, lord of Rathlin and Edward I's admiral in the North Channel, knew of or acquiesced in Robert's sojourn on the island, or that he assisted the Bruces. Had Robert landed among the Anglo-Irish lords of Ulster, they would have delivered him up to his enemies. As it was, even three men buying wine in Ulster for the royal stores at Carlisle were arrested on suspicion of being Scots.[3]

Professor Duncan suggests that if a landing on Rathlin occurred, it was probably unintentional, and suggests that the most likely refuge for the exiled court in 1306 was Islay, the centre of MacDonald power. In the Barbour narrative, before Robert embarked for Rathlin, Angus Óg MacDonald received the king, did homage and gave him his castle of Dunaverty.[4] Duncan considers that this episode may belong to the period after Robert's return from Rathlin, and that, since Dunaverty was held by Malcolm fitz Lengleys, Barbour's reference to Dunaverty may be mistaken and Angus's castle of Dunyveg on Islay intended. As Robert's murder of Comyn had earned him the lasting enmity of the MacDougalls, Angus Óg now did homage to Robert and placed at Robert's disposal the amphibious forces of the MacDonald lordship. The exiled king began to assemble a coalition built upon opposition to the MacDougalls; upon traditional alliances with MacDonald, MacRuairidh and Stewart; and upon the support of Gaelic Irish mercenaries. Christina MacRuairidh of the Isles, who held extensive lands in the isles and the west of Scotland, may well have contributed men and galleys.[5] A letter of King Robert, addressed 'to all the kings of Ireland, to the prelates and clergy, and the inhabitants of Ireland', surely belongs to this period. Citing common ties of custom, language and race between Scots and Irish, Robert asks credence for his envoys who are to discuss with the Irish how to restore 'our nation' to its pristine freedom. The letter survives as an exemplar in a formulary (or copy book for Scottish royal clerks) of the 1320s, preserved in a late fifteenth-century manuscript. In the text the capital letters 'T' and 'A' mark the places where clerks using the exemplar should insert the names of royal envoys.[6] Dr. Duffy points out that these initials could refer to Thomas and Alexander Bruce, both of whom were with Robert in exile at this time. Not everyone agrees that the letter belongs to this period, but the coincidence is too striking to be ignored.[7] Robert's envoys were therefore voyaging around the isles and the north of Ireland at this time, building alliances and collecting money. However close the ties of blood and sympathy with his allies, the galley crews and troops needed to effect a landing in Scotland would have to be paid. One chronicle claims that Robert landed in Kintyre around Michaelmas (29th September) 1306 'with many Irishmen and Scots' to collect the Martinmas rents from his earldom of Carrick, and there attacked the forces of Henry Percy. Dunaverty, however, had only just fallen to the English; and Robert's earldom must now have swarmed with English and Anglo-Scottish forces. An expedition to Carrick seems unlikely at this time and the episode may belong to the following year.[8]

The English and their allies were not ignorant of the Bruces' activities. They expected Robert to return and gathered intelligence as to the preparations being made. In April 1307 Edward I paid £10 to three Ulster noblemen and William Montecute 'for inquiring, regarding enemies and felons of Scotland who had come to Ireland and had been received . . . in the Liberty of Ulster', and for capturing them and bringing them to Dublin Castle.[9] But earlier in 1307 Edward seems to have considered that Robert was in Scotland and was endeavouring to escape to Ireland. In January 1307 Hugh Bisset was ordered to equip his fleet with utmost dispatch, to come to the isles off the coast of Scotland and to join John of Menteith in fighting Robert, to assist in cutting off his retreat. Edward I warned Bisset that he held this business 'greatly at heart'.[10] A royal envoy was sent to

Ulster to expedite matters, and Simon Montacute was put in formal command against rebels 'lurking in Scotland and the Isles between Scotland and Ireland'. Again to assist in cutting off Robert's retreat, the sheriff of Cumberland was ordered to scour the coast for vessels and send them to Ayr, and to see to it personally.[11] The Montacutes were not disinterested servants of Edward. They were barons of Somerset and show consistent interest in (and possibly entertained a claim to the lordship of) the Isle of Man.[12] By sea the western approaches were guarded by Montacute and William le Jettour, on land by Aymer de Valence and John of Menteith, and they waited at Ayr to oppose any landing. From 4th February they had a fleet of 15 vessels with 200 sailors, with which they patrolled the waters around Bute and Arran. With mounting impatience Edward I wrote twice from his sickbed at Lanercost Priory, demanding news from the forces at Ayr.[13] But already the Bruces and their supporters had landed in various places on the coast of southwest Scotland. They may well have done so in response to false rumours of Edward's death. One party disembarking from eighteen ships met with immediate and total disaster. It was led by Thomas and Alexander Bruce, Sir Reginald Crawford, Malcom fitz Lengleys the lord of Kintyre, and 'a certain Irish kinglet'. The Lanercost Chronicle says that they sought 'to avenge themselves upon the people of Galloway' for their failure to support Robert in 1306. But they encountered Gallovidians led by Dungal MacDowell and were wiped out but for a few who escaped in two galleys. Fitz Lengleys was beheaded straightaway; the two Bruce brothers and Crawford were taken, together with the heads of 'other traitors from parts of Ireland and Kintyre', to the Prince of Wales at Wetheral Priory on 19th February. In spite of his wounds sustained in the battle, Thomas Bruce was drawn by horses through the streets of Carlisle and executed; Alexander Bruce and Reginald Crawford were hanged and then beheaded. MacDowell received the substantial cash reward of £40 and a knighthood the following Easter.[14] The party led by Robert landed safely. The Cumberland militia was levied on 20th February to pursue him; and on 19th March, Edward I believed him to be 'hiding in the moors and marshes of Scotland'.[15] Determined that he should receive no further reinforcements from Ireland or the Western Isles, the English maintained a strong naval presence on the western seas. Hugh Bisset's fleet served for 40 days from 2nd May 1307, with 240 armed men and 260 'without arms' (presumably oarsmen) setting out for the islands of Scotland; and in June, John Bisset (Hugh's son) agreed to guard 'the Isles, the sea coast and the arms of the sea towards Kintyre' with four barges, manned by 100 men in return for 50 marks.[16] The Bruce attempt to revive the kingship of Scotland appeared to be doomed.

Robert's recovery of Scotland is recounted in several excellent works; here a narrative is merely sketched in, with notes relevant to the subsequent extension of the Wars of the Bruces. Robert I's survival during 1307

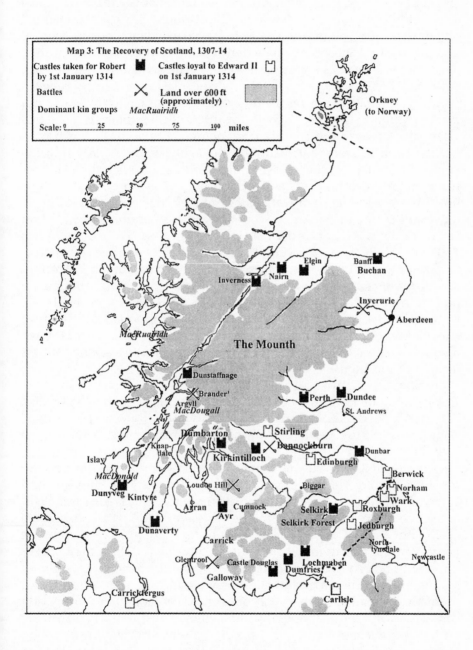

Map 3: The Recovery of Scotland, 1307-14

Castles taken for Robert by 1st January 1314

Castles loyal to Edward II on 1st January 1314

Battles

Land over 600 ft (approximately)

Dominant kin groups   *MacRuairidh*

Scale: 0   25   50   75   100   miles

Orkney (to Norway)

Elgin

Banff
Buchan

Inverness   Nairn

Inverurie

Aberdeen

MacRuairidh

The Mounth

Dunstaffnage

Brander
Argyll
MacDougall

Perth   Dundee

St. Andrews

Dumbarton   Stirling

Knapdale   Bannockburn

Islay   Kirkintilloch   Edinburgh   Dunbar

Loudon Hill   Berwick

MacDonald   Biggar   Norham

Dunyveg   Kintyre   Wark

Arran   Cumnock   Selkirk   Roxburgh

Ayr   Selkirk Forest   Jedburgh

Dunaverty

Carrick   North-
tynedale

Glentrool   Newcastle

Castle Douglas   Lochmaben

Galloway   Dumfries

Carrickfergus

Carlisle

was much more precarious than has hitherto been allowed.[17] The hero king was thought to have enjoyed progressively snowballing support, encouraged by consecutive victories in Galloway at Glentrool (in April) and Loudon Hill (around 10th May). But Duncan has recently pointed out that the Barbour narrative is highly dependent upon a Scottish account which exaggerates the extent of Robert's success at Glentrool. An entry in the English Wardrobe Account merely shows that on 30th May the English lost horses 'in the pursuit of Robert de Brus between Glentruyl and Glenheur, on the army's last day in Galloway'. Far from being a brilliant victory for Robert, the affair at Glentrool was a botched attempt to ambush the Treasurer of England. The ambush was beaten off, the guerrillas were pursued, and the evidence shows only that the English and their Anglo-Scottish allies were hot on his tail.[18] Another source relates that Robert besieged the port of Ayr around this time; but this episode has been transposed into the narrative of 1307 from an earlier period in the Anglo-Scottish war. Duncan argues that Robert could hardly have had resources to besiege a town the size of Ayr in 1307; and while he allows that at Loudon Hill Robert forced the English to withdraw, yet as English forces recovered so very rapidly, it cannot have been a significant victory. Even Barbour admits that the pursuit had by August 1307 assumed the character of a manhunt, led by he who was to become Robert's arch-enemy, John MacDougall, 'John of Argyll'. Barbour relates that John employed bloodhounds to track down the fugitive king; Bower that Robert 'hid among the bushes and thickets for fear of the English'.[19]

Cash and manpower now became crucial to King Robert's survival. At Glentrool, he had been after whatever cash had been in the English Treasurer's possession. Robert's mercenaries from the Western Isles must have been close to desertion. It was probably in September 1307 that he succeeded in preventing this by lifting the rents of Carrick.[20] In theory kingship gave Robert the authority to summon unpaid military service for 40 days. But how well the aura and authority of kingship had survived defeat, exile and inauspicious homecoming is far from clear. A further source of authority in the region was Robert's indisputable position as earl of Carrick, which could be used to extract rents from the peasantry. But threats and violence must have played the largest part in his mobilising of a guerrilla band. Robert seems also to have played upon regional antipathies, especially that between Carrick and Galloway. All these factors enabled him to call out a peasant levy from Carrick and conduct a rural terrorism against the Gallovidians, the Anglo-Scottish, and all who denied him their support – 'plundering and burning and inciting and compelling the inhabitants to rebel'.[21] Robert was not the only ousted aristocrat struggling against the English in the southwest. James Douglas of Douglasdale was pursuing his own feud against Robert

Clifford, the English lord who had been imposed upon Douglasdale by Edward I. Before Loudon Hill Douglas had been in contact with the English until the last moment, and presumably would have turned on Robert had he been offered a deal to his liking. Only victory confirmed his allegiance to Robert. Their partnership became the stuff of legend; but at this stage they were outlaws, rogue aristocrats of the sort that often infested the forests and wildernesses of the middle ages.

And yet as so often is the case with outlaws and terrorists, an air of expectation and romance began to cling to the Bruce cause. This was heightened immeasurably by the demise of Edward I, now surely imminent. In May 1307, as Edward I lay in terminal decline, a letter was dispatched to an English courtier at Carlisle. It was probably sent by the English commander at Forfar, and it is well worth reproducing:

> I hear that Bruce never had the good will of his own followers or of the people generally so much with him as now. It appears that God is with him, for he has destroyed King Edward's power both among English and Scots. The people believe that Bruce will carry all before him, exhorted by false preachers from Bruce's army . . . May it please God to prolong King Edward's life, for men say openly that when he is gone the victory will go to Bruce. For these preachers have told the people that they have found a prophecy of Merlin, that after the death of '*le Roy Coveytous*' the people of Scotland and the Welsh shall band together and have full lordship and live in peace together to the end of the world.[22]

So though at this date Robert was still hemmed in and many Scots still supported the English regime, much depended on the life of the old king. The air was alive with rumour, wild speculation and political prophecy. This letter suggests that hedge-priests had been fomenting mutiny among Edward's Welsh soldiery, beating the drum of celtic solidarity for all they were worth and successfully spreading an air of foreboding and expectation. In the event, Edward's death on 7th July did not blow the lid off a seething apocalyptic discontent; but it must have heightened tension, sapped English and Anglo-Scottish morale and contributed to the climate of change.

From 1306 Robert had been evolving a characteristic form of warfare, rules for survival from which he rarely deviated. There were four main elements: the slighting of castles; blackmail to ensure loyalty or neutrality; the painstaking destruction (harrying or 'herschip') of enemy lands; and retreat to what guerrillas of the 1960s used to call 'favourable ground', the forests, the moors and fastnesses where shelter and rugged terrain compensated for lack of manpower. Robert had witnessed Edward I's masterly reduction of Stirling Castle in 1304, which may have impressed upon him the impossibility of holding a castle against advanced siege technology. He had destroyed Ayr and Dumfries in 1306; Douglas destroyed his own castle in 1308 to deprive Clifford's garrison of security. Destruction of castles denied shelter to invaders of Scotland; and equally, it denied Scottish lairds the opportunity to sit out the war behind castle palisades without declaring commitment. Payment for peace was first imposed upon Gallovidian communities which preferred to buy off Robert's attacks rather than become refugees.[23] If he could not count upon their loyalty to himself as king, Robert could at least rely upon their loyalty to a financial investment in their own security. This policy brought him funds to pay mercenaries, to wage continuous 'low intensity' warfare; and it was eventually extended to secure financial support and grudging neutrality from communities in England. The third aspect, subjection of enemy territory to intensive wasting, was also eventually extended to Northumberland, Yorkshire and Ireland. Retreat to inaccessible districts was a traditional precaution for infantry forces apprehensive of cavalry attack. Already in 1306 after Methven Robert had taken this precaution; in 1307 the rugged terrain of Galloway had provided protection against the repeated mounted raids by the English.[24] The great forests of Selkirk (the 'cradle of insurrection', as Duncan calls it) and Ettrick which sprawled over the southern uplands provided shelter for Douglas and his men. These lands were 'forest' only in a technical or legal sense; they were not necessarily woodland, but uplands reserved for hunting which could provide refuge for guerrillas. Of these four elements, none was in any way novel, except perhaps the slighting of castles. The others were commonplaces of medieval warfare. Robert's combination of them however produced conditions in which he could 'choose the time and the place' for combat, and there would be no security for those who failed to support him.

An expedition under the uninspiring leadership of the new English king, Edward II, set out to search for Robert, splitting into three divisions. That led by Edward himself advanced to Cumnock, apparently to contain Robert in Carrick and Galloway, but it retired to Carlisle within the month, as the king was obliged to go to France to attend both to his impending marriage and to the Anglo-French alliance.[25] On Edward's retirement the next move for Robert may have been obvious, for the letter of May 1307 suggests that the north of Scotland was already on the brink of rebellion:

> I fully believe, as I have heard from Reginald Cheyne, Duncan of Frendraught and Gilbert of Glencarnie, who keep the peace beyond the Mounth and on this side, that if Bruce can get away in this direction or towards the parts of Ross he will find the people already at his will more entirely than ever . . .[26]

Northern districts were apparently clamouring for Robert's presence while he was at a distance. This takes some accounting for. Barrow's life's work has destroyed the myth that Robert was exclusively the champion of Gaelic Scotland as against the English-speaking southeast.[27] Intimidation and terrorism which Duncan highlights as characteristic weapons of the Bruces, can hardly have been responsible for such a surge of enthusiasm. Support for the Bruce monarchy in Ross can only have been due to MacRuairidh influence, and to the fact that distance and terrain preserved the northwest from English reprisal. Later, Edward Bruce would be able to rely on the allegiance of the Isles to advance his ambitions in the west; and throughout the period Robert was able to draw on the north of Scotland and the Western Isles for manpower.[28] Without denigrating the contribution of southeast Scotland in the struggle against English occupation, it is difficult to avoid the impression that the Bruce recovery of Scotland was powered by infantry manpower from the north and west.

Towards the end of September Robert was sufficiently confident to make his 'long march' to the north.[29] He marched rapidly northwards along the Great Glen, razing castles (Inverness, Nairn, Urquhart). Edward II ordered deployment of engines against Robert Bruce in October 1307, perhaps as a reaction to Robert's seizure of these strengths.[30] Confronting his enemies (John Comyn earl of Buchan, William Earl of Ross, and Reginald Cheyne) one at a time, and giving no opportunity for them to co-ordinate resistance, he forced each into disadvantageous truce. When at last they found the opportunity to unite, at Slioch in December, Robert was able to retreat to the fastnesses. During this winter campaign he exploited to the full the shortcomings of Edward II's allies and garrisons in the north. In the simple motte and bailey castles of northern Scotland, garrisons were isolated, ill-provisioned, demoralised and ultimately vulnerable. Robert also took a spiteful vengeance on the enemies of his family. At Inverurie in May 1308, he inflicted a severe defeat on the Comyn Earl of Buchan. The earl fled to the south, leaving his patrimony to be ravaged by Robert. A terrible example was made of this district and people sympathetic to King John; a devastation known to posterity as the 'herschip of Buchan'.

Edward II promised an expedition to Scotland in 1308.[31] He encouraged his adherents in Scotland to take truce until August, when he hoped to lead an army into Scotland. But at the English court the politics of magnate rivalry took precedence over a campaign in the far north of Scotland, and the expedition failed to materialise. But in August the council was advising the king to permit local commanders to take truce from the enemy 'as they have done hitherto'. It was thought that time was needed to victual castles; and the king wanted to be able 'to break the truce at pleasure', that is, to choose where and when to end the truce by surprise attack.[32] Yet time was on the side of Robert and this delay allowed him to become entrenched in the north. In July 1308 the Scottish king captured his first east-coast port, Aberdeen, an acquisition which put him in touch with the Flemish and German merchants who could equip and supply his growing army. Attacks on English ships victualling the castles of Scotland had already begun.[33] The submission of William Earl of Ross is evidence of the security of his position. Both Duncan and Barrow accept Barbour's claim that by the end of the summer Robert's position north of the Mounth was unassailable.[34] And in the southwest, Douglas had emerged from the forest to massacre Clifford's garrison in Castle Douglas and destroy the fortification in 1308.[35] Even before that time he may have been raiding border districts of England.

Robert's lieutenants meanwhile unleashed a campaign of devastation upon Galloway. Lanercost takes up the story:

> Edward de Brus, brother of the oft-mentioned Robert, and Alexander de Lindsey and Robert Boyd and James de Douglas, knights, with their following which they had from the outer isles of Scotland, invaded the people of Galloway, disregarding the tribute which they took from them, and in one day slew many of the gentry of Galloway, and made nearly all that district subject to them. Those Gallovidians however who could escape came to England to find refuge.[36]

The absence of corroborating evidence in administrative sources for this attack has aroused suspicion that this section of narrative belongs to either of the better-attested Galloway campaigns of September 1307 or of 1313. Yet the same episode appears in Barbour, Fordun and Bower, as well as Lanercost, and on that basis it may be admitted as fact. These sources add that Edward Bruce was supported by Donald of Islay (who may have been a cousin of Angus Óg); that he succeeded in capturing the Gallovidian chief Donald MacCan; in killing 'the knight Roland' (identified as Roland MacGachan); and in taking a fortress on the River Dee or Cree. This harrying of Galloway appears to be Edward Bruce's first independent action. Though found occasionally on the eastern march, Edward's interest was clearly focused on the west, and shortly after this campaign, Robert awarded him the title 'Lord of Galloway'.[37]

Despite Barbour's claim that Edward Bruce captured 13 castles in Galloway, all the main strengths remained in English or Anglo-Scottish hands; and castles, which bestowed security, were the concrete expression of lordship. Dungal MacDowell, driven off his lands by Edward Bruce's onslaught, was given command of the garrison at Dumfries and from that base was able to thwart Edward's ambitions to dominate the southwest. However, English garrisons throughout Scotland had been neglected and were already short of provisions. A letter of Edmund Hastings, commander at Perth, complained that his garrison's pay was twenty weeks in arrears, and asked that his authority be extended to include the town, indicating perhaps some friction between garrison and townspeople. He begged that the garrison be answerable to no judge but an Englishman, 'as it would be too much for them to be tried by a Scotsmen during the war', revealing the deep distrust between the English and their Scottish allies.[38] It is not surprising therefore that smaller castles in the south of Scotland began to fall into the hands of the Bruces from this time on. At Christmas 1308, the castle of Forfar was surprised by Robert's supporters and demolished. Similarly, Edward Bruce captured Rutherglen.[39]

Unable as yet to challenge the formidable castles and entrenched Anglo-Scottish interests of the southeast, Robert next turned to the southwest, where Alexander MacDougall, lord of Argyll, his son John of Argyll and the chiefs of Galloway had no intention of recognising the Bruce monarchy. Robert's first attack on Argyll may have taken place in 1308 or 1309, but the later date now seems more likely.[40] In a letter to Edward II which may be tentatively dated to March 1309 John of Argyll describes how Robert arrived near his castle of Dunstaffnage with a large army and galley-fleet. 'I am not sure of my neighbours in any direction', he wrote. Anxiously he assured Edward II that rumours of his own defection to Robert were unfounded. He had agreed to one truce; and had subsequently secured a second (either by payment or by some other means). In the absence of support he could do nothing else.[41] The letter obviously pre-dates the onslaught, and that it was written in 1309 is suggested by the fact that John's own father, Alexander MacDougall, the titular head of the family, had then been forced to do homage to Robert, creating a likely context for John's professions of loyalty. Alexander had been obliged to attend Robert's first known parliament at St. Andrews in March. John tried to ambush Bruce as he moved into Argyll, traditionally at the Pass of Brander. Duncan considers that the most probable site for the ambush is the north side of Ben Cruachan along the shore of Loch Etive. In addition to his main force passing along the shoreline, Robert had positioned men on the higher slopes, catching the Argyll men between two forces. John escaped to Ireland, Alexander soon returned to the allegiance of Edward II, and by December they had escaped to Ireland, from where John was to lead virulent Scottish resistance to the Bruces in the west and on the Irish Sea.

The erosion of the English position in Scotland was greatly facilitated by the temporising policies of Edward II. In early 1309 after mediation by King Philip and the pope a truce was agreed upon. Both sides were to return to their positions as they had been on the feast of St. James the Apostle (25th July 1308) and the truce was to last until All Saints (1st November). Robert restored nothing, however, and time and distance ensured that Edward was powerless to enforce the truce.[42] He again promised his Scottish adherents an expedition in the summer of 1309, but the only expedition to materialise was a powerful diplomatic mission led from Ireland by the earl of Ulster, which Edward II hoped would bolster John of Argyll's resistance to the Bruces in western Scotland. Piers Gaveston, in Ireland as King's Lieutenant, paid out over £2,000 in advances to Irish magnates due to cross to Scotland with the earl of Ulster, and after a conference with Gaveston at Drogheda, the Red Earl left for Scotland in August 1309. He had an impressive, perhaps intimidatory, following of magnates, men-at-arms, hobelars and foot.[43] But there is no record of the mission's having any impact. Irish ports however continued to supply Anglo-Scottish garrisons in the southwest of Scotland.[44]

In November English commanders had royal permission to re-open negotiations with the enemy, and on the 30th of that month English commanders at Berwick and Carlisle agreed a truce with the Scots until 14th January following. Guisborough states that money was paid to the Scots in return for this.[45] In December 1309 Edward II ordered his garrisons at Perth, Dundee, Banff and Ayr to take what truce they could until Whitsun (7th June 1310). A general truce was agreed upon, which lasted on and off until the summer of 1310. Banff, Edward II's last foothold in the north, fell to Robert in the interval.[46] The delay gave Robert time to consolidate; and important steps were taken during this period in the process of 'state-building'. Walter the Stewart now came out in open support of his kingship. This may have brought about a remarkable *volte-face* in Knapdale, where John of Menteith (a dependent of the Stewarts) came to Robert's allegiance and was made lord of Arran and Knapdale.[47] Robert's chancery emerges at this time as an effective administrative machine for collecting taxes and extracting performance of military services; and he enhanced his regality by holding a parliament at St. Andrews in March 1309. He organised a further ringing endorsement of his kingship by the Scottish church in the 'Declaration of the Clergy', intended to proclaim his kingship to all Christendom at the General Council of the Church at Vienne.[48] Also at this time diplomatic relations with the Papacy and Philip the Fair were opened. Though the alliance between England and France continued, Philip's sympathy for Scotland had begun to revive with the death of King John Balliol in 1306, and he had written a letter in 1308 inviting Robert to join his planned crusade. While remaining formally the ally of Edward II, Philip became increasingly alienated by Edward's infatuation with the Gascon knight Piers Gaveston.[49] Edward II for his part used this interval to provision his castles; but he later admitted that all the time he was losing ground to Robert.[50]

Truce or no truce, the 'Scottish war' was regularly spilling over the border into England from as early as 1307, at first from Douglas's lair in the Forest of Selkirk, then from North Tynedale. In September of that year Keepers of the Peace were appointed on the English west march, 'for the better preservation of those parts from incursions of the king's enemies and to punish rebels', and Cumberland magnate Thomas de Multon and four other local lords were ordered to assist them 'to meet the damages and wrongs sustained by the men of those parts, owing to the thievish incursions of Robert de Brus'.[51] Such language is suggestive of cattle raiding; and an incident in August 1308 bears this out. Patrick Lerebane, the receiver of Sir Alexander de Bastenthwaite, was driving animals from the fair at Bampton to Carlisle when he was robbed of them by 'enemies of the king of England'.[52] That same year three manor houses in Cumberland were licensed for crenellation (that is, conversion into castles): Dunmallogh and Drumburgh on the Solway, and Scaleby. It may be inferred from their locations that the raiders tended to avail themselves of the Solway fords.[53] On the eastern march too, there is evidence that the Scots were active from 1307. In November of that year Robert de Umfraville (earl of Angus, though an Englishman and a Northumberland magnate) and William de Ros were commissioned to protect Northumberland against 'incursions of the king's enemies'.[54] Past attachment to the Scottish crown and a history of lawlessness made the liberty of Tynedale especially vulnerable to infiltration and there are indications which betray that Tynedale and Redesdale were both restive.[55] In October 1309, 55 Cumberland landowners were ordered to repair to their demesnes on the border in readiness for defence,[56] but if hostilities took place they were on too small a scale to be recorded. Refugees from the war in southern Scotland were now streaming into England. Gallovidians drove their cattle to refuge in Inglewood Forest; and on the east march refugees 'coming from Scotland for fear of Robert de Brus' were liable to be robbed of their animals and held to ransom by brigands.[57] This waiting for the onslaught, this undermining of morale must in part account for the lack of resistance and swift payment of tribute by English counties when cross-border raiding suddenly intensified in 1311.

Prior to that, however, Robert I had to survive a second invasion of Scotland. Edward II had been converted to the need for action by political and diplomatic reasons which had little to do with Scotland. The author of the *Vita Edwardi II* considers that he went to Scotland in order to escape Philip the Fair's demands that he come to France to perform homage for his French fiefs.[58] Royal prises (arbitrary seizure of goods for which payment could be long deferred), over-generous grants to his curial favourites, heavy taxation on the pretext of Scottish war (contrasting with a marked lack of any achievement in Scotland), and the enormous unpopularity of Piers Gaveston had forged general agreement in England that government had to be taken out of the king's hands for at least a time. Edward was forced to consent to the appointment of Lords Ordainers to supervise his government.[59] The campaign of 1310–11 was intended to undermine the reforms of Ordainers, and to guarantee the personal safety of Gaveston (now seriously threatened by the magnates) in the presence of a royal host. Edward's removal of the exchequer and justices of the Bench to York, ostensibly indicative of a resolve to remain in the north, conveniently undermined the reform of government by the Ordainers in London. There were any number of sound military reasons why Edward ought to have embarked upon a campaign, as the policy of taking truces had given his enemy an opportunity to establish himself. Only in the southeast of Scotland did the English prevail; elsewhere their garrisons were becoming increasingly beleaguered; and alarm bells were now sounding for the safety of Perth. In a letter dated 16th June 1310 Edward reveals that a delegation of loyal Scottish magnates had advised him that unless he set out for the north in person all would be lost in Scotland.[60] The preparations were realistic enough. The whole of Scotland was put under the command of John de Segrave, Guardian or Warden, until the arrival of the king; and a new Chamberlain, John de Weston, was appointed to the administration in Berwick with funds to pay garrisons.[61] In June orders were dispatched for 5,000 infantry to muster in Wales, and to march to Berwick for 8th September. In July further levies were ordered from Lancashire, Cheshire, the Welsh Marches and the West Country.[62]

In October 1309 the attack from Ireland was planned. At Midsummer 1310 a fleet was to land Irish magnates led by the Red Earl at Ayr, presumably to support MacDougall resistance in Argyll.[63] Five hundred men, wearing the special body armour known as the hauberk, were to be provided by the Earl of Ulster; there were to be 300 hobelars and 2,000 foot.[64] The indications are however that, in Scotland, MacDougall power was already on the wane. In March John of Argyll had shown himself apprehensive of Bruce's army and fleet; during the course of 1309 the Macdougalls lost their castle of Dunstaffnage; and on 9th December John and his father Alexander arrived in Ireland, having found it too dangerous to remain.[65] An expedition was now essential for the maintenance of a foothold in western Scotland. Transport was to be provided by ships from Irish ports, joined by 45 ships from the west-country ports of England, and the combined fleet was to rendezvous at Dublin. As an added stimulus to this western effort Edward on 22nd July 1310 granted the land of Knapdale to John MacSween and his brothers if they could wrest control of it from John de Menteith. The MacSweens and Menteiths had been contesting Knapdale since 1262, an example of how long-standing local rivalries in the Gaeltacht aligned themselves with pro- and anti-Bruce positions. However, on 2nd August the expedition from Ireland was called off on account of unseasonal weather.[66] Around this time too, the MacSweens were driven out of Knapdale by John de Menteith; and their defeat may have been connected with the cancellation of the expedition. The rendezvous for the fleet was changed from Dublin to the Isle of Man, and the earl of Ulster's 500 hauberked men were ordered to join Simon Montacute on the Isle, which was now apparently vulnerable to attack.[67]

On the eastern flank the campaign went ahead. Foot soldiers began arriving at Berwick from the end of September 1310. There were about 3,000 infantry, 400 of them English, the remainder Welsh. In addition there arrived a company of a hundred crossbowmen financed by the city of London for the defence of Berwick.[68] From the magnates, however, there was a poor response. Only three earls accompanied the king: Gloucester, Warrene, and Gaveston who had been elevated to the earldom of Cornwall. Other earls showed solidarity with the Ordainers by boycotting the campaign.[69] Cavalry supplied by lesser magnates (John Segrave, John St. John, Henry Percy, Roger Mortimer and John Cromwell) was paid on a regular daily basis or in accordance with an agreed indenture. Altogether, the royal household paid a force of about 50 knights and bannerets and 200 squires or men-at-arms; and the large garrisons of Berwick and Roxburgh contained additional detachments.[70]

Edward II set off from Wark-on-Tweed on 1st September, down the valley of the Tweed.[71] His itinerary was a circular perambulation of his castles in southern Scotland, designed to strengthen and provision garrisons, and to recover his hold on Scotland south of the Forth. He visited Roxburgh and Selkirk, but skirted the 'bandit country' of Ettrick Forest on its northern side. He arrived at Biggar at the end of the month, then moved down the valley of the Clyde, west of Glasgow as far as Renfrew. By the end of October the royal expedition was at Linlithgow, having (presumably) traversed the country by way of Kirkintilloch and Falkirk. After a brief stop at Edinburgh, Edward retired, perhaps by sea, to Berwick which he reached by 3rd November. There he stayed for the next six months.

Predictably in the face of such odds, Robert retired into the north and refused to be brought to battle. There was nothing in the way of a pitched battle: '. . . as the army approached [Robert] kept to the trackless boggy mountain places, whither such an army could not easily penetrate'. No sooner had Edward retreated to Berwick than Robert attacked Lothian, his first foray into the strongly Anglo-Scottish southeast region. The English king again chased him northwards 'with a small force' before retiring a second time to Berwick.[72] The author of the *Vita Edwardi II* is unable to suppress his admiration for Robert and likens him to a second Aeneas, nimbly escaping his pursuers in fastnesses and wild places. The campaign had started so late in the year 1310 that Edward II could achieve little. Winter set in, and by the turn of the year most of the infantry force had returned home, their forty days' service having expired; and the English garrisons were confined to the towns and castles. In the Scottish winter campaigning on any scale was out of the question for the English because of the difficulties of finding forage for the animals. Significantly the one incident described in detail is an ambush of a detachment of English and Welsh infantry, out on a foraging expedition:

> One day, when some English and Welsh, always ready for plunder, had gone out on a raid, accompanied for protection by many horsemen from the army, Robert Bruce's men, who had been concealed in caves and in the woodlands, made a serious attack on our men. Our horsemen, seeing that they could not help the infantry, returned to the main force with a frightful uproar; all immediately leapt to arms and hastened with one accord to the help of those who had been left amongst the enemy; but assistance came too late to prevent the slaughter of our men . . . Before our knights arrived up to three hundred Welsh and English had been slaughtered, and the enemy returned to their caves. From such ambushes our men often suffered heavy losses.[73]

Nevertheless it suited Edward's purposes to stay in Scotland. Gaveston was safe, and he was saved from doing homage to the King of France. But progress against the Scots was unlikely. The Edwardian occupation of Scotland had depended to a very great extent upon occupation of castles; and at its height Edward I had held perhaps 40 castles, great and small, at various times. By the end of 1310 Robert is known to have taken and destroyed only nine minor strengths;[74] but by demolishing the castles he had taken Robert had made it extremely difficult for Edward II to restore the occupation to its previous strength. It is not surprising that there was little attempt by Edward to regain territory or initiative from the Scots; there was little that could be done in that respect without an expensive castle-building programme. It is surprising, though, that a contemplated assault on Aberdeen, which might have materially improved Edward's chances of retaining Scotland, was not attempted.[75] Relief of garrisons was supervised and regional commands were reorganised. A series of indentures was agreed with leading English magnates, most to last until the end of the regnal year, July 1311.[76] In the northernmost zone, 'beyond the Scottish Sea', Robert de Umfraville was appointed warden, from Easter 1311. He was to be based at Perth. Supporting him were Pain Tiptoft and Henry Percy, and altogether these three bannerets would be able to call on a force of 200 English men-at-arms besides other great Scottish lords.[77] The castle of Perth itself was entrusted to Henry Beaumont, a foreign adventurer and relative of the Queen.[78] Edmund Hastings, constable of Dundee, and Roger Mowbray were to act in support of Beaumont. In the southern zone, 'south of the Scottish Sea', Robert Clifford was appointed to overall command from Berwick. Roger Mortimer was installed as castellan at Roxburgh, having contracted to stay in Scotland for a year with 30 men at arms for £1,000. John Segrave was made warden of Annandale; but the marches of Galloway and Carrick were apparently recognised as lost to Robert's supporters. Some castles were held privately; Bothwell was commanded by Walter Fitz Gilbert for the earl of Hereford. Gascon mercenaries also received commands: Linlithgow was held by Peter Libaud and Stirling by Ebulo de Montibus. Still others were held by Anglo-Scots: Dirleton and Dalswinton by their respective lords, John de Vallibus and John Comyn (who may have been the son of the murdered Comyn). Dungal MacDowell remained at Dumfries; Ingram de Umfraville at Caerlaverock and Philip de Mowbray at Kirkintilloch.

Edward II grimly determined to see out the winter in Scotland rather than return to the censure of the Ordainers and risk separation from Gaveston. There may have been a political significance in the decision of the earls of Gloucester and Warrene to remain at private castles and on English soil. Gloucester stationed himself at the Bishop of Durham's castle of Norham; Warrene was at the Ros castle of Wark-on-Tweed. Both were just across the Tweed from Berwickshire. Gaveston was the only earl who wintered in Scotland, at Perth, where he remained until Umfraville and Percy took over at Easter. Lanercost says that Gaveston's brief was to prevent reinforcements from north of the Mounth from reaching Robert.[79] The difficulties of Edward's position were thrown into high relief by tension following the death of the moderate earl of Lincoln in February 1311. Thomas Earl of Lancaster, vociferous in opposing royal misgovernment, had inherited Lincoln's two earldoms, and now with a total of four earldoms at his disposal became by far the richest of the earls. Amid fears of civil war he travelled north to receive his inheritance from the king, but taking the strict Ordainer line of having nothing to do with the war in Scotland, he refused to leave the country by crossing the Tweed. Edward eventually gave in and made the crossing. Lancaster received his inheritance and performed fealty; but the king was much offended at his refusal to greet Gaveston.[80] The chronicles are firmly of the opinion that Edward II considered making peace with Robert I in return either for assistance against the Ordainers or for safe residence in Scotland for Gaveston.[81] Certainly there were contacts with Robert at this time. From a letter written in February it appears firstly that Robert Clifford and Robert fitz Payne had royal permission to attend a meeting with the Scottish king at Selkirk on 17th December 1310; and secondly that Gloucester and Gaveston were to have met with him at a place near Melrose. The second meeting did not take place because, the writer says, Robert was warned of treachery.[82] Interesting too is the report in February 1311, from a letter to the earl of Richmond, that Master John Walwayn, chancery clerk and putative author of the *Vita Edwardi II*, had been arrested and imprisoned in Berwick 'because he suddenly went towards those parts [the vicinity of Perth] to speak with Robert Bruce'. It is tempting to speculate that Walwayn acted as Edward's contact with Robert, imprisoned to appease the outcry when the king's secret contact with the Scots became known.[83]

While the English tightened their grip on eastern Scotland, the Scots were gaining ground everywhere else. From the northern port of Aberdeen Scottish privateers could prey on the North Sea supply routes; and a ship from Berwick carrying wine, flour and salt to Stirling was captured at night by Scottish privateers.[84] Furthermore in the forests of the interior the Scots were restive. The retinues of Gloucester and Warrene were deployed to pacify the Forest of Selkirk, which Edward II had not penetrated on his perambulation. But before this could be completed Gloucester was sent back to England to act as Guardian of the Realm, a key appointment, given the hostility of the Ordainers, which had been vacant since Lincoln's death.[85] From the Irish Sea in December 1310 rumour had reached Edward at Berwick that Robert had assembled a galley fleet in the Western Isles and that a Scottish attack on the Isle of Man was imminent. In February 1311 Robert was said to be marching towards Galloway. John of Argyll visited the court at Berwick over the winter; and probably as a result of his lobbying efforts on the western seas were renewed.[86] Early in 1311 Edward II ordered from Ireland 300 men-at-arms, 500 hobelars and 3,000 foot, to set out in June, with John of Argyll commanding. A fleet of 62 ships from English and Irish ports was to ferry this army to Ayr. This was no mere diversion, the king declaring that he was

> greatly desirous that the fleet which he had ordered to set sail for Scotland and the coast of Argyll, under the orders of his liege Sir John of Argyll, should be ready as soon as possible, seeing [that] it is one of the greatest movements of the Scottish war.[87]

By June, however, letters from English ports began to arrive, pleading all sorts of excuses for failure to provide ships.[88] Only a small force of men-at-arms and hobelars is known to have crossed from Ireland and made the journey to Berwick in July.[89] Clearly there was some action at sea; in October Edward wrote a letter of fulsome thanks to John for the repulse of his enemies, and to his sailors, English and Irish, for their labours in parts of Scotland.[90]

Spring arrived, and Edward showed no signs of returning to England; but he had neither troops with which to begin a campaign, nor money to pay for troops. To summon a parliament to obtain them was unthinkable as the magnates would support demands for reform. In the absence of parliamentary resources the king began to exert pressure on the rural communities of Northumberland to supply money, troops and provisions. In February the 'county community of Northumberland' paid a fine of £100 at the court of Roger Mortimer and Bartholomew Badlesmere 'for default of men-at-arms and foot of the said county, summoned to the king's service at a day and a place arranged.'[91] In common with many other parts of England, Northumberland had been subjected to purveyance and military service for some time already. In April the county communities of the north were ordered to aid Robert Clifford in the custody of the eastern march; and the king himself called up a part of the Northumberland militia. For three days (11th to 13th May) he paid for the raising of over 600 infantry in the northern wards of Northumberland.[91] What they were used for is unknown. Desperate to proceed with a campaign for the coming summer, on 20th May Edward took the extraordinary step of demanding troops without parliamentary sanction. A levy of one footsoldier from every vill in England was ordered to serve for seven weeks at the expense of the vills themselves, and to assemble at Roxburgh in mid-July.[93] Letters were also sent to magnates ordering a muster of cavalry for this date. The infantry levy was totally without precedent; and had been commanded without even the counsel and advice of the magnates. Only a trickle of infantry support arrived, however, and Edward was forced to call off the unparliamentary levy on 5th July. By this time, though, Edward had realised that the game was up and he would have to face the Ordainers in parliament. Accordingly on 16th June he issued a summons to parliament and the court left Berwick for England at the end of July.[94]

Scarcely had the English king left Berwick than Robert unleashed a savage destruction of northern England. The chronicles agree that he raided northern England twice in 1311, and this is borne out by the *compotus* of a manor taken into the king's hands. The keeper of Wark-in-Tynedale states that the manor was burned twice before Martinmas (11th November) in that year.[95] Lanercost, extremely well informed as to events on both marches, dates these raids to 12th–20th August and 8th–23rd September. The August raid is described in typically matter-of-fact style:

> ... having collected a great army, he [Robert] entered England at Solway on the Thursday before the feast of the Assumption; and he burned all the land of the lord of Gilsland and the vill of Haltwhistle and a great part of Tynedale, and after eight days he returned to Scotland, taking with him a great booty of animals; nevertheless he had killed few men apart from those who wished to defend themselves by resistance.[96]

Next month, about 8th September, Robert repeated the exercise:

> About the feast of the Nativity of the Blessed Virgin, Robert returned with an army into England, directing his march towards

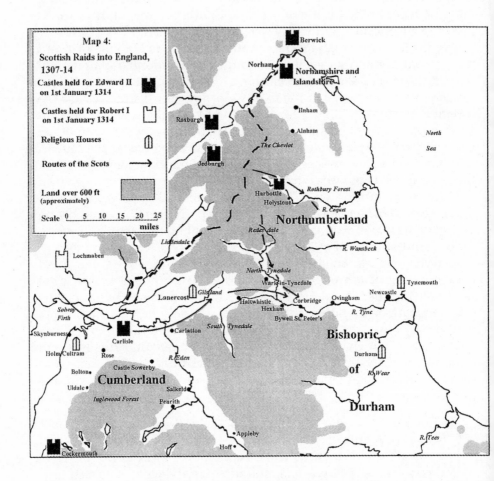

Map 4:

Scottish Raids into England, 1307-14

Castles held for Edward II on 1st January 1314

Castles held for Robert I on 1st January 1314

Religious Houses

Routes of the Scots

Land over 600 ft (approximately)

Scale 0   5   10   15   20   25
                                    miles

Berwick

Norham

Norhamshire and Islandshire

Ilnham

Roxburgh

Alnham

The Cheviot

North Sea

Jedburgh

Harbottle

Rothbury Forest

Holystone

R. Coquet

Northumberland

Redesdale

R. Wansbeck

Lochmaben

Liddesdale

North Tynedale

Warkin-Tynedale

Tynemouth

Lanercost Gilsland

Haltwhistle

Corbridge

Ovingham

Newcastle

Solway Firth

Hexham

Bywell St. Peter's

R. Tyne

South Tynedale

Skynburness

Carlatton

Bishopric

Carlisle

Holm Cultram

Rose

Durham

Bolton

Castle Sowerby

R. Eden

of   R. Wear

Uldale

Salkeld

Cumberland

Inglewood Forest

Peurith

Durham

Appleby

R. Tees

Cockermouth

Hoff

Northumberland, and passing by Harbottle and Holystone and Redesdale, he burnt the district about Corbridge, destroying everything; also he caused more men to be killed than on the former occasion. And so he turned into the valleys of North and South Tyne, laying waste those parts which he had previously spared, and returned into Scotland after fifteen days; nor could the wardens whom the King of England had stationed on the marches oppose so great a force of Scots as he brought with him.[97]

The attention which these expeditions receive from the chronicles suggest that the scale of raiding had increased dramatically; the forces employed were sufficiently large to discourage resistance; and the distances involved distinguish these expeditions from the cattle raids of the previous phase. They took place against a background of lesser incursions in the north and west of Northumberland. In a return to a writ for collection of arrears of a clerical tax, Bishop Kellaw of Durham names the parishes worst affected in Northumberland. Besides the Tynedale parishes of Haltwhistle, Ovingham and Bywell St. Peter's which lay in the path of Robert's expeditions, Alnham and Ilderton under Cheviot were both reported as destroyed by the Scots.[98]

The English and their Scottish allies despaired at Edward II's inability or unwillingness to lead a royal expedition against Robert, and Northumberland and those 'still of the king's peace' in the earldom of Dunbar hastened to buy off the raiders in September 1311, purchasing truces until 2nd February 1312.[99] Money forthcoming from these truces enabled Robert to prosecute the siege of Dundee, which lasted three months. Such a long siege exceeded the 40 days' free service he could expect from Scottish communities, and additional service had to be paid for.[100] The English made strenuous efforts to maintain Dundee. When the commander defending, William de Montefichet, made a pact for the surrender of the town in exchange for return of prisoners, Edward II angrily forbade it. William le Jettour was ordered to collect ships and barges to take heavily armoured infantry into Dundee by sea; but Robert captured the port in April, widening his window on Europe.[101] Meanwhile English districts stricken by raids witnessed an increase in lawlessness and banditry. In May 1312 Bishop Kellaw was unable to send the king money collected for arrears of taxation. He explained that there was great danger of robbery by *schavaldores*, indigenous bandits who sprang up in the wake of Scottish devastation, and on 1st July the sheriff of Northumberland was excused from rendering his farm at the exchequer to save him journeying to Westminster at a time of danger from the Scots.[102]

On 14th July 1312 an anonymous writer on the western march expected Edward Bruce to enter England while Robert attacked the castles of

Galloway and Dumfries.[103] Lanercost reports that in August Robert stayed three days at Lanercost Priory while his men burned Gilsland and Tynedale.[104] Attention in the lordly courts of England was however captured by the pursuit of Piers Gaveston, who was being hounded by the Earls of Lancaster and Warwick. Robert Clifford, hereditary sheriff of Westmorland and Cumbrian magnate, neglected the defence of his northern estates in order to participate in the hunt. Gaveston was ultimately murdered by them in the summer of 1312:

> When Robert Bruce heard of this discord in the south, having assembled a great army, he invaded England about the feast of the Assumption of the Blessed Virgin [15th August 1312] and burned the towns of Hexham and Corbridge and the western parts, and took booty and much spoil and prisoners, nor was there anyone who dared to resist. While he halted in peace and safety near Corbridge he sent part of his army as far as Durham, which, arriving there suddenly on market day, carried off all that was found in the town, and gave a great part of it to the flames, cruelly killing all who opposed them, but scarcely attacking the castle and priory.[105]

Lanercost's narrative is supported by that of the Durham chronicler, Robert de Graystanes, who adds that a large part of the bishopric was burnt, and also by the records of Durham Priory.[106] Wholly defenceless, the northern counties agreed to purchase truces. On 16th August 1312 the Bishopric of Durham bought a truce until Midsummer of the following year and the other border counties did likewise.[107] The truces did not entirely prevent violence: Lanercost records that the vill of Norham was burned and men and beasts carried off by the Scots as a reprisal against activities of the castle garrison.[108] Writs for collection of arrears of clerical taxes continued to be issued by the Bishop of Durham's chancery, but returns show that it was impossible to levy anything from the parishes of Norham and Ilderton (in the north) and Haltwhistle, Bywell St. Peters, and Ovingham in Tynedale.[109]

Although the truces purchased in August were to last until Midsummer 1313, there was an invasion scare in the spring. It could be that the northern counties were having difficulties in raising money: the Scots were exacting tribute at double the rate of 'normal' English taxation.[110] In March 1313 the Bishop of Durham, Richard Kellaw, excused himself from attending parliament on account of the threat from Scotland; and next month, in response to a plea for aid before Midsummer, the king simply ordered the men of Northumberland to do their utmost to defend the county against the Scots.[111] Despite the efforts of embassies from the Pope and King Philip, war was due to be renewed on that date. It was reported in June that the Scots were ready to attack in three places on the march, and on 5th August Kellaw again excused himself from parliament, writing that Robert 'has of late caused a great host to be assembled'. English northern counties, entirely at the mercy of the Scots, were again intimidated into negotiating for truces, and paid to have the truce extended until Michaelmas (29th September) 1314.[112]

From Christmas 1313 the system of buying truces was clearly breaking down on the western march. Collectors of the English lay subsidy granted in 1313 reported that the Scots invaded at that time because the people of Cumberland were unable to pay them for the truce, that most of the men of the county took flight, but that Andrew Harclay organised those remaining for the defence of the march. As a result of these disturbances the collectors were unable to carry out their task.[113] The county community of Cumberland then sent a messenger to inform the king of the emergency at a royal council on 20th May. By the spring, however, the patience of the King of Scots had worn out, and he dispatched his brother to exact the balance:

> On Tuesday after the octave of Easter [16th April] Edward de Brus, Robert's brother, invaded England by way of Carlisle, contrary to agreement, and remained there three days at the bishop's manor house, to wit, at Rose, and sent a strong detachment of his army to burn the southern and western districts during those three days. They burned many towns and two churches, taking men and women prisoners, and collected a great number of cattle in Inglewood Forest and elsewhere, driving them off with them on the Friday [19th April]; they killed few men except those who made determined resistance; but they made an attack upon the city of Carlisle because of the knights and the country people who were assembled there.[114]

Correcting the statement that this raid was in contravention of a truce, a later author with more local knowledge adds that 'the men of that March had not paid them the tribute which they had pledged themselves to pay on certain days'. This raid is well documented. It is described in the taxors' account, though there it is misdated.[115] The account of the keeper of the Honour of Penrith records that Penrith was burned on 17th April; and the fall in assized rents at Castle Sowerby is attributed to destruction of tenements by the Scots, 'who entered the vill after Easter'.[116] The Bishop of Carlisle struck a deal with Edward Bruce by agreeing to release two Scottish prisoners, the brothers Reginald and Alexander Lindsay, in return for Edward's sparing his manors at Rose and Linstock. These terms were not observed, however, for the Lindsay brothers were not released until after Bannockburn.[117]

At this stage (almost the eve of Bannockburn) an escheator's account for 1313–14 provides a useful list of manors in the king's hands which were affected, and these include High Crossby, Uldale, Bolton in Allerdale and even Hoff in Westmorland. The Cockermouth estates, on the other hand, remained unscathed until February 1315, the end of the period of account. The Cumbrian Mountains may still have marked the limit of Scottish depredations in the west. In Northumberland damage had spread further to the south and every one of the properties then in the king's hands showed signs of war damage.[118] Northern English communities were exhausted by unrewarded service in Scotland; by their efforts to resist the Scots or to raise money to stave off destruction; and by the devastating effects of the raids themselves. At last in the summer of 1314 Edward II's *grande armée* began to materialise. All the hopes of the northerners rested on the success of the royal expedition; for them there would be no escaping the price of failure.

Though his naval expeditions in 1310 and 1311 had no lasting success (so far as we can tell), Edward II's concern for the Irish Sea was justified by events. English control of the Isle of Man appears to have been weakened by a series of rapid changes of lordship. Gaveston had been given the Isle in 1307; then it had returned to Antony Bek, Bishop of Durham. Bek had died in 1311, and the Isle was granted to Henry Beaumont, titular constable of Dumfries.[119] It may have been at this time that Simon de Montacute attempted to realise his own claim to the Isle, for which he was forgiven in April 1313, on account of his good service to the king.[120] At any rate Robert I was able to take advantage of confusion or revolt on the Isle; and on 17th May 1313 he landed at Ramsay 'with a multitude of ships', besieged the castle of Rushen for five weeks, and eventually received its surrender.[121] Furthermore in 1313:

> On the last day of May, Robert de Brus sent certain galleys to parts of Ulster with his pirates to despoil them. The Ulstermen resisted them and manfully drove them off. It was said nevertheless that Robert landed by licence of the earl [of Ulster] who had taken a truce.[122]

The taking of tribute is very much in line with Robert's activities in the north of England; but it may here have had the specific purpose of supplying the Scots besieging Rushen. Disruption of the supplies to the English west march is another reason why Robert might wish to capture Man; but it also seems significant that the Anglo-Scottish commander at Rushen was Dungal MacDowell, who had recently surrendered Dumfries to Robert the previous February. Driven out of Galloway, Dungal had fled to Dumfries; driven out of Dumfries, he had retreated to Man; and now driven out of Man, he again shifted westwards, to Ireland.[123] Robert was pursuing an old enemy, a feud against the man who had delivered up his brothers to be killed, and also a logic which would carry the conflict with his Scottish opponents further and further to the west.

The departure of Edward II from Berwick in July 1311 surely gave a terrific boost to the morale of the Scots. Nine English garrisons in Scotland are not heard of after Edward's withdrawal, which suggests that they fell shortly afterwards.[124] From the middle of 1311 Robert was in a position to reduce the south-east of the country to obedience. It used to be thought that because Lothian was English-speaking or had been settled in the distant past by Anglian settlers, it was content with the English occupation and reluctant to embrace the Bruce monarchy. But Barrow has shown that many landowners of the southeast had resisted the occupation of Edward I and has drawn attention to several who declared support for Robert.[125] Until this time, however, the southeast had not suffered the ravages of war to anything like the same extent as other regions of Scotland. An inquisition as late as February 1312 shows the values of escheated estates to be just slightly below 50 percent of the peacetime values; this is not a catastrophic fall, and certainly not to be compared with what occurred in Northumberland in the 1310s.[126] The whole of southeast Scotland was dominated by a network of formidable castles – Dunbar, Edinburgh, Roxburgh, Stirling, Jedburgh, Berwick and lesser peles and fortalices besides – some with stone fortifications, all easily provisioned by sea and in close communication with one another. Robert now set about dismantling these castles and capturing the crucial east-coast ports which gave access to trade.

With relish Barbour describes the stealth and cunning of the Scots in capturing these strongholds. A stealth attack on Berwick was attempted, using ingenious rope-ladders, as early as 6th December 1312, which failed as the garrison was alerted by 'the barking of a dog'.[127] At Perth (taken on 8th January 1313) the Scots pretended to withdraw their siege, then returned at night to wade through the moat and climb the walls. At the peel of Linlithgow (taken between August 1313 and spring 1314) a loaded haywain concealing eight Scots was jammed into the gateway to provide access for others hidden outside. At Edinburgh (taken in 1314) they scaled the cliff to surprise the garrison at dead of night; and at Roxburgh (in 1314 as at Berwick in 1312) rope-ladders were secured to the parapets with grappling hooks. Only in the case of Linlithgow does Barbour omit to mention the destruction of the fortification that followed.[128] The implication of such stratagems is that the Scots had not the manpower or technology to storm a castle of any strength; and to judge from the references to folk-heroes who betrayed the garrisons, one also may be justified in inferring that the allegiance of the common people was increasingly being won over to the Bruces. It is interesting that the English Lanercost Chronicle records two opinions as to the sympathies of the Scots. In one passage it states that families were divided over allegiances; immediately after that, possibly in an interpolation by a later writer, it states:

> all those [Scots] who were with the English were merely feigning,
> either because it was the stronger party, or in order to save the
> lands they possessed in England; for their hearts were always with
> their own people, although their persons might not be so.[129]

Outrages committed by English garrisons on Scottish communities
loyal to Edward II accelerated the spread of Robert's support in the
southeast. The notorious behaviour of the garrisons of Roxburgh and
Edinburgh (robbery, holding to ransom, and spoiling of their truce
arrangements so expensively purchased) alienated what little support
the Anglo-Scottish regime had left. Leaders of opinion in Lothian and
Berwickshire communities, such as Adam Gordon and Patrick Earl of
March, protested bitterly to Edward II, receiving only assurances of
redress and thanks for their loyalty.[130]

So utterly absorbed were the English magnates by the pursuit of
Gaveston, his murder by the barons in June 1312 and the threat of
civil war that they could respond neither to the raiding of northern
England nor to the fall of Scottish castles. Perth was lost to Robert in
January 1313; Dumfries surrendered in February. To the royal council
in May the men of Cumberland had sent information of Edward Bruce's
depredations, but by that time the king was already committed to visiting
France. His departure on 23rd May was greatly criticised at the time and
has been since; but it was not as cavalier a move as has sometimes been
suggested. He was preparing to negotiate a huge loan from the papacy in
return for which he would temporarily surrender to the papacy control
of Gascon revenues. For this business the goodwill of Philip the Fair
was vital. Edward was aware of continuing French diplomatic efforts
to negotiate with Robert; and he himself sent a deputation to the north
to try to arrange a truce.[131] His relationship with Philip had improved
since Gaveston had been removed from the scene; and no doubt he also
sought assistance from the French king against his own magnates.[132]
On his return, however, on 16th July, he discovered that he had lost
the Isle of Man to the Scots. At the English parliament of September
and October northern affairs took second place to the repercussions of
Gaveston's murder. Only minor measures to enhance security in the north
were approved: grants to shore up the finances of the Berwick garrison;
and a commission headed by the Robert de Umfraville to inquire into
hostage taking and terrorism in Northumberland, Berwickshire and
Roxburghshire.[133] Only in November was a campaign decided upon;
in December the host was summoned to be at Berwick on 10th June
1314;[134] and meanwhile Scottish castles continued to fall to Robert –
Roxburgh in February, Edinburgh in March 1314.

Exactly what was it that prompted Edward II to decide in November

1313 to lead an expedition to Scotland? The established view, following Barbour, is that the fall of Stirling Castle was imminent; that Edward Bruce in summer 1313 had rashly agreed with the English commander of Stirling that unless the castle be relieved within one year, it should be surrendered to him. Duncan however has shown that Stirling was under no particular threat until February 1314; and has cited three independent English chronicles in support.[135] In November 1313 Edward II cannot have been reacting to any supposed danger to Stirling. His decision was a reaction to another event. In November 1313, Robert I proclaimed that his enemies had one year in which to come to his peace, or suffer perpetual disinheritance.[136] Edward II was indeed reacting to a one-year ultimatum as Barbour claims; but the ultimatum related not to Stirling Castle, but to this decree and the wholesale desertion by his Scottish supporters that it threatened to provoke. He was therefore forced to declare that his arrival in Scotland was imminent; and he also invited the Scottish magnates and prelates to declare fealty to him.[137]

In preparation for the campaign, Edward II now began to bolster the interests of dependable royal agents in the north. On the western march, curial favourite and Steward of the Royal Household Edmund de Mauley was installed as castellan at Cockermouth, and given lands to sustain his position.[138] Pembroke was appointed Keeper of Scotland with responsibility for receiving supplies. These were to be collected in the eastern counties of England and dispatched by Antonio Pessagno, Genoese banker and 'king's merchant'.[139] On 24th March the king summoned Lancaster and 21 other peers to be at Newcastle on 1st June for the campaign. Orders were sent to the counties to array over 10,000 infantry, including 3,000 from Wales. This was supplemented on 27th March by further writs demanding masons, carpenters and smiths from English counties. A further 10,000 troops were ordered chiefly from the northern counties on 20th April, all to be at Berwick for 19th May. As in 1311, there was to be a western offensive conducted simultaneously with the main effort in the east. John of Argyll was appointed admiral of the western fleet and the Red Earl was to lead the army including 4,000 Irish foot. Twenty-seven Irish peers were required to attend; and in an unprecedented move Edward II addressed letters to 25 Gaelic Irish leaders by name, asking for their participation.[140] Also as in 1311 there is scant record of action in the west. But there is evidence that forces were being raised in Ireland in the summer of 1314; gaol delivery at Drogheda shows that men were being sentenced to serve in John of Argyll's fleet from among supporters of a local rebellion staged by the gentry of Louth in April 1312.[141]

The size of the army which Edward II led to Bannockburn can only be guessed at. There is no Wardrobe Book to give details of the campaign. It is likeliest that one was never compiled, for horse lists, prests and other documentation used in the compilation were probably lost in the rout after the battle. The infantry turnout seems however to have been at first disappointing, for on 27th May (when the king was at Newminster Abbey) writs to Wales and the English counties were re-issued.[142] Chronicles expound the size and strength of the English army, and there is every reason to believe that it was on a par with all but the largest of Edward I's armies. The total demand was for 22,140 infantry (plus the 4,000 from Ireland); and it would be reasonable to estimate on the basis of Edward I's campaigns that half of this number of infantry materialised. As to cavalry, the earls Lancaster and Warwick failed to respond to the summons. But there were present three others (Gloucester, Hereford and Pembroke) and many substantial magnates below comital rank. Most of the cavalry is likely to have been paid by the royal wardrobe rather than supplied by earls. The *Vita Edwardi II* puts the number of cavalry at 2,000, which is unusually restrained for a chronicle estimate.[143] The accumulation of foodstuffs at Berwick and Carlisle in preparation for the campaign was also extremely impressive. Whatever else happened, Edward II's army would not starve. This is important, for continued victualling on this scale would enable English garrisons to remain in Scotland indefinitely.[144]

The Scottish army was predominantly an infantry force, estimated by Barrow at 5–6,000.[145] Judging by his later charters, Robert I had been meticulous in prescribing and insisting on military service from his adherents, and 'archer service' in particular. The Scottish infantry is described by the *Vita Edwardi II* as follows:

> Each [infantryman] was furnished with light armour, not easily penetrable by a sword. They had axes at their sides and carried spears in their hands. They advanced like a thick-set hedge, and such a phalanx could not easily be broken.[146]

Representations of Scottish infantrymen are included in the Carlisle charter. They wear the bascinet to protect the head, and carry a spear and a shield of wickerwork, but wear no body armour.[147] The Scots were also very short of cavalry. They had only 500 horse commanded by Sir Robert Keith, mostly light 'hackneys' as opposed to the great *destriers* used by English knights. The Scottish cavalry was further impoverished by the defection, practically on the eve of battle, of David de Strathbogie, Earl of Atholl. Atholl had been alienated by an affair between his sister Isabella and Edward Bruce.[148]

While at Newminster on 27th May, Edward II stated his belief that the Scots would assemble 'in strongholds and morasses between the king and Stirling', and Robert had indeed assembled the Scottish army in the Torwood to block the Roman road to Stirling.[149] As the English army drew nearer, the Scots showed every sign of following standard tactics for a small army facing overwhelming odds – retiring to cover against a cavalry charge, and withdrawal. They remained in the woodland and according to several sources were on the brink of retreat when on the afternoon of Sunday 23rd June, the great host of the enemy came into view. Robert, it seems, was determined to keep his options open for as long as possible. According to Barbour, he ordered his men to dig a series of pits on either side of the road, covering them with twigs, branches and grass to keep them invisible to charging cavalry until the last moment.[150] This strategem, likened by Barrow to the laying of a minefield, was designed to break up a cavalry charge. It is hard to say whether such a trap played any part in the battle.[151] If this is accurate, it would show that Robert had already selected a favourable battleground; but the other indications are that he was not yet committed to battle. Among historians the exact location of the battle is still disputed. Much depends upon the identity of the kirk mentioned by Barbour, and which is taken to be St. Ninian's by most modern commentators. However, the main features are clearly described in the chronicles: a narrow piece of ground, bordered by the trees of the New Park on one side and marsh on the other.

One has to agree with Duncan that Bannockburn was a gamble that Robert should not have taken. Faced similar situations in 1319 or in 1322, Robert chose not to attempt a repeat of this battle, but cautiously withdrew before the invaders, depriving them of shelter and sustenance by a thorough 'scorched earth' strategy.[152] Bannockburn is one of only two major occasions when King Robert threw caution to the wind and engaged directly with superior forces (the other being the defence of Berwick in 1319).

The author of the *Vita Edwardi II* says that when first sighted by the English vanguard 'the Scots were seen straggling under the trees as if in flight'. The sight gave false confidence to the arrogant young cavalrymen among the English who galloped towards the New Park. Once in the trees, some of them met with resistance stronger than anything they had anticipated. They came up against King Robert in person, and one of the English knights, Sir Henry de Boun, was felled by a great axe wielded by the Scottish king himself.[153] This incident took place in the woods, and was not visible to the main body of the English army. The English magnates were therefore still under the impression that the Scots were retreating as expected. It was to cut off this supposed retreat that the vanguard of heavy cavalry led by Robert Clifford and Henry Beaumont was dispatched around the New Park, keeping to open country well clear of the woods.[154] Others of the party were the Earl of Gloucester and Sir Thomas Gray, father of the author of *Scalacronica*. They halted on the Roman road to Stirling, blocking Robert's obvious line of retreat; but they were consequently out of touch with the main body of the

English army. Seizing the opportunity to take on this detachment while it was vulnerable, Robert ordered Moray to engage the enemy. Moray's infantry suddenly advanced out of the wood towards Clifford's cavalry, in schiltroms bristling with spears. The English, who must have halted too close to the woods, had neither time nor space to manoeuvre. Beaumont tried to get the cavalry back to organise for a proper charge; but with the Scottish infantry advancing at such speed he would have done better to retreat. The action that followed lasted for some time; but eventually the cavalry were overcome. Gloucester was unhorsed, an omen of what would happen on the morrow. Sir William Deyncourt was killed; and, his horse impaled upon the Scottish pikes, Sir Thomas Gray was captured on foot. The rest of the English cavalry was routed. Some fled to the safety of the Stirling Castle, others returned with Clifford and Gloucester to the main body of the army.

The 'evil, deep, wet marsh' where the English now made camp is identified by Barrow as the Carse of Balquiderock.[155] Having reached the site by forced march, they were exhausted from the toil they had undergone, and demoralised at the outcome of the initial engagements. Now they were forced to spend the whole night under arms and with horses bitted. While the infantry fortified themselves with Dutch courage, drinking and 'wassailing' into the short summer night, the cavalry crossed the Bannock Burn and the marshes with great difficulty. Roofs, doors and shutters of nearby dwellings were ripped off for use as planks to help horses and carts across the marsh. Communications with the castle appear to have been maintained, for some of these makeshift bridges were carried down from there.[156]

In spite of their signal successes of the 23rd, the Scots may yet have been preparing to withdraw to the more favourable terrain of Lennox. The *Scalacronica* of Sir Thomas Gray relates that a Scot in the service of Edward II, Sir Alexander de Seton, visited Robert's camp under cover of night to persuade him to stay and fight the battle.[157] In the early morning the English moved onto the firm ground that would facilitate cavalry manoeuvres. They prepared to drive off the Scottish magnates, strengthen the Stirling Castle garrison, and drive the remaining Scots out of the woods. There was no longer time for hesitation. Throwing caution to the wind Robert moved his army out from its cover into the open, offering battle. The English chronicles consistently describe the Scottish army as drawn up into three divisions; only Barbour mentions a fourth division, perhaps to give roles to each of the principal Scottish commanders.[158] They advanced into the open in schiltroms, blocking the whole width of the battlefield. Archers on both sides were the first to engage; but the English could not employ their bowmen in massed batteries as yet, so narrow was the space between the woods and the marsh. The English archers consequently failed to thin out or break up the schiltroms. Gloucester led the first charge. Probably the horses refused before the pikes, rearing up and throwing their riders:

> . . . when both armies engaged each other, and the great horses of the English charged the pikes of the Scots, as it were into a dense forest, there arose a great and terrible crash of spears broken and of *destriers* wounded to death.[159]

As the cavalry formation broke up, individual riders were surrounded by infantry and set upon. Gloucester was cut down. English chroniclers refer to this as the crucial event of the battle.[160] Other English magnates were similarly isolated and killed: Giles de Argentine, Pain Tiptoft, Edmund de Mauley and Robert Clifford. The narrowness of the battlefield prevented the English from making the most of their numbers, or from attacking the Scottish flank. With great difficulty English archers were massed and led to the front, where their volleys had some effect against the Scottish schiltroms. These batteries were however attacked and ridden down by a small contingent of Scottish cavalry under Keith. At the rear, the great mass of the English army, unable to engage the enemy, were quite powerless:

> The English in the rear could not reach the Scots because the leading division was in the way, nor could they do anything to help themselves, whereof there was nothing for it but to take flight.[161]

To Scottish onlookers at any rate it now appeared that the English had lost the battle. Confusion in the English ranks was added to by what they took to be the arrival of Scottish reinforcements. They were rather the *poveraille* or 'small folk', carters and labourers who had been guarding the Scottish camp, and who now joined the fray somewhat prematurely, anxious to secure their share of the pickings.[162] This sight dealt a final blow to English hopes. Edward II was escorted off the battlefield, and the sight of the royal standard leaving the field was the signal for a general retreat. Infantry and cavalry alike turned and fled into the marsh, and into the Bannock Burn.[163] One chronicle records the names of 75 English horsemen of knightly rank and above, killed or captured by the Scots;[164] of esquires, men-at-arms and lesser ranks no count was kept.

King Edward was escorted first to Stirling Castle; but the warden, Philip de Mowbray, refused to admit him. Relief of the castle having failed, it had now to be surrendered to the Scots, and Mowbray made his peace with Robert I. Edward II and his companions – Hugh Despenser and Henry Beaumont – fled to Dunbar, and from there took ship for Berwick and Bamburgh. Douglas pursued them; but he had not enough cavalry to engage. Pembroke escaped on foot, and led his Welsh retainers to safety in Carlisle. Others were not so fortunate. A large contingent led by Hereford and John de Segrave were received into safety by the commander at Bothwell Castle, who then made them all prisoner and turned them over to Robert.[165] Had Philip Mowbray delivered up Edward II in similar fashion, the war might conceivably have ended.

As it was, the repercussions of Bannockburn were immense. As a military technique, defeat of aristocratic heavy cavalry by mere infantry had been achieved only once in recent history, when at Courtrai in 1302 Flemish townsfolk had put to flight the knights of the French aristocracy. Sir Thomas Gray maintained (with hindsight) that 'the Scots had taken a lesson from the Flemings'.[166] Immense advantages accrued to the victor. The first-class castles of Stirling and Bothwell fell into his lap as their commanders changed sides. The *Vita Edwardi II*'s estimate of plunder worth £200,000 cannot be taken literally; but the haul of booty and armour was a godsend to Robert's impecunious administration and ill-equipped army. The value of the prisoners' ransoms was incalculable; the earl of Hereford alone was exchanged for Robert's queen, daughter and sister, and the Bishop of Glasgow. Robert de Umfraville earl of Angus, John Segrave, Maurice de Berkley and Antony Lucy were all redeemed for large sums. In England, the catastrophe discredited the royal administration headed by Pembroke, and forced the king to accept an unpalatable administration led by his cousin Lancaster.

In two crucial respects, however, the effects of the battle were muted. In the first place, it was no more than one battle in a very long war. It did not dissolve Edward II's claim to be the rightful lord of Scotland; nor did it alter the balance of power between England and Scotland. The English were still the stronger side by far, and they had no reason to give in. Secondly, although it brought more Scottish lords to his side, the battle did not vanquish the Scottish opposition to King Robert. Not surprisingly the air-brushed chronicles that have survived from his reign tell of a Scotland united under the Bruce banner; but the Balliol interest persisted. In Argyll and Ireland John of Argyll and other *émigrés* continued to whip up bitter resistance. Most dramatically, irredentist sentiment reappeared among the Scottish aristocracy in the Soules conspiracy of 1320. One prominent Anglo-Scot did defect to Robert after his capture at Bannockburn: Ingram de Umfraville. But there is no reason to believe that his example was widely followed, and Balliol himself left Scotland for France in 1320.[167]

The wailing tone of the English chronicles reflects the despair felt in the lordly courts after Bannockburn:

O famous race unconquered through the ages, why do you, who used to conquer knights, flee from mere footmen? . . . O day of vengeance and disaster, day of utter loss and shame, evil and accursed day, not to be reckoned in our calendar; that blemished the reputation of the English, despoiled them and enriched the Scots, in which our costly belongings were ravished to the value of £200,000 . . .[168]

But the real losers were vulnerable communities in the north of England, now defenceless in the face of the raiders.

NOTES

1 Barbour, *The Bruce* III, 725–762.
2 *Adae Murimuth Continuatio Chronicorum*, ed. E.M. Thompson (R.S., 1889), p. 30; *Vita Edwardi II*, p. 61. Various pardons and concessions were made to him in April 1306, perhaps to ensure loyalty, *CDI* v, nos. 507, 509, 510, 609.
3 *Calendar of the Justiciary Rolls of Ireland 1305–7*, ed. J. Mills (HMSO, Dublin, 1905), ii 234.
4 Barbour, *The Bruce* III, 659–67.
5 Barrow, *Robert Bruce*, p. 170.
6 *RRS* v no. 564, pp. 695–96 ; translated in Barrow, *Robert Bruce*, p. 314, and see note 9 on p. 379.
7 Duffy, 'Bruce Brothers', pp. 64–65. Duncan points out that the chances of documentation surviving from this shifting and restless period are slim; Phillips suggests an alternative context, see p. 199 below n.15.
8 *Guisborough*, p. 370; Barrow, *Robert Bruce*, p.169; but compare *Scalachronica*, pp. 34–35 and Barbour, *The Bruce* V, 89–119.
9 *CDI* v no. 633, p. 184.
10 *CCR 1302–7*, p. 482.
11 *CDS* ii nos. 1888, 1889, 1893.
12 S. Duffy, 'The 'Continuation' of Nicholas Trevet: A New Source for the Bruce Invasion', *PRIA* xci C (1991), 305–6.
13 *CDS* v no. 492 (ix), (xiv); *CDS* ii nos. 1895, 1896.
14 *Lanercost*, pp. 179–80; *CDS* iv, p. 489; *CDS* v no. 492, p. 216.
15 *CDS* ii nos. 1902, 1913.
16 *CDI* v, no. 627, p. 183; *CDS* ii no. 1941, p. 516.
17 This paragraph and the following are based upon A.A.M. Duncan, 'The War of the Scots, 1306–23', *TRHS* ii 6th series (1992), 138–41.
18 *CDS* v no. 490, p. 208.
19 Barbour, *The Bruce* VI, 536–674; *Bower* vi, 341. Barbour refers to John as 'John of Lorn', but this invites confusion with a later MacDougall chief.
20 *Guisborough*, p. 370, see note 8 above.
21 *CDS* iii no. 15, p. 3.
22 This is Barrow's translation, *Robert Bruce*, pp. 172–73.
23 There is evidence of displacement of the tenantry from southwest Scotland from September 1307, *CDS* iii nos. 11, 14.
24 *CDS* v nos. 485, 512.
25 *Lanercost*, pp. 183–84; *CDS* iii no. 2, p. 1; E.M.Hallam, *Itinerary of Edward*

II and his Household 1307–1328 (Lists and Indexes Society 211, 1984), pp. 21–23.

26 Barrow, *Robert Bruce*, pp. 172–73.

27 See for example Barrow, 'Lothian in the War of Independence', *SHR* lv (1976), 151–71.

28 References to the Bruces' reliance on northern and island manpower may be found in *Lanercost*, pp. 181, 188, 191; Barbour says that at Bannockburn, in Robert's own division there were men of Carrick, Argyll, Kintyre, and the Isles, *The Bruce* XI, 337–46; and *Melsa* ii, 346, where the army of 1322 is described as *exercitus Scottorum, Brandorum et Insulanorum*. See also Duffy, 'Continuation of Trevet', pp. 308, 311–12, 314.

29 The following narrative is based on Barrow, *Robert Bruce*, Chapters 10 and 11.

30 *CDS* iii no. 20, p. 4.

31 *Rot. Scot.* i, 55.

32 *CDS* iii no. 47, p. 9 (redated in *CDS* v p. 79 to August 1308).

33 See below, pp. 208–9.

34 Barbour, *The Bruce* IX, 302–100.

35 Duncan, 'War of the Scots', p. 140.

36 *Lanercost*, p. 188.

37 Barrow, *Robert Bruce*, pp. 181–82; *CDS* iii no. 69, p. 13; *Fordun* ii, 337; Barbour, *The Bruce* IX, 501–665; *Bower* vi, 343–45, 444–45. Edward was Lord of Galloway by the time of the St. Andrews Parliament of 1309, which he attended with Donald of Islay.

38 *CDS* iii no. 116, p. 22 (redated *CDS* v p.79).

39 Barbour, *The Bruce* IX, 311–24, X, 793–800; Duncan, 'War of the Scots', p. 143; Barrow, *Robert Bruce*, pp. 182, 190–91.

40 *Fordun* ii, 338.

41 The letter is translated in Barrow, *Robert Bruce*, p. 179. where the problems associated with it are discussed.

42 *Lanercost*, p. 189; *CDS* v, no. 526, p. 224.

43 J.S. Hamilton, *Piers Gaveston Earl of Cornwall, 1307–1312: Politics and Patronage in the Reign of Edward II* (Detroit, 1988), p. 62; J.F. Lydon, 'Ireland's Participation in the Military Activities of the English Kings in the Thirteenth and Fourteenth Century' (University of London Ph. D. thesis, 1955), p. 279. The Red Earl was paid £315 in expenses after the mission, *CDS* v no. 566, p. 232.

44 See below pp. 189, 203–4 n. 129.

45 *Rot. Scot.* i, 79–80; *Lanercost*, p. 190; *Guisborough*, p. 384.

46 *CDS* v no. 531, p. 226.

47 Barrow, *Robert Bruce*, p. 183.

48 Translation in *Anglo-Scottish Relations 1174–1328: Some Selected Documents*, ed. E.L.G. Stones (London, 1965), no. 36, pp. 140–43.

49 Maddicott, *Lancaster*, p. 83.

50 *CDS* v no. 531, p. 226.

51 *CPR 1307–13*, pp. 3–4; *CCR 1307–13*, p. 42; *Guisborough*, p. 384 dates the resurgence of Scottish raiding to 1308.

52 *Year Book of 12 Edward II* , ed. J.P. Collas (Selden Society, lxxxi, 1964) no. 62, pp. 53–54.

53 *CPR 1307–13*, pp. 8, 11.
54 *CPR 1307–13*, p. 14.
55 *CPR 1307–13*, pp. 39–40; *CDS* ii, no. 1806, pp. 484–85; *Rot. Scot.* i, 57.
56 *Rot. Scot.* i, 77–78.
57 Just 3/53/2, mm. 7,8.
58 *Vita Edwardi II*, pp. 10–11.
59 Maddicott, *Lancaster*, pp. 106–13.
60 Maddicott, *Lancaster*, p. 113; *CDS* iii no. 95, p. 18.
61 *CDS* iii nos. 137, 145, 152.
62 *Rot. Scot.*, i, 88–96.
63 *CDS* iii no. 156, p. 29; *Rot. Scot.* i, 78.
64 *Rot. Scot.*, i, 93.
65 *CCR 1307–13*, p. 205.
66 *Rot. Scot.*, i, 83, 90, 92.
67 Duffy, 'Bruce Brothers', p. 74.
68 BL MS Cotton Nero C viij, ff. 7–7d (*Debita peditum*), 45.
69 Maddicott, *Lancaster*, pp. 113–14.
70 BL MS Cotton Nero C viij, ff. 2–4d, 6, 6d, 8d, 9d, 10, 13, 13d, 15, 17, 41, 42, 43d.
71 *Itinerary of Edward II*, pp. 64–76.
72 *Lanercost*, pp. 190–91.
73 *Vita Edwardi II*, pp. 12, 13.
74 Aboyne, Banff, Dumbarton, Elgin, Forfar, Inverness, Nairn, Rutherglen, and Urquhart.
75 Duncan, 'War of the Scots', p. 149.
76 BL MS Cotton Nero C viij, ff. 42–45d; *CDS* iii nos. 170, 173, 184, 192.
77 *CDS* iii no. 202, pp. 40–41.
78 *CDS* iii nos. 201, 296.
79 *Lanercost*, p. 191.
80 Maddicott, *Lancaster*, p. 115; *Lanercost*, p. 192.
81 *Vita Edwardi II*, p. 22; *Lanercost*, p. 188.
82 *CDS* iii no. 197, p. 39.
83 *CDS* v no. 554, p. 229.
84 BL MS Cotton Nero C viij, ff. 67d - 71.
85 *Lanercost*, p. 191; Maddicott, *Lancaster*, p. 114.
86 *Calendar of Justiciary Rolls of Ireland* iii, 167, 219; *Rot. Scot.*, i, 96; *Lanercost*, p. 191.
87 Lydon, 'Ireland's Participation', p. 287; *CDS* iii no. 203, p. 41.
88 *Rot. Scot.* i, 103; *CDS* iii no. 216, p. 44; *CDS* v nos. 557, 558, 559, 560, 561, 563, 564, 565.
89 *CDS* iii Appendix VII, pp. 395–96.
90 *Rot. Scot.* i, 107.
91 E101/374/6, f. 2.
92 Bodleian Library MS Tanner 197, f. 46d.
93 Powicke, *Military Obligation*, pp. 139–40.
94 *Itinerary of Edward II*, p. 75.
95 *Fordun* ii, 338; E372/166, m. 32; *CCR 1307–13*, p. 397.
96 *Lanercost*, p. 194.
97 *Lanercost*, pp. 194–95; but Bishop Kellaw wrote that the invasion took place a week later, on 16th September, *RPD* i, 92–93.

 98 *RPD* ii, 847–51, 880.
 99 *Lanercost*, p. 195. See below p. 130.
100 Duncan, *RRS* v, p. 303; 'War of the Scots', p. 147.
101 *Rot. Scot.* i, 108,109.
102 *RPD* ii, 880; *CDS* iii no. 279, p. 55; E159/86, m. 85.
103 *CDS* iii no. 279, p. 55.
104 Described twice in *Lanercost*, p. 194 and again p. 197.
105 *Lanercost*, pp. 199–200.
106 Raine, *Scriptores Tres*, p. 94. M. Camsell cites a court case of 1340,
     which refers to the destruction of houses in St. Giles Street, Durham,
     and probably relates to this raid, 'The Development of a Northern
     Town in the later Middle Ages: the City of Durham c. 1250–1540'
     (York University D. Phil. thesis, 1985), i, 59.
107 Raine, *Scriptores Tres*, p. 94; *Lanercost*, p. 200; *The Chronicle of St. Mary's
     Abbey, York,* ed. H.H.E. Craster and M.E. Thornton (Surtees Society cxlviii,
     1933 for 1934), pp. 53–54; *RPD* i, 204–5.
108 *Lanercost*, p. 198.
109 *RPD* ii, 880–82.
110 See below p. 132.
111 *RPD* i, 301; *CPR 1313–17*, p. 559.
112 *Lanercost*, p, 203; *RPD* i, 301, 339, 386; *Rot. Scot.* i , 112, 113; *CDS* v nos.
     581, 583.
113 E159/100, m. 110d. See Chapter 4.
114 *Lanercost*, p. 205.
115 E159/100, m. 110d: 'the morrow of the Close of Easter' is given where
     other sources give 'the week after Easter'. Easter Sunday had fallen on
     7th April 1314.
116 E372/166, m. 32; *CCR 1313–18*, p. 56.
117 *Reg. Halton* i, 96–97. The Lindsay brothers had been prisoners since at
     least 1308, *CDS* iii no. 290, p. 57. They were included in the exchange
     for John Segrave after the battle, *Rot. Scot.,* i. 134.
118 E372/160, mm. 50, 50d.
119 Barrow, *Robert Bruce*, pp. 28–29, 191–93.
120 Duffy, 'Continuation of Trevet', pp. 305–7.
121 *Chronica Regum Manniae et Insularum, Facsimile of BL MS Julius A VII*
     (Douglas, 1924), p. 39.
122 *Chart. St. Mary's Dublin* ii, 342.
123 See p. 187. It is most surprising that Robert had allowed MacDowell
     to leave Dumfries with his life.
124 Cavers, Dalswinton, Dirleton, Kirkintilloch, Loch Doon, Luffness,
     Muckhart, Selkirk and Yester.
125 Barrow, 'Lothian in the War of Independence', pp. 162–71.
126 *CDS* iii no. 245, p. 50.
127 *Lanercost*, pp. 200–1.
128 Barbour, *The Bruce* IX, 331–63 (Perth); X, 136–252 (Linlithgow); 357–510
     (Roxburgh); X, 511–707 (Edinburgh). See also *Lanercost*, p. 204.
129 *Lanercost*, p. 195.
130 *Rot. Scot.* i, 111, 113–14.
131 *Foedera* ii (I), 215, 217; *CPR 1307–13*, p. 588; Maddicott, *Lancaster*,
     p. 149; Phillips, *Aymer de Valence*, pp. 62–64.

132 Maddicott, *Lancaster*, pp. 136, 152.

133 Phillips, *Aymer de Valence*, pp. 65–68; *Rot. Scot.* i, 114; *CPR 1313–17*, p. 71.

134 Phillips, *Aymer de Valence*, pp. 72–73; Maddicott, *Lancaster*, p. 157.

135 Duncan, 'War of the Scots', p. 150.

136 The decree of perpetual disinheritance was proclaimed one year later, at the parliament of Cambuskenneth, on 6th November 1314, *RRS* v no. 41, p. 330.

137 28th November 1313, *Rot. Scot.* i, 114; *Foedera* ii (I), 237.

138 *CPR 1313–17*, p. 128.

139 Phillips, *Aymer de Valence*, p. 73; *Rot. Scot.* i, 117. For Pessagno's contribution to the campaign, see Charts 3 and 4, p. 126.

140 *Rot. Scot.* i, 118–19, 119–21, 122, 124.

141 NAI KB2/7, pp. 3,4.

142 *Rot. Scot.* i, 126–27.

143 *Vita Edwardi II*, p. 50; Barrow, *Robert Bruce* , p. 207.

144 See Charts 3 and 4, p. 126.

145 Barrow, *Robert Bruce* , p. 208.

146 *Vita Edwardi II*, p. 52.

147 Plate 3.

148 *RRS* v no. 140, pp. 415–17.

149 The subsequent narrative follows Barrow, *Robert Bruce*, pp. 209–216.

150 Barrow, *Robert Bruce* , p. 217; Barbour, *The Bruce* XI, 363–80.

151 Such a trap is mentioned in the later *Chronicon Galfridi le Baker de Swynebroke*, ed. E.M. Thompson (Oxford, 1881), pp. 7–8; *Vita Edwardi II*, p. 54 mentions a ditch into which the English fell. But the trap has no place in either Barbour or any other narrative. See Barrow's map, *Robert Bruce*, p. 213.

152 Duncan, 'War of the Scots', p. 150.

153 *Vita Edwardi II*, p. 51.

154 *Scalacronica*, pp. 53–56; *Lanercost*, p. 207.

155 Barrow, *Robert Bruce* , p. 222.

156 *Vita Edwardi II*, pp. 51–52; *Scalacronica*, p. 55; Barbour, *The Bruce* XII, 390–408.

157 *Scalacronica*, p. 55.

158 *Vita Edwardi II*, p. 52; *Scalacronica*, p. 55; *Lanercost*, pp. 207–8. Barbour, *The Bruce* XI, 309–46 gives a division each to Edward Bruce, Douglas, Moray and King Robert. Compare accounts of the battle of Fochart, pp. 185–86.

159 *Lanercost*, p. 208.

160 Barrow, *Robert Bruce*, pp. 225–26.

161 *Lanercost*, p. 208.

162 Barbour, *The Bruce* XIII, 225–64.

163 *Vita Edwardi II*, p. 54; *Lanercost*, p. 208.

164 Duffy, 'Continuation of Trevet', p. 307.

165 *Vita Edwardi II*, p. 54–55; *Lanercost*, pp. 208–9; Phillips, *Aymer de Valence*, pp. 74–75.

166 *Scalacronica*, p. 55.

167 Ingram de Umfraville was not redeemed, but stayed in Scotland until 1320 and then left for France, Duncan, 'War of the Scots', p. 127.

168 *Vita Edwardi II*, p. 54.

CHAPTER THREE

The Raiding of Northern England, 1311–1322

'The longest stick that I have'

N ews of the astonishing defeat at Bannockburn was received in Northumberland with trepidation, as the report of two tax collectors shows:

> Richard and Robert began to tax the goods of the said men [of Northumberland] in the seventh year [of Edward II], and they sat at Morpeth in the said county; and suddenly there arrived Stephen Segrave and many others with him and they told them that the lord king was retreating from Stirling with his army and was coming towards England, and on this they were terrified. They fled, and, like others of the county, stayed in enclosed towns and castles and forts. And immediately afterwards, before the 1st August, there came Edward Bruce and Thomas Randolph leading the Scottish army . . .[1]

Lanercost names the leaders of this raid as Edward Bruce, James Douglas and 'John' Soules (by which presumably is meant William Soules, Lord of Liddesdale). The Scots entered Northumberland at Norham and marched the length of the county to Newburn on the Tyne, where they stayed three days, devastating, burning and intimidating Newcastle as William Wallace had done in 1297. Lanercost goes on to say that they crossed into Durham, but there they did not burn much because the inhabitants bought them off. However, they traversed the bishopric, carrying off cattle and prisoners. They crossed into Richmondshire but they did not enter the town of Richmond. Then, gathering together their forces, they turned north-west into Swaledale 'and other valleys', following the old Roman road. At Stainmore they carried off yet more cattle; but at the Reycross they met with resistance organised by Andrew Harclay of the Carlisle garrison. In the account of the king's receiver of victuals at Carlisle it is recorded that the garrison lost 16 horses in an action there on 4th August 1314,[2] a loss which suggests Harclay's detachment came off worse. They then burnt the towns of Brough, Appleby and Kirkoswald.[3] Kirkoswald's small castle is thought to have

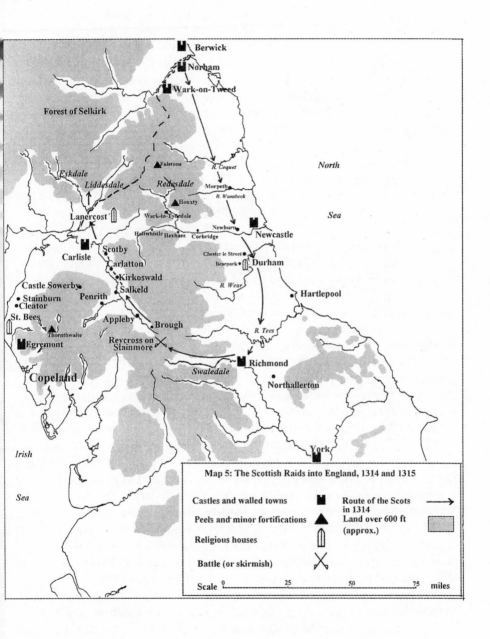

Map 5: The Scottish Raids into England, 1314 and 1315

Berwick
Norham
Wark-on-Tweed
Forest of Selkirk
Falstone
R. Coquet
North
Eskdale
Liddesdale   *Redesdale*   Morpeth
R. Wansbeck
Houxty
Lanercost
Wark-In-Tynedale
Sea
Newburn
Haltwhistle Hexham Corbridge
Newcastle
Scotby
Carlisle   Carlatton
Chester le Street
Bearpark   Durham
Kirkoswald
Castle Sowerby   Salkeld
R. Wear
Stainburn   Penrith
Hartlepool
Cleator
St. Bees
Appleby
Brough
R. Tees
Thornthwaite
Reycross on
Egremont   Stainmore
Richmond
Swaledale
Copeland
Northallerton
Irish
York
Sea

Castles and walled towns   Route of the Scots in 1314
Peels and minor fortifications   Land over 600 ft (approx.)
Religious houses
Battle (or skirmish)
Scale   0   25   50   75   miles

been destroyed on this occasion;[4] and it is recorded in a case in the court of King's Bench that Scots entered Westmorland on 8th August, the day on which the county court of Westmorland was due to be held; but the Scots came around the castle of Appleby and prevented the court from taking place.[5] Penrith did not lie directly in the raiders' path, but it seems to have sustained some damage, for the tenants of the Honour at Penrith and Castle Sowerby were subsequently granted a year's protection from purveyance 'on account of their losses during the late inroad of the Scots'.[6] Scotby had already been destroyed in July; at Carlatton a fall in bond rents was said to be due to burning of the vill by the Scots on the Thursday after the feast of St. Lawrence (15th August); and Salkeld, which did lie directly in the raiders' homeward path, had been visited in April by Edward Bruce's men and now suffered a further loss of rents and destruction of the watermill.[7] The raiders returned home by way of Lanercost Priory, trampling crops with their stolen cattle. By this it appears that they were making for Liddesdale, keeping well clear of the Carlisle garrison. On hearing of this raid, the people of Copeland bought off the Scots with 600 marks for peace from Christmas to Midsummer.

Prior to Bannockburn Robert I had concentrated on the tactical plane, throwing strategy to the wind in his efforts to survive. This first Scottish raid into England after Bannockburn appears to mark a new departure in the evolution of a broader Scottish strategy, inspired by victory in the open field. There is no documentary evidence for any change in the thinking of Robert and his commanders; this is, rather, an interpretation of events. The new Scottish strategy is characterised by increasingly long-distance raids carrying the devastation of hobelar warfare deep into northern England; secondly by concentrated pressure on two strategic points, Carlisle and Berwick; and thirdly by involvement in Ireland. The combination was only partially successful. The raids ravaged wide areas of northern England, but without forcing the English to make peace; of the strategic towns, only Berwick fell to the Scots and not until 1318, whereas Carlisle survived assault in 1315 and 1316; and intervention in Ireland ended in catastrophe in 1318. But Robert I continued long-distance raiding into northern England right up until 1322, and briefly revived it in 1327; and he persisted in interfering in Ireland. Altogether the period from Bannockburn to the peace of 1328 saw an unparalleled Scottish military hegemony in Britain, during which the mounted raids that swept across the north of England demonstrate the powerlessness of Edward II's government in the face of Scottish aggression. 'From the faces of two or three Scots, a hundred English would flee.'[8]

The outline narrative of these raids is familiar from the pages of Lanercost and other chronicles, but what is not so widely appreciated is the quality of independent evidence corroborating the narratives. The incursions they describe were spectacularly successful in demoralising the northern communities, in breaking the will to resist and most especially in the extraction of cash in return for truce. Discipline among the raiders was essential for such a system to work since English communities would not pay over large sums to the Scots if they thought that they were going to be robbed in any case. Comparison with the invasion led by Wallace in 1297 is instructive; Wallace's occupation seems at times to have degenerated into a riot of plundering; but breach of the terms of truce was unusual during the raids of Robert's reign.[9]

One does not have to search far for the motives of the Scots who participated. For the moss-troopers or hobelars on expeditions into England, patriotism, service to one's lord, and self-interest happily coincided. There was some looting of course; but the main object of raiding was cash, more efficiently extracted through the taking of hostages than through straightforward robbery. The loot was divided out between the Scottish lords and their men. According to later usage one third of a prisoner's ransom was reserved to the lord.[10] Apart from money, and captives taken to secure payment, the Scots sought to drive off cattle which in Scottish society was the most potent expression of wealth. Cattle hides were also valuable for making harness and light armour from boiled leather. In the border districts sheep and other farm animals were also driven off from English manors; but only cattle could make a longer journey to Scotland. Inanimate booty could include practically anything. There are references to the taking of grain,[11] but not enough to support the idea that raids were motivated by famine in Scotland. Precious metals, harness and armour were all especially sought after; while even household effects, books and muniments were carried off. The list of goods stolen from a Lancashire manor in 1322 included oxen, armour, weaponry, a chalice, vestments, books, bedclothes, and even pots and pans.[12] A commodity which the Scots valued particularly was iron. When they raided Furness in 1316, the Lanercost Chronicle relates how 'especially were they delighted with the abundance of iron which they found there, for Scotland is not rich in iron'.[13] The Scots needed iron for the manufacture of armour and weapons, of which they were chronically short, and which they were currently importing from Ireland and the Continent. This may also explain their many visits to Corbridge, 'the centre of the Tyneside ironware trade'.[14] Similarly, their arrival in Durham on market day may not have been entirely fortuitous. The Scots, then, could steal as much for utility as 'for gredynes'. While there were positive gains to be had for the Scots, the primary objective of the raids was negative: to drive off the enemy, burn crops, destroy his settlements, and steal his livestock. Whatever could not be easily carried off to Scotland on horseback was destroyed, and the main instrument of devastation was fire. Most contemporary buildings, churches and castles excepted, were of wood. Mills and barns were favourite targets. Growing crops burnt

readily in dry weather; in wet, they would be trampled down by the
stolen herds.[15] The Scots were remarkably thorough in both destroying
and in looting. At Hexham and Bearpark they cut down fruit trees; at
Bamburgh they even dug up the rabbit warren.[16]

Refinements in raiding tactics were adopted during the period. Chronicle accounts give an impression of significant changes in the nature of the
forces involved. Wallace's invasion had been predominantly an infantry
affair, and Robert I's raids prior to Bannockburn seem to have conformed
to this precedent. In the raids discussed in the previous chapter Robert is
said to have led 'a large army' and 'a great army', and this fits in with
the intensive wasting of the countryside described.[17] Presumably he used
horsemen to carry out the raid in 1312 on Durham, the only excursion
outside the border counties prior to 1314. Cavalry is not specified in
sources until after Bannockburn, from which point the increasingly long
distances traversed by the raiders leave no doubt that they were mounted.
The narrative of Jehan le Bel, describing the 1327 raid, confirms this
impression.[18] Robert's early raids, then, were infantry invasions; but they
differed in other respects from Wallace's invasion. Whereas Wallace had
confronted Berwick, Carlisle and even Newcastle, Robert took no interest
at this stage in major strategic prizes outside Scotland. Steering clear of
population centres and strong castles, he visited softer targets – manors,
villages and monasteries. Furthermore, while Wallace spent six weeks
in England, Robert's incursions, mounted or otherwise, were all of short
duration. The customary period of military service of course had a bearing
on the length of campaigns. In England and Scotland alike the period
of free service which the king was entitled to was 40 days; but though
Edward II might (sometimes) pay to maintain troops in the field after
that time had elapsed, one supposes that at first Robert I could not.

Another important (and obvious) development after Bannockburn is
that the Scots penetrated deeper and deeper into England. This was
partly a natural consequence of victory and growing audacity on the
part of Scottish commanders. But it was also a result of the thorough
pillaging of more northerly parts. Having made a wasteland of border
areas, they were forced to ride further south in search of plunder. The
reliance on mounted troops is confirmed by Jehan le Bel who participated
in the Weardale campaign of 1327. His vivid description of the Scots on
campaign is well known but still worth repeating briefly. The means of
transport were ideally suited to the terrain:

> . . . one and all are on horseback, except for the camp-followers [*la
> ribaudaille*], who are on foot, that is to say the knights and squires are
> mounted on great runcies, and the other folk of the country are all on
> little hackneys. And they do not bring wheeled vehicles, because of
> the various mountains through which they pass in this country.[19]

Camp-followers seem out of place in swift raiding parties; but it is easy to envisage a rabble of scavengers following in the wake of the mounted raiders, picking over leftovers in the devastated villages. The booty was carried home by sumpter horses. Much more mobile and versatile than heavily armoured knights, the raiders could not easily be brought to battle by the English. The dangers and discomforts of chasing the Scots in 1327 are narrated by Le Bel with vivid detail: the breakneck pursuit lasting several days; the pitfalls of trying to second-guess what direction the enemy might take; false reports and alleged sightings of the enemy; the misery of camping in the open; saddle sores, lack of sleep, food and water; and endless saturating rain. The Scots coped better than the English with the conditions. They brought nothing with them but little bags of oatmeal, which they baked into cakes on a flat stone, and gorged on the beef of stolen cattle. In this way they were able to move independently of supply lines. There were also changes in the routes adopted by the raiders. From 1314 to 1319 they came to prefer a characteristically U-shaped itinerary: down the Northumbrian plain on the east coast, across the Pennines by way of the great river valleys, and homewards through the western march. This route was determined by the distribution of wealth in the region, the Scots showing a greater interest in the richer eastern march than in the west. It was also dictated by prudence. Laden with spoil and slowed by prisoners and stolen cattle, they were more susceptible to attack on the homeward journey, and preferred to return by the mountains and moorlands of the west. As it was, they were ambushed by English garrisons on at least two occasions.[20] The precaution of riding homewards by the western route was inappropriate to the demonstrations of Scottish military strength in 1322 and 1327. These developments in tactics may relate to changes in the leadership of the expeditions. From Bannockburn to 1322 Robert I led only one raid into England; it is rather Thomas Randolph Earl of Moray and James Douglas who figure as the leaders of the mounted raids deep into England characteristic of the post-Bannockburn period.

The Scottish raids were intended by Robert I to goad the English into recognition of his title and sovereignty. It is questionable how effective they were in this respect; but there was a pattern: each raid was followed by a period of negotiation. Directly after the raid of August 1314 King Robert sent a letter directly to Edward II, expressing his desire for peace and giving credence to his emissary.[21] Truce was established on the marches from 6th October and continued until the following spring, but negotiations were interspersed with periodic recourse to arms by both sides. Talks between the English and Scots were scheduled to take place at Durham on 20th October, both about the exchange of prisoners taken in battle and about 'a perpetual peace'.[22] But the men of northern England put little faith in these negotiations and bought their own peace from the Scots. Moray was at Durham on the 17th, and before negotiations with envoys of the King of England opened he had guaranteed immunity from raiding to the 'Community of the Bishopric' in return for 800 marks.[23] Arrangements for an exchange of prisoners taken at Bannockburn were apparently finalised at these talks; but negotiations broke down soon afterwards, perhaps as soon as they proceeded to the substantive issue of Scottish kingship. On the 24th the garrison of Newcastle was ordered to be provisioned with arrows and victuals in apparent expectation of a raid; and the tax collectors in Northumberland reported that Robert himself led another invasion of Northumberland after the feast of St. Andrew (30th November).[24] This may have brought the English back to the table, for fresh negotiations began, this time at Dumfries. In October 1314, ostensibly at the request of King Philip, Edward II had 'granted' a truce to the Scots; but further negotiations which took place at Dumfries during this truce had collapsed by Christmas.[25] Early in 1315 another large invasion threatened. The alarm was not so much for Northumberland, now virtually overrun, as for Durham and Yorkshire. The Durham truce was due to expire on 20th January; and a special emergency conference of Yorkshire magnates held in York Minster reported to the king on 3rd January that an invasion was imminent. A muster at Northallerton was planned for 20th January; and a levy of 2d in the mark on parish valuations was taken to raise money to keep the forces of four captains in the field.[26] In response four keepers, recommended by the York assembly, were appointed by the king for the defence of Yorkshire, and 12 barons whose presence was needed on the eastern march were exempted from attending parliament. Fifteen other lords were ordered to attend them.[27] Scots were present in Durham in the week 3rd to 9th February 1315, but the source of this information, a marginal entry on the account of the cellarer of Durham Priory, may relate either to an embassy, or to Scots collecting the money due for the truce.[28] In February and March a proposal was under consideration which seems to have related to the kingship of Scotland.[29] If this was the case, it was confined to the Anglo-Scottish marches. Elsewhere hostilities continued unabated; in February the English recaptured the Isle of Man, and in May the Scots invaded Ireland.

From the end of 1314 chronicles lapse into general lamentations about the severity of raids, and it is impossible to tell from escheators' accounts whether devastation of any particular estate was recent or the result of previous incursions. It is no longer possible to discern the effects of particular Scottish incursions in the border counties; and resistance in Northumberland, beyond castles and walled towns, collapsed utterly. Clearly Robert was tightening his grip on northern England while negotiations continued. Tynedale, which since the twelfth century had been held by Kings of Scots as part of their English fiefs, returned to their faith. Scottish partisans had been active in that area since 1307 and many local lords had always supported the Scottish cause. Lanercost states that Tynedale did homage to the King of Scots and then attacked Gilsland, and the *Historia Aurea* bears this out:

> At this time the people of North Tynedale, deserting the King of England and his faith, gave themselves up completely to the King of Scotland. They treated their neighbours the Northumbrians inhumanely, carrying off their goods and taking them away as captives. The women too went riding in warlike manner, stealing the goods which their men did not care about, such as shorn wool and linen and carried them off.[30]

The Scots occupied North and South Tynedale, as well as the valley of the main river including Haltwhistle, Hexham and Corbridge. In 1315, 12 vills of South Tynedale complained to the English king's parliament, claiming that they had paid £20 15s. as a fine to William de Soules (to whom Robert had given the manor of Wark-in-Tynedale) in order that they should not have to do fealty to him and that they could remain outside his lordship. Soules had made them attend his court all the same; and the vills were consequently subjected to night-time raids by the men of Cumberland and Westmorland. They asked the king that they might be allowed to enter the neighbouring counties of Cumberland and Westmorland.[31] Referring to later events the *Historia Aurea* adds that 'King Robert of Scotland conferred that land of North Tynedale upon Sir Philip de Mowbray, who fortified for himself a stronghold near the chapel of Falstone.[32] It appears, then, that lands in Tynedale were being granted out by Robert, and that the Scots and their allies were fortifying their possessions. Clearly this was no temporary occupation; and such activities were not confined to the regalian liberty of Redesdale. Robert I also granted out other English lands: in Cumberland he granted lands belonging to Sir Richard de Kirkebride to Sir Walter Corri, his supporter.[33] These grants are not proof that Robert was thinking in terms of permanent conquest; it is rather the sort of aggressive posturing that might be expected. Destruction was not yet so widespread on the western march, where resistance was stiffer, and the mountains impeded the Scottish advance; and the western march continued taking truce much longer than the east.[34]

In June 1315 the Scots invaded Durham. Lanercost says they entered the bishopric around 29th June. Walter of Guisborough gives the most detailed account:

> In the year 1312 [sic] Sir Robert Bruce came into the Bishopric of Durham with a great army and so secretly had he come that he found people sleeping soundly in their beds. He sent Sir James

Douglas to the district of Hartlepool with many armed men while he himself remained at the vill of Chester [le Street]. Sir James despoiled the said town and he led back as captives many burgesses and many women. Having collected much booty from the whole countryside they all returned to their own country . . .[35]

Hartlepool may have been selected for two reasons: it had been one of the English fiefs of the Bruce family but now refused to recognise Robert's lordship; and it may already have been serving as a naval base for attacks on the Flemings and Scottish privateers. Lanercost adds that the townspeople took to sea in ships to escape the destruction. Inland, Robert de Graystanes tells how the complacent Prior Burdon of Durham was surprised by the Scots at his manor of Bearpark a week after Midsummer (1st July), losing much of the Priory's cattle and many of his own household accoutrements. There is confirmation of this story in the proceedings against Prior Burdon which led to his deposition in 1322.[36] As a result of this raid the bishopric bought truce in return for 1,600 marks, apparently for two years.[37]

Edward Bruce's presence in Ireland, from May 1315 to October 1318, seems to have profoundly affected the war in northern England. The Scottish effort now divided between northern England and Ireland, and the Scots seem never to have attacked in both theatres simultaneously. A massed attack in one theatre may have required a transfer of forces from the other. Raids on northern England from this point became less frequent but more penetrating, more spectacular and more destructive when they did occur. A striking illustration of the shift to a grand Irish Sea strategy is the siege of Carlisle (22nd July to 1st August 1315). Certainly it was provoked by the ambush at the Reycross and raids into Scotland by the Carlisle garrison;[38] but it was also a spectacular bid for a major strategic prize and was carried on in tandem with increased pressure on both Berwick and Carrickfergus.[39]

The best narrative of the siege is the original and vivid Lanercost account, clearly written by an eye-witness. Here there is space to mention only a few aspects. That the siege was attempted is testimony to the confidence of the Scots at this juncture; that it failed was due to their shortage of material and expertise:

> On every day of the siege [the Scots] assaulted one of the three gates of the city, sometimes all three at once; but never without loss, because there were discharged upon them from the walls such dense volleys of darts and arrows, likewise stones, that they asked one another whether stones bred and multiplied within the walls. Now on the fifth day of the siege they set up a machine for casting stones next to the Church of the Holy Trinity . . . but there were seven or eight similar machines within the city besides other engines of war.[40]

The Scots built a siege-tower (or 'belfry') but before it even reached the walls it stuck under its own weight in ground saturated by the torrential rains of the summer. In an effort to fill up the moat they poured in bundles of hay and corn, but the material was simply swallowed up in the swollen waters. Their drawbridges proved too heavy and sank into the moat altogether. Finally the chronicler's explanation for the abandonment of the siege, the approach of Pembroke's expedition, indicates that even after Bannockburn the Scots could not risk a major battle in open territory. The siege had two principal effects: firstly it established Andrew Harclay's reputation as valiant defender of the western march, and his role was acknowledged in the depiction of Harclay hurling spears from the battlements which adorned the initial capital on the charter subsequently granted to the city.[41] Secondly, Lanercost remarks on the devastation which befell the countryside surrounding Carlisle during the siege, and this is borne out by other sources.

Penrith, Carlatton and Castle Sowerby were raided by the Scots on St. James' Day (25th July 1315). At around this time James Douglas entered Copeland, harried the countryside around Egremont, despoiled the manors of Cleator and Stainburn, and robbed St. Bee's Priory.[42] On 30th July an all-out assault was launched on the eastern wall as a diversion, while Douglas's men tried to scale the western side. He may have been wounded in the assault. On 1st August Robert gave up the siege, abandoning his engines of war, and marched off in some disarray, which allowed the defenders to capture two Scottish knights, John de Morreve and Robert Bard.[43] The city remained under threat for some time to come, however, and its gates remained walled up until February 1316.

After the siege of Carlisle there were no significant raids into England for almost a year. Edward II permitted local commanders to take truces in February 1316 until Whitsun (30th May) or longer.[44] In March negotiations between the kings seem to have recommenced.[45] Probably a truce until Midsummer 1316 was eventually agreed at some level, though no documentary evidence of it exists. At any rate a stand-off prevailed. Scottish energies were absorbed by Ireland, where Edward Bruce had waged two campaigns back-to-back, and by the exertion of growing pressure on Berwick. English commanders (or *chevetaignes*) on the English marches deterred Scottish raids, but made only feeble attempts to advance into Scotland. The earls of Pembroke, Lancaster and Arundel were in turn given commands on the marches, but none of them carried an offensive deep into Scotland. Lack of money was a factor; famine caused the price of supplies to soar, and rendered it well-nigh impossible to assemble concentrations of armed men. Negotiations continued intermittently, but the Scots applied sustained pressure on Berwick and Carlisle.[46] The burning of the minor peel of

Thornthwaite in Cumberland in September 1315 is the only instance of Scottish activity in England at this time.[47]

Around Midsummer 1316 the Scots mounted their first serious attack on Yorkshire. There was a lull in the fighting in Ireland at this time, as resistance at Carrickfergus was ready to collapse, and veterans were probably withdrawn from there specially for this attack. A correspondent at York on 27th June reported that Robert was collecting his forces in the Park of Duns.[48] English chronicles indicate that the Scots rode down Tynedale and through the Bishopric of Durham.[49] Although the bishopric continued to purchase immunity from burning, there are signs of desertion by tenantry at Barnard Castle which might be due to this raid, for Pentecost rents due on 30th May were greatly reduced.[50] New sources for corroborating narrative accounts become available from 1316: the revisions of parish valuations for ecclesiastical taxation. On 16th July 1317 Archbishop Melton's official ordered a reassessment of valuations in the archdeanery of Richmond and this was completed by 27th July, entitled the *Prima Nova Taxatio* to distinguish it from subsequent revisions. The *Prima Nova Taxatio* covers the deaneries of Richmond, Catterick, Lonsdale and Copeland in the diocese of York, but not the northern dioceses of Carlisle or Durham.[51] While medieval parish valuations rarely correspond to the actual value of the livings,[52] it is reasonable to suppose that the worst affected parishes received the greatest relief. For the sake of clarity only parishes which received reductions of 50 percent or more on the original valuation are plotted on Map 6; they correspond well with the known route of the invaders. The *Prima Nova Taxatio* shows clearly that the Scots crossed the River Tees at Barnard Castle. Mortham was very severely affected; that parish was granted a reduction amounting to 98 per cent on its original valuation; and the vill of the same name was one of the very few settlements to be abandoned as a result of the destruction caused by these raids.[53] The Scots appear to have divided into three groups; one party rode up Teesdale into the Eden valley and burnt Penrith and Carlatton;[54] another approached Richmond and was bought off by the nobles of the liberty who negotiated with them from the safety of the castle.[55] The reduction in the valuation of West Witton in Wensleydale suggests that a third party of raiders followed the valley of the Ure into Lancashire. Perhaps payment of tribute had the desired effect of preserving property, for the parish of Richmond did not receive a substantial reduction in the assessment. Lanercost names Swaledale as the raiders' main route west, stating that they then rode to Furness, sixty miles to the west. The Scots crossed from Yorkshire into Kendal and Lonsdale. Lancashire was thus affected by Scottish raids for the first time, and it may be because of destruction by the Scots that the county did not contribute to the subsidy granted in 1315.[56] But it should be remembered that Thomas

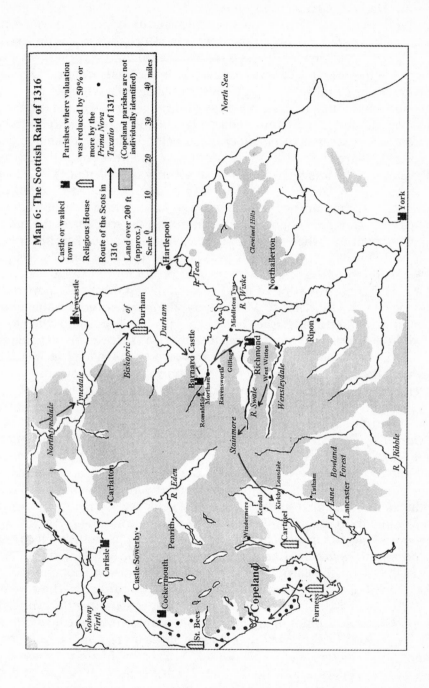

Map 6: The Scottish Raid of 1316

of Lancaster, now in the political ascendant, had every reason to protect his own Honour of Lancaster from taxation as the Scottish menace grew on the western march. The town of Lancaster itself cannot have been far from the raiders' path but there is no evidence that it was attacked on this occasion. Some of the Scots crossed the sands into Furness, where they were impressed by the abundance of iron.[57] They returned home by way of the Cumberland coast. This is unlikely to have been the first time the Scots entered Copeland; every parish except one in the deanery of Copeland had its valuation reduced by over 50 percent, and for that reason it is unnecessary to identify the Copeland parishes individually. A greatly enlarged English garrison at Cockermouth from 15th July to 5th August 1316 indicates the threat to security in this area.[58]

An attempt by Lancaster to mount a campaign in August 1316 failed abysmally in the midst of widespread crop failures and lack of will on the part of king and magnates. Scottish incursions continued; the mill, the whole vill and the corn of Scotby, in the Honour of Penrith, were reportedly burnt by the Scots on 29th October 1316.[59] From December 1316 to Spring 1318 it is unclear whether or not formal truces were in place. The English earl of Arundel successfully established a powerful presence on the marches to Midsummer 1317, but without launching a significant offensive. A truce had been agreed to last from November 1316 until Christmas, and it seems that this was successively extended, so that in the event Arundel's army was largely inactive.[60] In Ireland however the war continued unabated; and Robert and Edward Bruce together led a wide-ranging campaign from January to May 1317.[61]

On Robert's return to Scotland the English expected immediate resumption of hostilities, and planned a campaign for the summer. On 13th July Edward II wrote to Pembroke and Bartholomew Badlesmere that after Midsummer the Scots had been mustering, and he feared an invasion was already in progress.[62] Yet there are no reports of Scottish raids that summer; the English campaign was abandoned; and the stand-off endured. Until the next spring there is little evidence of hostilities on any scale either in Ireland or in England. The famine continued, preventing the mustering of armies; but this did not prevent Scottish intrigues in northern England. In September 1317 the Northumberland revolt erupted, led by the local knight Gilbert de Middleton, but probably inspired by Robert. It opened with the robbery of two cardinals. These were Luca Fieschi and Gaucelme de Jean, papal legates sent to settle a variety of ecclesiastical disputes in England, and to impose a two-year truce on the Anglo-Scottish conflict.[63] Robert ignored the truce, both because the papacy and legates failed to acknowledge his kingship, and because he was on the brink of capturing Berwick. He prevented publication of the papal bull in Scotland and had the cardinals' messengers assaulted and their letters torn up. In September 1317 the cardinals were on their way to Scotland to threaten Robert I with excommunication and to impose terms unacceptable to the Scots. It was obviously in Robert's interest to hire Northumbrian *schavaldores* to waylay the cardinals, thus escaping direct involvement in the scandal of such an assault, though there is no proof that Scots were directly involved. The English rebels had their own reasons for attacking the cardinals. They wanted to prevent Louis Beaumont from taking his seat as Bishop of Durham; and they held to ransom both Louis and his brother Henry. Aided by the Scots and possibly also by Lancaster, the *schavaldores* captured peels and castles in Northumberland and Yorkshire; one of the rebels, John de Lilleburne, captured the first-rank castle at Knaresborough and held it against the king in the name of the earl of Lancaster.

In the spring of 1318 the lull on the borders ended abruptly. On the night 1st to 2nd April 1318, the Scots led by Douglas scaled the wall of Berwick at a section where the guard had been bribed. The traitor is named as Peter or Sym of Spalding. The castle garrison, under Roger Horsley, held out until June 18th.[64] Wark-on-Tweed surrendered on 21st May; Harbottle and Mitford fell at around the same time 'because relief did not reach them on the appointed day',[65] and Scottish control of the east march became absolute. The following month, they seized the opportunity to launch a devastating raid, of scale and range hitherto unprecedented. The timing of this raid, late April or early May 1318, may have been significant. It took place during a truce between Robert I and the community of Durham, and it appears to have been partly intended as a sharp reminder to keep up with the instalments of tribute.[66] Furthermore it is possible that the Scots intended to support Lancastrian revolt in England. But whether or not there was any more elaborate reason for it, this raid was a pointed defiance of the two-year papal truce. In number of ways, therefore, this raid was intended to accelerate progress towards Scottish political aims. The leaders were Moray and Douglas.[67]

A principal source for tracing the routes of the invaders in Yorkshire in 1318 is the second revision of parish valuations to take account of war-damage, the *Nova Taxatio* made in 1318 to assist in collection of a papal tenth.[68] Northumberland was not included, ecclesiastical incomes in the devastated region having collapsed altogether. In the *Nova Taxatio* of Carlisle Diocese the valuation of every parish was reduced by over 50 percent, reflecting damage caused by raids since 1307, and the same is true of the deanery of Copeland, a part of the diocese of York. There is no point in mapping the reassessment for either of these areas. The Durham *Nova Taxatio* is not mapped here either; but it is significant that the greatest reductions in parish valuations there occur in the upland parishes (Stanhope, Middleton in Teesdale) and around Hartlepool, the target of a second assault in 1318, a reprisal for the capture of a Scottish

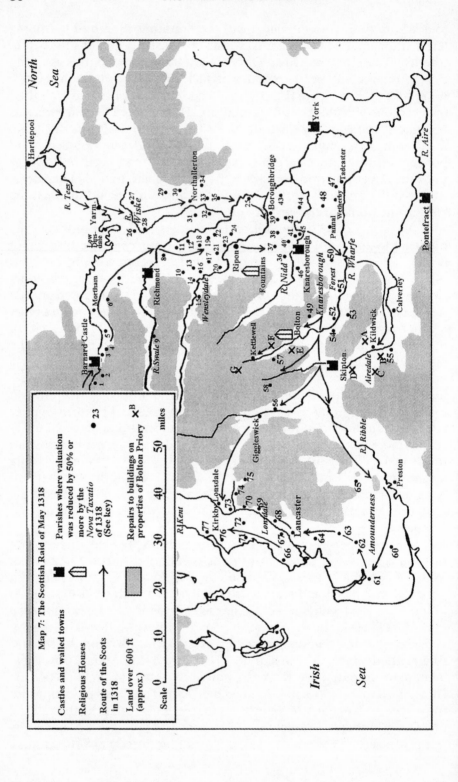

Map 7: The Scottish Raid of May 1318

Parishes where valuations were reduced by over 50% in the *Nova Taxatio* of 1318

1 Romaldkirk
2 Startforth
3 Rokeby
4 Brignall
5 Wycliffe
6 Kirkby Ravensworth
7 Gilling
8 Catterick
9 Grinton
10 Hauxwell
11 Kirkby Fleetham
12 Scruton
13 Finghall
14 Spennithorne
15 West Witton
16 Thornton Stewart
17 Thornton Watlass
18 Bedale
19 Burneston
20 Well
21 Kirklington
22 Pickhill
23 West Tanfield
24 Wath
25 Topcliffe
26 Great Smeaton
27 Rounton
28 Birkby
29 Osmotherley
30 Kirkby Sigston
31 Ainderby Steeple

32 Kirkby Wiske
33 Leake
34 Cowesby
35 Thornton le Street
36 Ripley
37 South Stainley
38 Copgrove
39 Staveley
40 Farnham
41 Alverton Mauleverer
42 Whixley
43 Great Ouseburh
44 Kirkby on the Moor -
   located as Kirkhammerton
45 Goldsborough
46 Hampsthwaite
47 Wighill
48 Kirk Deighton
49 Fewston
50 Kirkby Ferrers -
   located as Kirkby Overblow
51 Leathley
52 Weston
53 Guiseley
54 Ilkley
55 Bingley
56 Long Preston
57 Linton
58 Kirkby Malham
59 Marton
60 Kirkham

61 Poulton
62 St. Michael on Wyre
63 Garstang
64 Cockerham
65 Chipping
66 Heysham
67 Halton
68 Claughton
69 Tatham
70 Melling
71 Warton
72 Whittington
73 Tunstall
74 Burton
75 High Bentham
76 Beetham
77 Heversham

Repairs to Buildings on the possessions of
Bolton Priory
(Not specifically attributed to Scottish
raiders)

A KILDWICK
B EASTBURN
C COWLING
D CARLETON
E EMBSAY
F STEAD GRANGE
G MALHAM

ship by the townsfolk.[69] In Yorkshire, which the Scots had not previously penetrated to any great extent, the *Nova Taxatio* provides a striking illustration of the widespread extent of war damage; parishes where the valuation was reduced by 50 percent or more are plotted on Map 7.

The raids on Yorkshire in 1318 and 1319 have been the subject of a short but valuable study by Dr. Kershaw. In his discussion of the Scots' itinerary Kershaw did not attempt to distinguish between the two raids. He utilised not only the printed *Nova Taxatio* reassessments, but also repairs to buildings on the estates of Bolton Priory; lapsed rents on the Bolton Priory estates; and the exemptions of 46 named vills from the lay subsidy of 1319.[70] The exemptions of 1319 appear to be likelier to relate to consideration of that year's raid; but most of Kershaw's conclusions for 1318 hold good. The Scottish raiders entered Yorkshire at two points. One group crossed the Tees at Barnard Castle; another by way of Yarm or Low Dinsdale seems to represent those who had attacked Hartlepool. The western party was making for Richmond. Not all the chronicles record that Richmond was held to ransom a second time in 1318,[71] but this seems likely in view of its readiness to pay up in 1316. As the Scots continued their southward progress, raiding parties were dispatched into Wensleydale. The next town in the path of the main advance was Ripon, which they spared in return for 1,000 marks, a sum agreed by negotiation with the townsfolk who had crowded into the Minster for safety. Six hostages were taken by the raiders to secure payment, but the townsfolk avoided paying and did not redeem the hostages until ordered to by Edward II.[72] Nevertheless, the valuations of the church livings of Ripon are all greatly reduced in the *Nova Taxatio*. Nearby Fountains Abbey also paid the Scots a fine, but did not escape destruction of its property. In the *Nova Taxatio* Archbishop Melton reported to the exchequer that a large part of the Scottish army stayed at Fountains and many of the granges and outlying places were despoiled.[73] The Scots then rode on to Knaresborough.

The second, eastern raiding party rode directly down the centre of the Vale of York to Northallertonshire which was devastated by all accounts.[74] Not only was this liberty directly in the raiders' path, its destruction could also have been a warning to its lord, Louis de Beaumont, the new Bishop of Durham, not to upset the system of payment for immunity which the Scots had established with the bishopric. After burning Northallerton, the Scots rode along the course of the River Wiske as far as Ripon and Boroughbridge.[75] The front along which the raiders had been advancing, broad at first, had now narrowed considerably, both in order to avoid the city of York where resistance might be expected to concentrate, and in preparation for turning westwards up the Pennine dales. On the Sunday before the Ascension (28th May) the Scots burned Boroughbridge,[76] where they broke into the king's granary and carried away corn. Eleanor de Monkton, who had the farm of the town, was pardoned £30 in consideration of the damage they caused.

The two wings of the Scottish army converged in the Honour of Knaresborough. The current keeper of Knaresborough Castle was ordered to maintain horse and foot at the king's wages on the approach of the Scots on 28th May.[77] An inquisition bears out the Lanercost Chronicle's assertion that the town of Knaresborough was damaged. It claims that 140 houses were destroyed and only 20 left standing.[78] Damage was recorded at many other locations in the liberty, mostly in the Forest of Knaresborough, which was searched thoroughly for refugees hiding there with their cattle; and Archbishop Melton reported that the Scots stayed in the parish of Pannal and burned it on leaving.[79] Not all the looting, burning of homes and barns and trampling of crops in this area was actually related to the Scottish raid, for the surrounding countryside had been wasted while royalist forces besieged the Lancastrian garrison under Lilleburne in Knaresborough Castle from 5th October 1317 to 29th January 1318. A levy had been imposed throughout Yorkshire and cash was raised to buy off the rebels, but the king's tenants in Knaresborough and Clarhowe had been exempted from this by reason of the damage the siege had caused.[80] This raises the possibility that the Scots may not have arrived at Knaresborough by coincidence. In January the earl of Moray was rumoured to be approaching to relieve Lilleburne, and it is just possible that when Moray arrived in May he expected to find Lilleburne still holding the castle. The Scots camped in the Forest of Knaresborough, and rather than making a concentrated attack in the direction of York, they made sorties east and west from their lair. The parish of Tadcaster, eight miles from the city, was 'destroyed and wasted by the Scots'; and a petition complaining of war damage at Wetherby probably also relates to the activities of this expedition.[81]

Following the typical U-shaped itinerary, the raiders crossed the Pennines by several routes. The most southerly of these was through Airedale, where the parishes of Adel, Calverley, Guiseley, Bingley, Kildwick and others into Ribblesdale as far as Giggleswick were all awarded reductions in assessment on recognition of war damage; Hampsthwaite, Calverley (and Weston in Wharfedale) were described as 'scarcely sufficient to maintain a chaplain'.[82] Repairs were made to the buildings on the property of Bolton Priory at Cowling, Eastburn, Kildwick and Carleton. Another band of Scots proceeded along Wharfedale, laying waste the parishes of Leathley, Weston and Ilkley. Lanercost says that they attacked and laid waste the town of Skipton in Cravene. They certainly visited destruction on Bolton Priory's grange at Halton (where there were repairs to buildings and lapse of rents, servants fled, and demesne and tithe corn were taken and destroyed) but there is no evidence that they attacked the priory itself.[83] They followed the River Wharfe as far as

Arncliffe and Kettlewell where they crossed into Ribblesdale and thence into the valleys of the Greta and Wenning into Lonsdale. The Airedale raiders rode through Skipton and into Amounderness. Then, turning northwards, they linked up with the Wharfedale group, causing great destruction in the north of Lancashire. In the reassessment of parishes, the Scots are said to have burnt all the parishes of Lancaster for six days; Warton, Cockerham and Garstang were 'totally burnt'. Preston and Kirkham parishes were also described as 'burnt and destroyed',[84] but war damage this far south in Lancashire in 1318 is not corroborated by independent sources. However, the county was excused most of the lay subsidy of 1319, and the town of Lancaster was excused from contributing 'because the town was destroyed by diverse comings of the Scots, so it was said'.[85] Nothing further is known of the raiders' return journey. On 4th June the magnates of Yorkshire had been ordered to mobilise horse and foot in defence, but there is no record of resistance to the raiders.[86]

There were further alarms during the remainder of this year,[87] but there do not seem to have been any other significant raids. Robert I had other priorities during this period. He intended to send a reinforcement to Ireland in 1318 and may well have done so.[88] But the Irish adventure came to an end in October of that year, with the defeat and death of his brother Edward at the Battle of Fochart, and the recapture by the English of Carrickfergus Castle. At the beginning of 1319 the Scots attempted to destroy Dunstanburgh Castle in Northumberland (still under construction); while on the western march, Moray was negotiating a truce with the men of Cumberland and Westmorland on 25th January, for which he was demanding 600 marks.[89]

The sources for the invasion of 1319 are not so full as those for 1318. There is disagreement among the chronicles on some points; parish valuations were not re-adjusted to take account of the damage caused on this occasion; and the fact that the Scots traversed much the same ground as they had done the previous year renders it impossible to be certain what evidence relates to this expedition and what to the previous one. Far to the north the English besieged Berwick from 8th to 18th September, Lancaster and the king having mended fences in a desperate attempt to save honour and incomes.[90] Robert I was not in Berwick; but he was believed to have bound himself by oath to rescue the defenders before a certain time.[91] In launching the raid of 1319 he clearly intended to distract the English from pursuing the siege and advancing further into Scotland. The first that is heard of the Scots is that they entered Yorkshire before 3rd September, while the English army was approaching Berwick. The *Scalacronica* and *Brut* narratives say that the Scots entered England by the western march. They may have crossed to the eastern march by way of Tynedale, for according to the *Historia Aurea* they 'depopulated' Northumberland, the Bishopric of Durham and Northallertonshire on their way into Yorkshire.[92]

There was a widespread belief that the 1319 expedition was an attempt to capture Queen Isabella, then at York. This seems ambitious, worthy of any exploit by modern 'special forces'; but independent chronicles are consistent in their story of how a spy in York confessed the plot to Archbishop Melton and the citizens and offered to lead them to where the enemy lay in wait.[93] The *Flores Historiarum* alleges that an English guide, Edmund Darel, assisted the Scots who were again led by Moray and Douglas.[94] This chronicle and others suggest a stealth in the movements of the Scots which, while consistent with a plot to capture the Queen, is quite inconsistent with the idea that they wanted to draw the English army away from Berwick.[95] Either way this expedition follows the pattern of increasingly purposeful raids directed towards political ends, in this case the capture of a hostage so important as to force the English to sue for peace. As the author of the *Vita Edwardi II* says, 'Indeed if the Queen had at that time been captured, I believe that Scotland would have bought peace for herself'.[96]

There was no reassessment of parish valuations after the raid of 1319; but there survive two lists of vills exempted from the current lay subsidy: one in the Close Rolls, the other in the Enrolled Accounts of subsidies.[97] Together these name 49 North Riding vills and 57 in the West Riding exempted from the tax on account of burning by the Scots. Plotted on Map 8, they reveal a trail of destruction along the River Wiske in the Vale of York; a dense concentration just south of Northallerton; some damage around Boroughbridge and Myton-on-Swale (the scene of the battle); and finally a string of affected villages in Wharfedale, upper Ribblesdale and Lonsdale which mark the Scots' homeward routes. Care must be taken in the interpretation of these lists; much of the damage alluded to will relate to destruction caused in the raid of the previous year. Furthermore the exemptions were clearly the result of pressure from local lords, and a lord influential in court circles would have had no trouble in securing an exemption for his vills in the area. The Close Roll names the lord petitioning on behalf of each exempt vill: 22 vills belonged to Eleanor Percy; 16 to the Abbot of Fountains; and John de Haneby had a stake in 15 of the exempted vills. On the other hand, lords out of favour or without influence may have been unable to gain exemption for their vills, however badly affected. For example, the Scots are known to have visited Easingwold in 1319, but because its lord, the Earl of Lancaster, was out of favour at the time the lists were drawn up, no mention is made of it.

The English administration and the court of the Queen were both at York, and the city was convinced that it was the target of attack. A garrison was maintained at York Castle from 4th to 13th September,

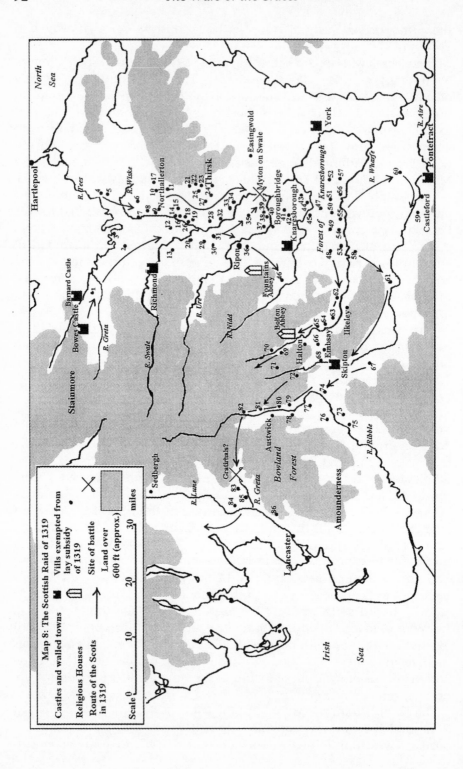

Map 8: The Scottish Raid of 1319

Vills exempted from payment of the lay subsidy of an eighteenth of 1319. Uncertain identifications are followed by (?).

a) North Riding
1 Rokeby
2 North Cowton
3 Eryholme
4 Yarm
5 Kirk Leavington
6 Welbury
7 Birkby
8 Brompton [? near Northallerton]
9 Romanby
10 Osmotherley
11 Thimbleby
12 Ainderby Steeple
13 Scruton
14 North Ottrington
15 Thornton le Beans
16 Thornton on the Moor
17 Kirkby Sigston
18 South Ottrington
19 Newby on Wiske
20 Maunby
21 Knayton
22 Thornton le Street
23 South Kilvington
24 Carlton Miniott
25 North Kilvington
26 Newsham
27 Sandhutton
28 Kirkby Wiske
29 Pickhill
30 Kirklington
31 Melmerby
32 Skipton on Swale
33 Topcliff

34 Asenby
35 Dishforth
36 Givendale
37 Newby
38 Langthorpe
39 Milby
40 Humberton

Unable to locate in the North Riding:
Cristwayt
Rennington
Neusom
Solbergh
Berghby
Hoton
Grisby
Newton on Swale
Kirkby on the Moor (which seems unlikely to have been Kirkby Moorside near Pickering, well off the raider's main course and not raided until 1322)

b) in the West Riding
41 Grafton
42 Marton
43 Hammerton
44 Hunsingore
45 Cowthorpe
46 Ripley
47 Follifoot
48 Timble
49 Lindley
50 Dunkeswick
51 Kirkby Overblow
52 Spofford

53 Stainburn
54 Leathley
55 Weeton
56 Colthorpe
57 Wetherby
58 Otley
59 Rothwell
60 Lede
61 Riddlesden
62 Weston
63 Middleton
64 Nessfield
65 Beamsley
66 Draughton
67 Silsden
68 Stirton
69 Linton
70 Grassington
71 Swinden End
72 Scosthorp
73 Gisburn
74 Newsholme
75 Westby
76 Paythorne
77 Wigglesworth
78 Gigglesworth
79 Settle
80 Langcliffe
81 Stainforth
82 Horton
83 Ingleton
84 Twilston
85 Burton
86 Bentham

and the Vicars Choral of York Minster paid a guard to keep watch along their section of the city wall for five nights consecutively. Queen Isabella was sent off to safety in Nottingham.[98] In fact the Scots never came nearer than 10 miles from the city;[99] but the story of a conspiracy to capture Isabella is not unrealistic. Subsequent attempts to capture individuals of importance were made no doubt to increase the Scots' diplomatic leverage; and in Yorkshire at this time allegations of spying or guiding the Scots are common.[100] The author of the *Vita Edwardi II* relates that a spy was captured and betrayed the plan. The invaders were discovered to be camped in secrecy at Myton-on-Swale. Archbishop Melton was instructed to resist the Scots; but only three days beforehand the king had ordered up to Berwick the whole of the Yorkshire militia.[101] 'Like another Thurstan', Melton improvised an army of citizens, peasantry from surrounding vills, and clergy which included the staff of the chancery and the chancellor himself, John de Hothum, Bishop of Ely. The predominance of clergy in his rabble gave to the episode the name the 'Chapter of Myton'. On 12th September Melton led this crowd out of York and across the Swale at Myton to confront the Scots.[102] Placing themselves between the bridge and the English, the Scots set fire to haystacks, and from behind this smokescreen attacked Melton's force. Fighting on foot, they easily overcame the English, who had no men-at-arms and were mostly inexperienced in war. Great slaughter ensued and many of the English drowned trying to cross the river. The mayor of York was killed, and several royal servants were taken prisoner including the notary Andrew Tang.[103]

News of the battle reached the English army before Berwick on 14th September. Immediately counsels divided. Northern lords, led by Lancaster, wanted to give up the siege and return to their estates to defend them against the Scots; the king and southern lords were anxious to press on with the siege, but the army began to melt away. Thus the 'Chapter of Myton' necessitated the abandonment of the siege of Berwick. Yet the victory was not followed up by the Scots in Yorkshire. Rather than advancing on York, they stayed in the vicinity of Myton, causing further damage at Boroughbridge,[104] and at the nearby vills of Milby, Langthorpe and Humberton. Two chronicles report that the Scots reached Castleford on the River Aire (the southernmost point which the Scots reached during this period)[105] and some followed the river westwards. On 13th October the York garrison was dismissed, so presumably the Scots were well clear of York by then.[106] Wharfedale seems to have been the route taken by the majority of raiders, judging by the succession of exempt vills through the Forest of Knaresborough and along the north bank of the Wharfe as far as Grassington. The grange at Halton, newly rebuilt by the canons of Bolton since the Scots' last visitation, was burnt again and 43 of the canons' oxen were stolen by the raiders; and their manor house and tithe barn at Embsay were also destroyed. The canons fled to safety in Skipton Castle.[107]

As a result of Scottish depredations Lancashire was excused payment of the current lay subsidy on 28th October,[108] so the Scots probably caused widespread destruction on their way northward. As in 1318, the Scots entered Lancashire by two routes, some through Lonsdale by way of Austwick and others by the valley of the Greta. One further incident seems to relate to the Scots' homeward journey, an ambush in a mountain ravine:

> In returning homewards through western parts of England, they were set upon by a throng of Englishmen at Gratirhals, a very narrow pass. But the Scots prevailed and the English were scattered, and many were killed, including Sir Henry Fitz Hugh, and they returned with great rejoicing to their own country taking many knights and squires with them.[109]

'Gratirhals' refers to the valley of the Greta; but there are two rivers of this name; one flows west–east from Stainmore through Bowes Forest and into the Tees, the other east–west into Lonsdale. As Henry fitz Hugh held Bowes Castle from the Earl of Richmond,[110] it may be that the tributary of the Tees is intended; but the Lonsdale location is more in keeping with the Scots' return journey. Edward II had meanwhile taken up position at Newminster Abbey in Northumberland to catch the Scots on their return, but he failed to guard the western march. This appalling lapse can only be explained by a reliance on faulty intelligence, and the earl of Lancaster was now blamed for this and much besides. Following his involvement in the Northumberland revolt, the earl was popularly believed to be corresponding with the Scots. The raiders escaped across the western marches 'like a puff of smoke' after three weeks in England.[111]

Before the end of the year the Scots mounted another raid, this time on the western march. It was of shorter range and duration, but appears to have been even more intensely destructive than those visited on Yorkshire. Yet again leadership of the raiders is credited to Moray and Douglas. They crossed into Gilsland around the feast of All Saints (1st November), laying waste houses and barns full of grain recently harvested; then ravaged as far south as Brough on Stainmore. They returned after ten or twelve days and devastated Cumberland before retiring to Scotland with a great spoil of cattle and prisoners.[112] The accounts of the receiver of victuals at Carlisle include large quantities of wheat, barley and beans taken by the Scots from his depot at Holm Cultram Abbey.[113] This raid could well have been retaliation for non-payment of a local truce.[114] Even before the Scots had returned home, the trusted English royal official Robert Baldock was on his way to Berwick with proposals for a truce.[115] It was agreed that the peace should last for two years, from 21st December 1319 to Christmas

1321.[116] The author of the *Vita Edwardi II* states that this was motivated by Edward II's need to go to France to perform homage in person; and as an afterthought adds that it was to relieve the sufferings of Edward's northern liegemen.[117] But some progress was being made towards a lasting peace. This two-year truce was to serve as the model for the thirteen-year truce of Bishopthorpe in 1323.[118]

From November 1319 to January 1322 there was peace on the borders for two years, giving Robert I a chance to recover from defeat in Ireland and Edward II an opportunity to confront and vanquish the baronial opposition. The year 1322 saw three Scottish raids into England, on Durham, Lancashire, and the East Riding of Yorkshire. The particularly severe raid on the Bishopric of Durham lasted from 15th to 30th January.[119] It was remembered simply as 'the burning of the bishopric', and by all accounts it was a terrible demonstration of the raiders' destructive capacity. We can only guess as to why the Scots targeted Durham at this stage. Durham Priory may have refused to resume paying tribute on the outbreak of war; and it is tempting to link this possibility with the deposition in January of the accommodating Prior Geoffrey de Burdon by the warlike Bishop Louis de Beaumont.[120] Furthermore the Scots probably acted in support of the earls of Lancaster and Hereford, leaders of a revolt currently raging in England. On 15th January Moray had issued letters of protection to Lancaster's emissary who was *en route* to ask for help from Robert; and according to an agreement later found on the corpse of the earl of Hereford after the battle of Boroughbridge, Moray, the Stewart and Douglas were to join Lancaster and Hereford in making war on their enemies in England, Wales and Ireland.[121] The actions of these three Scottish magnates in 1322 can be interpreted as a deliberate wasting of the power of Lancaster's enemies, the Beaumonts. Moray established himself at Darlington as though poised to intervene in the civil war further to the south. Walter the Stewart led a Scottish detachment to Richmondshire (a district which could be relied upon to pay up) and he extracted from it a fine to avoid devastation. Douglas ravaged the district around Hartlepool, another favourite target of the Scots.[122] The Scots did not venture far into Yorkshire but spent a fortnight in Durham, making a thorough job of the destruction of the bishopric. Robert de Graystanes asserts that the whole eastern plain of Durham was devastated, and that barns full of grain were burnt down causing famine in the following summer. Orders were given for fresh revision of parish valuations to take account of the devastation in Durham, but no schedule of revised valuations has been found.[123] The records of Durham Priory are very far from complete at this juncture, but a 'sudden and catastrophic' loss of income on Durham Priory's estates, known to have occurred sometime between 1319 and 1327, was surely the result of this devastating raid.[124]

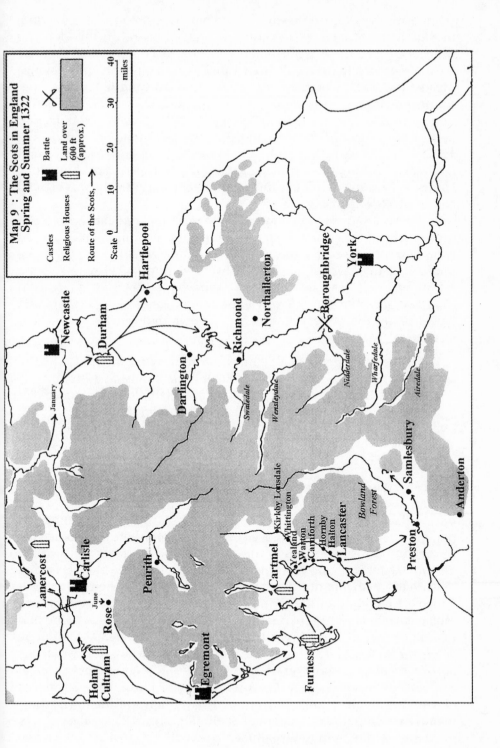

Map 9 : The Scots in England
Spring and Summer 1322

Castles

Religious Houses

Route of the Scots, →

Battle

Land over
600 ft
(approx.)

Scale

0   10   20   30   40
miles

Hartlepool

Newcastle

Durham

January

Richmond

Northallerton

Darlington

Boroughbridge

York

Swaledale

Wensleydale

Nidderdale

Wharfedale

Airedale

Lanercost

Carlisle

June

Rose

Penrith

Holm
Cultram

Egremont

Furness

Cartmel

Kirkby Lonsdale

Whittington

Yealand

Warton

Carnforth

Hornby

Halton

Lancaster

Bowland
Forest

Samlesbury

Anderton

Preston

The Scots maintained pressure on the marches throughout the spring. In March the mayor of Newcastle reported news of an invasion, for which however there is no other evidence.[125] On the west, too, the Scots threatened to attack. Andrew Harclay, having gone for assistance against the Scots to both factions in the civil war and having received satisfaction from neither, made a truce with the Scots, withdrew his forces from the border and marched to Boroughbridge to prevent a conjunction between the earl of Lancaster and the Scots.[126] There, on 16th March 1322, he defeated in battle the forces of the rebel earls Hereford and Lancaster, quelling the revolt against Edward II. Hereford died in battle; Lancaster was executed. For this valuable service Harclay was created earl of Carlisle.[127]

In March 1322 the Scots agreed to a truce until Michaelmas (29th September).[128] But English preparations for a campaign went on regardless and Robert I launched a pre-emptive strike to divert the impending invasion of Scotland. Edward II had called a muster for 1st August; on 1st July the Scots invaded on the west march. At least two separate forces crossed the border, one led by Robert and described by the Lanercost writer, and later that led by Moray and Douglas:

> Robert de Brus invaded England with an army by way of Carlisle in the week before the Nativity of S. John the Baptist [*c.* 17th June], and burnt the bishop's manor at Rose, and Allerdale, and plundered the monastery of Holm Cultram, notwithstanding that his father's body was buried there; and thence proceeded to lay waste and plunder Copeland, and so on beyond the sands of Duddon to Furness.[129]

Robert passed by Egremont, burning two of the castle's water mills around Midsummer.[130] Although the Abbot of Furness entertained him and paid a ransom to preserve his lands, the Scots nevertheless plundered and burned them, and then moved on to Cartmel (where they spared the priory) and across the sands towards the town of Lancaster. They visited Yealand Redmayne and Whittington, burned the vill of Netherkellet, and destroyed tenements at Torrisholme, driving refugees before them.[131] Lanercost reports that the town of Lancaster was burnt except for two religious houses. Here Robert met up with Moray and Douglas, who had arrived by way of Kendal, Whittington, Hornby Castle and Quernmore Forest on 2nd July. They had run into some resistance, for two of the Scots were taken prisoner on Hornby Moor. The Scots stayed at Lancaster for four days and nights in the fortnight after Midsummer. There was extensive damage, shown by a list of decayed rents in the town which mentions trampling of crops and spoliation. Townsfolk subsequently petitioned for the right to take timber to rebuild the town, and the castle too was burned.[132] The combined Scottish force then rode to Preston, visiting Moorholme and Skerton (where the whole village was burned, and corn in the fields trampled down) on the way. Lanercost says that here only the house of the Minorite Friars was spared from burning. A rent roll of tenants at will at Preston in 1324 shows slight evidence of destruction by the Scots, but perhaps recovery had been swift. Again the inhabitants had subsequently to petition for timber to help with rebuilding.[133] Some Scots rode 15 miles further south; and an inquisition reveals details of pillaging at Samlesbury manor a little to the east of Preston.[134] On the return journey the Scots stayed around Carlisle for five days trampling crops and destroying what they could. They crossed back into Scotland on 24th July. An entry in Bishop Halton's register supports this, but asserts that the Scots stayed about Carlisle for eight days.[135] In addition to being a necessary gathering of supplies in preparation for the impending English invasion of Scotland, the raid may have had other purposes. In Lancashire the Scots were probably searching for the great cattle herds of the recently executed earl of Lancaster, which they may previously have refrained from stealing. Furthermore the intensive wasting of Cumberland could well have been directed against the growing influence of Harclay on the western marches.

This spectacular raid on Lancashire could not of course prevent the English invasion of Scotland in August 1322. Edward II's huge army of almost 20,000 infantry, many heavily armed, bypassed Berwick and marched up Lauderdale towards Edinburgh. Robert had ordered the evacuation of all livestock from Lothian, a 'scorched-earth' retreat depriving the English of forage. Edward had arrived at Musselburgh on the coast near Edinburgh by 19th August without encountering any opposition; and at the port of Leith he awaited for two days the arrival of his supply ships. This fleet however had been scattered by Flemish privateers and wrecked by storms. Given the sheer size of the army, supplies must already have been low. Famine and disease were soon rife in the camp. Before the month was out the whole expedition was back across the border.[136] Edward returned to England on about 2nd September, but he announced his intention of remaining in the north. On 26th September he wrote from Durham to the constables of four northern castles, rebuking them for inactivity in the face of Scottish incursions. In his letter the Scots were said to be entrenched around Norham Castle and making a determined effort to capture it. The four were Bamburgh, Warkworth, Dunstanburgh and Alnwick – suggesting that Wark-on-Tweed was either in Scottish hands or had been slighted. The Scots were re-asserting their control of Northumberland, and refugees were now flooding into Yorkshire.[137]

On the western march, after the failed invasion of Scotland, Andrew Harclay commanded at Carlisle a huge concentration of cavalry, 280 men-at-arms (of whom four were bannerets and 30 knights) and 500 hobelars.[138] But this formidable power ceased to be in the king's pay at the end of September. It then disbanded, and Robert struck immediately. On 30th September he crossed the Solway Firth at Bowness and ravaged the vicinity of Carlisle for five days, until 5th October. The devastation of the district around Carlisle, the third recent wasting that the area had endured, had made it impossible for Harclay's army to regroup. Harclay went south into Lancashire to raise forces; but Robert swept on, raiding Castle Sowerby, Scotby and Carlatton on his way across the Pennines.[139] Lanercost alleges that he was from the first seeking a confrontation with Edward's entourage, and that he was informed of the whereabouts and meagreness of Edward's forces by spies. This expedition too can be interpreted as an attempt to force the English to concede sovereignty to Scotland by the capture of an important hostage.

English reactions were unco-ordinated. On 2nd October Edward II, travelling southwards from Barnard Castle, became aware of Robert's presence on the west march, and summoned ten northern magnates including Harclay to attend him at 'Blakehoumor', a location on the North Yorkshire Moors. They were to impose a levy of all able-bodied men between the ages of 16 and 60. Later the king was outraged when Harclay failed to appear.[140]But after the ravaging of his lands and dispersal of his men, Harclay could not give chase immediately to Robert; he went south into Lancashire to muster forces:

> This he did, having taken command of the county of Lancaster so that he had 30,000 men ready for battle; and since the Scots were in the eastern march, he brought his forces by western parts to reach the king.[141]

One of the Lanercost authors is favourable to Harclay, interpolating in the original text an explanation of Harclay's motives and actions; but Harclay may not still have been the devoted servant of Edward II. His regrouped force moved from Lancashire over the Pennines, but delayed long enough to ravage Airedale;[142] and he may have been awaiting the outcome of events rather than rushing to the king's aid. Edward can scarcely have believed that there was a threat to his personal safety as yet. With him were Pembroke, Richmond and the recently created earl of Louth, John de Birmingham, who had 74 mounted men-at-arms and 115 hobelars in his retinue; he expected to be met by Harclay with more troops.[143] Archbishop Melton at Nun Monkton thought the Scots were near Richmond as early as 5th October; but at this date his panic may yet have been unjustified, for according to most accounts Robert had not yet left Carlisle.[144] Then on 13th October Edward was informed that the Scots were at Northallerton. That evening, from his camp at Rievaulx, he began frantically issuing orders to Pembroke, Richmond and Beaumont to assemble magnates and militia 'to attend with all possible power' in the morning at 'Blakehoumor'. Moray was now only 15 miles away at Malton.[145]

Scottish movements in Yorkshire can only be interpreted as an attempt to confront the person of the English king. The main Scottish army occupied the Vale of York, destroying Thirsk and other parishes in that vicinity.[146] Some chronicles report that Ripon was attacked and many people killed, but a letter in the Chapter Act Book of Beverley says that the men of Ripon made a composition with the Scots.[147] Suddenly on 14th October from the west the Scots converged on the royal party, and Edward fled from Bylands Abbey to Rievaulx. The presence of Moray at Malton 15 miles to the north west of Rievaulx on the day before the battle, together with destruction of the coastal parishes of Whitby and Guisborough, implied by the revision of parish valuations,[148] suggests that Moray had been sent around the North Yorkshire Moors in pincer fashion to catch Edward in flight from the main Scottish force. As that force began advancing uphill towards Rievaulx, the English took up a hilltop position near Coxwold and Old Bylands to bar its progress and give Edward time to escape.[149] The earl of Richmond, the French magnate Henry de Sully and other prisoners were taken; and the Scots obtained a windfall of abandoned harness and silver plate from the royal household at Rievaulx.[150] Edward, 'chicken-hearted and luckless in war', was suddenly forced to flee via Pickering, Bridlington and Burstwick, taking ship to York, having abandoned all his valuable household effects to the Scots.[151]

Moray now occupied the Vale of Pickering, another of Lancaster's properties which he may have spared hitherto. At Malton he had made an agreement with the men of the Vale not to burn the district for a ransom of 300 marks.[152] Nevertheless a manor house was damaged by raiders at 'Kingthorpeworth', and the keeper of the Honour of Pickering was captured.[153] In 1327 parish valuations in the archdeaconries of Cleveland and the East Riding were revised, and this provides an indication of which areas were most severely affected by this raid.[154] Coastal parishes were destroyed, probably as the eastern wing of the Scottish army under Moray had advanced towards the English court.[155] On the flight of Edward II, the Scots took possession of the East Riding, unaffected by the raids until now. Most of the canons of Bridlington were evacuated. Those who remained sent an emissary to the Scots at Malton, choosing Robert de Bayntone, 'one of our canons, because his parents lived among them, so that the monastery and our manors might be spared from the flames'. When the Scots arrived, the canons offered accommodation and nine Scottish horsemen with 18 horses were billeted in the monastery.[156]

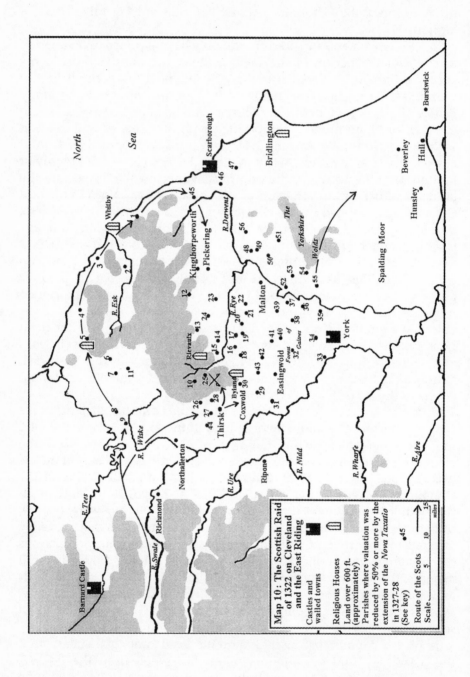

Map 10: The Scottish Raid of 1322 on Cleveland and the East Riding

Parishes where valuations were reduced by over 50% in the 1327 extension of the *Nova Taxatio* to Cleveland and the East Riding.

1 Fylingdales
2 Sneaton
3 Lythe
4 Skelton
5 Guisborough
6 Great Ayton
7 Stokesley
8 Crathorne
9 Welbury
10 Hawnby
11 Kirkby in Cleveland
12 Middleton
13 Kirkby Moorside
14 Kirkdale
15 Helmsley
16 Oswaldkirk
17 Stonegrave
18 Gilling East

19 Hovingham
20 Slingsby
21 Barton le Street
22 Appleton le Street
23 Kirkby Misperton
24 Normanby
25 Scawnton
26 Kirkby Knowle
27 South Kilvington
28 Felixkirk
29 Sessay
30 Coxwold
31 Brafferton
32 Sutton
33 Overton
34 Huntington
35 Upper Helmsley
36 Bossal

37 Crambe
38 Foston
39 Bulmer
40 Terrington
41 Sheriff Hutton
42 Dally
43 South Otterington
44 Brandsby
45 Hackness
46 Seamer
47 Folkton
48 Rillington
49 Thorpe Bassett
50 Settrington
51 Kirkby Grindalyth
52 Westow
53 Burythorpe
54 Kirkby Underdale
55 Skirpenbeck

The college of Beverley prepared to hide their treasures, as this letter shows:

> If the townspeople make a composition for the town and church, as Ripon did, well and good. But if sudden danger comes take Sir Alan with you and no one else, and secretly place the relics of the Saints and the inner chest [of St. John's shrine] in the treasury in the best place you know. And if great necessity arises, remove the silver plates of the outer chest and place them in a certain place.

The college also wrote to Robert on 20th October, begging protection, and according to Adam Murimuth they bought off the Scots for £400.[157] The men of Spaldingmoor and 'those north of the Humber' paid ransoms; and the Meaux chronicle records that the Scots 'raised their standard' at Hunsley, near Beverley.[158]

The chronicles are more struck by the audacity of the Scots in entering the East Riding than by the destruction they wrought there. Judging by the revised parish valuations in these southerly areas, the payment of ransoms did help to preserve property values. The map of revised valuations suggests that a part of the Scottish army, presumably that under Robert, had turned south after the battle, devastating Hovingham, Terrington, Sheriff Hutton and the Forest of Galtres, almost as far as York. Somewhere to the north of York Moray rejoined this force; but the united army probably turned back before 22nd October when the York garrison was reduced to its normal level.[159] There are a few clues as to how the Scots returned home. Ravaging was reported at Cottingley in Airedale; Barnard Castle estates are said to have been burnt around the feast of St. Jude (28th October); and finally at Skipton Castle the garrison was increased from 16th October to the 18th 'on account of great danger which then at that time threatened, in those parts, from the attacks of the Scots who burnt the said districts, despoiled and totally destroyed them'.[160] One of the chroniclers reports that the Scots were forced to return home because of the onset of winter, and this may be a reference to heavy rains and flooding which occurred in Yorkshire at this time.[161] One party of Scots raided Teesdale on their way home, on 28th October. Lanercost states that the raiders returned to Scotland on 2nd November, having been one month and three days in England,[162] the longest time they had yet spent there.

Even this raid, though disastrous for the north of England and for the' personal prestige of the monarch, had no effect on English policy towards Scotland. Edward II had no intention of giving up his claims and as early as February 1323 was preparing for yet another campaign.[163] But during the winter Andrew Harclay, who had been the north's most vigorous defender, made a unilateral peace with the Scots, surrendering all claim to Scotland.[164] The region was plunged once more into a state of emergency. The prospect of peace had considerable local support, according to the sympathetic author of the Lanercost Chronicle:

> ... the poor folk, middling people and farmers in the northern parts were not a little delighted that the King of Scotland should freely possess his own kingdom on such terms that they themselves might live in peace.[165]

Harclay was perhaps a natural leader; but he was also grasping, rapacious and commanded no broad base of support among the local gentry. Their jealousy of him brought about his downfall. He was surprised in Carlisle Castle, easily arrested and executed for treachery. Thus Edward II destroyed his kingdom's main bulwark against the Scots, but did not recognise it and in the spring of 1323 continued doggedly with preparations for a campaign. To increase pressure on Edward, the Scots began threatening another invasion of Lancashire. But the prospect of a French war now loomed, and Edward was forced to reconsider. At a council in Bishopthorpe on 30th May 1323 a thirteen years' truce with Scotland was resolved upon, pending conclusion of a final peace.[166] Even then, Robert's harrowing of the north was not quite over; there was more to come in 1327.

From 1314 to 1322 the Scottish raids into England became not only progressively more destructive and more wide ranging, but also increasingly purposeful in their timing, their methods and their targets. Realising the insensitivity of the English administration towards the north of the country Robert grasped the need to direct his attacks more pointedly at the administration. To achieve this dissident elements in England were offered and received military support; at first mere gentry such as Middleton and Lilleburne, and afterwards the heavy-weights, Lancaster and Harclay. He conceived of capturing an important prisoner whom the English could not fail to redeem, such as the Queen or Edward II himself. But Robert's growing ingenuity only illustrates the point that the devastation of northern England was not having the desired effect on the government. Before relinquishing their claims to Scotland Edward and his magnates abandoned the north to over a decade of destruction.

EFFECTS OF THE RAIDS ON RURAL COMMUNITIES

To gain some idea of how war affected agrarian society, we should survey the five main aspects of the rural economy: sheep-farming, cattle-farming, arable farming, rental incomes and the peasantry. The succession of natural disasters looms large: crop failures caused by torrential rainfall from 1315 to 1318; sheep disease in the years 1313–17; and cattle murrain from 1319. In his entry for 1316, the author of the *Flores Historiarum* states that 'in the kingdom of England three cruel scourges afflicted the people most horribly even unto death', and he identifies them as the raids of the Scots, the famine, and pestilence.[167]

During the years of the Scottish raids many of the sheep flocks of northern England diminished in size and wool exports sank dramatically. But the role of warfare in bringing this about can be exaggerated; and there is an alternative explanation of the disruption in the sheep epidemic of 1313–17, a result of heavy rainfall. A useful source for the fortunes of the peasant sheep farmer are the renders of wool and lamb tithes. The Prior of Durham was rector of the Northumberland parishes of Norhamshire and Islandshire (known jointly as 'North Durham') situated right against the Scottish border. It is estimated from the wool tithe receipts that as many as 3,600 sheep were maintained by wool producers in these parishes.[168] Up to 1314 the wool tithe from these parishes amounted to five or six sacks of wool.[169] Just across the Tweed from Scotland, these flocks should have been a prime target for marauding Scots; and the fact that renders showed no decline as late as 1314 is a strong indication that the Priory was buying off the Scots to secure immunity from raiding for these parishes.[170] After 1314 there is a hiatus in the accounts of the Priory which corresponds to the worst years of the Scottish raids, but during this time we know from chronicle sources that the area suffered dreadfully from the ravages of both Scottish and English armies. The next tithe proctor's account is a retrospective compilation covering the years 1317–20, which makes no mention of wool or lamb tithes.[171] The next available figure after that is for 1328, when only two sacks and 18 stone of wool were collected.[172] Yet by the accounting year 1330/31 the wool render had returned to its pre-war level of six sacks.[173] From this it seems that although wool production was very severely affected during the raids, the recovery was total and relatively swift. Undoubtedly many peasant producers had withdrawn their flocks as they themselves fled from the Scots. An increase in income from the 'small' tithes (of lambs, wool and other commodities) of these parishes in the 1330s leads Dr. Lomas to suggest that sheep farming was expanding at the expense of arable farming.[174] The evidence of a recovery in sheep farming at Norhamshire and Islandshire is supported by that of wool tithe renders of Ponteland.[175] During the truce year 1323/24 both the wool and the lamb render had made a recovery, with 140 lambs sold and 14 stone of wool. By 1329/30 income from wool tithes had surpassed the 1312 figure.[176] The remarkably swift recovery suggests that Northumberland flocks had been preserved, perhaps by evacuation of flocks from the war zone.

Further to the south, the records of Durham Priory allow some insight into the fortunes of a large-scale wool producer. Wool sales at Durham dropped dramatically during the 1310s and did not easily recover. In the 1308/9 account 20 sacks of good wool were sold; in 1318/19 sales had dropped to half of this.[177] The overall size of the flock at Durham is unknown; but what information there is suggests a serious decline in size. At Le Holm, the main Durham sheep farm, there were 1,195 sheep of all categories in 1310; in 1323 there were only 580.[178] The accounts of Durham's nearby cell of Jarrow may provide an analogy with what was happening to the flocks of the mother house. In 1313 the Jarrow monks had 275 sheep of all kinds and 133 lambs; in 1321 this had dropped to 168 sheep and 67 lambs; in 1326 to 10 sheep and 30 lambs.[179] The loss was not easily made good. But were the Scottish raiders to blame? They are known to have disrupted sheep farming in Durham on at least two occasions: in 1315 they drove off 'a large number' of sheep, and in 1322 during the 'burning of the Bishopric' flocks had to be evacuated to Cleveland and 40 of the better sheep were lost 'in the abominable depredations of the Scots and others'.[180] Yet these were exceptional occasions; as a rule Durham Priory was able to pay off the Scots to keep its livestock safe. Although there is no positive evidence either way, the serious decline in Durham wool sales and in the size of the Jarrow flocks is more likely to have been caused by disease, a much greater agent of sheep destruction than marauding Scots. Murrain was ravaging the flocks of other northern communities at around this time.[181]

On this evidence the tentative conclusion must be that the Scottish war was the cause of serious but temporary disruption to sheep farming along the borders; but that further south, in Durham, sheep murrain of 1315 was chiefly responsible for a severe and long-lasting decline in the size of the Priory's flock. On this basis one has to remain sceptical of the testimony of the 'Inquisitions of the Ninth' in 1341, which suggest that the Scottish raids of this period had a lasting impact upon wool and lamb tithes in Yorkshire and Lancashire; though it is possible that the evidence of the Inquisitions for other sectors may be perfectly valid.

Medieval cattle were also vulnerable to disease. Lanercost records the spread of the cattle murrain:

> (1319) At the same time the plague and the murrain of cattle which had lasted through the two preceding years in the southern districts broke out in the northern districts among oxen and cows, which after a short sickness generally died; and few animals of that kind were left so that men had to plough that year with horses.[182]

Dr. Kershaw has tentatively identified the disease as rinderpest; and its effects were devastating. At Bolton Priory the number of oxen on demesnes fell from 139 in 1318/19 to 53 in 1320/21; and the cattle herd fell in size from 225 head in 1318/19 to only 31 before the Scots arrived in 1319. Nostell Priory lost 59 oxen and 400 cows and calves to the epidemic. Further north, at Ponteland, six oxen died in 1319/20 'of the pest current in the countryside'.[183] But cattle were also the prime target of the Scottish raiders. It is difficult to escape the view that the north of England must have been progressively denuded of cattle during most of the period 1312–1322. The absence of cattle from the region during the 1310s and early 1320s is evident from three recurring features in manorial accounts: shortage of plough oxen; the near impossibility of finding tenants for pasture, described either as 'herbage' or 'agistment'; and abandonment of the woodland and high seasonal grazings or 'sheilings.' The most widespread complaint in manorial accounts is not physical damage by the Scots, but rather the inability to obtain a decent price for grazings as a result of the flight of the tenantry and the evacuation of herds. At Hexham winter and summer agistments in Alwentondale, worth £20 in peacetime, brought in only 10s. in 1315; at Barnard Castle revenue from grazings was greatly reduced 'because of the lack of animals on account of the Scottish raids'; at Moorholme, Cockermouth, Skipton, and almost every other manorial account which survives from the war years the same excuse is offered.[184] As the cattle were driven off by raiders or evacuated by their owners, so the sheilings were abandoned. On the Alnwick estates, a sheiling at Alnham on the slopes of the Cheviots paid no rent from 1315/16 until the account ended in 1318. The keeper of Hexham provides a list of abandoned tenements in the Allendale district, which, to judge by the placenames, are all seasonal pastures – Eskynscheles, Yarrug, Grenerrug, Botland and *Nove Terre*. These, too, do not recover during the period of account (1315–17). Pastures in Inglewood, which earlier in the war were used to conceal cattle, were also abandoned. They also seem to have been among the last tenements on the western march to recover: during the truce, in 1323/24, the holdings of Highhead and Selwra in Inglewood still paid no rent, while rents in Plumpton and from seven other agistments were reduced 'for default of animals and destruction of the countryside by the Scots'.[185] The Earl of Lancaster's great cattle-ranching operation in the western Pennines seems to have been greatly diminished by the raid of 1322. The rental of the lands formerly belonging to the earl shows that the productivity of vaccaries in Blesedale and Wyresdale was reduced because 'all other of the lord's beasts there were driven away by the Scots', making it impossible to 'demise' (or let out) herbage. In Blackburnshire positive evidence of Scottish activity is limited, but here, where previously the de Lacy earls had maintained 2,400 head of cattle at the turn of the century, there were at Michaelmas 1324 only 415 recorded.[186]

But the sector most severely affected by the Scottish war was surely tillage, vulnerable at every stage to devastation. Ploughing was inhibited by the theft of draught oxen by the raiders, or their evacuation by the owners; and plough oxen were more liable to abduction than other cattle because they were kept at the manor farm during the summer months, whereas other cattle were safe on the high sheilings. At Wark-on-Tweed, the keeper of the estate accounted for the reduction in profit from arable demesne with the claim that 'there were beasts enough neither to graze nor till the land'.[187] Sowing was also occasionally disrupted by war. Antony Lucy, keeper of the Liberty of Hexham in 1315/16, reported that the demesne lands (the lands which the lord reserved to his own use) rendered no profit:

> nor was it possible for the said land to be sown by the keeper during the said time, on account of the frequent attacks of the Scots, nor did any one wish to take herbage on the said land for the same reason, and also on account of the shortage of animals.[188]

Crops were especially vulnerable when growing, and the burning of crops is referred to repeatedly in both chronicles and manorial accounts. Hay and corn were burnt when the Scots arrived unexpectedly at Bearpark in Durham in 1315.[189] Demesne rents at Salkeld near Penrith were reduced in 1323/24 'because the tenants were so destroyed by the Scots who burnt the vill and the corn entirely on the first of this year'.[190] Standing crops were also trampled by the herds of stolen cattle driven north; for the Scots this appears to have been a favourite and effortless means of destroying livelihoods.[191] Harvesting at Stamfordham near Embleton was interrupted in 1313/14 when the labourers tying up sheaves were attacked by the Scots.[192] Grain remained vulnerable even after it had been gathered in, for barns were invariably of wooden construction and burned easily. Reference has already been made to the burning of barns on the western march in the autumn of 1319, and in Durham early in 1322, which caused severe scarcity that summer.[193] Mills, too, were obvious targets for the Scots, and destruction of water and windmills is noted at Norham, Bamburgh, Penrith and many other places.[194] These expensive structures represented considerable investment and could not easily be replaced. It is this destruction of capital equipment that explains the slowness of arable farming to recover.

The effects of war on grain production are illustrated by the cash income from the sheaf tithes of Durham Priory's churches at Norhamshire and Islandshire (Chart 1).[195] The tithes were extremely sensitive to military activity; this we might expect from two parishes situated on the border itself. Yet Durham Priory's ability to buy off the Scots staved off the impact of war until relatively late; these border parishes seem to have been protected until 1315/16. But then as with the wool tithes in the same parishes, a dramatic fall occurs. Although the price of wheat soared on account of the crop failure, the cash income from the sheaf tithe plummeted, indicating that grain production had fallen away to almost nothing in 1316. No explanation for the fall is given in the sources; but given the exposed position of these parishes, one can scarcely ascribe the collapse of these revenues to harvest failure. The

Scots must have destroyed the miserable harvest of 1316 and the two succeeding years, probably because the priory failed to pay protection money. Thereafter, the tithes of 1319 are said to have been 'destroyed' by the English army, then encamped nearby at the siege of Berwick.[196] These tithe incomes never fully recovered, and in that respect the contrast with the swift recovery of sheep farming in the same area is striking. The same sources also contain records of 'mulcture' or income from the mills in these parishes. From 1300 this had been a steady £3.10s., dropping to £1 in 1313 but recovering in 1314 and 1315. The Bursar's Account Roll for 1316/17, however, contains a note to the effect that all the mills in the parishes had been destroyed. This is repeated in the subsequent roll; and income from this source is not mentioned again until 1329, when the much reduced figure of £1. 3s. 0d. is recorded. This same pattern, a sudden collapse of income during the 1310s, is replicated in the records of the sheaf tithes of Holy Island, Durham's cell in the parish of the same name. Holy Island tithes had brought in £112 *per annum*, but in 1326 they were worth only £47, and they continued to decline, to £21 in 1327 and £15 in 1328.[197]

Another aspect of the war's impact on arable farming is a curtailment of arable acreage. *Terra frisca* or *terra vasta*, both of which are usually translated as 'wasteland', was not necessarily unproductive,[198] but in the wake of the Scottish raids countless acres of ploughland, demesne, husbandlands and bovates are recorded as *frisc*, and it is evident that these lands which had once regularly produced corn were now greatly under-exploited if not abandoned. The desertion of arable land is especially marked in Northumberland. When accounts begin at Wark-on-Tweed in 1323 there were 936 acres of arable demesne 'which no-one dared to cultivate for fear of the Scots' and 416 of untilled husbandland.[199] All over Northumberland, the situation was the same: Hexham, Little Ryhill, Shotton and Alnwick all had the same problem, the mass desertion of tenants.[200] West of the Pennines the situation was the same: Robert Tilliol's manor of Scaleby, which included 24 acres of demesne and 40 bovates, rendered nothing in 1321 because the country was so wasted by the Scots.[201] At Penrith only 15 acres of demesne land out of 120 were demised to tenants in 1317/18; and at Castle Sowerby all 254½ acres of demesne, together with 664 acres of assartments, lay *frisc* and uncultivated.[202] Examples could be multiplied, but these instances give some idea of the extent of the waste caused by the desertion of the tenantry.

The catastrophic effect of the war on rental income of all kinds is attested by constant repetition of the same refrain in manorial accounts throughout the north of England: 'unable to rent out for more on account of the frequent raids of the Scots' or 'on account of the poverty of the tenants'. From the frequency with which these phrases appear it

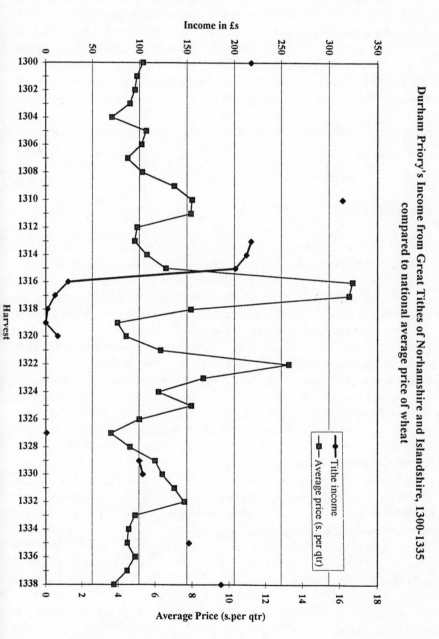

Chart 1

Durham Priory's Income from Great Tithes of Norhamshire and Islandshire, 1300-1335 compared to national average price of wheat

seems that the flight of the tenantry from the war zone was a much more widespread problem than the actual depredations of the raiders. Detailed and accurate pictures of how raiding affected the payment of rent can be constructed from accounts of two individual estates. The first is at Alnwick, where an account covers the period 1314–18; and Dr. Scammell calculated that agricultural rents on the estates fell by 4.1, 16.5 and 28.6 per cent in successive years.[203] The account reveals successive rent reductions in an effort to retain tenants, and a steady diminution in the acreage rented out:

Demesne or Common Field	Acreage & Peacetime Rent	1314/15	1315/16	1316/17	1317/18	1318
Beyond Aln (demesne)	77 @ 15d.	77 @ 15d.	77 @ 12d.	77 @ 12d.	77 @ 12d.	77 @ 12d.
Bondgate (demesne)	94 @ 18d.	94 @ 18d.	16 @ 18d.	11 @ 4d.	11 @ 3d.	n.r.
Westfield	19 @ 15d.	n.r.	n.r.	n.r.	n.r.	n.r.
Southfield	36 @ 4d.	36 @ 3d.	n.r.	n.r.	n.r.	n.r.

n.r.=*non respondent*, nothing paid

The explanations offered for this catastrophic decline in rental income are: 'the destruction made in the countryside by frequent Scottish attacks'; 'the impoverishment of the countryside' by the same; and simply 'default of tenants'. Rents kept up best on the demesne lands, demesne being generally better quality land than bondland or land in common fields and therefore the last to be abandoned.

Another estate for which detail is available is the Honour of Penrith (Chart 2).[204] Here the decline of rental income may be related to specific raids through a set of accounts spanning the period 1307/8 to 1329/30. The graph shows income from all rents (soke, bond and demesne) in these years. But the nature of the evidence requires that it be handled with caution. The graphs are not independent of one another; the same official, the keeper, accounted to the exchequer for all the manors. The uniformity of the first five years reveals the artificiality of the process; here the keeper of the Honour simply paid the exchequer the sum which it had come to expect. No explanation is available for the sudden hike of 1312/13; and thereafter the keeper seizes upon the Scottish raids as excuses for reducing his render. It becomes clear that fluctuations in rental income are only loosely related to the Scottish raids; in several instances income rises even though that manor had been raided the previous year. Most strikingly, the raids of 1322 and 1327 fail to prevent a rise in the income from all the manors. There are, then, many other factors at work besides the Scots, though the only indication of natural disaster is an isolated reference to flooding in 1317, and another to a storm in 1327/28.[205] The gradual recovery after 1322 may be due to the truce with Scotland, to genuine improvement in economic conditions, or to a more stringent supervision of incomes following the reform of the exchequer.

Rental Income from Manors in the Honour of Penrith, 1307-1330

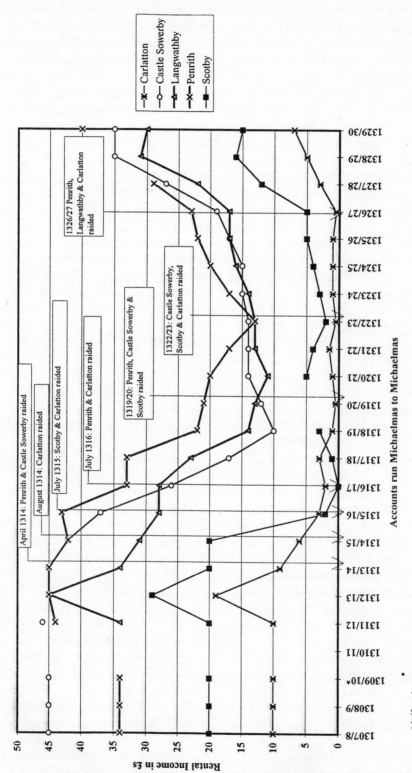

Legend:
- ✕ — Carlatton
- ○ — Castle Sowerby
- △ — Langwathby
- ✕ — Penrith
- ■ — Scotby

April 1314: Penrith & Castle Sowerby raided

August 1314: Carlatton raided

July 1315: Scotby & Carlatton raided

July 1316: Penrith & Carlatton raided

1319/20: Penrith, Castle Sowerby & Scotby raided

1322/23: Castle Sowerby, Scotby & Carlatton raided

1326/27 Penrith, Langwathby & Carlatton raided

Rental Income in £s

Accounts run Michaelmas to Michaelmas

*
A half yearly rent
paid twice yearly
doubled up

Despite all the *caveats*, however, the impact of the four raids in successive years from 1314 had a depressing effect upon the levels of this category of revenue; and the accounts repeatedly complain of 'the poverty and destruction of the tenant', 'lack of tenants' and an 'inability to let at a dearer rent'. Altogether the revenues from the Penrith manors bear out Dr. Miller's suggestion that the cumulative effect of repeated raids was the real cause of the chronic impoverishment of the region.[206]

In the 1310s, the Bishopric of Durham affords a stark contrast to the desolation of Northumberland and Cumberland. The rental income of Durham Priory *infra aquas* (that is, between the waters of Tyne and Tees, the bishopric) increased steadily from £356 in 1291/92 to £455 in 1316/17, the war having no apparent detrimental effect. [207] No records survive for the lands of the Bishop of Durham; but during episcopal vacancies the lands of the Bishop of Durham were taken into the king's hands, so that after the death of each bishop and before the appointment of the next, the royal accounts afford a window on episcopal estates. Episcopal vacancies occurred in 1311, 1316/17 and 1333. There is mention of Scottish activity during the vacancy of 1316/17, when assized rents stood at £432, but the fall in rents since the account of 1311 was a mere three percent.[208] It seems that rental incomes in Durham barely suffered at all during the very period when they fell dramatically at Alnwick and Penrith; the only factor that can account for this is that the policy of purchasing immunity from raiding by the Scots endured longer in Durham than elsewhere, protecting rents and agricultural incomes. But at some time in the 1320s rental income in Durham had suffered a serious reverse. By 1329/30 the rents of the Priory had fallen to £391, a drop of 14 percent on the figure for 1316.[209] The likeliest occasion of the fall is the 'burning of the bishopric' in 1322, so the rents in 1329/30 were probably recovering from this earlier nadir.

In evaluating the evidence of Penrith, Alnwick and other estates, the rents of the Bishop and Prior of Durham serve to some extent as a 'control'. Estates in Durham were protected from Scottish raids longer than any others in the north by the payments for truces. The stability of rents in the bishopric up to *c*.1317 provides powerful support for the view that war was responsible for the collapse of rental income elsewhere in the region. Famine, murrain and flooding were common throughout the north; auditors and accountants presumably exaggerated losses to the same extent in Durham as elsewhere in the north. War was the only factor that did not obtain in Durham, and the maintenance of high levels of rental income in Durham while they fell dramatically elsewhere shows that war damage was chiefly responsible for the devastation of the north in these years.

Before leaving the topic one might ask, 'What of the individual peasant cultivators?' Professor Barrow has stressed with every justification that

King Robert showed humanity and restraint in the aftermath of Bannockburn;[210] but it should be remembered that for the English peasantry his war spelt high taxes, military service, poverty, ruin and death. While non-payment of rent is no proof of depopulation, there are many references to the flight of the tenantry. At Christmas in 1313 it is recorded that a great part of the men of Cumberland 'took their goods with them to divers parts of the kingdom in flight as best they could for fear of the Scots'.[211] Bishop Halton of Carlisle, confirming the church of Addingham to Carlisle Priory, accused the Scots of having 'wasted and robbed their lands and possessions [and] killed their men and farmworkers'.[212]

The depopulation of Northumberland is remarkable. On the manor of Acomb only two individuals remained on their holdings, others having left, taking their goods and chattels; two others remained at Wall; and at Erington, only one man and his son stayed on, in spite of the raids.[213] Across the Pennines at Stenton it was reported in 1316 that no-one had lived there for four years past.[214] Not that this depopulation resulted from the actions of the Scots alone; at Cockermouth the English garrison were also partly responsible for driving people away from the area.[215]

One document more than any other conveys the full impact of the Scottish raids on the northern peasantry. It is an inquisition, taken on 10th January 1326 as to the ability of the men of Easingwold and Huby to pay the farm of 260 acres in the former township and 60 in the latter.[216] Easingwold and Huby are situated in the Forest of Galtres in the Vale of York, ten miles north of York city. They were smitten by Scottish raids in 1319 and again in 1322. Brief explanations are offered in the case of each tenant. At Easingwold 84 tenants are described as unable to pay the farm. The Scots were blamed specifically for the ruin of 57 of these: 13 had been killed at the Battle of Myton in 1319; nine at the Battle of Bylands in 1322; and another nine killed by the Scots either at Easingwold or at places unspecified. Among these last, one John Baker, tenant at will of an acre and a half, was burnt to death in his house at Easingwold when the Scots arrived there in 1322. Seven other tenants had been driven from the neighbourhood by poverty or destruction caused by the Scots; 10 died in poverty; 17 were reduced to beggary; and the holdings of 17 others are described simply as 'impoverished, burnt and destroyed'. The tenants of Huby suffered similar fates. It is a rare glimpse of the fate of individual peasants; and a reminder of the brutality of the war.

NOTES

1   E159/102, m.114d; *Lanercost*, pp. 210–11; *Bridlington*, p. 47 and *Melsa* ii, 332.

2   E101/14/31, ff. 9d, 10; discussed in J.E. Morris, 'Cumberland and

Westmorland Military Levies in the time of Edward II', *CWAAS* new series, iii (1903), 317–19.

3 *Lanercost*, p. 211; E372/166, m. 32.

4 J.F. Curwen, *Castles and Towers* (*CWAAS*, Extra Series xiii, Kendal 1913), pp. 150–53.

5 KB27/218, m. 72d.; *CCR 1313–18*, pp. 127–28.

6 *CPR 1313–17*, p. 186.

7 E372/166, m. 32. Destruction of Carlatton is included in 7 Edward II, and therefore reads literally as 1313; but since that was a time of truce, this seems to be a mistake.

8 *Walsingham* i, 142.

9 C. McNamee, 'William Wallace's Invasion of Northern England, 1297', *NH* xxvi (1990), 40–58.

10 D. Hay, 'Booty and Border Warfare', *TDGNHAS* 3rd Series xxxi (1954), 157–63.

11 *CIM* ii, nos. 385, 408; Merton College MCR 5987; E101/378/4, f. 8d; *CCR 1318–23*, p. 65.

12 Hay, *op. cit.*, pp. 149–53; Farrer, *Lancashire Inquests*, ii, 163.

13 *Lanercost*, pp. 216–17.

14 C.M. Fraser, 'The Pattern of Trade in the North-East of England, 1265–1350', *NH* iv (1969), 47. See also F.W. Dendy, 'Purchases at Corbridge Fair in 1298', *AA* 2nd series ii (1906), 1–8; *Rot. Scot.* i, 115 .

15 *Lanercost*, pp. 211, 238.

16 SC6/1144/3; *Correspondence, Inventories, Account Rolls and Law Proceedings of the Priory of Coldingham*, ed. J. Raine (Surtees Society, xii, 1841), pp. 22–23; SC6/950/3.

17 *Lanercost*, pp. 194, 197.

18 *Le Bel*, pp. 47–48.

19 *Le Bel*, pp. 47–48.

20 See pp. 72, 93.

21 *RRS* v no. 40, pp. 328–30.

22 *Rot. Scot.* i, 131; *CDS* v no. 593, p. 238.

23 Raine, *Scriptores Tres*, Appendix XCIV, p. cxiii.

24 E159/102, m. 114d; *Lanercost*, p. 212; Barbour, *The Bruce* XIII, 742–54.

25 *Rot. Scot.* i, 133.

26 SC1/35/37, calendared in *CDS* v no. 598, p. 239; *Reg. Greenfield* i, 103, 155, 271; v, 43–45; Raine, *Northern Registers*, pp. 243–49.

27 *Rot. Scot.* i, 136–37; *CCR 1313–18*, p. 205; Maddicott, *Lancaster*, pp. 167–8.

28 DCD Cellarer's Roll, 1313–14, m. 4.

29 *CDS* iii no. 474, p. 91; a notary was assigned to draw up a process on Anglo-Scottish relations, Phillips, *Aymer de Valence*, p. 85; Raine, *Northern Registers*, p. 237.

30 *Lanercost*, p. 212; *Melsa*, ii, 333; V.H. Galbraith, 'Extracts from the *Historia Aurea* and a French *Brut*', *EHR* xliii (1928), 209.

31 *Rot. Parl.* i, 293; G.W.S. Barrow, 'A note on Falstone', *AA* (5th Series) ii, 149–50; *RRS*, no. 424, p. 665.

32 'Historia Aurea', 209. Duncan dates this grant to the second half of 1317, *RRS* v no. 428, p. 665

33 Summerson, *Medieval Carlisle* ii, 219; Duncan, 'War of the Scots', p. 129.

34 See below pp. 133, 135.
35 *Guisborough*, p. 396; *Lanercost*, p. 213; *Priory of Coldingham*, ed. J. Raine (Surtees Society, xii, 1841), pp. 22–23, which Raine dates incorrectly to 1327.
36 Barrow, *Robert Bruce*, p. 198; Raine, *Scriptores Tres*, p. 96; *Coldingham*, ed. Raine, pp. 22–23; DCD Loc. XXVII, 30, 31, described in Scammell, 'Robert I', p. 329.
37 See below pp. 135, 160 n.50.
38 See above p. 72, below, p. 154.
39 *Vita Edwardi II*, pp. 61–62.
40 *Lanercost*, pp. 213–15 and also *English Historical Documents*, ed. D.C. Douglas (London, 1975) iii, 265–67; and discussed in detail and with map by Summerson, *Medieval Carlisle* i, 215–19.
41 Plate [ ].
42 E372/166, m. 34; *The Chronicle of St. Mary's Abbey, York*, ed. H.H.E. Craster and M.E. Thornton (Surtees Society cxlviii, 1933 for 1934), p. 68.
43 *CDS* iii no. 465, p. 88.
44 *Rot. Scot.* i, 153.
45 *Rot. Scot.* i, 154.
46 See below pp. 149–51.
47 *CDS* v no. 628, p. 244.
48 *CDS* iii no. 440, p. 83, which I would be inclined to date to 29th June 1316; Duncan, *RRS* v 'Introduction', p. 138 and no. 99, pp. 376–77.
49 *Lanercost* p. 216; *Melsa* ii, 333; BL MS Cotton Domitian A XII, f. 41d.
50 E372/167, m. 34.
51 E179/67/9, m. 37. This bears no relation to the printed *Nova Taxatio* in *Taxatio Ecclesiastica Angliae et Walliae Auctoritate P. Nicholai IV circa A.D. 1291*, ed. J. Topham (Record Commission, 1802), pp. 306–9.
52 I. Kershaw, *Bolton Priory* (Oxford, 1973), pp. 67–68.
53 M. Beresford, 'The Lost Villages of Yorkshire, Part II', *Yorkshire Archaeological Journal* xxxviii (1952–55), 217.
54 E372/166, m. 32.
55 *Lanercost*, p. 216.
56 J.F. Willard, 'The Scotch Raids and the Fourteenth Century Taxation of Northern England', *University of Colorado Studies* v, No. 4 (1908), 239.
57 *Lanercost*, pp. 216–17.
58 *CCR 1313–18*, p. 496; E159/92, m. 40.
59 E372/166, m. 32.
60 *Rot. Scot.*, i, 166–68;
61 See below pp. 182–84.
62 *CDS* iii, no. 562, p. 108.
63 M. Prestwich, 'Gilbert de Middleton and the Attack on the Cardinals, 1317', in *Warriors and Churchmen in the High Middle Ages: Essays to Karl Leyser*, ed. T. Reuter (London, 1992), pp. 179–194; Duncan, *RRS* Introduction, pp. 140–43; R. Hill, 'An English Archbishop and the Scottish War of Independence', *Innes Review* xxii (1971), 65–66; *Foedera* i (II), 317.
64 Peter of Spalding is well attested as a man at arms at Berwick, from 1310 Bodleian Library MS Tanner 197, f. 11d; Barbour, *The Bruce* XVII, 23; *Scalacronica*, p. 58.

65 Society of Antiquaries MS 121, f. 30; *Lanercost*, p. 220.
66 *Lanercost*, p. 221; *Bridlington*, p. 55; 'Historia Aurea', p. 209. See below pp. 137–38.
67 *Le Livere de reis de Brittanie*, ed. J. Glover (R.S., 1865), p. 334.
68 E179/67/9, m. 26. *Taxatio Ecclesiastica*, pp. 297–309.
69 *CDS* iii no. 602, p. 114; SC1/19/142; E179/67/9, m. 25.
70 I. Kershaw, 'The Scots in the West Riding, 1318–19', *NH* xvii (1981), 233 and 236.
71 *Melsa* ii, 335 and BL MS Cotton Domitian A XII, f. 42d report this; but 'Historia Aurea' and *Lanercost* do not.
72 *Lanercost*, p. 221; *Melsa*, p. 335; KB27/248, m. 70d; E179/67/9, m. 23.
73 *Melsa* ii, 335; BL MS Cotton Domitian A XII, f. 42d; E179/67/9, mm. 26.
74 *Reg. Melton* i, no. 394, p. 120.
75 E179/67/9, m. 23 details destruction of the Archbishop of York's manors at Ripon, Monkton, Thorp, Northlathes and Otley.
76 *CIM* ii no. 385, p. 95; E372/166, m. 18d; *CCR 1318–23*, p. 65.
77 *CPR 1313–18*, p. 544.
78 *Lanercost* , p. 221; *CIM* ii no. 392, pp. 98–99.
79 E179/67/9, m. 26.
80 SC8/204/10165; *CCR 1313–18*, p. 575; *CPR 1327–30*, p. 152.
81 E179/67/9, m. 26; *Le Livere de reis de Brittanie*, p. 334 confirms that they came within eight miles of York; *CDS* iii no. 856, pp. 156–57.
82 E179/67/9, m. 26.
83 *Lanercost*, p. 221; Kershaw, *Bolton Priory*, p. 15. Only *Bridlington* p. 55 claims that Bolton Priory was sacked.
84 E179/67/9, m. 23.
85 E359/14, m. 13d; Willard, 'Scotch Raids', p. 239.
86 *Rot. Scot.* i, 182.
87 *Rot. Scot.* i, 189, 190–91.
88 See below, p. 185.
89 Duncan, *RRS* v, Introduction, pp. 145–46.
90 Maddicott, *Lancaster*, pp. 247–51.
91 *CCW 1244–1326*, pp. 501–2.
92 *Scalacronica* , p. 66; 'Historia Aurea', pp. 210–11.
93 *Vita Edwardi II*, p. 95; *Trokelowe*, p. 103; *Flores Hist.* iii, 188–89.
94 *Flores Hist.* iii, 188–89; *Lanercost*, p. 226.
95 BL MS Cotton Cleopatra D III, f. 153d.
96 *Vita Edwardi II*, p. 95.
97 *CCR 1313–18*, pp. 166–67, dated 25th November 1319; E359/14, mm. 12d, 13d.
98 E159/93, m. 23d; York Minster Library, VC6/2/4.
99 They reached Walton, 10 miles from York, *CIM* ii no. 453, p. 112.
100 E372/168, mm. 42–44d ; JUST 3/75, m. 34 and JUST 3/76, mm. 26d, 31, 36.
101 *Vita Edwardi II*, p. 95; *CDS* iii, no. 664, p. 124.
102 The best accounts are in BL MS Cotton Cleopatra D III, f. 153d, and *Vita Edwardi II*, pp. 95–97; *Bridlington*, p. 56. Thurstan was a twelfth-century archbishop who defeated the Scots at the Battle of the Standard in 1138.

103 *CDS* iii no. 680, p. 129.

104 *CIM* ii no. 489, p. 121; E359/14, m. 12d.

105 *Bridlington*, p. 58; *Melsa* ii, 337.

106 E159/93, m. 23.

107 Kershaw, *Bolton Priory*, pp. 16, 124.

108 E159/100, m. 37d; Willard, 'Scotch Raids', p. 239.

109 'Historia Aurea', p. 209, which dates the incident to 1318. *Bridlington*, p. 58 confirms that the Scots took this route homewards in 1319.

110 'Historia Aurea', p. 209.

111 *Trokelowe*, p. 103; *Vita Edwardi II*, pp. 97–98 ; *Lanercost*, p. 227; Maddicott, *Lancaster*, pp. 248–51.

112 *Lanercost*, pp. 227–28.

113 E101/378/4, f. 8d.

114 Duncan, *RRS* v Introduction, pp. 145–46.

115 BL MS Add. 17362, f. 9d.

116 *RRS* v no. 162, pp. 433–37.

117 *Vita Edwardi II* , pp. 102–3.

118 Duncan, *RRS* v, Introduction, pp. 147, 161.

119 BL MS Cotton Julius D IV, f. 123 says it took place after the feast of St Hilary (13th January); Fraser, *Northern Petitions* no. 133, pp. 179–81 specifies 15th to 31st January.

120 J. Scammell, 'Some Aspects of Medieval English Monastic Government: The Case of Geoffrey de Burdon, Prior of Durham (1313–1321)', *Revue Bénédictine* lxviii (1958), 226–50.

121 Maddicott, *Lancaster*, pp. 301–2.

122 Raine, *Scriptores Tres*, pp. 102–3; *Lanercost*, p. 230; Fraser, *Northern Petitions*, no. 133, pp. 179–81.

123 E159/96, m. 28; the printed *Nova Taxatio* for Durham is substantially that of 1318.

124 R.A. Lomas, 'Durham Cathedral Priory as a Landowner and Landlord, 1290–1540' (Durham University Ph.D Thesis, 1973), p. 150. Other traces of this destruction may survive in later records, c.f. Raine, *Scriptores Tres*, pp. 46–47 where damage to the manors of Ketton and Wardley is mentioned, and R. Surtees, *History and Antiquities of the County Palatinate of Durham* (London, 1816) i (I), 2–3, a record of damage to the parishes of Dalton, Morton and Hesilden.

125 *CDS* iii no. 749, p. 140.

126 Summerson, *Medieval Carlisle* i, 247; *Lanercost*, p. 230.

127 *CPR 1321–24*, p. 90; *Vita Edwardi II*, pp. 120–21; *Lanercost*, pp. 231–35; Maddicott, *Lancaster*, pp. 310–11.

128 *CDS* iii no. 747, p. 140.

129 *Lanercost*, pp. 237–38; *Fordun* ii, 349; *Reg. Halton* ii, 216–17 says that the raid began on 6th June, and this may refer to Douglas and Moray's raiders.

130 E372/172, m. 48d.

131 W. Greenwood, *The Redmans of Levens and Harewood* (Kendal, 1905), pp. 31–32; E159/102, m. 177d; Farrer, *Lancashire Inquests* ii, 165, 178n; E159/97, m. 55. *South Lancashire in the Reign of Edward II*, ed. G.H. Tuppling (Chetham Society i, 3rd series, 1949), pp. xxxvi-xxxvii.

132 Farrer, *Lancashire Inquests* ii, 116, 168, 172; *CDS* iii no. 761, p. 142.

133 Farrer, *Lancashire Inquests* ii, 163, 107, 172–73, 175, 178; *CDS* iii no. 838, pp. 154–55; *CCR 1323–27*, p. 679.
134 Tuppling, *South Lancashire*, pp. xxvi, xxvii; *CCR 1323–27*, pp. 207–8; Farrer, *Lancashire Inquests* ii, 162–63.
135 *Lanercost*, p. 238; *Reg. Halton* ii, 216–17.
136 Fryde, *Tyranny and Fall*, pp. 129–30.
137 *CDS* iii nos. 783, 784; *CCR 1323–27*, p. 679.
138 *Lanercost*, p. 239; BL MS Stowe 553, f. 61d.
139 E372/173, m. 48d.
140 *CCR 1318–23*, p. 680; *Lanercost*, p. 239; *Bridlington*, p. 79; Fryde, *Tyranny and Fall*, pp. 130–31.
141 *Lanercost*, p. 239.
142 *Bridlington*, p. 82; E372/173, mm. 48–49.
143 E101/16/16, m. 1.
144 MS Reg. Melton, OF 442v, NF 562v, calendared in *Reg. Melton* i, no. 61, p. 19; R.M. Hill, *The Labourer in the Vineyard* (Borthwick Papers No. 35, 1968), pp. 12–13.
145 *CCR 1318–23*, p. 681; Barrow, *Robert Bruce*, p. 243; SC1/49/52.
146 JUST 3/76, m. 26d; E372/168, mm. 42–45.
147 *Adae Murimuth Continuatio Chronicorum*, ed. E.M. Thompson (R.S., 1889), pp. 37–38; *Memorials of Beverley Minster*, ed. A. F. Leach (Surtees Society cviii, 1903) ii, 20.
148 See n. 155 below.
149 *Le Livere de Reis de Brittanie*, p. 345–46; Barbour, *The Bruce* XVIII, 348–522; A.D.H. Leadman, 'The Battle of Bylands Abbey', *Yorkshire Archaeological Journal* viii (1884), 475–88. Barrow, *Robert Bruce*, pp. 243–44 identifies the place as Scawton Moor.
150 BL MS Stowe 553, ff. 69, 112d.
151 *CDS* iii no. 791, p. 147; *Bridlington*, pp. 79–80.
152 *CIM* ii no. 891, p. 222.
153 *North Riding Record Society*, new series ii (1895), 245–46.
154 E179/67/9, m. 23. This is the *Nova Taxatio* for Cleveland and the East Riding. The map drawn by D. Robinson shows all the parishes, *Beneficed Clergy in Cleveland and the East Riding,1306–1340* (Borthwick Papers no. 37, 1969).
155 E179/67/9, m. 23.
156 *Bridlington*, pp. 79–82.
157 Leach, *Memorials of Beverley Minster*, ii, 20–21; *Murimuth*, pp. 37–38.
158 BL MS Cotton Domitian A XII, f. 43; *Melsa* ii, 346.
159 BL MS Stowe 553, f. 63.
160 E159/100, m. 125; E372/172, mm. 51–53; E159/103, m. 176.
161 *Murimuth,*pp. 37–38. The mill of Kirkdale was flooded at Michaelmas, JUST 1/1119A, m. 3.
162 *Lanercost*, p. 241.
163 *CCR 1318–23*, pp. 645–46.
164 See below pp. 154–55.
165 *Lanercost*, p. 242.
166 See below pp. 234–37.
167 *Flores Hist.* iii, 173–74.
168 *AHE* ii, 409. A sack or bale of wool is generally taken to be 364lbs,

the produce of 240 to 280 sheep, E.M. Carus-Wilson and O. Coleman, *England's Export Trade, 1275–1547* (Oxford, 1963), p. 13.

169 DCD BAR 1308/9; DCD PNA 1314/15.

170 See below pp. 132–33.

171 DCD PNA 1317–20.

172 DCD PNA 1328(B).

173 DCD PNA 1330/31.

174 R. Lomas, *North-East England in the Middle Ages* (Edinburgh, 1992), p. 59.

175 The rector of Ponteland was Merton College, Oxford. Merton College MCR, nos. 5983, 5984, 5985, 5986, m. 2.

176 Merton College MCR, nos. 5995a, 5995b.

177 DCD BAR 1308/9, 1318/19.

178 DCD Livestock Accounts, 1310, 1323.

179 *The Inventories and Account Rolls of Jarrow and Monkwearmouth*, ed. J. Raine (Surtees Society xxix, 1854), pp. 11–15.

180 *Priory of Coldingham*, ed. Raine, pp. 22–23; DCD Livestock Account, 1323.

181 *AHE*, ii, 727, 755; I. Kershaw, 'The Great Famine and Agrarian Crisis in England', *P&P* lix (1973), 20–22; Kershaw, *Bolton Priory*, pp. 80–84.

182 *Lanercost*, p. 228. There is evidence of ploughing with horses at the Hospital of St. Giles in Hexham, *The Priory of Hexham*, ed. J. Raine (Surtees Society xlvi, 1865) ii, 131.

183 Kershaw, 'Great Famine', pp. 25–26; Kershaw, *Bolton Priory*, Tables XI and XII, pp. 96–98; W. Dugdale, *Monasticon Anglicanum* (London, 1846) vi, Part I, 90; Merton College MCR, no. 5988.

184 SC6/1144/3, m. 1; SC6/835/2, m. 2; Farrer, *Lancashire Inquests*, ii, 164; SC6/824/18, m. 2; SC6/1147/23 (Skipton, where there is evidence of murrain as well as of war damage). One could keep adding to this: e.g., E372/164, m. 34 (Wigton, Melmerby, Stenton and Kirkebride in Cumberland, 1316); E372/174, m. 51 (Bamburgh, 1318–24).

185 SC6/950/1 (Alnwick); SC6/1144/3 (Hexham); E372/171, mm. 40, 40d.

186 Farrer, *Lancashire Inquisitions*, pp. 177–78, 185, n. 1; G.H. Tuppling, *An Economic History of Rossendale* (Chetham Society, 1927), comparing Tables I and II with pp. 31–32.

187 SC6/952/12, 13.

188 SC6/1144/3, m. 1.

189 *Coldingham*, ed. Raine, p. 22.

190 E372/173, m. 49d.

191 *Lanercost*, pp. 213, 238; Farrer, *Lancashire Inquests* ii, 172–73.

192 DL29/1/3, m. 2d, an apparently isolated case of the Scots molesting the estates of the Earl of Lancaster.

193 *Lanercost*, pp. 227–28; Raine, *Scriptores Tres*, p. 102.

194 DCD PNA 1330–1; SC6/950/3; E372/166, m. 32; Kershaw, *Bolton Priory*, pp. 123–24; SC6/952/12 (Wark-on-Tweed). K.M. Longley, 'The Scottish Invasion of 1327: A Glimpse of the Aftermath' (Wigton Church Accounts, 1328–9), *CWAAS* 2nd series lxxxiii (1983), 65 shows a tithe mill at Waverton rendering nothing because burnt by the Scots, and another at Dockray destroyed by flood.

195 Sources are as follows:

1300	DCD PNA 1300–1	1319	DCD PNA 1317–21
1310	DCD BAR 1310–11	1320	"　　　" 　　　　"
1313	DCD BAR 1314–15(B)	1327	DCD PNA 1327–8
1314	DCD PNA 1314–15	1329	DCD PNA 1329–30
1315	DCD PNA 1315–16(B)	1330	DCD PNA 1330–31
1316	DCD BAR 1316–17(B)	1335	DCD PNA 1335–6
1317	DCD PNA 1317–21	1338	Lomas, *North-East*
1318	"　　　" 　　　　"		*England*, p. 59.

The national average wheat prices is taken from T.H. Lloyd, *The Movement of Wool Prices in Medieval England* (EcHR Supplement 6, 1973). They are intended only as a general guide.

196 PNA 1317/21.
197 DCD Holy Island Status 1326, 1328.
198 *NCH* viii, 214, n.4; B. Harvey, 'The Population Trend in England between 1300 and 1348', *TRHS* 5th series xvi (1966), 33.
199 SC6/952/12.
200 SC6/ 1144/3; *Calender of Inquisitions Post Mortem* vi no. 560, p. 357; SC6/ 950/1.
201 *Calender of Inquisitions Post Mortem* vi no. 279, p. 166.
202 E372/173, m. 48.
203 SC6/950/1; Scammell, 'Robert I', p. 387.
204 Sources are as follows:
　　1307–8　SC6/824/28
　　1308–9　SC6/824/29
　　1311–17 E372/166, m. 32
　　1317–27 E372/173, mm. 48–49
　　1327–30 SC6/824/31
205 E372/166, m. 32; E372/173, m. 49.
206 E. Miller, *War in the North* (University of Hull Publication, 1960), pp. 8–12.
207 Lomas, 'Durham Cathedral Priory,' pp. 100–4.
208 Comparing SC6/1144/17 (1311) with E372/164, m. 34 (1316–17).
209 Lomas, 'Durham Cathedral Priory', p. 101.
210 Barrow, *Robert Bruce*, p. 231.
211 E159/100, m. 110d.
212 Summerson, *Medieval Carlisle* i, 220.
213 SC6/1144/3, m. 1.
214 E372/172, m. 51.
215 *CIM* ii no. 297, p. 75.
216 E159/100, m. 37; G.C. Cowling, *The History of Easingwold and the Forest of Galtres* (Huddersfield, 1967), p. 29.

CHAPTER FOUR

The Defence of Northern England, 1311–1322

'. . . our strong men are become tyrants, our defenders destroyers, our protectors traitors'

There is no mystery as to why the English were losing the Wars of the Bruces: on the one hand, the preoccupation with domestic discord reduced even defence of the realm to a lesser priority in the eyes of king and magnates; on the other, crop failures from 1315 to 1318 and widespread social distress made it difficult to exact purveyance sufficient to keep armies in supplies. For the defence of northern England the consequences were disastrous. Edward II neglected – or was unable – to carry war into Scotland. Payment of cash by English communities in return for truces allowed all initiative to pass to the Scots. Logistical support for garrisons and the maintenance of fortifications were woefully inadequate. Expeditions of magnates to the north of England became mere exercises in containment, achieving only a temporary and partial security. Finally, deployment of mounted free companies contributed to the collapse of all authority in that region.

EDWARD II: DEFENCE OF ENGLAND, INVASIONS OF SCOTLAND

The most telling criticism of Edward II's handling of the war is his failure to carry war into Scotland. He could only have regained control by showing single-minded dedication to victory, demonstrated by a constant royal presence in the north, invasions of Scotland, and maintenance of garrisons to control that country. In a petition of uncertain date men of the west marches stressed that the king should come in person and with force:

> And sire our allegiance will not suffer that we keep from you any longer the truth, which is that you waste your money on Keepers of the Marches towards Scotland, because, sire, no Keeper can arrest the force of your Scottish enemies without the presence of you and your great army . . .[1]

Foremost in Edward's list of priorities was the defeat of a baronial opposition led by his cousin, Thomas Earl of Lancaster. A successful offensive required the undivided energy of the kingdom; but when the opposition forced the king to choose between his domestic priorities and firm action against the Scots, he always chose the former. Royal expeditions therefore took place only when the king was freed from domestic pressures, or when he felt he could use the war as a means to thwart his opponents. Thus his expedition of 1310/11 was embarked upon to undermine the work of the Ordainers and to protect Piers Gaveston;[2] that of 1319 was made possible by the 'reconciliation' with Lancaster brought about by the Treaty of Leake;[3] and that of 1322 by his victory over Lancaster. The priority which Edward accorded to defeat of his domestic enemies is illustrated by an episode in 1322: when Andrew Harclay travelled to Gloucester to inform the king that the truce with the Scots had expired, his response was merely to empower Harclay to negotiate an extension of that truce until he had dealt with the baronial revolt.[4]

But Edward II was not alone among the English aristocracy in giving low priority to the defence of northern England. He was denied support from his magnates while he pursued domestic policies of which they did not approve. Most refused to join his expedition of 1310/11; Lancaster and Warwick refused to participate in the Bannockburn campaign.[5] There are other reasons, too, for the failure of Edward II's administration to take resolute action. The untimely death of several northern magnates, Robert Clifford (1314), Thomas de Multon of Gilsland (1314) and Henry Percy (1315), undoubtedly left regional interests under-represented in the counsels of the king. And whereas the French alliance was undoubtedly an advantage to Edward in many respects, Philip the Fair's sympathy for Scotland could bridle his efforts to subdue the Scots, and in 1313 the need to visit France diverted attention from the war.[6] A crippling lack of funds was another element accounting for Edward II's failure to provide adequately for the war, at a time when the king's freedom to manage was hedged about in every direction.[7] His father had bequeathed to him £200,000 in debts; and since local communities and baronage were already outraged by the incidence of purveyances, prises and additional export duties, scope for taxation was very restricted. From 1311 the Ordinances denied Edward the right to collect duties from alien merchants and required the dismissal of his Italian bankers the Frescobaldi; from 1315–19 customs revenues declined as the wool exports were sent into depression by murrain of sheep, famine and the general economic malaise.

In spite of all this Edward II mounted four royal expeditions into Scotland: 1310–11, 1314, 1319 and 1322 (that of 1307 had already been organised by his father). All were formidable; that of 1322 involved an infantry force just short of 20,000 men, almost as large as Edward I's army of Falkirk.[8] But of these, the first was undermined by baronial dissent; the second and third were defeated by the Scots; and the fourth was abandoned because storms wrecked the supply fleet. The enormous effort which government put into the recovery of Scotland is again illustrated by the victualling record. The main obstacle to the English occupation and permanent conquest of Scotland was shortage of provisions for an occupying army. Records survive for most years of the victualling of Berwick and Carlisle, the main supply depots; and receipts of victuals at these bases are represented in Charts 3–6.[9] A wide variety of goods and materials were stockpiled at the bases, but for clarity the analysis is confined to two staple foods, wheat and oats. For comparison the figures for the later years of Edward I's reign are included. They show the consistently high stocks maintained under Edward I, contrasting with erratic though generally low levels of stores under his successor. They also illustrate the relative importance of the victualling effort at Berwick on the eastern march, the preferred route of English armies bound for Scotland, over that on the poorer, western march supplied from Carlisle.[10] In 1316 difficulties of access to Berwick became so acute that the receiver's office on the east coast had to be removed to Newcastle. Preparations were also made for royal expeditions in 1308, 1309, 1316, 1317, 1318 and 1323; all of which involved strenuous logistical exertions, and all of which came to nothing.[11]

One of the more obvious points is that the victualling effort for the Bannockburn campaign exceeded anything that had been achieved by Edward I. The Carlisle charts, showing the flow of provisions from Ireland to sustain defence of the west march are of particular interest for the next chapter. Highlighted on the Berwick chart is the role of Italian merchants in supplying the English war effort on the east. Of these, Antonio Pessagno was the most important.[12] Banker, diplomat and war-contractor, Pessagno's ascendancy at the English court is demonstrated by a letter of 1313, in which he is described as 'a stronger runner' than Gaveston in his heyday. Pembroke was said to be supporting him with all his influence, and opinion had it that 'the court is led according to his judgement and will'. Pessagno made possible the Bannockburn expedition of 1314: by negotiating a huge loan from Pope Clement V for the English king of 160,000 florins (£25,000) in return for papal control of the revenues of Gascony; by lending, in the months leading up to the campaign, at least £21,000 to the exchequer; and by supplying three quarters of the wheat and oats received at Berwick. As security for vast sums lent to Edward II – in excess of £145,000 to the crown between 1310 and 1319 – Pessagno had received custody of the English crown jewels. He was instrumental in supplying wheat for the next major expedition in the north, that of Arundel in 1317. Edward II was forced in November 1317 to appoint him as Seneschal of Gascony, to

Chart 3

Net Receipts of Wheat at Berwick and Newcastle in Quarters of Wheat

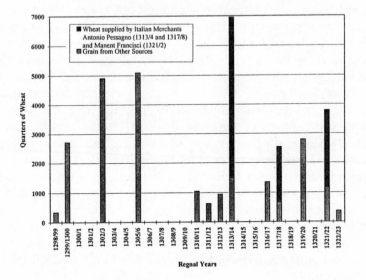

Chart 4

Net Receipts of Oats at Berwick and Newcastle in Quarters of Oats

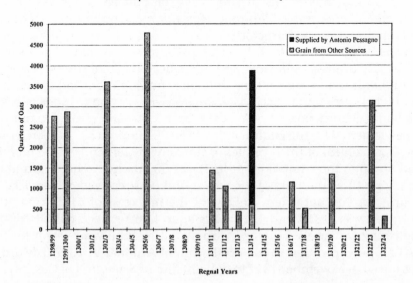

Chart 5

Net Receipts of Wheat at Carlisle in Quarters of Wheat
(showing quantities received from Ireland)

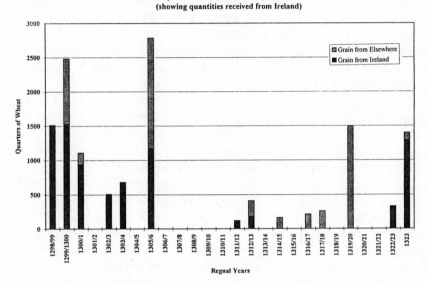

Chart 6

Net Receipts of Oats at Carlisle in Quarters of Oats
(showing quantities received from Ireland)

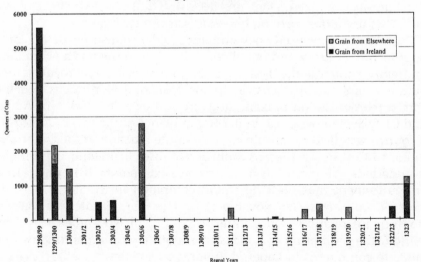

assist in the recovery of the revenues of Gascony from the papacy. But even from Gascony he strove to facilitate the war with Scotland, and undertook to furnish a small army of 200 knights and 2,000 men-at-arms from the resources of the duchy, and galleys for the Irish Sea. He proved inept at dealing with the Gascon nobility, however, and when he embarrassed the administration he was arrested in November 1318, and subsequently left the service of Edward II – to the enormous detriment of the royal finances. By the time of Edward's last invasion of Scotland in 1322 another Italian merchant had been found to take Pessagno's place. Manentius Francisci provided £2,735 worth of wheat (2,614 quarters), bought in London and St. Botulph's and from the Archbishop of Canterbury.[13]

No financial wizard, however, could insure England's war effort against the effects of famine, murrain, widespread discontent at taxes and purveyance and baronial opposition – all of which inhibited Edward II from defending the north with conviction. But Edward was nevertheless guilty of a serious miscalculation; after Bannockburn he became preoccupied by the need to invade Scotland with heavily armoured foot spearmen. He pursued the assembly of this force relentlessly, and in spite of the glaring fact that the north of England, devastated by Scottish raids, required a totally different sort of defence lightly armoured and highly mobile cavalry to bring the Scottish raiders to battle. He further strained the loyalty of local communities by persistent attempts to shift the financial burden of military service onto their shoulders, by extending the period of military service and by insisting on more elaborate armour. In his defence it may be said that Edward was raising the level of preparedness in northern communities by increasing requirements for possession of armour.[14] Furthermore, in his preparations for campaigning in 1323 he recognised the need for speed and mobility, anticipating that fighting would be on foot, and declaring that wheeled vehicles would not be as useful for carrying baggage as sumpter horses.[15]

On occasions Edward II's government could demonstrate an integrated approach to military and naval crises facing it in the north of England, in Ireland and on the Irish Sea. In March 1315 the royal council planned joint naval offensives in the Irish and North Seas, together with a reorganisation of commands in northern England.[16] In August and early September 1315, under the influence of the earl of Lancaster, a council was held at Lincoln to co-ordinate reaction to the continuing threat to Carlisle and recent Scottish successes in Ireland. Presumably it undertook the planning of Lancaster's campaign. It resulted in an announcement that the king would campaign in the north from the feast of All Saints (1st November) and in the despatch of John de Hothum to Ireland.[17] On another occasion, in November 1316, and without the prompting of Lancaster, simultaneous appointments were made to commands in England, Ireland and Wales.[18]

THE PURCHASE OF PEACE

Toleration and encouragement of *suffrances de guerre* or short-term, purchased truces was an early and grievous mistake on the part of Edward II. It allowed Robert I to become established in Scotland as a plausible alternative source of authority; and it supplied the Bruces with a steady flow of funds and foodstuffs. For Edward II the truces were a short-term alternative to military action which he resorted to for two reasons: since the king did not have to pay for them, they were cheaper than campaigning; and they also saved Edward from compromises he might have to make on domestic issues in return for taxation to launch a campaign. Only as the situation in the north deteriorated did Edward show a gradual awareness that the taking of such truces was eroding his authority, and he began to prohibit them from 1315.[19]

From the first days of his reign Robert I used extortion widely as he struggled to survive. Robert effectively had an 'official' truce with Edward II from 1308 until 1310; but during this time the position of English garrisons deteriorated, and commanders were permitted to make whatever deals were necessary to retain their positions. Measures recommended by the English royal council in August 1308 stipulated that, while the king himself should take no truce or *suffrance* from Robert, 'wardens of Scotland may take such as long as possible, as they have done hitherto of their own power or by commission'. Here there is no sense that the royal dignity was being compromised by these small-scale, temporary agreements in distant localities. The document implies that truces were a military necessity to gain time for victualling and garrisoning. As to whether the king should be bound by the truces of his commanders, the council shows a very relaxed attitude: 'he may break the truce at pleasure, if others will yield this point; but if they will not, the truce is to be made without it'.[20] Resistance to Robert I was therefore from the first neither principled nor dogmatic, but shaped by day-to-day contingencies.

In the temporising climate of 1308–10, however, when English garrisons were compelled to strike deals with the Bruces, truce also began to be taken by Scottish rural communities which were unarmed, isolated and vulnerable to intimidation. The word *tributa* is used to describe the payments made; but its translation as 'tribute' is scarcely accurate, for no obeisance or recognition of lordship was implied. There are examples of communities paying in order to remain outside the lordship of an aggressor.[21] It was common for defenders to take the initiative in proposing truce. The first that comes to notice was made in 1308 when the Bruces took *tributa* from Galloway 'under agreement that it should be left in peace'. In that same year Edward Bruce and Robert's other lieutenants invaded Galloway, 'disregarding the *tributa* which they took from them'.[22] Truces, then, were not always observed, though subsequent events show that the Bruces did not generally violate these arrangements without reason.

The purchase of peace is next recorded when Robert I was closing in on Lothian and Berwickshire after Edward II's withdrawal in 1311. Not enough information is available to allow meaningful generalisation about their cost, duration or how they were negotiated. There were at least five truces for south-east Scotland but probably many more, spanning most of the whole period from Edward II's withdrawal in summer 1311 and Bannockburn. What little is known is as follows:[23]

Time Span	Duration	Cost
Sept 1311–2 Feb 1312	4 months	[Unknown]
Feb 1312 – [Unknown]	[Unknown]	[Unknown]
[Unknown] – 24 June 1313	[Unknown]	[Unknown]
24 June 1313 – 9 July 1313	15 days	[Unknown]
9 July 1313 – Nov 1313	5 months	1,000 qtrs corn

After Robert I's raid of September 1311 'those of the earldom of Dunbar, next to Berwick in Scotland, who were still of the King of England's peace, were very heavily taxed for a truce until the Purification (2nd February 1312)'.[24] The men of the earldom were evidently paying with Robert to remain outside his lordship, for this truce was later justified as necessary 'for the safety of the country and their allegiance'.[25] In January 1312 Edward II gave power to David de Atholl, Alexander de Abernethy, Adam Gordon and others to negotiate with the enemy on behalf of the 'people of Scotland' in preparation for renewal of the arrangement; and in November he ordered sheriffs and constables in what remained of his Scottish territories to contribute cash towards the truces and to curb abuses perpetrated by their garrisons which threatened to disrupt them.[26] These agreements were organised by nobles of the district calling themselves the 'commune' or 'people' of Scotland, and led by Adam Gordon and Patrick Dunbar Earl of March. They embraced the three remaining Anglo-Scottish sheriffdoms of Berwick, Roxburgh and Edinburgh, and the total cost of truce seems to have been apportioned to each sheriffdom, with Edinburgh expected to pay a quarter of the cost. The 'commune of Scotland', however, did not have co-operation from English garrisons and wrote to the king complaining bitterly of purveyance, seizure of goods and persons, extortion of ransoms, and in particular of arrests which endangered the truce.[27]

The next petition from 'the people of Scotland' reveals a five-month truce costing a thousand quarters of corn, and further rampant excesses by English garrisons. Distrustful of all Scots and irregularly paid, garrisons made no distinction between the Bruces' partisans and other Scots and terrorised the population with wholesale arrests, extortions and seizures.

Left: Effigy of Bricius McKinnon from Iona, showing details of armour worn by the mercenaries of Western Scotland upon whom the Bruce brothers placed considerable reliance. The surcoat or 'aketon' is probably of two layers of material sewn together with lines of vertical stitching. Wool was then stuffed into the tubes thus created in the garment to make a protective padding. The open-faced helmet or 'bascinet', gauntlets and thrusting spear are all clearly visible. *Courtesy of Historic Scotland.*

Below: The 'Rodel Ship', a roughly contemporary carving, showing the type of ship available to Thomas Dun and John of Argyll in their struggle for control of the Irish Sea. Seventeen oar-fittings are shown along the hull, implying 34 oars. Robert I made several demands for ship service from Man, Argyll and the Isles, usually specifying vessels of 26 oars. Ships of the main Irish sea ports and on the North Sea tended to be larger, designed for bulk carrying and powered by sail alone.

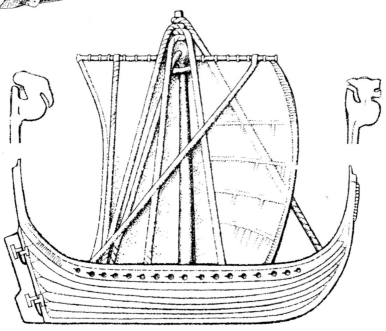

A fifteenth-century representation of the battle of Bannockburn. The castle and town of Stirling are in the background and the Torwood is represented in the bottom left corner. The Scottish army, fighting left to right, is predominantly infantry and armed with spears, but the axe-bearing figure in the centre, mounted on a caparisoned horse, could be Robert I. To the right of centre, the unhorsing of a mounted knight by an infantryman with thrusting spear could represent the death of the earl of Gloucester. From the manuscript of Fordun's *Scotichronicon*, *Corpus Christi College, Cambridge.*

The Carlisle Charter of 1316, granted in acknowledgement of the citizens' defence of the city in 1315. Embellishment of the initial 'E' was the work of a local scribe. The plumed and visored knight is Andrew Harclay, for the shield bears his armorial device. The figure beside him, operating a windlass, prepares to launch a bolt from a *springald*. Others fend off the assault with spears and stones. The Scots are shown to be unarmoured but for bascinets. Some undermine the city walls; one who has mounted a storming ladder is transfixed by a spear. The Scottish catapult has been identified as a *trebuchet*. At the siege the Scots had only one machine for casting stones, whereas the English had seven or eight within the city. *Courtesy of Cumbria County Record Office.*

Dunstanburgh Castle, built by Thomas Earl of Lancaster from 1313 to 1322. The twin cylindrical towers which make up the gatehouse keep represented the latest in defensive architecture. They are finished with fine ashlar. The scale of this castle (the curtain wall is ten feet thick in places) suggests that it was built not just to defend the earl's manor of Embleton, but to prepare for decisive intervention by the earl in the Scottish war. But as a result of the earl's treason and execution the first garrison housed in Dunstanburgh was that of Edward II in 1322. *Courtesy of English Heritage.*

Carrickfergus Castle, the main residence of the earls of Ulster, which guards the sea lanes of the North Channel. The Bruces appear to have attached almost as much importance to the capture of this stone fortress as to Carlisle or Berwick; but the Red Earl of Ulster had recently rebuilt the gatehouse to incorporate a series of defensive features. It was besieged by Edward Bruce from the summer of 1315 to September 1316, when Robert may have journeyed to Ireland to demand its surrender in person. *Courtesy of the Department of the Environment for Northern Ireland.*

Greencastle, Co. Down. This lesser residence of the earls of Ulster was protected by a rock-cut ditch and possessed a magnificent great hall. It fell to Edward Bruce in 1315, possibly as a result of defection by the garrison. Later, in 1327, when Robert I arrived in Ulster he invited the English king's Justiciar of Ireland to a conference at Greencastle. *Courtesy of the Department of the Environment for Northern Ireland.*

Left: The *Declaration of Arbroath*, addressed from the Scottish earls and barons 'and the whole community of the realm' to Pope John XXII, dated at Arbroath 6 April 1320. It stands in a tradition of appeals from peoples of the British Isles to the papal curia. Edward I had arranged such a letter articulating his own claim to Scotland in 1301; Robert I obtained a *Declaration of the Scottish Clergy* in his own favour intended for the Council of Vienne in 1311; and Robert may have inspired Domnall O Neill's *Remonstrance of the Irish Princes* against English rule in 1317. About 50 seals were collected from Scottish barons for appendage to this document. But the collection of magnates' personal seals seems to have aroused indignation, culminating in conspiracy against Robert that same year. *Courtesy of the Scottish Record Office.*

Below: Impression of the second great seal of Robert I. Depictions on both sides are highly stylised and are intended to convey the majesty of the Scottish monarchy through symbols. An earlier great seal had been in use until 1316. It may have been replaced as a ploy to raise money, if the holders of Robert's charters were charged to have documents renewed under the new seal.

But diplomatic and foreign considerations seem to hold the explanation. The earlier great seal had features characteristic of English great seals, whereas the second version appears to have been inspired by that of Louis X of France. *Courtesy of the Scottish Record Office.*

The alabaster effigy of Edward II of England, from his tomb in Gloucester Cathedral. As Prince of Wales, Edward of Caernarvon served his father as a commander in Scotland, and during this time Edward Bruce was attached to his household. As king, Edward II presided over the loss of his father's conquests in Scotland, and came close to losing Ireland. Edward was torn between his anxiety to promote and protect his court favourites and the prosecution of the war against the Bruces, which led a contemporary chronicler to compare him to one trying to hunt two hares at once. From: L. Stone, *Sculpture in Britain: The Middle Ages* (Harmondsworth, 1955).

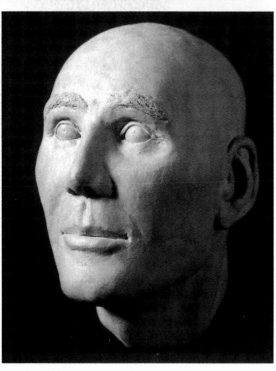

A cast of the skull of Robert I, and below it a terracotta model of the king's head. This was constructed from the cast in 1996 by Brian Hill of Newcastle Dental Hospital, using standard soft tissue depth measurements. Robert's body had been buried in Dunfermline Abbey but briefly exhumed during building work there in 1819. It was then observed that the breastbone had been sawn apart to facilitate removal of the heart for embalming. Barbour relates how the embalmed heart was borne into battle against the infidel in Spain by Robert's companion James Douglas. Subsequently the heart was returned to Scotland and buried at Melrose Abbey. It was exhumed in 1921 and again in 1996. The fate of Edward Bruce's mortal remains is uncertain. *Courtesy of the Scottish National Portrait Gallery.*

The hero king: Pilkington Jackson's monument to Robert I at Bannockburn. It was modelled on the equestrian representation on the second seal and unveiled in 1964 on the occasion of the 650th anniversary of the battle. Robert I's image as a heroic defender of Scottish liberty and identity remains virtually unchallenged to this day. There is no such monument to his brother Edward Bruce, whose intervention in Ireland invited only universal opprobrium. There is some irony in this judgement of posterity as the brothers must have had shared aims and values. *Courtesy of the National Trust for Scotland.*

The random and insensitive activities of the commander at Roxburgh added to the cost of the truce when he arrested some individuals for whose ransom the community had to pay 80 marks to the Roxburgh garrison, plus a further 160 marks to the enemy as a fine for breach of the truce. Adam Gordon, leader of the Anglo-Scottish community, was arrested while remonstrating with the warden of Berwick. Edward II did respond to the petitions of the community: the keeper of Berwick was ordered not to jeopardise truces; inquiries were made into the pay of the garrison at Berwick; a letter of thanks was dispatched to Anglo-Scottish communities; the outraged Adam Gordon was exonerated (though only after after appearing before the king at Westminster to protest his innocence); and the keeper of Berwick was replaced.[28] The conflict of interest between the King of England and his liegemen of Scotland was now glaring. Why should Anglo-Scottish communities continue to pay to remain loyal to a king who would not protect them?

The extraction of cash in return for peace was such a lucrative business that the Bruces could hardly fail to extend it beyond Scotland as soon as the opportunity arose. The Earl of Ulster was forced to buy truce in 1313, though when Robert's galleys came to collect, they were beaten off by the Ulstermen.[29] Fourteen years later Robert again descended on Ulster and this time there is no doubt as to the terms of the truce exacted. The transcript of an indenture between the King of Scotland and the seneschal or stewart of the earldom of Ulster survives. It is dated 12th July 1327 and shows that a year's peace was purchased in return for a hundred chaldrons of wheat and a hundred of barley to be paid half at Martinmas, half at Whitsun. In monetary terms this was a fairly minor exaction; at four English quarters to the chaldron and at current prices in Scotland its monetary value comes to about £260.[30]

The north of England offered far greater returns. The 'men of Northumberland' are said by Lanercost to have bought three truces from the Scots:

From	To	Total Cost	Cost per Day
Mid Sept 1311	2 Feb 1312	£2,000	£13.6
15 Aug 1312	24 June 1313	£2,000	£ 6.3
24 June 1313	29 Sept 1314	['a very large sum']	[Unknown]

Northumberland paid up after the raid of September 1311, and after the August raid of 1312; and at Midsummer 1313 Robert had only to make threatening noises for them to pay up again. The source for this information is the Lanercost Chronicle, but Northumberland truces are referred to elsewhere.[31] Lanercost states that in the autumn of 1311 'the men of Northumberland' sent envoys to King Robert. This deputation negotiated for the whole county as a 'commune', but presumably it was

dominated by the interests of the chief lords. It may have availed itself
of the formal sanction of the county court. There was not much unity of
purpose or community feeling in northern English counties at the time,
and county courts were often forums for the stewards of the rival lordships
to fight out their long-standing and bitter local rivalries; but in so far as
the fourteenth-century county had any unity, it was as a tax-paying,
money-raising entity. During the wars in Scotland comparable bargains
were made with English kings over loans and provision of troops in the
name of the county community of Northumberland.[32]

Whether or not the county court was consulted, there seems to
have been a correspondence between methods used to raise cash
for these truces and the forms of regular taxation. Northumberland
raised money for Robert I's exactions as though for regular subsidies
payable to Edward II. The established distinction in regular taxation
between 'temporalities' (secular property, such as manors, which paid
the lay subsidy) and 'spiritualities' (property pertaining to the church,
such as tithe income from benefices, which paid the clerical subsidy)
seems to have been adhered to in levies for the truce. Traces of levies
on temporalities in Northumberland survive in the records of Durham
Priory, where bursar's account rolls for 1313/14 and 1314/15 record that
the Priory paid a levy for its Northumberland manors, Wallsend and
Willington.[33] It is not known what assessment was used to levy the
money. There were also levies on spiritualities; in 1312/13 a tenth was
levied on Northumberland benefices through the normal machinery of
ecclesiastical taxation and described as 'conceded to Sir Robert Bruce for
the defence of the see'.[34] The sum of £2,000 may be a stock figure used by
the Lanercost chronicler simply to denote a large sum of money. But it is a
not improbable sum; and something very like it was paid by the western
march in 1312. It is roughly double the amount paid by Northumberland
to Edward I in the lay subsidy of 1296, and it represents 24 percent of the
wealth of the county as assessed.[35] To levy this twice, maybe three times
in as many years, was to extract a ruinous tribute. Surprisingly the cost
of peace per day fell from £13 in 1311 to £6 in 1312. The cost (in these
terms) appears to have declined for all the county communities on the
border in these years. It is difficult to account for this. Certainly county
communities would have found it increasingly difficult to pay, but this
is not something the Scots would have allowed for.

Besides these quasi-regular lay and ecclesiastical subsidies paid for
property and parishes within the bounds of Northumberland, Durham
Priory also paid additional sums for immunity for its northern liberty, the
parishes of Norhamshire and Islandshire which technically lay outside
the county. The sums paid for this area, £25 in 1313–14 and £17. 19s. the
following year, represent contributions to a separate deal, independent
of the county levy, and designed to prevent repetition of the burning

of Norham in 1312.[36] The payment in 1314–15 'to have a truce' for Norham and Islandshire must have been one of the last payments for the enclave.[37] There were also more occasional sweeteners to be provided. Bribes were paid to Scottish agents and go-betweens, usually referred to as 'spies'. In 1311 the accounts of Ponteland show 12d. paid 'as a gift to a certain spy for the Scots', and in 1317 or 1318 Durham paid 2s. to 'Scottish spies'.[38] Ultimately it was all in vain. As the graph of tithe income from those parishes reveals, the Scots destroyed North Durham in 1316; by 1318–19 the only income from Durham's Northumberland possessions was £10 from the tithes of Ellingham parish; every other revenue rendered nothing on account of the burning of the Scots.[39]

On the English west march four truces are known to have been bought. Here again the cost per day of truces may have fallen in successive years:[40]

Purchased by	From	To	Sum	Cost per day
'Westmorland, Copeland, Cumberland and other borderers'	15 Aug 1312	24 June 1313	[Unknown]	[Unknown]
[the county of Cumberland]	24 June 1313	29 Sept 1314	£1,466	£3.1
'the people of Copeland'	1 Aug 1314	[Unknown]	[Unknown]	[Unknown]
'the county of Cumberland alone' under negotiation	25 Dec 1314	24 June 1315	£400	£2.2
'Cumberland and Westmorland'	c. 25 Jan 1319	[Unknown]	£400	[Unknown]

One can be less confident however that truces bought by 'the men of the western march' or 'the men of Cumberland' relate to whole counties. Historically the western march was much more fragmented than the eastern, being divided formally into wards and in more practical terms into liberties and lordships, each jealous of its independence. The entry for 1312 in the Chronicle of St. Mary's Abbey, York records that the truces of 1312 were bought by 'Northumbria, Gilsland, Cumberland, Allerdale and Copeland'.[41] This suggests that the western communities could on occasion bargain with the Scots in units much smaller than the county, namely the constituent lordships.

But the truce of 1313 to 1314 extended all over the county of Cumberland and was paid for on the basis of an assessed levy. On 4th October 1314 Edward II ordered the audit of a levy taken for use of his Scottish enemies by William de Mulcaster, Richard de Kirkebride and Alexander de Bastenthwaite.[42] The final membrane of the account survives, giving assessments, receipts, and sums outstanding for a part of the ward of Allerdale, for the liberties of Penrith, Sowerby, the Bishop and the Prior of Carlisle and for Alston Moor. The surviving part of the Allerdale section is detailed, giving the contributions of separate vills and of individual parish clergymen. The sum of 2,200 marks (£1,466) was due to 'Robert Bruce', to be paid in two instalments, at the Assumption (15th August 1313) and Easter (7th April 1314). Assessment was probably based upon the abandoned lay subsidy of 1312, and funds originally collected for that tax may have been diverted to buying off the Scots, prompting the king to have the account audited. Unusually, spiritualities and temporalities are both included in this levy; the usual practice was separate levies for each. The total assessment came to only 2,202 marks, so practically no margin had been built into the assessment to cover expenses of collection. Only 1,540 marks (£1,026) was actually raised and, out of this, hefty expenses were paid to a few local gentry, including bribes to intermediaries, costs of travelling to Scotland and maintenance of hostages. The levy was therefore managed very badly.[43]

The total expenses came to 1,550 marks (£2,325). Of this, 1,290 marks (£860 or 59 percent of the sum demanded) found its way to King Robert. Philip de Lindsay, a Scot still formally loyal to Edward II, was paid £8 for travelling to Scotland twice on business concerning the truce. Presumably he was delivering cash. Bribes paid to intermediaries, perhaps essential to maintaining trust, came to £32. They included 20 chaldrons of oaten flour (80 qtrs.) to King Robert; and £12 in cash, a salmon and two measures of wine to Brother Robert de Morton, King Robert's 'attorney'. Expenses of collection paid to the organisers came to £40; but other payments, including £90 paid for the maintenance of the sons of local knights as hostages in Scotland, allowed the organisers scope for creaming off a profit. At first the levy was supervised by Richard de Kirkebride with Alexander de Bastenthwaite assisting. Both had an interest in its success, having given sons to the Scots as hostages. Three sergeants of the peace traversed the county from August 1313 to Easter 1314 collecting money. The brief Scottish raid at Christmas 1313 suggests that already payments were behind. Collectors of the lay subsidy granted to Edward II in 1313 reported that the Scots then invaded Cumberland because the people were unable to pay for the truce. Needless to say, the collectors were unable to carry out their task. Towards Easter, when it became clear that not enough would be raised to pay the second instalment, panic set in and Bastenthwaite and others rode for six days with a posse of foot and horse, scouring the countryside for cash to stave off invasion. When this failed to raise enough to propitiate the Scots, Edward Bruce invaded to collect in person.[44]

On the east march the system of buying truce collapsed after Bannockburn. Northumberland was already descending into chaos. In September 1314 Edward II ordered an investigation into burnings and depredations by 'malefactors' in Northumberland who had 'broken truces made between the commonalty of the county, for the peace and tranquillity of the king's people there, and the king's Scottish enemies'.[45] The terrorism of local bandits known as *schavaldores* seems to have been blamed for provoking the Scottish raids of 1314. But whatever the precise cause of the breakdown, there was no longer any sense in buying time since the longed-for royal expedition had arrived, gone to Scotland and been defeated. In the anarchy which then descended on the east march, it became impossible to arrange truces for the whole county. Instead the Scots were free to extort relatively large amounts from terrified, isolated communities. But Scottish gains would have been subject to diminishing returns, as the flight of tenantry restricted the productivity of the land, and famine and animal murrain destroyed incomes. About the year 1315 the earl of Moray was demanding a colossal £270 from the terrified burgesses of Bamburgh; but the half-bushel of wheat given to Philip de Moubray by the reeve of Ponteland 'to have a truce' may have been more typical of Scottish gains on the east march at that time.[46] On the west march the uneasy peace of the truces gave way to the violent years of 1315 and 1316, but later there occurred a revival of truce-taking. Moray was at Lochmaben in early 1319 offering the men of Cumberland and Westmorland truce in return for 600 marks. The relative security of the western march is apparent in its ability to provide manpower and grain for the campaign of 1319, in contrast to the meagre contributions of Northumberland.[47]

The Bishopric of Durham continued to pay for truces long after the Scots had overrun Northumberland. Mrs. Scammell explained this in terms of Durham's long tradition as a compact political unit and its social and geographical cohesion;[48] however, distance from the border was equally important. English border counties had been in the front line of the Scottish attack since 1311 and had spent much manpower and resources in Scotland.[49] Sheltered from the war, Durham may have been better able to meet Scottish demands. Six truces were taken in the name of the 'community of the bishopric of Durham'.[50]

From	To	Total Cost	Cost per Day	Levy on Spiritualities
16 Aug 1312	24 June 1313	[900 marks?]	£1.9	10d in £
24 June 1313	[Unknown]			20d in £
17 Oct 1314	20 Jan 1315	800 marks	£5.6	6d in £
1 July 1315	[Unknown]	[1,600 marks?]		9d in £
				30d in £
11 Nov 1317	11 Nov 1318	800 marks	£2.9	6d in £
29 Sept 1327	11 Nov 1328	1,000 marks	£1.8	12d in £

No doubt 'the community' effectively meant, as in Scotland and Northumberland, the principal lords of the bishopric: the bishop, the prior, Richard Fitz Marmaduke, Robert de Neville and his brothers. Payments are described vaguely as 'contribution to Robert Bruce'. The cost of three truces is known for certain; and for two others there is a basis for estimate. In view of the size of the sum agreed to in 1315, this truce was probably to last two years. In terms of the cost per day, that of 1314–15 was the most expensive, probably because the Scots were most difficult to appease just after Bannockburn. Moray himself was present in Durham on 7th October 1314, so there cannot have been much scope for haggling on that occasion.[51] As with the border communities, however, the general trend was for the price of peace per day to fall. The gravity of the Scottish threat during these years is brought out by the fact that in 1344 Durham was able to purchase truce for a year in return for as little as £160, that is less than 10s per day.[52]

As in Northumberland and Cumberland, money for the Durham truces was raised by assessed levies. For the first truce of 1312 the sub-prior of Durham acted as treasurer and Bishop Kellaw lent authority to the raising of money. He wrote to the earl of Warwick asking that Warwick's lands in Sadberge should contribute to the cost of the immunity that they enjoyed.[53] For the truce of 1317–18 a levy was paid on the temporalities of the bishop elect, Louis de Beaumont.[54] William de Kellaw, an important figure in the financial administration of the palatinate, paid over money to intermediaries and also seems to have supervised the collection of funds. The distinction between lay holdings and benefices was consistently observed. Lay contributions are best documented in the truce of 1327. Surviving receipts show that payment was by manor with collectors assigned to each ward of the bishopric.[55] Contributions do not relate to any extant assessment; but a rental of episcopal lands was drawn up by Bishop Beaumont, possibly as an aid to assessment, at some unknown date.[56] By 1344 there was in existence an assessment which had long been used specifically for collecting money to buy off the Scots.[57] How much landed income was siphoned off to the Scots in these levies? Comparing the money paid to the Scots in 1327 with the cash income of the priory's manors, as recorded in 1299–1303, it appears that Ketton and Bearpark manors were paying a little under 20 percent of their former income to the collectors of tribute.[58] Taking into account the fall in agricultural incomes in the 1310s, Mrs. Scammell's estimate that one third of the annual value of the Durham manors went in tribute to Robert would not be far off the mark.[59] Levies on benefices or spiritualities, on the other hand, were paid according to the established assessment, the *Taxation of Pope Nicholas IV*. Since the assessment did not change until 1318, the yield was fixed; a levy of 6d in the pound brought in £65, one of 9d brought in £97, and so forth. Durham Priory recorded these as 'contributions to Robert Bruce' for the safety of its parishes within the waters of Tyne and Tees, that is, within the bishopric. Almost £20 was paid in 1313–14, and £4.10s. in the following year.[60] To pay for the 1317–18 truce, an extraordinarily harsh levy of 30d in the pound was imposed.[61]

In emergency the community seized whatever funds it could to buy off the Scots. In 1312 time was short; the truce had been agreed on 16th August and the first instalment of 450 marks was due at Holm Cultram at Michaelmas (29th September).[62] Cash was seized from individuals by episcopal officers, but paid back in December as the levy came in.[63] Another crisis loomed late in 1315. According to the truce taken in June, the community was to pay 800 marks by Christmas, apparently the first instalment of 1,600 marks promised altogether.[64] Payment must have lapsed, for on 25th November news reached Durham that the Scots had again invaded. A house-to-house search for money was initiated. Conducting the search, William de Kellaw seized £70 from the house of William de Hebburn. Later Hebburn sued Kellaw successfully; but judgement was reversed by the episcopal court on the ground that Hebburn had consented to the communal decision to buy off the Scots. Hebburn then took the matter to the king's court, but the final decision is not recorded. There was another, more spectacular, violation of property rights. At some time unspecified Richard Fitz Marmaduke, a leading member of the Durham gentry and cousin of Robert I (and consequently a man thought to have influence with the Scots), seized £240 from funds in the cathedral accumulated for payment of a regular clerical subsidy, the 12d in the mark granted to Edward II in 1316. Fitz Marmaduke too acted by consent of the community; but the Durham clergy had later to repay the missing tenth to the king and in 1325 they were levying money for this purpose.[65]

Until the winter of 1317–18 payment for these truces was delivered to the Scots by a monk of Durham, Brother Robert de Ditchburn.[66] That winter Ditchburn set out for Scotland as usual, but vanished with the money.[67] This event seems to have had an effect on the amount of information recorded, as though while Ditchburn was courier, business was conducted on a face-to-face basis with little or nothing written down. By contrast, in the year after Ditchburn's disappearance, there are numerous receipts acknowledging sums paid by William de Kellaw and William de London, the collectors. The receipts show that the expenses of the community did not stop at sums agreed with the Scots but, as with the Cumberland truce of 1313–14, involved a range of additional costs. At Martinmas (11th November) 1317 the community entered into truce for one year in return for 1,000 marks (£666).[68] The known expenditure of the community during that year is analysed as follows:

Payments	to Robert Bruce	£628. 3. 4.
	to fitz Marmaduke and Neville	£205. 6. 8.
	for the expenses of hostages	£ 39.14. 4.
	to *schavaldores*	£310. 2. 8.
Other Payments		£ 32. 0. 0.
Total known expenditure of the Community		£1,215. 7. 0.

The community was paying out almost twice the sum agreed with

Robert I for the ransom of the bishopric. Payments to the Scots were made irregularly. From Martinmas 1317 to February 1318 small sums were being paid to William de Denum. They amount to only 72 marks (£48).[69] Presumably Denum was amassing these for transmission to Scotland. The next payment 'for the purposes of Robert Bruce' was of 200 marks, on 1st May;[70] and then at the end of June Richard fitz Marmaduke handed over £411 in cash for Robert Bruce.[71] This may have included the £260 which he had lifted from the cathedral treasury. The size of this sum, representing 60 percent of the 1,000 marks due, and the drastic levy of 30d in the pound authorised only days beforehand[72] reveal a panic in the bishopric at this stage. In May a powerful Scottish force had passed through the bishopric on its way to raid Yorkshire where the bishop's liberty of Northallertonshire was destroyed, a sharp reminder to the bishopric to pay up on time.[73] The crisis may have had its origin in the disappearance of Robert de Ditchburn.

The size of the sums paid to fitz Marmaduke and Robert de Neville highlights the inefficiency of dealing with the Scots indirectly, and the tendency of local lords to profit wherever possible from the situation. Of the £205 paid out to these two, only £37 was specifically for travelling expenses. Fitz Marmaduke and Neville were rival leaders of the Durham gentry. Their competition for the profits of the truce revenues was one of several factors which led to a combat on the Framwellgate Bridge at Durham in December 1318, in which fitz Marmaduke was killed by Neville amid accusations of treachery.[74] The amount spent on hostages seems paltry compared with the £90 paid by Cumberland. While the Cumberland lords considered the maintenance of their sons and heirs in Scotland to be a priority, the community of Durham could be cavalier in its attitude to hostages. John de Wessington was taken hostage in surety of payment by Durham and he remained in Scotland because the community failed to pay 36 marks owing for a truce. In the end he had to pay the sum himself and, receiving no recompense from the community, he petitioned the king for redress.[75] Payments to *schavaldores* (Gilbert de Middleton and Adam Swinburne) accounted for over 20 per cent of the year's expenditure. The *schavaldores* were at their most active during the episcopal vacancy of 1317–18, and this is unlikely to have been an item in other years. It is interesting that in addition to paying off the King of Scots, the community had to buy off other Scottish lords. In the current year 1317–18 payments were made to Philip de Mowbray, and earlier the liberty of Norham had had to buy off William de Prendergast. Probably these other lords were paid in return for using their influence with Robert I in some matter or other, but one cannot entirely discount the possibility that they extracted money on their own account.[76]

There is no question but that the Scots dictated the terms of these truces. In 1312 they reserved to themselves the right to ride through the bishopric into Yorkshire; and they availed themselves of this on three occasions.[77] On a separate occasion they specifically excluded Hartlepool from the truce and attacked it.[78] Payment for peace, then, did not keep the Scots out of Durham nor did it immunise the bishopric from other effects of war: passage of armies or ravages of castle garrisons. In 1322 on the expiry of the 'official' two-year truce there was in place no unofficial agreement with the Scots to protect Durham. A decision not to purchase one may have been associated with the deposition of the accommodating Prior Geoffrey de Burdon or with the policy of the new Bishop Louis de Beaumont, whose family was so virulently in favour of war. In the single raid known as 'the burning of the bishopric' in that year, all that had been protected at such expense from the ravages of war went up in smoke.

Yorkshire was too large and divided to make deals for comprehensive truces, and in the 1310s ransoms tended to involve only individual 'shires' or localities. Negotiating from the safety of castle walls in 1316, the nobles of Richmondshire struck a deal with the Scots and organised a levy in the name of the 'Community of Richmond' to finance it. Collectors for a clerical subsidy provided some of the money for the Scots.[79] In May 1318, from the security of the Minster, the men of Ripon promised the Scots 1,000 marks to spare their town. There and then 240 marks were paid and six hostages given. The remainder was to be paid before August. But the wives of the six hostages petitioned the king in 1324, claiming that they could get no satisfaction from officials of the liberty: 'commune and franchise do nothing, suffering them to languish and die'. The town bailiff claimed to have sent over £500 (750 marks) to Scotland; but only £50 had been received, and the Scots released three of the hostages to speed up payment. These men sued the bailiff, and at length the sheriff of York was ordered to levy the outstanding sum.[80] In another case three hostages of the Vale of Pickering petitioned Edward II from prison in Scotland to order collection of £400 which men of that district had promised to pay to the Scots for their release. Their neighbours, having agreed to the deal, had totally abandoned them.[81] These cases illustrate the complacency of southerly districts, who believed that they could give the Scots some unimportant individuals as hostages and then safely forget about them. But in 1327 the Scots returned to Yorkshire. Richmondshire and Cleveland are said to have bought peace. Northallertonshire certainly did; in July 1328 the vicar of Northallerton paid 17s. 6d. to the bailiff of the liberty for the expenses of messengers and hostages in Scotland.[82]

How much money was extracted from the north of England? If Lanercost's figures are even vaguely correct, the three Northumberland truces may have yielded around £7,000. The yield from the more divided western march is more difficult to estimate. Perhaps, since they were still negotiating in 1319, £5,000 might have been forthcoming from

Cumberland, Westmorland and the various western lordships. Durham paid perhaps £4,000. Add to this the sums extracted from isolated rural communities on the border after 1315 and substantial payments from Yorkshire communities, and the total probably exceeded £20,000. The £40,000 suggested by the author of the *Vita Edwardi II* strains the bounds of credibility.[83] What the Bruces did with the money is easier to say. Some found its way into the pockets of the petty kings of Ireland by way of subsidies and payments for provision of mercenaries. Most was used in Scotland, to pay for the prolonged periods of infantry service necessary for the sieges of Dundee and Berwick in 1312, Perth in 1313, Edinburgh and Stirling in 1314, and Berwick from 1316 to 1319. Gradually it would have percolated into the domestic economy. The anxiety of merchants in Ireland, the Netherlands, Germany and in England to trade with Scotland whatever the political or military conditions suggests that there may be a basis in fact to Fordun's swaggering assertion that Scotland 'overflowed with boundless wealth' in the years after 1314.[84] No doubt this tangible profit of military success helped to stabilise the Bruce regime.

FORTIFICATIONS

Castles, like truces, had implications for seigneurial authority, since only in the possession of castles did there reside all-year-round control of the surrounding territory. As the English had the resources to hold castles but he did not, Robert I set about dismantling castles throughout the Scottish theatre of war. Apart from Berwick, the last Scottish castle to remain in English hands may have been Jedburgh, whose defenders were pardoned their misdemeanours by Edward II for good service in January 1315.[85] The destruction of castles was first extended beyond Scotland when Rushen Castle on Man was demolished in 1313; and the fortified manor house at Aydon in Northumberland was destroyed by the Scots in 1315.[86] In Ireland, too, the minor castle at Dundonald was reportedly destroyed 'by the war of the Scots'; another at Dunadry was said to have been 'thrown down and waste from the time of the war of the Scots'.[87]

Carrickfergus, however, built of stone and virtually impregnable, was not destroyed when it was at last starved into surrender in 1316. From this point Robert abandoned his concentration on denying castles to the English, and strove instead to possess them, perhaps because the influx of money from truces enabled him to pay for garrisons. He launched a serious drive against English castles in 1318. Berwick was taken in April 1318; Wark surrendered on 21st May 1318; Mitford and Harbottle followed.[88] The author of *Scalacronica* states that both Wark and Harbottle were slighted by the Scots. Mitford certainly became a ruin about this time, whatever the cause. Only Berwick was judged strong enough to be held against determined opposition. But the crucial strengths of Bamburgh and Alnwick also came very close to falling to the Scots, for their garrisons were negotiating with the rebels, 'the one by means of hostages, the other by collusion'.[89] Subsequently, the Scots attacked the site of Dunstanburgh where a large castle was being built.[90] Danger of losing castles, with all the implications that carried for loss of lordship, persuaded the English to sue for peace in 1327.[91]

Robert I's attack on England did not prompt the building of new stone castles. The only major stone castle built anew in northern England was the earl of Lancaster's at Dunstanburgh on his own manor of Embleton in Northumberland, under construction in 1314/15 and probably for years afterwards.[92] In many ways it is a strange site for such an enormous castle. Dunstanburgh guards no cross-roads or river ford, and serves no obvious strategic purpose. Its great size suggests that it might have been intended to accommodate refugees, not just from Embleton but from a far wider area; and its out-of-the-way location has prompted speculation that the earl was preparing a bolt-hole in anticipation of attack by his royal cousin. Whatever the truth of this, Dunstanburgh was certainly intended as a northern base for anticipated involvement in the Scottish wars. While few could afford to build on this scale, many other magnates acquired castles in this theatre of war: Isabella de Beaumont had control of Bamburgh Castle until 1310 and her brothers Henry and Louis had control of castles in the Bishopric of Durham from November 1316. Pembroke acquired Mitford Castle for his northern campaign in 1314.[93] Lancaster did not live to garrison his state-of-the-art fortress; and after his execution in 1322 it housed a royal garrison.[94]

Other building was on a smaller scale. The Prior of Tynemouth was moved by the sacking of Hexham Priory by the Scots in 1296 to construct a castle to protect his monastery.[95] It was unusual for a religious house to adopt such impressive defences, but as the Scottish raids began to bite, other monasteries also invested in fortifications. At Bolton Priory the canons began to build ring defences, peels and ditches at their properties of Bolton Moor and Ryther in response to the raids of 1318, 1319 and 1322.[96] As a result of the Scottish raids of 1296 and 1297, other lords improved existing castles. Robert Clifford built an elaborate gatehouse at Brougham;[97] Henry Percy added a gatehouse and barbican at Alnwick;[98] and John Clavering improved the curtain walls of Warkworth Castle and added a flanking tower.[99] These were probably exceptional cases; generally northern castles were far from prepared for Robert I's raids. Clavering's expenditure on Warkworth contributed to his bankruptcy.[100] Cockermouth was badly dilapidated.[101] The buildings at Egremont were in ruins.[102] The Umfraville Earls of Angus saw their vulnerable castle at Harbottle fall into dilapidation through lack of funds and constant Scottish attacks. Harbottle was captured by the Scots in 1318;

then it was returned as provided for in the terms of the two-year truce of December 1319.[103]

Because of Edward's lack of money, royal building was restricted to usually long overdue renovations of existing structures. The defences of both Carlisle and Berwick had been improved by Edward I. Carlisle had recently been restored at a cost of £217, and was thus in good shape when war first broke out in 1296. Edward II continued the work at Carlisle. An East Gatehouse was added at a cost of £654, and from 1308 to 1312 a further £925 was spent, chiefly on a tower in the inner bailey. But only minor repairs were made during the 1310s. A survey of 1321 reveals that during this most dangerous period the castle had become seriously dilapidated. Two sections of curtain wall were ready to collapse, and a forty-foot stretch of the outer bailey, and the vault above the main gate, had actually fallen in. During the truces of 1319–21 and 1323–27 major repairs were carried out to Carlisle, including the erection of peels where the curtain wall had collapsed.[104] Dr. Summerson makes the intriguing suggestion that the crumbling state of Carlisle's defences could have been a factor in persuading Andrew Harclay to seek a separate peace with Robert I.[105] Defences were in better shape at Berwick. Both castle and town had been radically improved by Edward I. The castle acquired sally ports and a bridge to the town and the gate had been repaired. Major repairs were ordered to turrets and brattices and the formidable Douglas Tower was built. In the case of Berwick Castle, there may have been little for Edward II to improve upon. In 1318 the castle could not be taken by the Scots and had to be starved into surrender.[106] Edward II engaged in a serious building programme at only one other site, Pickering, where the castle was enlarged to double its original size at a cost of £953.[107] Accounts are too piecemeal and disjointed for calculation of an exact total spent on castles, but over the whole period the royal outlay on building and repairs to northern castles might have been in the region of £15,000. A significant investment perhaps; but it is unlikely to have been anything like enough; and that Carlisle should have been on the verge of collapse in 1321 was inexcusable.

Whereas Edward I's Welsh wars had spawned a magnificent series of stone castles around the north coast of Wales, in Scotland he had preferred to build in wood and earth, probably to save money. Wood and earth remained the preferred building materials throughout the Wars of the Bruces. Stone castles retained an important strategic and perhaps psychological role, but the real initiative in fortification at this time was in minor defensive works - towers, strong-houses and 'peels'.[108] A proliferation of such weak defences is characteristic of an unsettled 'march' territory; in Ireland, for example, the trend towards minor fortifications appears to have been well established. In 1316 the Scots were said to be sheltering in forts in the vicinity of Leix; tenants at Crumlin were to be distrained to construct a 'fortalice' there.[109] The term 'peel tower' is a confusion of two very different fortifications which came into vogue around this time. During this period in the north of England, 18 licences to crenellate were granted, 16 of which were for minor fortifications. Small stone towers, two or three stories high and with vaulted basement, began to be built. This sort of construction is notoriously difficult to date; but examples which seem to belong to this period include the 'Vicar's Peel' at Corbridge, and the towers at Dalley, Tarset and Heaton in Northumberland, Drumburgh, Lanercost and Wythop in Cumberland.[110] They were relatively cheap to build and easy to defend. The tower at Melmerby cost about £100 to construct, and could be held by a dozen men.[111] 'Peels', however, were the most flexible of the lesser fortifications. The term originally meant a palisade of wood daubed with clay to make it fireproof, often supplemented by earthworks. Even cheaper to build than stone towers, peels were sufficient to provide short-term security for goods and livestock,[112] and were often combined with existing castles to increase accommodation or to improve defences; but they also existed independently as low-cost fortifications. Edward I had found peels useful in extending English lordship into the wilder parts of Dumfriesshire and Galloway, where they provided shelter for his forces in hostile country, and bases for raiding deeper into Scotland. The peel of Selkirk projected English authority deep into the forest; other peels at Dumfries and Lochmaben enlarged the capacity of existing castles to provide safety. When the war zone spread south into England, peels began to appear in that theatre too, at Bolton, Horton and Whittingham in Northumberland, Highhead and Scaleby in Cumberland, and Northallerton in Yorkshire.[113] Thirdly, manor houses could be adapted to war conditions by the addition of defensive features: Plessy in Northumberland acquired a wall and ditch; Aydon sprouted battlemented parapets; Aykhurst (also known as Hay) in Cumberland was strengthened by a simple wall; and Houghall in Durham by a moat.[114]

Robert I and his supporters are known to have been building such minor fortifications in Northumberland. Reference has already been made to Sir Philip de Mowbray's fort near the chapel of Falstone in Tynedale, and a similar fort was built by a Northumberland *schavaldor* at Houxty in the same area.[115] These lesser fortifications may be described as tactical, as distinct from strategic, defences, in that they were designed for the defence of a few individuals and their possessions. They were built to be cost-effective (not to require constant attention and investment); to hold off lightly armed horsemen for a short time (not to 'laugh a siege to scorn'); and to escape attention (rather than to bar the path of invaders). Altogether they represented a more flexible response to the problem of raiding than the great impregnable monuments to earlier wars.

In terms of victualling and manning of castles, the reign of Edward II compares badly with the careful estimates and generous margins for error which characterise the administration of Scottish castles in his father's reign.[116] The garrisons of northern England relied more heavily on local sources of foodstuffs than the English garrisons in Scotland had done. Edward I had been able to sustain his garrisons by bulk transportation of grain into Scotland; but by 1315–16 Edward II had made arrangements with clerks in his service who held benefices in the north to supply tithe grain to neighbouring castles.[117] But local sources of victuals were depleted by the famine of 1315–17 and by the flight of the northern peasantry in the face of Scottish raids. Inventories of stores and equipment in northern castles reveal a serious lack of logistical support.[118] Berwick Castle, Harbottle and Wark surrendered to the Scots for lack of victuals, or because 'relief did not reach them on the appointed day'.[119]

There were many complaints against castle garrisons, and seizures of foodstuffs figure prominently in them. As early as 1309 Alexander de Bassenthwaite had to seize wheat and oats from the Prior of Carlisle's manor of Crossby in Allerdale to victual Carlisle and Dumfries. The sheriff of Westmorland also took grain from the prior for the supply of Appleby and Brougham garrisons.[120] In 1313 the Berwick garrison was alleged to have robbed the surrounding countryside of 300 fat beasts, and 4,000 sheep and horses.[121] Outrageous 'prises' or seizures were said to have been taken by the keeper of Cockermouth Castle, causing the decay of rents and depopulation in surrounding vills.[122] Roger Horsley, castellan at Bamburgh, was notoriously rapacious.[123] The Prior of Nostell complained in 1318 that constables of Bamburgh, Alnwick and Norham took tithe grain worth almost £250 over a number of years.[124] Similarly Nicholas de Swinburne complained that for six years the garrison of Staworth Peel had lived off the issues of his own lands.[125]

In addition to prises by garrisons, local people were further burdened by the taking of 'access money', that is extraction of a fine from those seeking security within castle walls for their persons, goods or livestock. John de Felton at Alnwick included among his receipts for 1314–16 money for 'the lodging of diverse men of the neighbourhood within the said castle'.[126] At Bamburgh, Roger Horsley was said to charge 12d. each for a plot of ground on which possessions might be stored safely in times of danger. Free access to the castle was a repeated demand of the Bamburgh tenants,[127] and Horsley was finally ordered to stop exacting access money on 27th November 1318.[128] It has been pointed out that Horsley may not have been the worst offender in this respect; a petition alleges that castles in the west march charged 5s. or half a mark for two or three nights' accommodation, and the locals threatened to evacuate the area rather than pay such outrageous demands.[129]

The victualling of Berwick and Carlisle was absolutely crucial to containing the Scottish threat, since they served as supply depots for border garrisons. It may be seen from the victualling record that the safety margins in these depots were in some years very slim.[130] Letters reveal that the Berwick garrison were actually starving in the spring of 1316.[131] Payment of garrisons was an associated problem; the men needed their wages to buy victuals, and if unpaid, would just walk away. From 1314 there was great danger that both Carlisle and Berwick garrisons would desert through hunger and lack of pay. In June 1314 the sheriff at Carlisle complained that he was unable to pay his troops; in November he was seizing foodstuffs coming into the town; and in March 1315 it seemed unlikely that the garrison would stay until Whitsun (11th May).[132] In the autumn of the same year (September 1315) letters from Berwick were again received complaining of lack of pay and victuals; later that month the king wrote to the chancellor and treasurer that he was receiving daily appeals from Carlisle and Berwick, and that 'many of the people of the garrisons have departed for lack of sustenance . . .'[133] A letter dated 18th February 1316 from Maurice de Berkely, warden at Berwick, reveals that the town garrison were deserting daily, leaving only the castle garrison, itself depleted by casualties and hunger.[134] Bitter rows over the distribution of rations are revealed by proceedings against Ranulph Benton, keeper of victuals at Berwick. Benton was accused of every conceivable form of cheating: giving short measure; exchanging foodstuffs he had received for others of inferior quality and keeping the profit; selling off stores on the quiet; and buying poor quality victuals.[135] In November 1316 the king was sent an urgent request for a transfer of money to Carlisle, because of the number of desertions from the garrison due to non-payment of wages.[136] All of Edward II's castellans were chronically short of money. The difficulties of John de Felton, keeper of Alnwick, are typical.[137] Over a period of about one year (4th January - 30th December 1315) Felton put his expenditure - in pay, replacement of horses and maintenance of the estate - at £1,252. Receipts from the estate and the exchequer came to only £875, leaving him £376 short. In 1317 his garrison at Alnwick went on strike: the 50 men-at-arms and 60 hobelars withdrew to the town demanding their arrears of pay, and Felton had to write urgently to the king for leave to account in the Wardrobe.[138]

Most castles were owned by lords other than the king; but private castles vulnerable to capture by the Scots were public liabilities. However, far from taking command of private castles in this emergency, Edward II preferred to ensure that, as far as possible, the expense of maintaining garrisons should fall on shoulders other than his own. Only Berwick and Carlisle had permanent royal garrisons prior to 1314. Even at the vital royal castle of Bamburgh there is no evidence of a garrison, though the bishop of Durham maintained a garrison at his castle of Norham. After Bannockburn, Roger Horsley was ordered to maintain 20 men-at-arms and 30 hobelars in Bamburgh.[139] Several private castles came into the king's hands through minorities on the deaths of the northern magnates Henry Percy (Alnwick) and Robert Clifford (Brougham, Brough, Appleby and Pendragon). From 1315 the regional commanders known as *chevetaignes* took greater care to maintain garrisons in the north; but not so Edward II. He was so anxious to disburden himself that he returned Alnwick and the Clifford castles to under-age heirs.[140] Norham, vital to the defence of Northumberland, passed several times between the bishop of Durham and the king.[141] But the strain of maintaining castle garrisons was too much for many local lords. An undated petition by John de Denum, asking for royal aid, asserted that he was no longer able to pay the 12 men-at-arms at his tower of Melmerby.[142] Ultimately Edward was obliged to take over the reversion of Warkworth and Wark-on-Tweed (belonging to John de Clavering and William de Ros respectively) as a result of their owners' financial difficulties.[143]

The fluctuations in the size of castle garrisons make it difficult to estimate costs to the crown. But two Wardrobe Books give totals of annual expenditure. In the year 1316/17 northern garrisons cost about £8,000, and in 1317/18 roughly the same.[144] To this figure must be added the annual cost of the Berwick and Carlisle garrisons, which works out at about £8,571 and £5,002 respectively in 1315/16.[145] The annual cost of manning and supplying northern garrisons probably came to around £20,000 at the height of the Scottish raids. By comparison Edward I had spent £18,368 on garrison pay and supplies to maintain the occupation of Scotland in 1299/1300; £13,769 in 1300/01; and £10,019 in 1303/4.[146] In the years of the Scottish onslaught in the north it was therefore costing Edward II much more just to hold his own than it had cost his father to subdue Scotland.

The difficulties of raising such sums on time to prevent garrisons from starving or deserting were immense. No money was being raised locally: estates were ravaged; taxes ceased to be collected in border counties from 1309; and customs revenue fell away as a result of privateering and disruption to trade. Garrisons meanwhile exploited local communities to make good the shortfall. Royal control of castellans clearly diminished as the military situation deteriorated. Isolated by the chaos, some constables behaved as independent warlords. John le Irroys, sent north with a force which was allowed access to castles, exacted purveyance from the people of Bamburgh and embarked on a short career of terrorism during which he abducted Lady Clifford to Barnard Castle.[147] Eventually he sought refuge at Tynemouth Castle.[148] Tynemouth was a place of sanctuary, and the garrison there was allegedly composed of criminals and fugitives from justice. The constable of Newcastle had them all arrested in 1322.[149] John de Eure, Pembroke's constable at Mitford, put that castle at the disposal of the Northumberland rebels in 1317.[150] The rebels were able to capture many of the minor peels: Horton, Bolton and Whittingham; and the peels of Northallerton, Redham, Daneby and Laneburn fell to rebels in the associated disturbances in Yorkshire.[151] Eustace le Constable of Warkworth and others plundered a ship loaded at Hartlepool carrying corn, flour and salt to Berwick, and driven by attacks of privateers into Warkworth.[152] Altogether the North of England's castles ought to have been its salvation from the Scottish raids. The failure of the crown to pay and provision garrisons adequately, and to exercise control over castellans, left them to prey on those they were supposed to defend.

THE EXPEDITIONS OF THE CHEVETAIGNES

The border districts rapidly developed early-warning systems to counter Scottish raids; the earliest mention of beacons on the hillsides dates to 1298.[153] But the reactions of the royal administration to the long-range mounted raids of the 1310s were so much slower than local responses as to be ineffective. Generally an array of foot and horse over a wide area would be ordered. In 1314, for example, the Scots invaded Yorkshire around 1st August; on 10th August Pembroke was appointed keeper of the region from Trent to Berwick, and the Yorkshire militia, the 'fencible' (able-bodied) men between the ages 15 and 50, were ordered to be arrayed. But already by 4th August the Scots had safely escaped over Stainmore into Westmorland.[154] With a little warning local authorities could arrange more effective precautions. The conference in York Minster at the beginning of 1315 was able to appoint four local magnates as commanders, and a subsidy of 2d. in the mark was levied from the clergy to support their efforts.[155] These measures were successful in keeping the Scots out of Yorkshire, but rarely was there such warning of Scottish intentions. Yorkshire was caught unprepared when the truce of February to Midsummer 1316 lapsed. The Scots raided Yorkshire at Midsummer (24th June), but it was 4th July before orders were issued for an array of foot and a general muster at Newcastle on 10th August.[156] The Scots had probably returned over the border by 5th August.[157]

To keep the marches during intervals between truces and campaigns, the English began to dispatch expeditions to the war zone, led by great magnates, *chevetaignes* or 'Superior Captains'.[158] These *chevetaignes* had plenipotentiary powers over wide areas (often from Trent to the Border), and they were obviously intended to be a substitute for the royal presence. Subordinate to the *chevetaignes* were Wardens of the Marches, the existing unpaid local officials. This hierarchy was intended to facilitate mobilisation of the whole region in resistance to Scottish raiders. After the defeat of Bannockburn, successive *chevetaignes*

– the earls of Pembroke, Lancaster, Arundel and John de Cromwell and the earl of Angus jointly – led expeditions to keep the north free from raiders, with varying degrees of success.

The efforts of the first two magnates are detailed in their biographies. Pembroke's appointment in 1315 was probably a reaction to the arrival at court of a letter from Ralph fitz William and Simon Ward (keeper of Berwick) which reported that Robert I was preparing to attack York or besiege Berwick and advised a levy of troops.[159] On 4th May 1315, 500 hobelars from Pembroke's Irish estates were ordered to Newcastle. His mission was to hold the north until a royal army could muster at Newcastle on 15th August, but it was given a new urgency by the Scottish assault on Carlisle.[160] An indenture was drawn up between Pembroke and the king by which the earl agreed to stay in the marches from 24th June to 1st November with 100 men-at-arms for 4,000 marks (£2,666). Additional forces were hired, and when the expedition assembled at York on 21st-23rd July, its total strength exceeded 300 men-at-arms.[161] Pembroke arrived at Newcastle on 3rd August and advanced towards Carlisle by way of Barnard Castle and Kendal.[162] Robert I called off the siege of Carlisle at his approach; but Pembroke rode as far as Lanercost to harass the retreating Scots. Leaving the west march in the charge of Ralph fitz William, he returned to Newcastle through Tynedale. After a short stay at Newcastle, Pembroke ventured northwards. It is scarcely credible that he intended to invade Scotland on his own; it is more likely that he intended a punitive raid to relieve the growing pressure on Berwick.[163] The continuator of Walter of Guisborough's chronicle accuses the earl's forces of wanton destruction while moving through Northumberland.[164] He encountered a Scottish force, was lured into Scotland by feigned flight, and was defeated at Longridge, near Berwick. By 1st October Pembroke had retired to Newminster. He remained in the north until relieved by Henry Beaumont, appointed on 18th October to keep the march during the winter.[165] Though Pembroke himself left for the south, his retinue remained for a time under William de Felton, and 10 horses were lost in a clash with the Scots at Rothbury in Northumberland on 31st October.[166]

The promised royal army of 1315 never materialised; but Pembroke's appointment had formally been superseded since 8th August when the earl of Lancaster took over the job of defending the north.[167] This may have been because the fall of Carlisle was anticipated, and the Honour of Lancaster was considered to be in the front line of defence. In October and November Lancaster made requests to religious houses for horses and carts in preparation for a campaign. The replies must have made depressing reading: citing famine, murrain, depredations by magnates and the burden of purveyance, the monasteries declined to help or offered only token assistance. Nevertheless at the Parliament of Lincoln in January 1316 Lancaster succeeded in securing a grant of one footsoldier from every vill in the kingdom and a lay subsidy of one fifteenth from the shires. Orders were issued for a muster at Newcastle on 8th July 1316. Over 2,000 Welsh foot arrived at Newcastle in preparation for the campaign.[168] The administration, however, soon became swamped by problems: the revolt of Adam Banaster in Lancashire; the rebellion of Llywelyn Bren in Glamorgan; civil unrest at Bristol; and the widespread misery of famine. The king was at first distracted from the campaign when a son was born to him; then he became over-enthusiastic and issued demands for military service in violation of the Ordinances. This angered Lancaster, who considered himself guardian of the Ordinances. A violent quarrel ensued, and Lancaster began to distance himself from the administration. The muster was postponed, first to August, then to 6th October, and finally the campaign was abandoned. Government had been paralysed, both by agrarian distress which rendered provisioning a campaign impossible, and by personal antagonism between Lancaster and the king.

On Lancaster's throwing up the reins of government, Edmund fitz Alan, earl of Arundel, was appointed *chevetaigne* from 20th November 1316 to Midsummer 1317. His terms of service are preserved in his indenture with the king, dated 19th November; and his appointment coincides with a raft of measures designed to bring the war once more under the control of the administration. In simultaneous appointments Roger Mortimer of Wigmore (who held extensive lands in Meath) was made Keeper and King's Lieutenant in Ireland; and Roger Mortimer of Chirk, Justice of North Wales.[169] A survey of armaments and manning levels of northern castles was initiated, and Pembroke was dispatched to Avignon to assist in recovering the revenues of Gascony from the Pope.[170]

Arundel was to serve with 100 men-at-arms of his own retinue, receiving £3,000 for expenses; and was to be supported by 16 other captains, who contracted to supply men-at-arms and hobelars. On the west march, for example, William Dacre and Antony Lucy each contracted to serve with 65 men-at-arms and 100 hobelars for a year.[171] Arundel's indenture reveals a plan to station a total force of 799 men-at-arms and 750 hobelars on the marches. The main feature of this plan was the deployment of cavalry at 19 castles and peels throughout the region. Based in these castles, 299 men-at-arms and 470 hobelars were stationed as a mobile reserve to counter infiltration and support Arundel's field forces. Map 11 shows how these forces were distributed throughout the region. Most of the hobelars were provided by northern lords, Arundel's own forces being mostly men-at-arms. Another new departure was that the king, who had tended to rely on other English lords to defend their own castles, now provided garrisons in 13 castles not in his own hands.[172] At the same time negotiations with the Scots were renewed. Although their outcome is

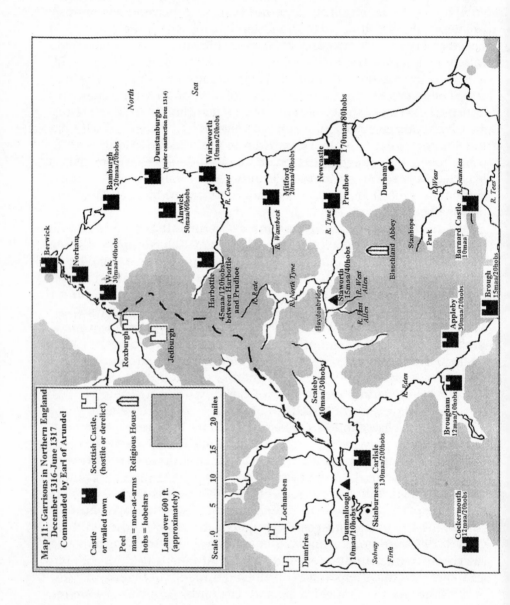

Map 11: Garrisons in Northern England
December 1316–June 1317
Commanded by Earl of Arundel

Castle or walled town

Scottish Castle, (hostile or derelict)

Peel

Religious House

maa = men-at-arms
hobs = hobelars

Land over 600 ft. (approximately)

Scale : 0   5   10   15   20 miles

not known, it is possible that a truce for six months was agreed upon for the Anglo-Scottish marches. This is suggested by Robert I's decision to leave Scotland and cross to Ireland in January.[173] At any rate Robert was apparently confident that Arundel would not attempt a serious invasion of Scotland. If there was a truce at this time, the English decided not to rely on it, for the deployment of Arundel's forces went ahead. Probably the English government intended no full-scale attack on Scotland before Midsummer, for estimates were made as to what sums could be raised by that date.[174] In the meantime Antonio Pessagno undertook to supply 17,000 quarters of wheat and 2,600 tuns of wine to maintain Arundel's garrisons. The contract was fulfilled, despite the famine conditions which prevailed over most of the British Isles.[175]

In March 1317 Arundel took advantage of Robert I's absence in Ireland to lead an incursion into Scotland.[176] It can hardly have been intended as an invasion aimed at permanent recovery of Scottish territory. Advancing into Jedwood Forest, his men hewed down trees to deny cover to the Scots. But the advance guard led by Thomas de Richmond was ambushed at Lintilee by James Douglas. Richmond was killed; and the expedition halted. Douglas's capture of a nearby peel from a band of *schavaldores* deterred Arundel from further advance and he retreated into England. Arundel also tested the Scots by sea, sending ships to raid the east coast of Scotland.[177] Robert returned to Scotland in May to meet the planned invasion, but in the desperate famine conditions that prevailed, a campaign was out of the question, and the truce was successively extended. In view of the 'near miracle' achieved by Pessagno in keeping these garrisons in place, Arundel ought to have achieved much more.

The period from September 1317 to 1319 was another disastrous phase for the English, with enmity between Lancaster and Edward II threatening to plunge the country into civil war. No *chevetaigne* was appointed; and the Middleton rebellion caused the temporary loss of many minor fortifications.[178] By May 1318 Robert I had captured Berwick, taken Wark and Harbottle castles, and raided Yorkshire. In August, however, Lancaster and the king settled their differences in a compromise known as the Treaty of Leake. But by this time it was already too late for action on the marches, and an expedition had to wait until the following season.[179]

Edward II's presence at Berwick in the autumn of 1319 lent some temporary semblance of security to the eastern marches. On his retreat from Berwick and in reaction to the ravages by the Scots after Myton, on 28th September Edward appointed John Cromwell and Robert de Umfraville, Earl of Angus, as wardens of the march with full powers. Each contributed 30 men-at-arms of his own retinue and the king provided a further 140, making 200 men-at-arms in all. They were to keep the march, secure Newcastle, and maintain garrisons. Other contingents were added, and 249 men-at-arms were listed as staying on the march from 28th September until 26th June 1320. Aside from this, special provision was made for additional cavalry to be stationed in the Northumberland garrisons after the fashion of the Arundel plan, though on a smaller scale. Bamburgh was to have an extra 30 men-at-arms; Alnwick 20 men-at-arms and 20 hobelars; Warkworth four men-at-arms and eight hobelars; and at Newcastle, 10 men-at-arms and 46 crossbowmen. Noticeably absent from the list of castles are Wark, which had fallen to the Scots in May 1318, and Norham, currently under siege.[180] Cromwell and Angus's force was to complement that which Andrew Harclay had built up in the west since he had been appointed keeper there in April. But the *chevetaignes* were not immediately commissioned. Arrangements were reviewed at a council meeting on 13th October; this decided that the king was to stay at York with 600 men-at-arms, and gave detailed instructions for an array of Yorkshire foot with special heavy armour. Simultaneously Edward authorised negotiations with the Scots.[181] It appears that the commissioning of the wardens on 27th October (when a Scottish raid was expected on the eastern march) and the Scottish raid on the west march in November were part of the posturing by both sides for diplomatic leverage, prior to the two-year truce, declared at Christmas 1319. Cromwell and Angus's forces were maintained until 31st January, when they were paid off.

These expeditions of the *chevetaignes*, which provided for forces to be on permanent standby in the north, may have seemed a reasonable response to the problem of hit-and-run raids. They were successful in reducing the degree of Scottish activity in England, but they were not popular with inhabitants of the region, as the chroniclers emphasise:

> In past years the king had been in the habit of strengthening the March with wardens throughout the winter, but their oppression was more injurious to the people than the persecution of their enemies. For the Scots used to spare the inhabitants of Northumbria for a time in return for a moderate tribute, but those who were supposed to be set over them for their protection were constantly at leisure to oppress them every day.[182]

Of these defensive expeditions, Arundel's expedition was the largest by far and the most expensive. His field forces alone cost £9,272, and the additional forces in castles and peels an extra £4,380.[183] Pembroke's expedition cost about £7,000; Cromwell and Angus (confined to the eastern march) would have cost £3,563 had the expedition not been cut short.[184] All three had some success in keeping the Scots out of England. But as defensive expeditions they could achieve nothing more, and none of them made any serious attempt to penetrate Scotland.

ANDREW HARCLAY: HOBELARS AND SCHAVALDORES

Besides royal expeditions against Scotland and occupations of the north by *chevetaignes*, local forces offered such resistance to the Scots as they could muster. Castle garrisons harried them where possible,[185] and there were many small-scale actions against Scots and *schavaldores*. But there was no organisation of local defence on the east march. Roving gangs of mounted outlaws terrorised Northumberland; among the analogies that suggest themselves are the American western frontier, or in the more recent past the 'bandit country' of the Irish border. Duels were fought, the most famous being that between Marmaduke and Neville on Framwellgate Bridge in Durham.[186] Reputations could be made. In an episode glamourised by Sir Thomas Gray and immortalised by Sir Walter Scott, the young knight Marmion arrived at Norham to win valour on the border.[187] No reputation stood higher than that of Douglas who, having seen off Arundel in 1317, slew Robert de Neville, 'the peacock of the north', and took prisoner his three brothers during a fight near Berwick on 6th June 1319.[188] Barbour relates:

> When Neville thus was brought to ground,
> And likewise Sir Edmund of Calhou,
> The dread of the Lord Douglas
> And his renown was so great
> Throughout the marches of England
> That all were in Dread of him
> As the very Devil from Hell!

Barbour does not exaggerate the terror of the Black Douglas. In July 1326 one Hugh de Croxton was hauled before the court of exchequer and convicted of 'telling falsely in public that James Douglas and other enemies and rebels of the king of Scotland had entered England, to the fear and trembling of the people and to the disturbance of the king's peace'. He spent a week in Fleet Prison.[189]

The activities of the *chevetaignes* were largely concentrated on the east march, and while conditions in the west are still unlikely to have been anything other than miserable, there are signs that this theatre underwent some recovery in the period 1316 to 1319, when there were no serious Scottish raids on the area. In 1319–20 John de Louthre, keeper of victuals at Carlisle, was able to obtain for the first time in the reign of Edward II a significant quantity of grain from Cumberland and Westmorland.[190] Each of these counties was able to present Edward II with a small aid for carriage of the king's victuals for the invasion of Scotland in 1322, to ward off requisitioning of vehicles by royal officials.[191] Most strikingly, Andrew Harclay seems to have amassed large numbers of light cavalry, which acted as a deterrent to all but the most powerful Scottish forces.

Perhaps because it was well-protected, Moray offered truce to the west march in 1319.[192]

Harclay had shown himself to be a formidable opponent. He had shown courageous leadership during the Scottish invasion of Christmas 1314, and his inspired defence of Carlisle in the following year encouraged retaliation for Scottish ravages. In August 1314 the Carlisle garrison ambushed the Scots returning over the Pennines from Yorkshire, and in November they raided Pennersaughs in Scotland.[193] Losses suggest that these actions were unsuccessful; but two important prisoners were taken in the aftermath of the siege of Carlisle, and heavy ransoms were extracted.[194] Harclay raided Annandale on 22nd August 1315, and in January 1316 he was involved in an action against the Scots at Morton near Carlisle. Undoubtedly his dominance of the west march was made easier by the absence in Ireland of the Lord of Galloway, Edward Bruce. When Harclay was finally captured by John de Soules, probably on 26th January 1316, it was in Eskdale, raiding Scotland yet again.[195] During Harclay's imprisonment the aggressive policy was continued; Ralph fitz William tried to organise similar raids into Scotland. Harclay was back in power from 1319; and he may already have had the capacity to act independently of royal authority. He certainly had a powerful retinue. As warden of Carlisle in 1319 Andrew Harclay led three knights, 13 men-at-arms, 361 hobelars and 980 foot to aid Edward II at Berwick; and for the invasion of Scotland in 1322 he was able to assemble 113 men-at-arms, 1,435 hobelars and 2,069 foot.[196] As reward for his defeat of the Lancastrian rebels at Boroughbridge in 1322, he was created Earl of Carlisle.[197] From 1319, however, Robert I concentrated on the west march, either because it had recovered slightly from his onslaughts of 1315 and 1316, or because he perceived the growing threat. Harclay was forced into a succession of mistakes. He led all his forces to Berwick in August 1319, allowing Douglas's raiders to slip into Yorkshire and return the same way. Harclay also followed the king to York after the campaign, leaving the west exposed to Robert's raid of November 1319.[198] He was unable to prevent the raid into Lancashire in June 1322;[199] and after the royal expedition to Scotland, his forces disbanded too soon, allowing Robert to ravage for five days before riding through into Yorkshire.[200] His subsequent failure to arrive in time to save the king from humiliation at Bylands lost him the favour he had enjoyed since Boroughbridge;[201] by this stage the raids of 1319 and 1322 had seriously weakened that area's capacity for resistance.

Harclay therefore had his own reasons as a regional potentate for making a unilateral peace with Robert I in December 1322.[202] The abortive treaty stipulated that England and Scotland should be separate and independent kingdoms; that Scotland should be free from all claims of English overlordship; and that Harclay and Robert should bind themselves to impose the treaty on those who dissented from it – this of course being a reference to Edward II. Should Edward accept the treaty, Robert promised to found a monastery in Scotland for the souls of those killed in the fighting between the two kingdoms; to pay the English king 40,000 marks over ten years; and to marry his male heir (at that time Robert Stewart) to a blood-relation of the English king. The treaty survives in two versions; one is the authoritative version; the other differs in ways designed to attract support from among the northern English. The 'English version' describes itself as a treaty on behalf of 'all those in England who wish to be spared and saved from war with Robert Bruce and all his followers'. Both refer to a committee of 12 lords, six Scottish and six English. But whereas in the authoritative version the committee of 12 was to settle points of dispute between Robert I and Harclay, in the English version this committee wass empowered to take all measures necessary for the common profit of both realms. This language was an echo of the Ordinances, and was intended to appeal to latent Lancastrian sentiment.

It was a remarkably generous offer from Robert I: security for the north was to be had in return for simple recognition of Scottish independence, and into the bargain Robert was prepared to pay an enormous cash sum for the peace. Harclay undertook to win the retrospective acquiescence of Edward II to this agreement, and to this end he began to extract oaths of adherence to the peace and to himself from individuals and communities.[203] He was preparing to force Edward II to abandon the war, and his agreement that the English king should be distrained to adhere to the treaty was of course intolerable to Edward II. Harclay was sufficiently unpopular among the Cumbrian gentry to be arrested and executed with ease.[204] Though he was grasping and rapacious, he deserves credit for defence of the western march to 1316 and for carrying the war into Scotland. It would be unfair to blame him for failure to prevent the Scottish raids of 1315, 1319 and 1322; the reality is that hobelar raids could not be guarded against. The only practical response was retaliation.

In the past Harclay has been lionised as a pioneer of hobelar warfare, but this view has now been discredited. It was to be expected that Irish mercenaries and irregular cavalry should gather around the city of Carlisle looking for employment. Following Edward I's campaigns, some Irish hobelars apparently stayed on the Anglo-Scottish marches. In 1299 Clifford had ordered the receiver at Carlisle to pay Richard le Bret, an Irish hobelar, retained to spy on the enemy, 'lest he should desert for want of sustenance'. Richard le Bret shows up again in 1303, leading 60 archers of Cumberland into Scotland; and again in 1307, leading 97 foot and 50 archers; he continued in the garrison at Carlisle until 1320.[205] But early in Edward II's reign few hobelars remained in the king's pay: in 1311 there were 20 at Berwick, and in 1312 six at Carlisle.[206] Following the success of Robert I's mounted raids from 1314, the use of light horse came back into vogue, since light cavalry could be used to pursue the raiders and bring them to battle.[207] When the northern castles were garrisoned in late 1314, hobelars were again employed: 40 at Alnwick, and 30 each at Carlisle and Bamburgh.[208] In preparation for his campaign Pembroke ordered 500 hobelars from his own Irish estates in 1315.[209] But Pembroke's expedition is known to have included 412 Northumberland hobelars, which proves that this style of warfare did not depend upon manpower from Ireland and must have been rapidly adopted in the north of England. In November 1315 a small number of Irish hobelars arrived to reinforce Henry Beaumont's force holding the east march.[210] In 1316/17, 80 men-at-arms and 80 hobelars accompanied sheriff Adam de Swynburne in Northumberland.[211] Arundel, as we have seen, had deployed hobelars all over the region; but the largest concentrations were still on the western march. Harclay tends to get the credit for introducing hobelar warfare;[212] but their presence in the west predates Harclay's rise to power and may simply have been due to the proximity of Ireland. Harclay had no monopoly in their use; in 1316–18 John de Castre (Harclay's local rival) had over 70 hobelars at Carlisle.[213]

The employment in garrisons of autonomous companies, Irish mercenaries and local bandits was however damaging to the fabric of society in the north of England, as they were wholly insensitive to the needs of local communities. Letters of marque were given to the leaders of armed bands from 1315, permitting the plundering of enemy goods. The letter granted to Thomas de Fishburn junior in December 1315 was typical. He could keep all the plunder he might gain from the enemy and the ransoms of prisoners, though the king might buy any of his prisoners for 100 marks. A similar privilige was granted to John de Whelpedale and his brothers, allowing them to keep all goods and moveables they could seize from the enemy, on condition that they did not interfere with people in the king's peace or jeopardise local truces with the Scots.[214] But there was no way of enforcing these conditions. The sort of anarchy that ensued is illustrated by a complaint in 1317 by Roger Mauduit, from which it appears that Mauduit had captured a band of Scots raiding Tynedale, but that Thomas de Fishburn junior and his gang stole his prisoners, set most of them free and claimed the reward for the most valuable one. Mauduit added that another set of his Scottish prisoners, whom he imprisoned at Mitford, were ransomed for his own use by the castellan at Mitford, John de Lilburne.[215] Free companies such as Fishburn's, or that led by John le Irroys, could hardly be prevented from doing exactly as they liked to the detriment of all authority.

Hobelars were essentially an offensive arm, best deployed in hostile or occupied territory to destroy farms, disrupt the fabric of economy and society and make settlement impossible. In practice, there can have been little distinction between the hobelars and *schavaldores*, the mounted brigands of the east march. The earliest use of the word *schavaldores* or *schavaldi* dates from 1312, when Robert of Graystanes uses it to describe the outlaw John de Werdale.[216] The word is probably a form of *chevalier*, 'a horseman'. But in this context its meaning is quite clear: a mounted bandit, often of the Pennine dales, a product of the militarisation of the border and of hobelar warfare. Its use is unknown outside this context.[217] Bishop Richard Kellaw wrote in 1312 that banditry was daily on the increase; and Graystanes writes approvingly of Kellaw's curbing of outlaws in the bishopric.[218] It is highly significant in this respect that hobelars originated in the 'land of war', on the margins of the beleaguered Irish colony; and their increasing number in northern England was a far from healthy symptom. The bitterness expressed in a 'Song on the Times' seems relevant to the woes of the peasantry of northern England. It bemoans the increase in crime and robbery, and calls on the church to lay her interdict on all robbers, especially the mounted horsemen:

> And those hobelars in particular,
>> Who take from the husbandman the tillage of the ground.
>> Men ought not to bury them in any church,
>> But to throw them out like a dog![219]

In summary, we may say that, given Edward II's refusal to dedicate his resources to the recovery of Scotland, the survival of an independent Scotland was guaranteed. Edward's reliance upon northern communities to purchase truces was tantamount to the surrender of revenues to the enemy. He himself could levy no taxation from the north after 1311. His neglect of northern castles, in terms of fabric, victualling and manning was unpardonable. Nowhere was the king's attitude more explicit than in his reluctance to shoulder the financial burden of the northern castles. But his greatest mistake was to have squandered the early years of his reign, allowing Bruce to become entrenched. His reliance upon free companies of hobelars to defend the north was to have lasting consequences. There was a contemporary confusion between the terms 'hobelar' and *schavaldor*, which is telling. During the War of St. Sardos Edward II ordered *schavaldores* of Northumberland to be sent to fight the French.[220] The careers of Gilbert de Middleton, John de Werdale and John le Irroys show how easily these troopers could turn bandit. If the man-at-arms (like the castle) reflected dependence upon lordship, the hobelar (and the peel) implied loyalty to no-one.

NOTES

1 SC1/34/179, printed by *Chronicon de Lanercost*, ed. J. Stevenson (Maitland Club, Edinburgh, 1839), p. 538.

2 *Vita Edwardi II*, pp. 11, 13–14.

3 Maddicott, *Lancaster*, p. 240.

4 *Vita Edwardi II*, p. 120; *CDS* iii no. 745, p. 139.

5 *Vita Edwardi II*, pp. 10–11; Maddicott, *Lancaster*, pp. 157–58.

6 *Rot. Scot.* i, 133; Maddicott, *Lancaster*, pp. 149–50 (1313).

7 W. Childs, 'Finance and Trade under Edward II', *Politics and Crisis in Fourteenth Century England*, ed. J.Taylor and W. Childs (Gloucester, 1990), pp. 19, 25, 26.

8 BL MS Stowe 553, ff. 56–62, 80–84; Fryde's figure of 21,700 infantry in *Tyranny and Fall*, p. 128 includes 2,100 hobelars.

9 The sources for Charts 3 to 6 are as follows:

Berwick:	1298/91	BL Add MS 37654.
	1299/1300	*Liber Quot.*, pp. 113–16.
	1302/03	BL Add MS 17360.
	1305/06	E101/369/11, f. 84.
	1310/11	BL Cotton Nero C viij, ff. 66–71.
	1311/12	Ibid., ff. 75–76d.
	1312/13	E101/375/8, f. 23–24d.
	1313/14	BL MS Cotton Nero C viij, ff. 153–178d.
Newcastle:	1316/17	Society of Antiquaries MS 120, ff. 40d–41d.
	1317/18	Society of Antiquaries MS 121, ff. 24–24d.
	1319/20	E101/378/4, f. 6d–8.
	1322/23	BL MS Stowe 553, ff. 51d–54.
	(July–October) 1323	Ibid., ff. 123–124d.
Carlisle:	1298/99	Liber Quot., pp. 120–21.
	1299/00	*Liber Quot.*, pp. 122–25.
	1300/01	BL Add MS 7966A, ff. 58d–59d.
	1302/03	E101/11/19.
	1303/04	BL Add MS 8835, f. 35.
	1305/06	E101/369/11, ff. 83–84.
	1311/12	BL Cotton Nero C viij, ff. 77d–78.
	1312/13	E101/375/8, f. 22–22d.
	1316/17	Society of Antiquaries MS 120, ff. 42–43.
	1317/18	Society of Antiquaries MS 121, ff. 25–26.
	1319/20	E101/378/4, ff. 8d–14.
	May 1322–Jan 1323	BL MS Stowe 553, ff. 47–d.
	January–July 1323	Ibid., ff. 124–124d.

10 Provisioning at Carlisle is further discussed in on pp. 189–90 and 203-4.

11 (1309) *Rot. Scot.* i, 67–76; (1316) *Ibid.* i, 155–6; Society of Antiquaries. MS 120, f. 66; *CCR 1313–18*, pp. 426, 460, 524; (1317) *Rot. Scot.* i, 170–76; (1318) *Ibid.*, pp. 183–9; (1323) *CPR 1321–24*, pp. 261–68.

12 N. Fryde, 'Antonio Pessagno of Genoa, King's Merchant of Edward II of England', *Studi in Memoria di Federigo Melis* (Rome 1978), ii, 161–62.

13 BL MS Stowe 553, f. 49.

14 Powicke, *Military Obligation*, pp. 140–49; *CDS* v no. 615, pp. 241–42.

15 *CCR 1318–23*, p. 708.

16 *Rot. Scot.* i, 136–41; Phillips, *Aymer de Valence*, pp. 83–86.

17 Phillips, *Aymer de Valence*, pp. 92–93; *CCR 1313–18*, p. 310.

18 See below, p. 149.

19 *Rot. Scot.* i, 151; *Historical Papers and Letters from Northern Registers*, ed. J. Raine (R.S., 1873), pp. 285–86.

20 *CDS* iii no. 47, p. 9.

21 See for example pp. 79, 130 above.

22 *Lanercost*, pp. 185, 188.

23 *Lanercost*, p. 195; *CDS* iii no. 337, pp. 65–66.

24 *Lanercost*, p. 195.

25 *CDS* iii no. 186, p. 34.

26 *Rot. Scot.* i, 107, 111.

27 *CDS* iii no. 186, pp. 34–35 (dated by *CDS* v p. 81 to 1312).

28 *Rot. Scot.* i, 113–14; *CPR 1313–17*, p. 47.

29 See p. 58 above.

30 E. Gemmill and N. Mayhew, *Changing values in medieval Scotland: A study of prices, money and weights and measures* (Cambridge,1995), pp. 147, 163, 390. The author of the document claims however that the quantity stipulated amounted to in excess of a thousand quarters of grain, Sayles, *Documents* no. 155, p. 128.

31 *Lanercost*, pp. 195, 198, 199–200, 203; *The Chronicle of St. Mary's Abbey, York*, ed. H.H.E. Craster and M.E. Thornton (Surtees Society cxlviii, 1933 for 1934), pp. 53–54; *Vita Edwardi II*, pp. 31, 48.

32 These include a negotiated loan of 1303, BL Add. MS 7966A, f. 54; payment of a fine for failure to provide foot soldiers, see p. 52 II; and the county communities of Cumberland and Westmorland in 1322 reached agreement with the king over provision of carriage, BL MS Stowe 553, f. 19.

33 DCD BAR 1313–14(B), dorse, £6.13.4, which includes the priory's parish of Bedlington; BAR 1314–15 (A), dorse, 115s. for the manors alone.

34 *RPD* i, 208; DCD MC 4941.

35 *The Northumberland Lay Subsidy of 1296*, ed. C.M. Fraser (Society of Antiquaries of Newcastle upon Tyne, 1968), pp. xxi, 181.

36 DCD BAR 1313–14(B), dorse; BAR 1314–15 (A), dorse; *Lanercost*, p. 198.

37 DCD BAR 1314–15 (A)

38 Merton College MCR, 5983, part ii, m. 1; DCD BAR 1317–18.

39 DCD BAR 1318–19.

40 *Lanercost*, pp. 199–200, 203, 211, 212; C. McNamee, 'Buying off Robert Bruce: An Account of Monies Paid to the Scots by Cumberland Communities in 1313–14', *CWAAS* new series xcii (1992), 77–89; Duncan, *RRS* v Introduction, pp. 145–46. A letter cited in Maddicott, *Lancaster*, p. 162 [C81/1706/17] suggests that the 1314–15 truce may have been only until Pentecost.

41 *Chronicle of St. Mary's York*, pp. 53–54. This is a puzzling entry: *et exhibitum fuit per Comitatum Karleolensem. Northimbria post vastacionem factam per idem R[obertum] viij^a libras; a Couplandia viij^xx marcas*, which seems to imply that Copeland paid 160 marks, but that the men of Carlisle delivered the cash. The reference to Northumberland is puzzling.

42 *CPR 1313–17*, pp. 240–41.

43 McNamee, 'Buying off Robert Bruce', pp. 86–89.

44 See p. 57 above.

45 *CPR 1313–17*, p. 237.
46 Fraser, *Ancient Petitions*, no. 22, pp. 26–27; Merton College MCR, 5978 dorse.
47 E101/378/4, ff. 6d–8d, 18d–32.
48 Scammell, 'Robert I', pp. 389–90.
49 See above pp. 52–53.
50 The sources are as follows:

    1312–13   *RPD* i, 204, where 450 marks are paid, apparently as a moiety; Raine, *Scriptores Tres*, p. 94 states that the total cost of the truce was 1,000 marks.

    1313   *Lanercost*, p. 200 ; DCD MC 4416; *RPD* i, 469; DCD BAR 1313–14 (B), dorse.

    1314–15   Raine, *Scriptores Tres*, Appendix XCIV, p. cxiii; *RPD* i, 63; DCD MC 4702; DCD BAR 1313–14(B).

    1315   DCD MC 4254. Raine, *Scriptores Tres*, p. 96 reports this as a truce until Christmas 1315 for 800 marks. But *RPD* iv, 159–65 reveals that the agreement was made on 25th November 1315 and that the sum involved was 1,600 marks, of which some had to be paid immediately. I suggest that Robert de Graystanes, the chronicler, has mistaken a termly instalment for the total cost of the truce.

    1317–18   DCD MC 4111, 4265, 4712

    1327–28   DCD MC 4354*, 4609

    A levy on benefices of 1325 is mistaken by Scammell as a collection of tribute for the Scots, 'Robert I' p. 369 citing DCD MC 4198; but DCD MC 5060 identifies this as a levy to replace the proceeds of a regular clerical subsidy which were taken from for Durham Cathedral treasury in 1315–16. See note 65 below.

51 Raine, *Scriptores Tres*, Appendix XCIV, p. cxiii.
52 *RPD* iv, 273–76.
53 *RPD* i, 191.
54 DCD MC 4111.
55 DCD MC 4605, 4606, 4607, 4607*, 4608, 4609, 4610, 4354.
56 *Bishop Hatfield's Survey*, ed. W. Greenwell (Surtees Society xxxii, 1857), p. 51.
57 *RPD* iv, 273–76.
58 E.M. Halcrow, 'The Administration and Agrarian Policy of the Manors of the Cathedral Priory of Durham' (Oxford University B. Litt. thesis 1949), p. 137, compared with DCD MC 4607, 4605.
59 Scammell, 'Robert I', p. 397.
60 DCD BAR 1313–14(B), dorse; DCD BAR 1314–15(A).
61 DCD MC 4712.
62 *RPD* i, 204.
63 DCD MC 4091, 5055, 6035.
64 Raine, *Scriptores Tres*, p. 96; DCD MC 4254; *RPD* iv, 159–65.
65 E159/95, m. 112d; DCD MC 5060; H.S. Offler, 'Murder on Framwellgate Bridge', *AA* 5th series xvi (1988), 196.
66 DCD BAR 1313–14 (B); DCD BAR 1314–15(A).
67 Scammell, 'Robert I', p. 395.
68 DCD MC 4265.

69 DCD MC 3531, 3623, 4439.
70 DCD MC 4265.
71 DCD MC 4399.
72 DCD MC 4712.
73 See above p. 85.
74 Offler, 'Murder on Framwellgate Bridge', 193–211.
75 Fraser, *Northern Petitions* no. 128, pp. 173–74.
76 DCD MC 4086, 4399; DCD PNA 1314/15.
77 *Lanercost*, pp. 200, 216, 221, 230.
78 Fraser, *Northern Petitions* no. 131, pp. 177–78.
79 *Lanercost*, p. 216; *CPR 1317–21*, p. 482.
80 *Lanercost*, p. 221; *CDS* iii nos. 707, 858; *CIM* ii no. 452, pp. 111–12; *Memorials of the Church of SS. Peter and Wilfrid, Ripon* (Surtees Society lxxviii, 1886) ii, 86; KB27/240, m. 70d; KB27/ 250, m. 88d.
81 *CIM* ii no. 891, p. 222.
82 *Melsa* ii, 357; DCD MC 4105.
83 *Vita Edwardi II*, p. 48.
84 *Fordun* ii, 340.
85 *CPR 1313–17*, p. 210; *CCR 1313–18*, p. 160.
86 *NCH* x, 345.
87 *Chart. St. Mary's Dublin* ii, 343; *CIPM* vii no. 537, p. 374.
88 *Lanercost*, pp. 219–20; *Scalacronica*, p. 60; Society of Antiquaries MS 121, f. 20 where 'Wark' can only mean Wark-on-Tweed; there was no significant castle at Wark-in-Tynedale.
89 *Scalacronica*, p. 60.
90 Duncan, *RRS* v Introduction, pp. 145–46.
91 R. Nicholson, 'The Last Campaign of Robert Bruce', *EHR* lxxvii (1962), 243–5.
92 *NCH* ii, 196–216; Maddicott, *Lancaster*, pp. 25–26; W.D. Simpson, 'Dunstanburgh Castle', *AA* 4th Series xvi (1939), 31–42 and 'Further Notes on Dunstanburgh Castle', *AA* 4th series xxvii, 1–28.
93 M. Prestwich, 'Isabella de Vescy and the Custody of Bamburgh Castle', *Bulletin of the Institute of Historical Research* xliv (1971), 148–52; *Rot. Scot.* i, 167 ; *NCH* ii, 24–25.
94 BL MS Stowe 553, f. 56d.
95 *CPR 1292–1301*, p. 197; *NCH* viii, 83.
96 Furness Abbey, *VCH Lancashire* ii, 118; Cartmel Priory, J.C. Dickinson, *The Land of Cartmel: A History* (Kendal, 1980), pp. 18, 83. Kershaw, *Bolton Priory*, pp. 122–23. At Holm Cultram Abbey Edward I had built a peel, E101/369/11, f. 188, E101/369/16, f. 4d.
97 *Inventory of the County of Westmorland* (RCHM, 1936), pp. 57–62.
98 G. Tate, *History of the Borough, Castle and Barony of Alnwick* (Alnwick, 1866) i, 83–6, 134–42, 372–88.
99 W.D. Simpson, 'Warkworth: A Castle of Livery and Maintenance', *AA* 4th series xv, 115–24.
100 *NCH* v, 26–31.
101 Extensive repairs had to be ordered in November 1316, *CCR 1313–18*, p. 374.
102 E372/172, m. 48d; Fraser, *Northern Petitions* no. 65, pp. 98–99.
103 SC1/21/25, dated 1336; *RRS* v no. 162, pp. 433–37.

104 R.A. Brown, H.M. Colvin, A.J. Taylor, *The History of the King's Works: The Middle Ages* (HMSO, 1963) ii, 597–98; *Reg. Halton* i, 178–181; *CCR 1313–18*, p. 366; *CCR 1318–23*, pp. 15, 161; E101/13/36 (33); *CCR 1323–27*, p. 115.

105 Summerson, *Medieval Carlisle* i, 229, 257.

106 E101/619/61; *The History of the King's Works* ii, 563–66; E101/68/1 (25c, 27); BM Add. MS 17360, ff. 12d, 28, where, however, the cost of the Douglas Tower is not included in the account; *Lanercost*, pp. 219–20.

107 *The History of the King's Works* ii, 780.

108 D.J. Cathcart King, *Castellarium Anglicanum, an Index and Bibliography of the Castles in England, Wales and the Islands* (Millwood New York and London, 1983), ii, 81–101, 133–41, 243–51, 325–78, 489–96, 511–41.

109 NAI RC8/10, p. 212.

110 Cathcart King, *Castellarium Anglicanum* ii, 331, 341–2, 335; i, 85, 88 (No. 2), 91.

111 Fraser, *Northern Petitions* no. 104, pp. 137–38.

112 G. Neilson, *Peel: Its Meaning and Derivation* (Glasgow, 1893).

113 Cathcart King, *Castellarium Anglicanum* ii, 346, 350, 344; i, 93, 90; ii, 522.

114 Northumberland Record Office ZRI/1 (68); *NCH* x, 350–86; *CPR 1321–24*, p. 82; R. Surtees, *History and Antiquities of the County Palatinate of Durham* (London, 1840) iv (Part II), 94.

115 See above p. 79; Neilson, *Peel*, p. 19; and the treaty of 1319 seems to imply that Robert was building fortifications in southern Scotland, *RRS* v no. 162, pp. 433–37.

116 See M. Prestwich, 'Victualling Estimates for English Garrisons in Scotland during the Early Fourteenth Century', *EHR* lxxxii (1967), 536–43.

117 E101/376/7, ff. 116d–117.

118 E.g., Bamburgh, *NCH* i, 37–9, citing SC6/950/3, m. 2d; also M. Prestwich, 'English Castles in the Reign of Edward II', *Journal of Medieval History* viii (1982), 164–65.

119 *Lanercost*, p. 235.

120 E159/88, m. 89, in *CDS* iii no. 524, pp. 100–1.

121 *CDS* iii no. 337, pp. 65–66.

122 Fraser, *Northern Petitions* no. 112, pp. 145–46; *CIM* ii no. 297, p. 75.

123 *CPR 1313–17*, p. 309; Fraser, *Ancient Petitions* no. 22, pp. 26–27.

124 E159/93, m. 14d.

125 Fraser, *Ancient Petitions* no. 133, pp. 159–60.

126 E372/166, m. 29.

127 Fraser, *Ancient Petitions* nos. 22, 156, 157.

128 *CCR 1318–23*, p. 40.

129 Fraser, *Northern Petitions* no. 112, p. 145; *CIM* ii no. 297, p. 75.

130 Charts 3–6, pp. 126–27.

131 *CDS* iii nos. 470, 477.

132 Summerson, *Medieval Carlisle* i, 215.

133 *CCW 1244–1326*, pp. 422, 424.

134 *CDS* iii no. 470, pp. 89–90. See below p. 217.

135 Fraser, *Northern Petitions* no. 30, pp. 59–61.

136 Maddicott, *Lancaster*, p. 162.

137 Tate, *History of Alnwick* i, 136.

138 Fraser, *Ancient Petitions* no. 131, pp. 158–9.

139 E 101/376/7, f. 62.

140 Prestwich, 'English Castles in the Reign of Edward II', p. 162.

141 *CPR 1313–17*, p. 163, where the king, having borrowed Norham Castle from the Bishop for three years, returned it before that term had elapsed; *RPD* i, 547, 598, 666, 670; ii, 1013; iv, 481, 488, 497, 506, 507, 510, 514, 521, 523, 528, 530; *CDS* iii no. 507, p. 97.

142 Fraser, *Northern Petitions* no. 104, p. 137.

143 *CPR 1313–18*, pp. 569–70; *NCH* v, 30.

144 Society of Antiquaries MS 120, f. 46 gives £17,065 for total of section entitled *Garnistura Castrorum* (1316/17); MS 121, f. 22 gives £10,465 (1317/18); I have deducted costs of field forces included in those sections.

145 In 1315/16 the Berwick garrison cost £4,993 for 208 days, or £8,761 per annum, E101/376/7, f. 113d; Carlisle cost £2,851 for the same 208 days, a rate of £5,002 per annum, Ibid., ff. 116–17.

146 *Liber Quot.*, p. 154; BL Add. MS 7966A, f. 65; BL Add. MS 8835, f. 38.

147 *Rot. Scot.* i, 131; *CDS* iii no. 458, p. 86; Fraser, *Northern Petitions* nos. 31, 32; Fraser, *Ancient Petitions* no. 22, pp. 26–27.

148 *NCH* viii, 86–87, n. 1.

149 C.M. Fraser and K. Emsley, 'Law and Society in Northumberland and Durham, 1290–1350', *AA* 4th Series xlvii (1969), 66–7; *NCH* viii, 88–89.

150 A.E. Middleton, *Sir Gilbert de Middleton* (Newcastle, 1918), p. 34; Phillips, *Aymer de Valence*, pp. 126–27.

151 Fraser, *Ancient Petitions* no. 23, pp. 27–28; Just 3/74/4, mm. 1, 1d, 2, 3.

152 *CPR 1313–17*, p. 597.

153 *Scotland in 1298*, ed. H. Gough (London, 1888), pp. 127–28.

154 *Rot. Scot.* i, 129–30; E101/14/13, f. 9d; see above pp. 72–74.

155 See above p. 78.

156 *Rot. Scot.* i, 156–57.

157 See p. 84.

158 M.L. Boyle, 'The Early History of the Wardens of the Marches of England towards Scotland, 1296–1377' (Hull University M.A. thesis 1980), pp. 66–67.

159 *CDS* iii no. 440, p. 83; Phillips, *Aymer de Valence*, pp. 88–91.

160 *Rot. Scot.* i, 143, 145.

161 The indenture is alluded to in E101/376/7, f. 59.

162 E101/376/7, ff. 60d - 62.

163 On 3rd October men were reportedly dying of hunger in Berwick, *CDS* iii no. 452, pp. 84–5.

164 *Guisborough*, p. 397.

165 *Ibid.*, p. 90; *Rot. Scot.* i, 150.

166 Phillips, *Aymer de Valence*, p. 90.

167 Lancaster's efforts at mounting a campaign are detailed in Maddicott, *Lancaster*, pp. 173–87.

168 Society of Antiquaries MS 120, f. 66.

169 *Rot. Scot.* i, 166–67; E101/68/2 (39); *CPR 1313–17*, p. 563; *CFR 1307–19*, p. 312.

170 Phillips, *Aymer de Valence,* pp. 107–11.

171 *Ibid.;* Society of Antiquaries MS 121, f. 40.

172 E101/68/2 (39).

173 Duncan, *RRS* v, Introduction, p. 140.

174 *CDS* v, no. 627, p. 244.

175 Fryde, 'Antonio Pessagno', p. 173.

176 'Historia Aurea', p. 208; Barbour, *The Bruce* XVI, 335–492; Society of Antiquaries MS 120, f. 52 dates the skirmish at Lintilee to March 1317.

177 See below pp. 213–14.

178 Fraser, *Ancient Petitions* no. 23, pp. 27–28; *CPR 1317–21,* pp. 73, 135, 141; JUST 3/74/4, m. 1.

179 Maddicott, *Lancaster,* pp. 225–29, 232.

180 E101/15/26, printed in *Proceedings of the Society of Antiquaries of Newcastle upon Tyne* 3rd Series, iv (1909–10), 21–25.

181 Maddicott, *Lancaster,* p. 251; *Rot. Scot.* i, 203–4.

182 *Vita Edwardi II,* p. 103; see also *Lanercost,* p. 195.

183 Society of Antiquaries MS 120, ff. 44–6.

184 E101/376/7, ff. 59–62d; *Proceedings of the Society of Antiquaries of Newcastle,* 24.

185 Society of Antiquaries. MS 120, f. 53, shows that the Norham garrison lost 10 horses in the king's service, February to June 1317.

186 *Bridlington,* p. 57; *Scalacronica,* p. 58.

187 *Scalacronica,* p. 62

188 Fraser, *Northern Petitions* no. 132, pp. 178–79; Barbour, *The Bruce* XV, 425–550.

189 Barbour, *The Bruce* XV, 551–557; E159/102, m. 138.

190 E101/378/4 f8d, 330 quarters of oats, all the grain that appears under that year.

191 BL MS Stowe 553, ff. 19.

192 Duncan *RRS* v Introduction, pp. 145–46.

193 E101/14/31, ff. 9d,10.

194 *CDS* iii, nos. 456, 515, 697.

195 E101/14/31, ff. 9d, 10; Barbour, *The Bruce* XVI, 516–30.

196 Summerson, *Medieval Carlisle,* i, 235; BL MS Stowe 553, f. 61d.

197 *CPR 1321–24,* p. 93, 25th March 1322.

198 I. Hall, 'The Lords and Lordships of the English West March' (Durham University Ph. D. thesis, 1986), pp. 328–30.

199 See pp. 98–99.

200 *Lanercost,* p. 239.

201 Fryde, *Tyranny and Fall,* pp. 130–31.

202 *RRS* v no. 215, pp. 480–85, and see also p.162; translation is given in *Anglo-Scottish Relations 1174–1328, Some Selected Documents,* ed. E.L.G. Stones (London, 1965), no. 39.

203 E159/103, m. 176; *Lanercost,* p. 242.

204 Summerson, *Medieval Carlisle* i, 230–56.

205 *CDS* ii, no. 1084, p. 275; BL Add. MS 8835, f. 77; E101/373/15, ff. 13–17d; *CDS* v no. 562, p. 230; P. Connolly, 'Irish Material in the Class of Ancient Petitions', *Analecta Hibernica* xxxiv (1987), pp. 7, 28.

206 E101/374/16, f. 5d; E101/375/8, f. 25d.

207 J.E. Morris, 'Mounted Infantry in Medieval Warfare', *TRHS* 3rd series viii (1914), 87–91.
208 E101/14/39 (4); E101/14/31, schedule; E101/376/7, f. 62.
209 *Rot. Scot.* i, 143.
210 E101/376/7, ff. 60d-61, 62d.
211 *Rot. Scot.* i, 151; Society of Antiquaries. MS 120, f. 45.
212 Morris, 'Mounted Infantry in Medieval Warfare', pp. 82–85; Hall, 'Lords and Lordships', pp. 372–73 sees no reason to credit Harclay with introduction of the hobelar.
213 Society of Antiquaries. MS 120, f. 45d; MS 121, f. 21d.
214 *CPR 1313–17*, pp. 372, 373. *Rot. Scot.* i, 131 to John de Whelpedale alone is the earliest of these letters of marque, 18th September 1314.
215 *CPR 1313–17*, p. 687.
216 Raine, *Scriptore Tres*, p. 94.
217 *RPD* iii, pp. ci-ii; Middleton, *Gilbert de Middleton*, Appendix.
218 *RPD* ii, 868; Raine, *Scriptore Tres*, p. 94.
219 T. Wright, *Political Songs* (Camden Society, 1839), p. 196.
220 P. Chaplais, *The War of Saint-Sardos (1323–1325)* (Camden 3rd Series, lxxxvii, 1954), p. 66.

CHAPTER FIVE

The Bruce Intervention in Ireland, 1315–1322

The Earl of Carrick, Sir Edward
Who was braver than a leopard
Thought that Scotland was too small
For himself and his brother both
And therefore to one and all announced
That he of Ireland would be king.

O f all the aspects of the Wars of the Bruces, the intervention in Ireland is the most curious. The themes are weighty: strategy, on a scale grander even than that conceived by Edward I; professions of 'pan-celtic' brotherhood, purporting to span centuries and seas with equal ease; and kingship, produced as by magic like a rabbit from a hat. Of the sources, no chronicle as full and reliable as Lanercost exists to provide a framework for the interpretation of events.[1] Although the other main sources have been in print for some time,[2] crucial aspects have eluded the light. Not surprisingly an authoritative interpretation of the Bruce involvement in Ireland has yet to emerge though the subject has attracted many scholars.[3]

Robert I showed a consistent interest in Ireland and visited the country on at least four occasions. Edward his brother led a Scottish invasion of Ireland in 1315, used the title 'King of Ireland' and died in battle against the Anglo-Irish at Fochart in 1318. The Bruces represented their interest in terms of a pan-celtic solidarity against the common enemy. An illustration of how they wanted to be seen in Ireland is the letter of Robert I to 'all the kings of Ireland, to the prelates and clergy, and to the inhabitants of all Ireland, his friends'.[4] Enigmatic and undated, it is a letter of credence for envoys, claiming for the Irish and Scots a common national ancestry, a common language and common customs. It is justly famous for its use of the phrase 'our nation', clearly intended to embrace both peoples: an expression of that pan-celtic sentiment which occasionally surfaces in medieval literature, but only rarely in history or politics. In their appeals to the common culture and the common mythology of the Scots and Irish, and their similar overtures to the Welsh, the Bruces laid claim to leadership of a Celtic Alliance against the English; and in their interventions in

Ireland from 1315 to 1318, this claim appears to have been sustained with blood and steel.

Yet the most basic questions surrounding the Bruces' involvement in the celtic world remain unanswered. Why was the letter to the Irish written? Why did the Bruces embark upon the costly invasion of Ireland? Were they gradually sucked into intervention, or did they grasp a sudden opportunity? How did they think they could unite the multiplicity of warring kingdoms of the Gaeltacht? And how far was what happened in Ireland related to events in Britain? There is no end to the questions; and there are many possible answers. The anxiety to stop the flow of provisions from Ireland to the English western march is one explanation for the occupation of Ulster, but it does not account for the Bruces' campaigns in Leinster and Thomond. The desire to enlist the Gaelic-speaking peoples of the west against a common Anglo-Saxon foe was noised abroad by both brothers, but their own actions and those of their Gaelic allies suggest that this was propaganda rather than substance. The arrogance of Edward Bruce is well attested by narrative sources, and his desire to achieve kingly status is borne out by his stated ambitions in Wales and reported interest in the Western Isles; but the persistent involvement of King Robert and his willingness to divert resources to assist in the subjugation of Ireland suggests that the King of Scots had his own reasons for wanting to see his brother become King of Ireland. On the whole the evidence suggests that Scottish intervention in Ireland was driven primarily by the dynastic ambitions of Edward Bruce, but also that these ambitions were being made to serve the war aims of Robert I.

Fortunately the broad outline of events in Ireland is no longer in question, so it is possible to provide a summary narrative incorporating the findings of recent research and relying where possible on documentary sources rather than the accounts of the Irish annalists. Related aspects and interpretations of the Irish episode may then be examined: the presence in the 'Irish Sea province' of Scottish lords whom the Bruces had exiled from Argyll and Galloway; Ireland as a source of supply for the warring kingdoms of Britain; the development by the Bruces of the Celtic Alliance, embracing Wales as well as Ireland; and finally the implications of Edward Bruce's claim to the kingship of Ireland. But it would be wise to begin by setting these narrative, military, logistical and political questions within the overwhelming economic reality of the time – the crop failures of 1315–18.

Historical evidence for the Irish manifestation of the Great European Famine does not extend much further than the stock epithets and images of the native annalists:

Then reigned many diseases generally throughout the whole kingdom, a great loss of the inhabitants, great scarcity of victuals, great slaughter of people, and in summer, ugly and foul weather.[5]

Occasionally in the annals the hard times are depicted with a ghoulish horror which cannot quite be accepted at face-value:

Also it was said truly that some evil men were so distraught by famine that they dragged out of cemeteries the corpses of the buried, and roasted the bodies on spits and ate every single one of them; and women ate their sons for hunger.[6]

The lurid imaginings of the annalist were included only as entertainment for the reader; but there is no mistaking the fact that the famine of 1315–18 was worse than anything in living memory. Heavy rainfall ruined successive harvests; and the Scottish invasion coincided exactly with scarcity, crop failure and animal and human epidemics. Not surprisingly, the annalists drew a direct connection between the dearth and the presence of Edward Bruce.[7] Campaigning inevitably involved deliberate destruction of agricultural productivity, but 'friendly' armies were almost as destructive as the hostile. The Annals of Connacht describe the rival armies passing through Ulster:

. . . between them they left neither wood nor lea, nor corn nor crop nor stead nor barn nor church, but fired and burnt them all.[8]

What evidence there is from manorial accounts tends to confirm the impression of great hardship, hunger and increased human mortality. In the atrocious summer of 1315, the meadows on four manors of the Archbishop of Dublin could not be mown; and turf at Finglas could not be cut.[9] The difficulties of keeping the armies supplied continually impinge upon the narratives of marches and battles. Edward Bruce is portrayed as highly reliant upon his Gaelic Irish allies for supplies. In the winter retreat from Leinster in February 1316 many of the Scots are said to have perished from hunger and cold. Under the year 1316, the Scottish account by Fordun records that during King Robert's visit in 1317 'many perished through confusion and scarcity of provisions; for such dearth prevailed there that many fed on horse flesh'.[10] In Britain famine conditions affected the English, who had relied for their superiority upon large concentrations of infantry; but in the Irish campaigns, where there was no discernible difference between the armies of the Scots and those of their opponents, the dearth favoured neither side.[11]

The famines and pestilences of the early fourteenth century were at least as responsible as the Wars of the Bruces for accelerating the long-term decline of the Anglo-Irish colony. But there was a much longer-standing drain on the resources of the lordship: the exploitative policies of English kings. From the start of Edward I's reign to 1311, over £53,000 had been paid from Irish sources directly into the royal wardrobe for the king's business elsewhere. Much more probably went unrecorded. War against the Irish, economic malaise and the diminishing size of the colony were at the same time bringing about a dramatic decrease in the revenues of Ireland. The Ordainers had attempted to preserve the resources of the colony by declaring that all revenue from Irish customs was to be paid into the Dublin exchequer and expended on the colony's defence, rather than sent over to the royal wardrobe. But when the Ordainers were sidestepped and Edward II regained control of his government in 1312, this concern went by the board.[12] Furthermore, from 1312 to 1314 a further £2,000 of the revenues of Ireland were made over to Antonio Pessagno in part-payment of the king's debts to him.[13] During this reign the Irish colony, formerly a net contributor to royal finances, became a liability.

THE IRISH CAMPAIGNS

An escalation of the war in the Irish Sea forms the background to the Scottish invasion of Ireland; and the event which immediately preceded it was the recapture of the Isle of Man for the English by John of Argyll shortly before 18th February 1315. Duncan MacGoffrey, John's deputy, captured the Scottish garrison on the Isle, Murtagh MacKennedy and 22 of his comrades.[14] John may have been anticipating a Scottish offensive. In the spring of 1315 the Scots were preparing to receive a convoy of 'thirteen great cogs' from Flanders, loaded with foodstuffs and weaponry; and a Scottish expedition may have been advertised in Ireland with a view to acquiring allies, for among eight Scots arrested and imprisoned in Dublin by16th February was a messenger of the Scottish king called Henry.[15] But the English and their allies had also laid plans for an offensive. On 18th February the Irish justiciar, treasurer and chancellor had been ordered to raise 10,000 men in Ireland and a fleet of 60 ships manned at double strength to be commanded by John, and this was to be ready by 6th April 1315 for an expedition against the Scots. John was ordered to 'receive to the king's peace' magnates and communities of the Western Isles, including Edward Bruce's ally Donald of Islay. His appointment as captain of the western fleet coincided with that of John de Botetourt on the North Sea. The ports of Seaford and Shoreham were to supply four ships and Bristol 14 ships, all with double crews. The co-operation of the Cinque Ports fleet was secured probably just as news of the Scottish invasion of Ireland reached Westminster.[16] It is not really possible therefore to say which side was taking the initiative in the Irish Sea; Edward Bruce's invasion of Ireland appears to have averted this invasion of western Scotland by John of Argyll.

On St. Augustine's Day (26th May) 1315, a Scottish fleet left Ayr, where the nobles of the kingdom had congregated for a Great Council, and landed on the Antrim coast. The annals do not agree as to the precise location of the landing; some give it as Glendun which was Bisset territory, others Ulfreksfiord (the modern Larne) where Robert himself was to land in 1327.[17] There being no Scottish royal fleet, Edward Bruce had to rely upon galleys of MacDonald and MacRuairidh, and upon the existing commercial carrying network for transport. Larne was an established crossing point, and would have been a source of ships and crews.[18] We do not know the size of Edward Bruce's force. Chronicles employ a stock figure of 300 ships which is probably a gross exaggeration. But judging from the *kudos* of the personnel accompanying him, this expedition represented a substantial investment in both material and psychological terms. Barbour lists the Scottish heroes who accompanied Edward Bruce. They include the great magnates Thomas Randolph Earl of Moray, John Soules and Philip Mowbray, none of whom had any particular interest in Ireland or the Irish Sea. But there were others who had traditional territorial interests in the region. John Stewart who accompanied the expedition was perhaps a brother of Walter the Stewart, whose expansionist ambitions in the region were well established and who had married a sister of the Red Earl of Ulster. Less is known of Fergus of Ardrossan, but the toponymic suggests an interest in the western sea routes.[19] Most Scottish lords involved in Ireland came and went as opportunities for plunder arose and abated. There is no firm evidence that the Scots were accompanied by Irish exiles, but the Laud Annals alone mention the presence of John Bisset, the son of Hugh and a former commander of Edward I's North Channel squadron. The Ulster Bissets seem to have been casual in their allegiances.[20] That no Gaelic presence is specified is probably due to dependence upon non-Gaelic sources, for prominent Irish and Scots Gaelic lords are known to have participated at later stages. Dr. Duffy has drawn attention to the ambition of Edward to become King of Ireland and the Western Isles, and he was accompanied by a strong force of 'galloglasses', as Gaelic mercenaries were called.[21]

Edward Bruce was immediately opposed by the leaders of the Ulster gentry. Barbour lists as his adversaries De Mandeville, Bisset, Logan and Savage, though Bisset and Logan are described in documentary sources as supporting the Scots during the early stages of the expedition.[22] It is worth noting, too, that even from this early stage contemporaries were convinced that the Bruces aimed at outright conquest of all Ireland, and as rapidly as possible. Gaelic Irish rapidly submitted to Edward; and from this point onwards Edward Bruce was never without Gaelic allies.[23] Domnall Ó Néill, the powerful king of Tyrone, was probably Edward's ally from an early stage. The Scots proceeded against Carrickfergus Castle, an obvious target for any lord interested in controlling the North Channel, but a virtually impregnable stone keep. Edward's siege of Carrickfergus commenced at around the same time that King Robert began his siege of Carlisle (22nd July) just across the Irish Sea.[24] The Scots' lack of the means to reduce elaborate fortifications, so evident at Carlisle, was once again apparent at Carrickfergus. According to Barbour, the garrison agreed to surrender 'when the folk of Ulster were wholly come over' to the side of Bruce.[25]

Leaving men to invest Carrickfergus, Edward Bruce led his force southwards in the early summer to confront Dundalk. On the way there was widespread destruction of the countryside.[26] He can hardly have ignored the chief manorial centres on the coast, Dundrum and Downpatrick. There is no record of his capturing either, though from November 1315 the Bishop of Down was maintained as a refugee in Dublin castle, having been expelled by Edward Bruce.[27] Greencastle, Co. Down, was taken and a Scottish garrison installed which was commanded by an Irishman, Robert of Coulrath. Duncan suggests that Robert had been the Anglo-Irish warden, and had surrendered to the Scots on their approach.[28] However, there may already have been many Irish in the pay of the Bruces. MacKennedy's garrison on the Isle of Man includes men with Irish toponymics. In the marches of Uriel at 'Innermallane' the Scots were ambushed by enemies whom Barbour names as 'Makgullane' and 'Makartane.'[29] The Laud Annals date the capture of Dundalk to 29th June. Barbour's assertion that an abundance of wine was discovered in the town rings true; Dundalk, Drogheda and other east-coast ports of Ireland functioned as supply depots for English campaigns in Scotland. Edward stayed three days in Dundalk. Chronicles agree that the town was razed and the inhabitants slaughtered; and documentary sources record damage.[30] Devastation of Louth followed upon the fall of Dundalk, and the towns of Ardee and Rathmore are also said to have been burnt.[31]

By July the Justiciar, Edmund Butler, Richard de Burgh the Red Earl of Ulster and their Anglo-Irish and Gaelic allies advanced against the Scots.[32] Among them was John de Barry, who described to Edward II the advance from Dublin, through Dundalk and Carlingford between 3rd and 18th July.[33] At this time the *Annals of Clonmacnoise* place Edward Bruce at Inniskeen, an archepiscopal manor.[34] The Prior of St. Mary's Abbey Louth was later accused of

> warning the said Scots at Iniskeen ... that the Justiciar and [ ] of Ireland and many more nobles and magnates of Ireland were coming, with a great army of the king, and his banner displayed, to fight the Scots by means of which warning the Scots who would have been slain, as it was hoped if such warning had not been given, then retreated in flight through fear of the arrival of the army to the town of Coulrath [Coleraine] in Ulster.[35]

While the Scots retreated into Ulster, the Red Earl, anxious to preserve his

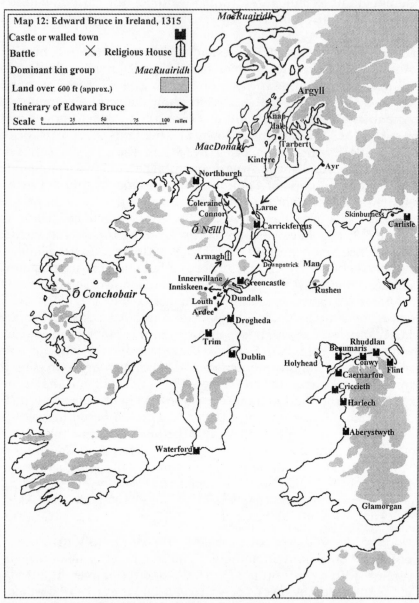

Map 12: Edward Bruce in Ireland, 1315

Castle or walled town

Battle   Religious House

Dominant kin group   *MacRuairidh*

Land over 600 ft (approx.)

Itinerary of Edward Bruce

Scale 0   25   50   75   100 miles

Based on maps by J.F. Lydon in *An Historical Atlas of Scotland, c. 400 - c.1600* (St. Andrews, 1975), pp. 168-69.

lands from the passage of such a great host, persuaded the Justiciar and other magnates to leave the pursuit of the Scots to him and his Gaelic ally Fedlimid Ó Conchobair. John de Barry, David fitz Alexander de la Roche and other Anglo-Irish lords returned home with the Justiciar.[36] But John le Poer of Dunoyl stayed with the earl, and followed the Scots into Ulster 'for five weeks', and he gives a valuable report of the campaign. The Scottish retreat northwards to the banks of the lower Bann is reported by the annalists' accounts, and it is clear that the Scots were led back, through the lands of the earldom which they had already wasted, and to the east of Lough Neagh. At Coleraine they crossed the bridge over the Bann and then demolished it to prevent its being used by the earl's army which was following them.[37] In the Barbour narrative there occurs at this point a mysterious anecdote. It is related that the Scots trusted an Irish king called O'Dempsey, who nevertheless deprived them of cattle, flooded their camp and abandoned them to starve in a desolate place by the River Bann, until they were ferried across the river by Thomas of Downe, who arrived with four ships. This hero of the hour was Thomas Dun, a privateer operating with increasing success against English vessels on the Irish Sea. The identity of O'Dempsey is more of a mystery as the family name O'Dempsey is not common to the north of Ireland. Professor Frame suggests that the anecdote belongs to a later, more southerly episode in the Scottish intervention. However, the story seems to fit the context of distrust between the Scots and their Gaelic allies in Ulster, and it is consistent perhaps with the meanness of a Gaelic ally forced to provide hospitality yet determined to prevent the passage of the Scots through his land in a year of scarcity. The presence of the Scots did indeed place a strain on the resources of the Gaelic lords, and Domnall Ó Néill was obliged at one point to guarantee the immunity of certain ecclesiastical lands against subsidies and imposts 'for ourselves or for our Scottish allies'.[38] Furthermore the *Annals of Inisfallen* seem aware that lack of hospitality had been alleged:

> . . . it was reported that in the Scottish camp four quarters of a sheep fetched 2s. sterling. On account of this dearth, however, the people of the countryside, principally ÓNeill, Ó Cathain and Ó Flainn, did not fail to provide for them as best they could.[39]

The O'Dempsey of the Barbour text can only be Ó Néill, who was in Bruce's company at Iniskeen, whose territories lay west of the Bann, and who appears as an ally in the subsequent battle.[40]

In the chronicle accounts the armies faced one another across the Bann at És Craibe, the Salmon Leap opposite Coleraine:

> they were severed from each other by the deep, spacious and

smooth-running waters or river. Nevertheless, they had a daily shooting of arrows . . .[41]

Edward Bruce then became involved in negotiations between rival factions of the Ó Conchobairs. He was approached by Ruairidh Ó Conchobair, enemy and rival of Fedlimid, for an alliance against the English. But Fedlimid also parleyed with him, trying to outbid Ruairidh for Edward's support. Edward tried to retain the allegiance of both Ó Conchobair factions by granting Rory alliance on the condition that he did not attack the lands of Felimid. In this Edward displays naiveté in dealing with Irish kings; the feud between Ruairidh and Fedlimid was of such immediacy that it was bound to take precedence over any alliance against the English. Ruairidh returned to Connacht and straightaway began to attack the lands of his rival. For Edward there was however a favourable outcome to these discussions, for Fedlimid Ó Conchobair was forced to withdraw from the earl's army to defend his own lands in Connacht.[42] This gave the Scots an opportunity to attack. A letter of John le Poer written on 3rd October reports to Edward II that

. . . by chance on Monday after the feast of the Decollation of St. John the Baptist [1st September] it happened that Ó Néill and the other Irish of Ulster and your said enemies [the Scots], attacked us suddenly at Connor and found us vulnerable there through the negligence of our scouts who ought to have warned us and in whom we trusted. Some of the company of the said earl [of Ulster] fought them and in the fight Sir John Stewart and Sir John de Bosco were mortally wounded, and a great number of their people were killed as I heard. But the place remained theirs at the end. And at that action on our side, William de Burgh was captured and wounded and is said to have been sent to Scotland.'[43]

Le Poer is putting a brave face on what was a significant defeat. Barbour and the Irish annals record this as a rout, though they give the date as 10th September.[44] The Red Earl abandoned the defence of his possessions in Ulster and went to Connacht to try to save his lands there from devastation in the Ó Conchobair wars. After this Moray left Ireland on 15th September 1315, taking the captive William de Burgh (a nephew of the Red Earl) and four ships of Thomas Dun, possibly to collect on the peace agreement which he had made with Durham Priory the previous October.[45] Presumably the Irish adventure was costing all the Scottish magnates a great deal of money; but the capture of prisoners would have helped to offset their expenses. Already Gaelic Irish as far away as Desmond were rebelling against the English; Maurice fitz Thomas reported to Edward II that he had been unable to take part in the Ulster campaign because the Irish of Desmond had risen against him and that all the Irish were emboldened by the presence of the Scots.[46] If the Ulster gentry had initially opposed the Scots, as Barbour suggests, they were now coming to heel. A letter written to Edward II on 18th October 1315 states that

> since their [i.e. the Scots'] arrival in your said land, he [Edward Bruce] has been received and sustained by the Irish who are in the march of Ulster and of Uriel and by those English who are of his company, that is to say the Bissets and the Logans.[47]

Much later, the Mandevilles, Logans, Bissets and Savages were all accused of riding in the company of Robert and Edward Bruce through Louth. But these allegations could well be spurious, for among the Ulster gentry bitter recriminations persisted long after the Scots had been vanquished.[48] At this time, too, an amphibious night attack was launched from English ports against the Scots before Carrickfergus, and the attackers carried away the tents and gear of the besiegers, allegedly killing 40 of them.[49]

The crucial importance of Carrickfergus lay in its relation to the sea lanes between Ireland and Scotland. The 'birlings' of the north-western sealanes did not differ greatly from their predecessors of Viking times. Contemporary sculptures show single masted, clinker-built vessels, with high stem and stern, even sometimes bearing the grotesque figureheads that are popularly associated with Viking ships.[50] But they were ideally suited to the strong currents of the North Channel. Thomas Dun's ferrying of Edward Bruce's men across the Bann and of Moray to Scotland suggests a high degree of co-ordination between these Scottish forces in the western theatre of war. This was not the case with the English and their allies. Until quite late in the summer Edward II seems to have had little idea of the crisis facing his Irish colony, and he pressed ahead with plans for a naval offensive against western Scotland. The involvement of the Cinque Ports fleet, however, seems to have necessitated a change of commissions, for William de Creye and Thomas de Hewys were appointed admirals and John of Argyll relegated to captain.[51] All the king's debts in Ireland were to be collected and directed towards the maintenance of the fleet, and the money was to be ready three weeks from Midsummer. An unspecified sum was sent to pay the wages of the Cinque Ports fleet; and sailors were being pressed into service in Bristol and Gloucestershire by John of Athy and Alexander le Convers. In July, Athy was given his own command of 11 ships in Bristol.[52] In the event the campaign of 1315 in Britain never materialised; and most of the fleet was held up in Portsmouth by contrary winds. Some service was obtained; Alexander le Convers accounted for £466 which he received in 1315–16 for wages of the Cinque Ports fleet, 'who came from Ireland in the company of Alexander and went from there to Scotland in the king's service'.[53] Other ships too were in the Irish Sea on royal service. But probably even if a landing in Scotland was effected, little was achieved. The money ran out; and in October the king wrote to the mayor and bailiffs of Winchelsea, allowing them to recall the 17 ships which they had granted as an aid to the king for the Scottish War, and which were languishing in Portsmouth harbour unable to set out on account of contrary winds and tempests.[54]

While this English fleet rode at anchor, Scottish privateers threatened the Isle of Man in July,[55] and carried out a particularly spectacular exploit off Anglesey. On 12th September 1315, shortly after Edward Bruce had defeated the Red Earl on the River Bann, Thomas Dun sailed into the harbour of Holyhead on Anglesey and captured a laden cargo ship, the *James* of Caernarvon.[56] In a petition to Edward II for relief, her captain voiced suspicions that local officials had colluded with the Scots. He claimed that Tudor ap Candelo, 'rhingyl' (or official) of the county, had sent a boat out to Dun's ship and had contacted the privateer. The captain accused Tudor of failing to raise the alarm with urgency and of allowing the Scots to make off with the prize. The incident is doubly significant: firstly, it is the earliest indication that the Bruces might have the capacity to influence events in Wales; secondly, the name of Thomas Dun is henceforth encountered repeatedly in the sources as 'a perpetrator of depredations on the sea' and 'a cruel pirate'.[57] His reputation spread rapidly; but though Dun is said in the petition to have entered the port with 'a great navy', he is twice described as commanding only four ships.[58] The names of three other privateers are given in the captain's petition. It may be that Dun's three companions on the Holyhead raid were the captains of his three other ships and that this may have been the whole strength of the privateer squadron. The privateers may not even have been exclusively Scottish; one of Dun's accomplices is named as William of Cashemary in Ireland, and Thomas Dun himself may have come from *An Dun* or Downpatrick. Probably the privateer squadron had originated in the North Channel as carriers and supply vessels for Edward I, turning to piracy as the work dried up, and then turning for employment to the Bruces. To counter the threat posed by the privateers, John of Argyll wrote to Edward II before 27th September pleading that six ships remain with him in Irish ports to harass the enemy during the coming winter.[59] Shortly after this, however, he was forced to retire to London, 'impotent in body and his lands in Scotland totally destroyed'.[60]

That autumn at the Council of Lincoln it was decided that the resistance of the Irish colony to Edward Bruce should be stiffened by the dispatch of a trusted royal servant. John de Hotham Bishop of Ely crossed to Ireland in order to take charge. He had to be escorted by 86 *satellites* and crossbowmen, 'to secure his passage and because Thomas Dun and divers other enemies, robbers on the sea between the lands of England, Wales and Ireland are doing much mischief and daily perpetrate evil'.[61] Hotham's background was that of a trusted official, experienced in Irish affairs, and his arrival in Ireland had a salutary effect on the inefficient and impoverished Dublin government. He had been invested with wide powers of patronage, including the capacity to grant pardons, wardships and marriages, to remit debts and to replace incompetent officials. Changes in the Anglo-Irish administration followed, and oaths and hostages were taken to secure the loyalty of the magnates; but it was probably his judicious use of pardons, grants and privileges that contributed most in this most dangerous situation.[62] Hotham's success in organising resistance to the Scots was due to his astute handling of relations with the Anglo-Irish magnates; but it would take time before his report to the English council could result in military or financial assistance.

With winter coming on, Edward Bruce again marched south out of Ulster. Barbour makes no mention of this expedition; but the Anglo-Irish had been expecting a winter campaign.[63] The town of Dundalk had been reoccupied and, presumably, fortified, for the Scots bypassed it. The Laud Annal lists the locations through which the Scots passed. At Dundalk they met Moray returning from Scotland with 500 men. Advancing into Meath, they encountered at Kells Roger Mortimer of Wigmore, defending his lordship of Trim, and put him to flight. They were guided by Mortimer's inveterate foes and tenants, Walter and Hugh de Lacy, who when later charged with treason responded that they parleyed with the Scots only at Mortimer's request and led them among the lands of the king's Irish enemies, in order to spare the revenues of the king and his lieges.[64] Mortimer left Ireland after this defeat, crossing to Wales to defend his estates there against the revolt of Llywelyn Bren. Edward Bruce spent Christmas at the de Verdun manor of Loughsewdy, because Mortimer's retainer Walter Cusack held Trim Castle against him. The citizens of Dublin began to prepare for the worst. The castle was repaired and provisioned; and the bell tower of St. Mary del Dam was demolished and the materials used in the repair of the castle.[65] Surprisingly, however, they did not attack Dublin but continued to advance southwards.[66] At Ardscull near Skerries the leading Anglo-Irish magnates of Leinster turned out in force to oppose the Scots on 26th January 1316. By all accounts, the Anglo-Irish should have won the day. A draft report to Edward II read as follows:

> There were assembled more than enough men-at-arms, hobelars, and foot soldiers and they met with the enemy in open field but they withdrew from the place, without warlike exploits on the enemy and without losing any of their people except for one man, as men beaten on the day, each on his own, and by ill luck the enemy kept the field but the enemy lost on the day some of their best men.[67]

In a comment on the size of Edward Bruce's force, the Laud Annal

Map 13: Edward Bruce in Ireland, 1315-16

Castle or walled town

Battle

Dominant kin group   *MacRuairidh*

Land over 600 ft (approx.)

Itinerary of Edward Bruce

Scale 0   25   50   75   100 miles

Based on maps by J.F. Lydon in *An Historical Atlas of Scotland, c. 400 - c.1600* (St. Andrews, 1975), pp. 168-69.

remarks that even one of the Anglo-Irish magnates assembled against him (Edmund Butler, John fitz Thomas or Arnold le Poer) should have been able to defeat the Scots. Although they had scattered the Anglo-Irish, the Scots incurred the loss of two captains, Fergus of Ardrossan and Walter de Moray. The Gaelic Irish of Leinster were inspired to rise in revolt, taking advantage of the situation to attack the Anglo-Irish colony. The Irish destroyed Bray; the Scots and Irish together devastated Carlow. As far away as Desmond the Irish clans O'Donnegan, Ó Conchobair and O'Kennedy rose in sympathy and anticipation.[68] The Scots besieged Kildare Castle briefly, but then began to withdraw.[69] On account of lack of supplies probably, Edward then withdrew into fortified places (*forceletz*) in the vicinity of Leix, while the Anglo-Irish regrouped near Kildare. The Scots burnt Lea Castle and the church of the new town of Leix, and were at Geashill in Offaly on 14th February; but they began to suffer from a shortage of provisions:

> The Scots suffered from such famine that many of them died of hunger, and on account of this, they secretly marched towards Fore in Meath. On the Sunday following, they were so weakened, both from hunger and from exhaustion, that many of them began to die.[70]

They did indeed visit Fore, for the prior and convent wrote to the king complaining that they lost their charters in the destruction caused by the Scots. As Professor Phillips has put it, the Scottish retreat after Ardscull is a better measure of their military situation than their temporary possession of the battlefield. The purpose of Edward Bruce's campaign of early 1316 is difficult to fathom; shortage of food was bound to compel withdrawal. Frame does not mince his words: 'It is hard to see how any commander in his right mind would have freely chosen to campaign in the early months of 1316 or 1317'.[71] One possible explanation, though perhaps a far-fetched one, is that Edward Bruce was anxious to take advantage of conditions in South Wales (where the Welsh prince Llywelyn Bren had commenced an insurrection against the English on 18th January) and might have been working to a timetable which admitted of no delay on account of the weather.

In the early spring of 1316 Edward Bruce's depleted force returned to Ulster; and in March 1316 he seems to have been consolidating his authority there. The Laud annalist states that about the end of March Edward Bruce 'held the pleas of Ulster', 'killed the Logans' and captured Sir Alan Fitz Warin and led him to Scotland. The earl of Moray left once again for Scotland, in the first week of March, tempted away by the prospect of an expiring truce on the Anglo-Scottish border. As the Scots' most able leader he was present on most of the Bruce brothers' major enterprises, and his departure may be taken as a sign that it had been decided to cease campaigning in Ireland for the foreseeable future.[72] Now confined to Ulster, Edward's main difficulty was the continued resistance of Carrickfergus. The Anglo-Irish were making determined efforts to reinforce the castle. On 17th March Thomas de Mandeville was granted permission to negotiate with those English and Irish against the peace of the king, that is, to foment opposition to Bruce in Ulster. At Drogheda ships were arrested and pressed into service; provisions accumulated; and a relief expedition was launched.[73]

Mandeville's force of 15 ships arrived on 8th April during an Easter truce between garrison and besiegers. The Land Annal relates that he met with initial success, putting to flight the Scots and killing 20 of them. On the eve of Easter, 10th April, he attacked the Scots a second time, but the Scots were reinforced by John MacNakill, with 200 spearmen, who succeeded in capturing four or five of the ships. Thomas de Mandeville was cut down in desperate street fighting, and so the attempt to relieve the castle failed. Yet the garrison grimly held out.[74] During negotiations at Midsummer the garrison seized 30 Scots and put them in irons as hostages. The defenders were now reduced to eating animal hides and, according to one source, they devoured eight of their Scottish prisoners.[75] The garrison was not assisted by the action of the Red Earl, who commandeered eight supply ships destined for Carrickfergus towards the ransom of his nephew in Scotland. Other supplies were diverted to Whitehaven and Skinburness, either by accident or for personal gain.[76] For Carrickfergus the end was now very close and it is not surprising to discover from subsequent legal proceedings that the garrison began to compromise. An officer of the garrison, Henry de Thrapston, agreed to a month's truce with Edward Bruce. Thomas Dun was admitted to the castle, treated to food and given cloth for a cloak; perhaps this buttering up was in the hope that he could moderate the surrender terms.[77] Carrickfergus had fallen by 30th September 1316 when Edward had returned to Scotland.[78] A hitherto unnoticed entry in the Laud Annals may explain why. The annalist records under 1316 that news came to Dublin that Robert Bruce, King of Scotland, entered Ireland to help his brother Edward and that the castle of Carrickfergus was besieged by the said Scots so Carrickfergus may have surrendered not to Edward but to Robert himself.

In the Irish Sea the summer of 1316 saw the English on the offensive, and a naval presence continued to be maintained off the coast of Ulster. Nicholas de Balscot, royal clerk, had spent £578 in the year 1315–16 (which included pay of the forces of the justiciar, men-at-arms, hobelars and foot, besides the pay of sailors); and £262 in the year 1316–17 was spent on the pay of sailors alone.[79] The naval activity that this expenditure represents seems to have been sufficient to keep Thomas Dun's privateers at bay. There is evidence of strenuous activity in the

Irish Sea ports; 10 ships from the ports around Dublin were ordered to be commandeered; and all the shipping around Drogheda was ordered to patrol and search out Thomas Dun and his privateers, described as 'lurking in maritime places between Ulster and Scotland'.[80] Edward II, however, had plans for a much greater initiative. He contracted with his Genoese banker, Antonio Pessagno, for the provision from Genoa of five galleys, each with 200 men, to leave Genoa for Ireland on 1st April 1317. Pessagno was to take these vessels into the Irish Sea, and use them to escort victuals to Skinburness to provision a campaign in the summer of 1317. For this he was to be paid 250 marks per galley per month, and that rate was guaranteed as long as the ships remained in his employ.[81] Pessagno delivered enormous quantities of victuals on the east coast of England; but the Irish aspects of the plan were not carried out. Later he undertook to furnish a small army of 200 men-at-arms and 2,000 foot in Gascony for Ireland, and claimed to have paid £500 to begin recruitment. But Edward's plans were bigger than his purse, and the scheme collapsed 'for want of payment'.[82] Nevertheless these plans are remarkable testimony to the anxiety of Edward II to regain control of the Irish Sea, and to guarantee the safety of his supply convoys for the English western march.

After the surrender of Carrickfergus, Edward and Moray both returned to Scotland. On 30th September King Robert confirmed a grant to Moray of the Isle of Man, with the assent of Edward 'King of Ireland'. Moray had already been granted the Isle by July 1316; but this confirmation may have been necessary to record the assent of Edward Bruce, whose established western interests it affected. Since at this time Man was in English hands, it provided an incentive for Moray to wrest the Isle from them.[83] It was most certainly a return for Moray's service in Ireland; and it provided a basis for co-operation for these three principals in a third Irish campaign. In January 1317 King Robert and Moray sailed from Loch Ryan in Galloway to Carrickfergus. The timing of this expedition calls for comment. There was probably a truce on the marches of England, for Robert would hardly have left Scotland at this time with the earl of Arundel maintaining a powerful presence on the borders. In Britain between 1315 and 1317 there had been sieges of Carlisle and Berwick, but only one Scottish attack deep into England. In Ireland, by contrast, this was the third campaign in two years and the second consecutive winter campaign. Robert was then sufficiently confident of his position in Britain to put things on hold; but in Ireland he was impatient for victory. Edward Bruce's position in Ulster may have been increasingly unstable; chronicles report that in November 1316 John Logan and Hugh Bisset killed 300 Scots. Sir Alan Stewart had been taken prisoner by the Anglo-Irish.[84] Moreover, Roger Mortimer of Wigmore had been appointed Keeper and King's Lieutenant in Ireland on 23rd November with wide powers, and he was to go to Ireland with 150 horse and 500 foot in February. Like the original invasion of 1315, this expedition may have been intended to fend off an impending English offensive.[85]

Robert landed at Larne, and together with Edward and Moray he continued southwards onto the plain of Meath. The Scots are said to have beeen at Slane on 16th February 1317, where yet again 'they laid waste the whole country'. They attacked the manor of the Red Earl at Ratoath; and the earl, then in residence, was forced to flee to Dublin. The Scots then advanced to Castleknock, within striking distance of Dublin, clearly intending to intimidate the city into surrender.[86] On their approach Dublin began to prepare a second time for a desperate defence. Suburbs were destroyed to deprive the attackers of cover; the bridge over the Liffey was broken; and the tower of the church of St. Saviour was demolished to provide material for barricades. Within the city, the earl of Ulster was arrested on charges of treachery. There is no evidence that he was anything but a faithful vassal of Edward II; but his daughter's marriage to Robert I naturally made him an object of constant suspicion, and the citizens may have felt that by arresting Robert's father-in-law they were taking a hostage. But for a second time the Scots decided against an assault. They may have been impressed by the defences of the city, or doubted their own capacity to hold it. Moving away from the city in a south-westerly direction, they marched towards the valleys of the Nore and Barrow, where Edward had campaigned the previous year. Map 14 shows their itinerary through Leinster and Munster as given by the Laud Annals. Edmund Butler the Justiciar, and now provocatively bearing Edward Bruce's own title 'Earl of Carrick', had mustered a force but dared not commit it to battle. There survives an account of wages paid to this Anglo-Irish army in the period 24th February to 17th April, which provides information on the movements of the Anglo-Irish force shadowing the Scots, and hence by implication, on the movements of the Scots themselves.[87] On 18th and 19th March the Scots were at Cashel. From there they turned north towards Nenagh where they wasted lands belonging to Edmund Butler. Responding to an appeal from an Ó Briain faction, Clann Briain Ruad, for assistance against their enemies, the Bruces moved westwards into Thomond. Early in April they were approaching the city of Limerick, their movements followed cautiously at a distance by Edmund Butler.[88] Butler had at this time a force of 220 men-at-arms, 300 hobelars and 400 foot. It may be inferred that the Bruces had an army superior to this.

The English administration had been ordered to accelerate preparations for Mortimer's expedition at the end of January,[89] but it was April before the army materialised. A convoy of 'twenty great ships' was assembled from Bristol and surrounding ports by John of Athy, to ferry across the army under Roger Mortimer. This was landed at Youghal on 7th April;

Map 14:   The Bruces in Ireland, 1317

Castle or walled town

Battle

Dominant kin group   *MacRuairidh*

Land over. 600 ft (approx.)

Itinerary of the Bruces

Scale

Based on maps by J.F. Lydon in *An Historical Atlas of Scotland, c. 400 - c.1600* (St. Andrews, 1975), pp. 168-69.

but Athy had orders 'to stay at sea for the defence of Ireland and the king's land of Scotland'.[90] Limerick had refused to admit the Scots; and in Thomond the Bruces were met not by their allies from Clann Briain Ruad, but by the hostile Ó Briain faction Clann Taid, who had recently triumphed over their rivals.[91] Short of supplies, they had no choice but to retreat, first to Leinster, where on 17th April there was the merest brush with Edmund Butler's hobelars at Eliogarty, and then to Meath. Here even Scottish writers admit they were 'nearly perished with hunger and fatigue, and many were left there dead'. After a painful retreat to Ulster, Robert left for Scotland to meet the threatened invasion of 1317, since the current truce on the Anglo-Scottish border was about to expire.[92]

On the Irish Sea meanwhile the English continued to be frustrated by the presence of the privateers, and the smuggling of provisions to Scotland. Simon de Montecute and others were ordered in April to prevent the people of southwest England from trading corn, victuals and armour to Scotland. Grain from these counties (Somerset, Devon, Dorset, Cornwall and Gloucestershire) was currently arriving at Carlisle, and it appears that the merchants carrying these supplies also traded with the Scots.[93] Just as Robert I left Ireland, in May 1317, Edward II commissioned Nicholas Dauney and Geoffrey de Modiworthe to provide a good ship from one of seven English ports, to be equipped at the expense of the king 'to destroy Thomas *le mariner*, who is infesting the sea towards the west with a crew of Scots, doing great damage to trade coming to England'. Modiworthe had already paid for a 140–man galley, a very large vessel by the standards of the Irish Sea and probably therefore faster than anything else afloat.[94] On 2nd July John of Athy caught up with Thomas Dun, and in the greatest sea battle of the war 40 of the privateers are said to have been slain. Geoffrey de Coigners captured the privateer chief and received a reward of £10 from Edward II.[95] Before his execution Dun was made to reveal that Moray was ready to mount an attack on the Isle of Man 'and intends to attempt Anglesey by aid of some English traitors'. The Scottish presence on the Irish Sea was indeed far from finished. In October 1317 Edward II believed that he still controlled Man, but Moray was in possession of it shortly afterwards.[96]

We have no information as to what occurred between the departure of Robert and Moray in May 1317 and the Battle of Fochart in October 1318, a period of over eighteen months. Famine provides a plausible explanation for this hiatus in what had been vigorous campaigning in Ireland; but the absence of Moray, who was raiding in England, generally coincided with lulls in the Irish theatre of war. We do not know whether Edward Bruce was comfortably maintaining his position in Ulster; or whether it was being slowly eroded by famine, defections or deteriorating relations with local allies. The Scots may have been starving. There is one indication that they had to be supplied from outside Ireland: a local official in Meath was accused of taking bribes to permit a 'foreign' ship to furnish the Scots with victuals. The Laud annalist claims they were reduced to cannibalism.[97] Dublin at any rate still considered Edward a threat; it retained the emergency fortifications which had been thrown up in 1317, for at least a year afterwards.[98]

It was not until the summer of 1318 that a good harvest caused grain prices to fall.[99] The availability of food enabled Edward Bruce to advance out of Ulster on his fourth and final campaign. One source, the Continuation of Nicholas Trevet, contains the names of 29 commanders who, it is alleged, fought and died with Edward Bruce. The list probably includes all those who ever sided with him, regardless of the many comings and goings of the Scottish lords and the many changes of sides by the Irish. The Scottish commanders are named as Philip de Mowbray, John Soules, John Stewart and the brothers Walter and Alan Stewart. Among those of Anglo-Irish descent there were said to be four members of the de Lacy family; and from Ulster there were said to be Robert and John Savage. Gaelic Irish allies were also present, though according to Barbour they refused to participate in the battle. Bruce is known to have had the support of Scots-Gaelic lords, including Alexander MacRuairidh, 'King of the Western Isles', his long-time ally Donald of Islay and also Alexander Óg MacDonald.[100] Ranged against him on the Anglo-Irish side were three prominent magnates: Edmund Butler, John de Birmingham, and Archbishop Roland Joyce of Armagh. We also know the names of many lesser lords and others who claimed to have taken part on the winning side, from the petitions for reimbursement for losses, among them burgesses of Drogheda. Judging by the names of those petitioning, Edward did not encounter on this occasion the assembled might of the Anglo-Irish colony, but rather a force hastily gathered together from Meath.[101] This suggests that the Scots and their allies were on the offensive.

The battle was fought at Fochart near Dundalk on 14th October 1318. According to Barbour, Edward's undoing was his overweening pride and arrogance, in his refusal to share the glory with a reinforcement. 'Sir John Stewart' is given a speech in which he pleads with Edward to wait, saying that his brother is leading 15,000 men to his aid (the numeral, of course, has been plucked from the air). The Gaelic Irish allegedly refused to fight while the Anglo-Irish heavily outnumbered them.[102] The Annals of Clonmacnoise agree with Barbour about Edward's rash judgement, stating that 'anxious to obtain the victory for himself, he did not wait for his brother'.[103] But there is a third account, in the Lanercost Chronicle, which states that the reinforcement had already arrived. It claims that Edward approached Dundalk 'with a great army of Scots which had newly arrived in Ireland'. Edward, who had been inactive for so long, did not venture out of Ulster without reinforcements. Lanercost gives the clearest description of the battle:

They [the Scots] were in three columns at such a distance from each other that the first was done with before the second came up, and then the second before the third, with which Edward was marching, could render any aid. Thus the third column was routed, just as the two preceding ones had been. Edward fell at the same time and was beheaded after death; his body being divided into four quarters, which were sent to the four chief quarters of Ireland.[104]

There died at Fochart the heads of the MacDonald and MacRuairidh clans, and Robert I's only surviving brother.[105] News of the defeat must have come as a bitter blow to Robert, which he may have attributed to the curse of Malachy, the twelfth-century Irish saint, on the Bruce family.[106] Furthermore the battle was followed by a collapse of the Scottish position in Ulster. Carrickfergus was retaken and garrisoned by John de Athy, by 2nd December 1318 at the latest. John de Birmingham received most of the credit for the defeat of the Scots in Ireland; and he was elevated to the earldom of Louth for his part in the defeat of the Scottish invasion.[107] Fochart, however, by no means brought an end Robert's interest in Ireland. In 1319 five ships from Devon had to be sent to John of Athy 'for repelling the Scots', and until July 1320 Athy had to maintain a strong garrison at Carrickfergus, 20 men-at-arms and 15 crossbowmen 'because at that time great danger threatened the castle by the presence and the frequent arrival of Scots and other enemies of the king in the districts around the castle'.[108] Athy was assisted in this by Colman 'Megulhan'. This individual appears to be MacDuilechain, Gaelic lord of Clan Breasail, a territory just east of the Bann and south of Lough Neagh. In 1319 Edward II wrote to MacDuilechain thanking him for his consistent support.[109] But Athy never regained control of the North Channel. The Mayor of Dublin reported in October 1321 a rumour that the Scots were descending once more upon Ireland in haste and with great force.[110] There was a need for constant patrols in the North Channel: Duncan MacGoffrey was patrolling the sea between Ireland and Scotland in 1320 and 1321 and subsequently John of Athy was appointed to the custody of the sea between Ireland and Scotland.[111].When in May 1322 huge purveyances were ordered in Ireland to supply the English invasion of Scotland, they were ordered to be kept near the coast until a naval escort under the admiral Robert de Leyburn should arrive, 'as the sea between Ireland and Skinburness is infested by the king's enemies, with the intention of taking the victuals'.[112]

SCOTTISH EMIGRÉS IN IRELAND, MAN AND THE IRISH SEA

An essential part of the background to the invasion of Ireland is the presence in lands bordering on the Irish Sea of Scottish exiles who had shifted operations to Ireland after expulsion from western Scotland. The most active of these exiles was of course John of Argyll. An indefatigable enemy of the Bruces, and a cousin of that John Comyn who had been murdered by Robert Bruce at Dumfries in 1306, John first arrived in Ireland with his father on 9th December 1309, having been driven out of Argyll. He travelled from Ireland to Berwick to attend the king, and no doubt to press the case for western offensives.[113] Having captured the Isle of Man in February 1315, he sent the Bruces' garrison led by Murtagh MacKennedy to Dublin, preferring to see them behind bars in Dublin Castle rather than to release them for ransom.[114] One of John's knights in the Irish Sea was Duncan MacGoffrey, later to command at Newcastle McKynegan during the invasion of Robert and Edward.[115] Another was that veteran of resistance to the Bruces, Dungal MacDowell. In one English source Dungal is described as 'hated by the enemy', and with good reason; he had handed over Thomas and Alexander Bruce for execution in 1307.[116] He had been sheriff and constable of Dumfries from 1311 to 1313, and then as commander of Rushen he had held out against Robert I for six weeks. With MacGoffrey he served in John's fleet during the years 1315 to 1316; and after the defeat of Edward Bruce both he and MacGoffrey appear in the garrison at Carlisle.[117] Dungal de Gyvelestone, a Scottish exile who had been serving in Ireland, also shows up in John's fleet in 1315. In March 1315 Edward II made over to de Gyvelestone, for the good service of himself and his father, all the lands of Suny Magurke in Knapdale and 'Glenarowyle', currently held by Robert's liegeman, John de Menteith. In 1319 he was serving in Northumberland.[118] Another exile, Duncan Makouri, was ordered to Ireland in 1316; he too appears as a deputy of John of Argyll, keeping the Isle of Man, and claimed to have lost his own father and had his lands destroyed by 'the Scots' in serving John.[119] This network of exiles was thus operating in the Irish Sea, thirsting for revenge against the Bruces and their MacDonald and MacRuairidh allies, and in 1315 their forces were poised on the Isle of Man to attack the western approaches of Scotland.

It would be wrong to see the invasion of Ireland purely as a response to John of Argyll's capture of Man; it would have been a wholly disproportionate response on the part of the Scots, and in any case there are many indications that the Scots were, prior to February 1315, preparing an offensive in the western theatre of war. But the invasion of Ireland must be seen in the context of an escalation of activity in the region by both sides; and against a background of very personal animosities, in which context it served as a crushing response to the exile presence in the Irish Sea. One of Edward Bruce's first objectives may have been destruction of the sources of supply for John's fleet on the Isle. When Robert had seized

Man in 1313, he had sailed to Ulster to secure provisions and no doubt John of Argyll depended upon the same source. The wasting of Ulster, the progress of Edward Bruce through Ireland, his destruction of Dundalk and his repeated wastings of Meath must have been a source of mounting anxiety to John. Similarly the capture of Northburgh, Greencastle and above all Carrickfergus deprived John of harbours.

Furthermore the Irish expedition was one prong of a dual attack on MacDougalls. Edward's crossing to Antrim and initial victory in Ulster was complemented by a simultaneous campaign by King Robert in the west. After the Council at Ayr Robert had moved into the western Gaeltacht to take the homage of the western lords. According to Barbour, the same fleet that carried Edward to Ireland then proceeded against Argyll. Walter the Stewart accompanied the king on this expedition, just as his relative John accompanied Edward in Ireland. At Tarbert Robert established a new royal sheriffdom; and Barbour tells how he had galleys hauled over the isthmus of Tarbert, fulfilling the ancient prophecy that dominion over the Isles would come to one who made ships sail overland. Barbour's claim that 'John of Lorn' (which is his name for John of Argyll) was captured on this occasion cannot be correct; nevertheless this campaign dealt a terrible blow to MacDougall influence, for the MacDonald chief who fell with Edward Bruce at Fochart, Alexander Óg, was known as 'King of Argyll'.[120] On either side of the North Channel the brothers were co-operating to reduce MacDougall influence in Argyll and to secure the western approaches of Scotland from attack by the exiles.

IRELAND, CARLISLE AND THE ENGLISH WEST MARCH

Squeezing the MacDougalls was only one minor advantage of the invasion of Ireland; the Scots could expect to achieve more from the pressure which a Scottish presence in Ireland exerted on Carlisle. Edward's investing of Carrickfergus (around Midsummer 1315) mirrors his brother's assault on Carlisle (from 22nd July to 1st August) and, in the broader picture, the intermittent siege which was applied to Berwick after Bannockburn.[121] Long recognised as the pivotal points of war on the Anglo-Scottish border, Carlisle and Berwick dominated the western and eastern marches respectively; but the importance which the Scots attached to the capture of Carrickfergus suggests that they saw this castle in the same light, as a third English forward garrison, threatening a flank vulnerable to MacDougall influence. The author of the *Vita Edwardi II* makes the invasion of Ireland simultaneous with the siege of Carlisle; and considers a rumour of defeat in Ireland as one of the factors which persuaded Robert I to abandon the siege of Carlisle:

> A false report meanwhile spread throughout England that our army in Ireland had scattered the Scots, that Edward Bruce was dead, and that hardly one of the Scots remained alive. Hence Robert Bruce, both on account of these wild rumours and because he heard that the Earl of Pembroke had recently arrived with many men at arms, gave up the siege and set out towards Scotland.[122]

Another link between Carlisle and Ireland was the significant Irish presence on the west march, often in the shape of light cavalry or hobelars for whom employment on the Anglo-Scottish border was guaranteed.[123] During the siege of Carlisle, there were 40 Irish archers in the town; besides these, the crossbowmen in Cockermouth Castle appear to have been Irish.[124] Some of Pembroke's relieving force is likely to have been raised from his Irish estates.[125]

Ireland was also a potential source of supply for both warring kingdoms. The author of the *Vita Edwardi II* maintains that in 1315 the English blockade was creating scarcity in Scotland; a more obvious cause of dearth was perhaps the atrocious weather of that year. Whatever the cause, it is not surprising to read that in that year the earl of Moray brought back to Scotland 'four pirate ships full of the goods of the earth of Ireland', one of which sank.[126] But the overwhelming image of Edward Bruce's campaigns in Ireland is one of wholesale wastage of agricultural production. About this, too, there is nothing that surprises; it was a practice common to all armies of the day. But Edward's wastage of Irish resources weakened the resilience not only of the Anglo-Irish colony, but also of the city of Carlisle. Reports reaching the English chancery show that supplies at Carlisle were at their lowest in March and September 1315, immediately before and immediately following the Irish expedition. A state of virtual siege seems to have existed at Carlisle for some time before and after the assault of late July 1315. During the siege and for six months afterwards the gates were bricked up, and the citizens lost all access to their lands and possessions outside the walls.[127] The Bruce invasion of Ireland came, then, at a critical time for Carlisle, and one effect of the invasion was to make the supply of Carlisle difficult and dangerous. The accounts of royal receivers at Carlisle, preserved in the records of the royal wardrobe, show that the English had relied heavily upon provisions from Ireland to sustain their occupation of south-western Scotland from 1299 to 1306.[128] No receivers' accounts for the years 1307 to 1311 have been found, but the records of grain shipped to Ireland by the purveyors at Irish ports are preserved. These have been analysed by Professor Lydon, and they show that Ireland continued to supply large quantities of grain to the depot at Carlisle from 1307 until Bannockburn.[129] There was therefore no decline in the provisions forthcoming from Ireland in the years prior to the Scottish invasion, as the receivers' accounts alone might lead one to suppose. But from July 1315 to the end of 1318 neither the receivers' accounts nor the records of the Irish purveyors show that any provisions were shipped to Carlisle or anywhere else in England. Not realising how serious the situation in Ireland was, Edward II still ordered victuals to be accumulated for shipping to Carlisle and to Welsh castles; but nothing very much can have been forthcoming.[130] Rather, stores at Dublin destined for Skinburness were diverted to the provisioning of Carrickfergus, Northburgh and Dundalk, and to the fleet on the coast of Ulster.[131] During these years Carlisle had to be provisioned at great risk and expense across the privateer-infested Irish Sea, from Somerset and Dorset, Gloucestershire, Cheshire, Beaumaris, and Devon.

The cessation at Carlisle of receipts of grain from Ireland between 1315 and 1318 may be accounted for by a variety of factors, among them: the decline of Edward I's purveyance machine in the reign of his successor; the presence of Thomas Dun's privateers in the Irish Sea; the cessation of English campaigns on the west march; and of course the famine, raging in England and Ireland from 1315 to 1318. But Carlisle depended on supplies from Ireland, and the Scottish occupation of Ulster coincided with a sustained attempt to capture Carlisle. One of the benefits which Robert I expected to flow from his brother's presence in Ireland was additional leverage in his own attempts to crack the English stronghold at Carlisle.

CELTIC ALLIANCE – OR ANGLO-NORMAN ADVENTURISM?

Edward Bruce's invasion of Ireland therefore served the purposes of his brother Robert, in that it helped bring pressure on the *émigrés* threatening Scotland from the Irish Sea, and brought pressure to bear on Carlisle, a city 'hateful to the Scots'. It is quite impossible to prove that either provided any motivation for the Scottish involvement in Ireland, but most historians would agree that they could well have done. It is worth looking at another explanation, which though it is offered by medieval writers, is more difficult to credit, namely that Edward Bruce (and later Robert I in 1327) invaded Ireland with a view to intervening in Wales. It is clear from their letters to Irish and Welsh lords that the Bruces appealed to pan-celtic sentiment; and furthermore English writers and contemporaries were convinced that the Bruce invasion of Ireland was part of a wider strategy of 'Celtic Alliance'. The author of the *Vita Edwardi II* relates:

> And there was a rumour that if he [Edward Bruce] achieved his wish there [in Ireland], he would at once cross to Wales, and raise the Welsh likewise against our king. For these two races are easily roused to rebellion; they bear hardly the yoke of slavery, and curse the lordship of the English.[132]

Perhaps given the recent history of colonising the celtic countries, English authors were bound to interpret any Scottish intervention in Ireland or Wales as part of a plot to unite the celtic peoples against them.

The chain of stone castles along the coast of North Wales, still under construction, had been designed by Edward I to surround the Welsh; but Edward II also considered that they had a role in controlling the Irish Sea. Immediately upon recapturing the Isle of Man in February 1315, he gave orders that armour for 100 crossbowmen and 20 foot should be purchased in London and taken to Beaumaris, and that provisions should be sent from Ireland for the use of the chamberlain at Caernarvon.[133] The security of Man was seen as depending upon the Welsh castles; and it may also have been that the security of Wales was considered to depend upon that of Man and Ireland. Because of the arrival of the Scots in Ireland Edward II gave orders in June 1315 for Welsh castles to be provisioned and the Welsh coast to be defended. Justices of Wales were ordered to look to coastal defences.[134] After the salutary shock of Thomas Dun's raid on Holyhead in September, a commission was appointed to take precautions against the danger of invasion by the Scots. They were ordered to 'speak and treat with the people, so that if the Scottish enemies come thither, they may have no power to land'.[135] A general rising of the Welsh was to be avoided at all costs. Messengers were sent to constables and all the other ministers of the king in North Wales with gifts; and 18s. was spent on 'various men assigned by the Justice and Chamberlain to watch the sea coasts and to examine and listen in on gossip among the Welsh on account of the coming by sea of Thomas Dun the pirate, and the attacks of Scots and Irish by the same means'. This may have been in response to a petition, presumably from English settlers, which requested that the coast of Wales be well guarded against Thomas Dun and other Scottish felons, who might come from Ireland to Wales.[136] The authorities considered that trouble was brewing throughout Wales. The castles of North Wales were prepared; Beaumaris, St. Briavels, Aberconway, Hardelagh and Crukyn were all to be provisioned and made ready, and the quay of Caernarvon repaired.[137] Finally, a messenger of a 'Bishop Enadens' of Ireland was taken at Caernarvon with suspicious letters and held for 96 days in the castle; one of a number of incidents that provoked Edward II to write to Pope John XXII in March 1317 complaining that some Irish prelates were supporting the Scots.[138]

What were these letters? Richard, the bishop's messenger, may have been carrying a personal correspondence, but it is more likely that he was caught with the open letter which Edward Bruce directed to the Welsh, addressed to 'all those who desire to be delivered from servitude'. This manifesto is comparable to that written by his brother to the Irish, in respect of its claims of primeval kinship between the *Albanicus* and the *Britannicus*. But Edward's letter is more wordy, much more explicit in its invitation to rebel against the English, and contains not only a promise of military aid to the Welsh but also a less than self-sacrificing offer to assume chief lordship over them in return for such assistance.[139] Material of this sort would have been copied and circulated in Wales by Irish or Scottish travellers and traders, wherever there was a likelihood of attracting the attention of the disaffected. The manifesto used much the same terminology as that of Robert's letter to the Irish, and the themes of slavery and deliverance come across strongly:

> Since each Christian man is obliged to assist his neighbour in every difficulty, so also should those who proceed from a common root, who share the same race, ancestors, and country of origin. On that account we have now and for a long time been overwhelmed by sympathy with you in your servitude and oppression. Affronted by the vexations of the English, we are bound to attend to your plight, and, with the help of the Most High, to expel from the borders of your land with all force the unnatural and barbaric servitude imposed by the English, so that, as from earliest times, the Albanic and British people having expelled their enemies, should become one in perpetuity.
>
> Since no enemy is dispersed willingly or easily, and since the English yoke bears as heavily upon you as it did recently depress the Scottish people, we intend that by your own efforts and with our irresistible assistance, you will be able to recover your just rights and to possess peacefully your property and inheritance.[140]

Edward did not conceal that he expected a *quid pro quo*, and asked the Welsh magnates to consider whether 'you wish to commit to us the prosecution of your case and right, or indeed the chief lordship of your people, which until now your other prince [that is, Edward II] was accustomed to possess . . .' The manifesto ended with a promise that all traditional rights, inheritances and customs would be restored to the Welsh if they agreed.

This, then, was the sort of propaganda that the Bruces were putting about in Ireland and Wales, but, as Edward's offer of assistance to the Welsh, conditional upon their accepting him as Prince of Wales, suggests, the Bruces had their sights fixed firmly on their own aggrandisement. Claims to common racial origin and awareness of common language and customs among the Irish, Scots and (more rarely) Welsh were long-established themes in Gaelic and Welsh poetry, but manifestations of pan-celtic sentiment seldom occurred outside the world of literature. There was however one precedent of some importance within living memory; in 1260 the Irish king Briain Ó Néill built up a coalition of Irish kings and appealed to the Scots for assistance against the English.

Brian died in battle the following year and the rebellion was put down. More significant perhaps was the accelerating pace of conflict in the late thirteenth century between the English crown and the rulers of the celtic-speaking regions. A revival of Gaelic culture had been underway in Ireland since about the middle of the thirteenth century with a growing tendency among Anglo-Irish lords to show interest in and adopt the customs of the Gaelic Irish.[141] The Bruces were familiar with the Gaelic world; and, while they themselves had more in common with the Red Earl of Ulster and his peers than with the petty kings of the Gaeltacht, it may have seemed natural to their Irish allies to cast their struggle against the English in terms of Gaedhil against Gall.

The Bruces may be seen exploiting pan-celtic sentiment wherever they felt they could turn it to their advantage. There is no mistaking the excitement which the Scots invasion of Ireland stirred up among the Gaelic Irish. On arrival Edward was aided by the Irish of Ulster and Uriel. In the autumn of 1315 the Irish of far away Desmond were in rebellion because of the coming of the Scots. Edward's campaign of 1316 in Leinster clearly involved wide co-operation with native chiefs. Yet Edward Bruce had as many Gaelic enemies as allies. He was welcomed by several kings in Ulster, but was treacherously attacked by 'Makgullane' and 'Makartane'. Barbour seems to indicate that many of the Scots felt shoddily treated by Domnall Ó Néill's failure to provide adequate supplies for them. While in Ireland the brothers seem to have seriously underestimated the factional strife that pervaded the Gaeltacht. Twice the Scots were inveigled into participation in the struggles of rival Gaelic factions. Edward was manipulated by factions of the Ó Conchobairs who each sought his support in 1315; and in 1317 both he and Robert were diverted far to the west by the promises of an Ó Briain faction. These instances, in which the Bruces expected to find and exploit commitment to an anti-English crusade in Ireland, show how foreign to them were the shifting alliances and all-absorbing local conflicts of the Gaeltacht. As Professor Frame points out, 'Political fragmentation and disputed successions had a long history and a long future' and bedevilled the Bruce's attempt to form a broad alliance against the English.[142]

No doubt the same fragmentation would have stymied any Bruce intervention in Wales. But there are aspects of the invasion of Ireland that are difficult to account for unless by reference to a strategy involving Wales as well as Ireland. In February 1316 the rebellion of Llywelyn Bren erupted in Glamorgan, the result of famine, of instability proceeding from the death of the earl of Gloucester at Bannockburn, and of deep-seated grievances against the English.[143] The coincidence of this revolt with Edward Bruce's winter campaign in Ireland is striking, and the idea that the Bruces in Ireland and Britain were working to pre-arranged times affords a tempting explanation of this midwinter campaign and their indecent haste to conquer Ireland. The text of a reply to Edward Bruce's manifesto survives, written by the Welsh magnate Gruffydd Llwyd. It is couched in the same rhetoric as Edward's manifesto, professing common racial origins and common hatred of the English. Llwyd states that if Edward were to come to Wales, or if he were to send someone with even a few men, then the nobles of Wales would all be prepared to join him. Llwyd was arrested in December 1316, and his son removed to the English court.[144]

In practical terms the evidence amounts only to a Scottish interest in keeping the Welsh pot boiling. There is no evidence of Scottish involvement in the rebellion of Llywelyn Bren; and evidence for the Scottish interest in Wales amounts only to the raid of Thomas Dun in 1315, and Edward's manifesto, 'a typical piece of Bruce fishing in troubled waters'.[145] When Robert I returned to Ireland in 1327 and 1328, he appears to pay much more attention to winning over Anglo-Irish allies than Gaelic Irish. Yet the idea that the Bruces actively sought a 'celtic alliance' embracing Welsh as well as Irish cannot be dismissed until it is known quite why Edward Bruce felt the need to campaign in Ireland in the bleak winter of 1315–16; why the Scots were in such a hurry to conquer Ireland from 1315 onwards; and what it was that attracted first Edward, then Edward and Robert together, to the south-east of Ireland. At a time when Scottish raids in England were increasingly purposeful, deliberate, and beginning to be aimed at the achievement of very specific objectives, it is difficult to credit that Edward Bruce, and Moray and Robert I, were floundering aimlessly in Ireland.

THE KINGSHIP OF EDWARD BRUCE

It has been pointed out that the Scottish intervention in Ireland served the purposes of Robert I, and also that the Scots were reacting to events and dangers in the Irish Sea. Yet Edward Bruce's desire for conquest, martial glory and a throne was probably the most powerful motivation for the invasion of Ireland. Edward must surely rank as one of the great opportunists of history, and his pride, arrogance and ambition were all noted by chroniclers. Barbour praises Edward's hardiness, but claims that, in contrast to Robert, he lacked 'measure', or prudence. Fordun hints at bad feeling between Robert and Edward:

> The cause of this [Irish] war was this. Edward was a very mettlesome and high-spirited man, and would not dwell together with his brother in peace unless he had half the kingdom for himself, and for this reason war was stirred up in Ireland.[146]

Edward's actions are those of a man possessed by ambition to achieve kingly status. He wrote to the nobles of Wales asking to be made Prince of Wales; he is said to have addressed a similar letter to the nobles of Ireland; and he also sought dominion over the Western Isles.[147] In Ireland he was successful in gaining a degree of recognition and was addressed as King of Ireland on 30th September 1316 by his brother, and at an uncertain date by Domnall Ó Néill.[148] Edward II of course made no acknowledgement of such claims; but his elevation of Edmund Butler to Edward Bruce's own title 'Earl of Carrick' before November 1316 may have been a deliberate scorning of Bruce's adoption of the grandiose title 'King of Ireland'.[149]

Were the date of his inauguration known for certain; it would help identify the priorities of the Scots in Ireland. If after the invasion a year or two elapsed before Edward assumed the title, this would indicate that the motivation was military or logistical and that Edward's ambition was subordinate to the purposes of Robert I; it might also lend weight to the idea that the Scots were being drawn into Ireland by degrees. If, as seems more likely, it took place shortly after the landing, it would support the idea that the initiative came from Scotland, from Edward Bruce himself, and that he was embarked upon a war of conquest and hellbent on becoming a king. A time early in the expedition seems to be most probable. Native annals all agree in placing the inauguration in the year 1315. The *Annals of Connacht, Loch Cé* and *Clonmacnoise*, all working from the same source, describe it as follows:

> ... [Edward] then burned Ardee and took the hostages and lordship of the whole Province without opposition, and the Ulstermen consented to his being proclaimed King of Ireland and all the Gaels of Ireland agreed to grant him lordship and they called him King of Ireland.[150]

Only the Laud Annals, in its entry for the year 1315, offers a more precise date, 'very soon after the feast of Saints Philip and James [1st May]'.[151] But Edward Bruce was not in Ireland on 1st May 1315; he had arrived only on 26th May. This has led some authors to conclude that Edward was inaugurated on 1st May in the following year, 1316 (despite the annals including it under 1315). Duncan has another suggestion: that the feast originally intended was not that of Philip and James, but that of Philip the Deacon (6th June).[152] This timing would allow the inauguration to coincide broadly with an early submission to Edward made by Irish kings of Ulster mentioned in the Barbour narrative.

But it is the settlement of the succession to the Scottish throne, agreed at Ayr in 1315 (just before the expedition sailed), that confirms the Scottish intervention as motivated primarily by conquest and by Edward's ambition. It suggests that the Scots had agreed among themselves that Edward would become King of Ireland.[153] While Robert's queen was a prisoner in England, Edward had stood a fair chance of becoming King of Scotland. But following the release of Queen Elizabeth in January 1315, Robert could expect an heir; and Edward's chances of succeeding in Scotland were suddenly diminished. The royal tailzie (or entail) of 1315 settled the succession on King Robert's heirs male; and only if Robert failed to have a son would Edward succeed to the throne. Furthermore, if Robert were to die leaving an infant son, the regent was not to be Edward, but Moray. Both Edward and Moray were leaving for Ireland, but the tailzie implies that Edward was expected to be permanently absent from Scotland. Finally, relations between Edward and Robert, or perhaps Edward and Moray, may not have been cordial. Edward's pride and arrogance loom large in Barbour.[154] Among Anglo-Norman families it was often the burning ambition of all younger brothers to acquire lands and titles equal to those of the first-born. Barbour and Fordun are in no doubt that it was Edward's personal ambition to become a king that was responsible for the extension of the war to Ireland. Edward had clearly been culpable in alienating David Earl of Atholl on the eve of Bannockburn. It is remarkable too that, leading up to the siege of Carlisle, King Robert should not require the earl of Carrick and lord of Galloway to assist in the assault on the city. The kingship of Ireland would both compensate Edward for the loss of his hopes to succeed in Scotland, and might have had the further advantage from Robert's point of view of removing an awkward personality from a crucial theatre of war. For all these reasons, then, it appears that the intervention in Ireland may have been propelled by internal Scottish considerations. The early date of Edward's inauguration has further implications. It suggests that Edward's kingly ambitions were as significant in prompting the invasion as any strategic design. It also points to a strong impulse for expansion from Scotland, rather than to a response to any pressing invitation from Irish magnates; and it means that the Scots were bent upon outright conquest of the country rather than limited strategic aims and objectives.

In the sources the inauguration is mentioned, but not described by Barbour or any of the annalists. From Anglo-Irish and Gaelic perspectives alike, Armagh's ecclesiastical importance and regalian associations make it a likely location for the event. One source mentions Armagh in the itinerary of the Scots from Iniskeen to Coleraine.[155] At an uncertain date Domnall Ó Néill made a confirmation of privileges to the Archbishop, Dean and Chapter of Armagh, citing 'Edward King of Ireland' as guarantor, and since 'King of Ireland' was not a title ever used by Edward II, this can only refer to Edward Bruce. The document suggests that Edward Bruce was an acceptable intermediary and (perhaps) that his regal status was accepted by both parties.[156] Probably at such a place as Armagh a deal was struck between Edward Bruce and Domnall Ó Néill, enlisting the Scots as Ó Néill's allies against the Red Earl; in return for which Edward Bruce was acclaimed King of Ireland. The essential elements common to both Scottish and Irish inaugurations would probably have been observed: the placing of the king on a ceremonial stone, recitation of genealogy, acclamation by the assembly and ratification by the clergy. Coronation of course was unknown in either country at this date.

In all probability, the Gaelic Irish reacted to the arrival of the Scots in much the same fashion as their compatriots of 150 years before had reacted to the coming of Henry II and King John.[157] Desperate to win the powerful invaders to their side, and anxious to use them against their neighbours, they swore every oath, made every promise. Falling over one another in the rush to acquire the Scots as allies in local struggles, they might readily have conceded Edward's claims to overkingship or superior lordship. There are sources which suggest an invitation from the Gaelic Irish; indeed, if such an invitation was not spontaneous, Edward Bruce would have been able to procure one with the same ease that he procured an invitation from the Welsh.[158] The 'Remonstrance of the Irish Princes' written on behalf of Domnall Ó Néill illustrates the point. This document, addressed to the newly elected Pope John XXII and dated to summer or autumn of 1317, recites a list of oppressions by the English and invokes papal approval for redress against them. It is accepted (though not without misgivings) as a genuine text rather than a fourteenth-century forgery. It is thought to have been written both to take advantage of the presence of the two cardinals in England, and to undermine the success of the English envoys at the papal court. It is of Irish provenance, although it survives only in a Scottish source and may have been composed under Scottish influence or transmitted to the papal court *via* Scottish envoys.[159] Contained in the Remonstrance is a declaration that Edward Bruce has been acclaimed as King of Ireland:

> And in order to achieve our aim more swiftly and more fitly in this matter, we call to our help and assistance the illustrious Edward de Bruce earl of Carrick, the brother of the lord Robert by the grace of God the most illustrious king of Scots, and sprung from our noblest ancestors. And as each person is free to give up his right and transfer it to another, all the right which is recognised to pertain to us in the said kingdom as its true heirs we have given and granted to him by our letter patent so that he may dispense judgement with justice and equity there, which, as a result of the inadequacy of the prince have utterly failed there. We have unanimously established him as our king and lord, and set him over us in our aforesaid kingdom . . .

This is very gracious lip service. As the royal visits to Ireland by Henry II, John and Richard II demonstrate, Gaelic lords had no qualms about conceding grand titles to powerful allies, for overkingship had almost no meaning amid the constantly shifting local alliances that prevailed in Gaelic Ireland, where no allegiance was for ever. The text of the Remonstrance itself illustrates this, as some paragraphs further on it turns out to be a most comprehensive statement of Ó Néill regality, claiming for Domnall Ó Néill lineal descent from 136 kings 'without admixture of alien blood'.

Edward Bruce's inauguration cut little ice with the annalists, and probably less with his Gaelic allies. In the climate of ever-shifting alliances and temporary allegiances which prevailed in Gaelic Ireland, Edward Bruce's Kingship of Ireland cannot have meant very much outside Ulster; but it seems to have been of crucial importance to the Scots. King Robert may have had a vision of allied neighbouring monarchies, bound by ties of blood. But the sense that Edward Bruce had been something of a liability in Scotland runs strong in Barbour; and Robert may have been relieved to see the back of him. The invasion of Ireland, however, still served Robert's immediate and long-term aims: pursuit of the MacDougalls and the other Scottish *émigrés*; destruction of Ulster as a source of supply for Man and for the English west march; and the capture of Carrickfergus as a step towards controlling the whole of the Irish Sea. The motives behind the Scottish invasion of Ireland were probably very mixed.

It is not quite accurate to say that Edward's stirring up of trouble in Ireland provided a diversion in support of Robert's own offensives, since campaigns in both theatres never coincided. Nor can it be said that the English were forced to divert resources to Ireland; for the colony patently received very little help. Scottish failure in Ireland stands in contrast to success in Britain. Whereas long-range raids of the Scots into the relatively prosperous north of England enriched the Scots at the expense of their enemies, expeditions into relatively impoverished and war-ridden Ireland could never compete in terms of plunder or chivalric lustre. But the failure of the Irish adventure should not be taken for granted; by all accounts the Scots came close to conquering Ireland; and Scottish involvement in Ireland may indirectly have contributed to success in Britain. The occupation of Ulster for three years (a considerable achievement in years of famine) no doubt assisted in anchoring the Bruce regime by taking the war to the MacDougalls and their allies. However, support for the Gaelic Irish tended to alienate the Anglo-Irish who controlled that part of the country most relevant to Bruce ambitions. The administrations of Westminster and Dublin both recognised this and took critical steps to secure the allegiance of the Anglo-Irish lords. The Bruces would have done better to drop the pan-celtic rhetoric, appeal instead to Anglo-Irish lords, and thus maintain a presence on the east coast. Instead of fighting the Red Earl, they should have been wooing him and his peers to their cause. Moreover, the capture of sea ports ought to have been a priority.

From Westminster the presence of a Scottish army in the north of Ireland was uncomfortable and threatening; but the capture of Dublin might have given the Bruces sufficient diplomatic leverage to impose a peace upon England.

NOTES

1 Besides Barbour, *The Bruce* XIV, XV, 1–266 and XVIII, the most reliable narrative source is the Laud Annals in *Chartularies of St. Mary's Abbey, Dublin*, ii, 303–98. Other narratives include: *The Annals of Connacht*, ed. A.M. Freeman (Dublin, 1944) [*Ann. Connacht*]; *The Annals of Clonmacnoise*, ed. D. Murphy (Dublin, 1896) [*Ann. Clonmacnoise*]; *The Annals of Inisfallen*, ed. S. Mac Airt (Dublin, 1951) [*Ann. Inisfallen*]; *The Annals of Loch Cé*, ed. W.M. Hennessy, (2 vols.) (R.S., 1871) [*Ann. Loch Cé*]; *The Annals of Ireland by Friar John Clyn and Thady Dowling*, ed. R. Butler (Dublin, 1849) [*Clyn*]; and *Jacobi Grace, Kilkenniensis, Annales Hiberniae*, ed. R. Butler (Irish Archaeological Society, 1842) [*Grace*].

2 Phillips, 'Documents'; Sayles, *Affairs of Ireland*; Gilbert, *Hist. Mun. Docs.* One text has been unmasked as a forgery: S. Duffy, 'The Gaelic Account of The Bruce Invasion, *Cath Fhochairte Brighite*: Medieval Romance or Modern Forgery', *Seanchas Ard Macha* xiii (1988), 59–121; and there is doubt as to the authenticity of another: D. O'Murchadha, 'Is the O'Neill–MacCarthy Letter of 1317 a Forgery?', *IHS* xxiii (1982–83), 61–67.

3 The modern starting point is R. Frame, 'The Bruces in Ireland, 1315–18', *IHS* xix (1974), 3–37. Since then: J.F. Lydon, 'The Impact of the Bruce Invasion', *NHI* ii, 275–302; Duncan, 'Scots Invasion', pp. 100–17; and Duffy, 'Bruce Brothers', pp. 55–86.

4 See above p. 37.

5 *Ann. Clonmacnoise*, p. 275 (1315).

6 *Chart. St. Mary's Dublin* ii, 358.

7 *Ann. Clonmacnoise*, p. 282; *Ann. Connacht*, p. 253.

8 *Ann. Connacht*, p. 233.

9 *Reports of the Deputy Keeper of the Public Records of Ireland* xxxix (1907), 65.

10 *Fordun* ii, 340; *Bower* vi, 381; *Pluscarden* ii, 186.

11 Frame makes this point with regard to the decision by Edward Bruce to campaign during the winter of 1316, 'The Bruces in Ireland', p. 11, n. 35.

12 J.F. Lydon, 'Edward II and the Revenues of Ireland in 1311–12', *IHS* xiv (1964), 39–49, Appendix pp. 56–57; *NHI* ii, 275–76.

13 P. Connolly, 'List of Irish entries on the Memoranda Rolls of the English Exchequer, 1307–27', *Analecta Hibernica* xxxvi (Irish Manuscripts Commission, 1995), no. 51, p. 184.

14 E101/237/2 and E372/166, m.26. Fourteen of the garrison are named on NAI KB2/7, pp. 31–32.

15 *CCR 1313–18*, p. 218; NAI RC8/7, p. 760. Professor Phillips suggested this as the occasion for Robert's letter to the kings, prelates, clergy and inhabitants of Ireland, 'Mission of John de Hothum' *England*

and Ireland in the Later Middle Ages ed. J.F. Lyndon (Dublin 1981), pp. 66–67.

16 *Rot. Scot.*, i, 138–39, 143–44.

17 *NHI* ii, 282; *Grace*, p. 63 gives the location as 'Glondonne'. None of these locations is far from Carrickfergus, *CDS* iii no. 216, p. 44.

18 Larne had been the rendezvous for the Anglo-Irish fleet of 1311, *CDS* v nos. 557, 559, 560, 563, 564.

19 G.W.S. Barrow and A. Royan, 'James Fifth Stewart of Scotland', in *Essays on the Nobility of Medieval Scotland*, ed. K.J. Stringer (Edinburgh, 1985), pp. 167–69. Barbour, *The Bruce* XIV, 23–32 mentions also Ramsay of Ouchtirhouse, and *Grace*, p. 63, 'the Earl of Menteith' (which might be a mistake for John of Menteith, who was closely associated with the Stewarts), John Bosco, and John Bisset.

20 John Bisset of Antrim received a commission from Edward II in March 1315, *Rot. Scot.* i, 139.

21 Duffy, 'Continuation of Trivet', p. 308; *Ann. Connacht*, p. 249.

22 J.R. Greeves, 'Robert I and the De Mandevilles of Ulster', *TDGNHAS* (3rd Ser.) xxxiv (1955–56), 60; Phillips, 'Documents', no. 8, pp. 257–58; Barbour, *The Bruce* XIV, 46–60; *Clyn*, p. 12: 'almost all the Irish of the land' of Ulster adhered to the Scots.

23 *Vita Edwardi II*, p. 61; Phillips, 'Documents', nos. 15, 16; *Clyn*, p. 12: 'almost all the Irish of the land' adhered to the Scots.

24 See above p. 80.

25 Barbour, *The Bruce* XIV, 97–98.

26 *Ann. Connacht*, p. 231; *Ann. Loch Cé*, i, 563.

27 E101/237/4, m. 1.

28 E101/237/5, m. 5; *Chart. St. Mary's Dublin* ii, 345; Duncan, 'Scots' Invasion', p. 105.

29 Barbour, *The Bruce* XIV, 101–12; Phillips, 'Documents', no. 8, pp. 257–58. The placename 'Innermallane' or 'Inderwillane' is generally used to refer to the Moiry Pass, between Newry and Dundalk. The former personal name may indicate Colman Megulhan whom Edward II thanked in 1319 (see p. 186), the latter is surely MacArtaín.

30 *Chart. St. Mary's Dublin* ii, 345 ; Barbour, *The Bruce* XIV, 224–32; *Clyn*, p. 12; E101/237/4, m. 1, £46 paid to attorneys of the town 'recently robbed and burned by the Scots', for its rebuilding and repair.

31 Duncan, 'Scots Invasion', p. 107; *Ann. Clonmacnoise*, p. 268; *Ann. Inisfallen*, p. 419.

32 Barbour does refer to Butler, but not to de Burgh; however, he consistently names Edward Bruce's arch-opponent in Ireland as 'Richard de Clare'. This was the name of an Anglo-Irish magnate who fought Bruce in Ireland, but he was not one of the lordship's leading magnates.

33 Phillips, 'Documents', no. 18, pp. 264–65.

34 *Ann. Clonmacnoise*, p. 269.

35 NAI KB2/7, pp. 58–59. Printed in D. Mac Iomhair, 'Bruce's Invasion and the First Campaign in County Louth', *Irish Sword* x (1971–72), 201.

36 Phillips, 'Documents', nos. 18, 9,

37 Phillips, 'Documents', no. 17, pp. 263–64. *Ann. Clonmacnoise*, p. 269; *Ann. Connacht*, p. 233.

38 PRONI DIO 4/2/2, f. 39.

39 *Ann. Inisfallen*, pp. 419–20.

40 Barbour, *The Bruce* XIV, 329–66; *Ann. Inisfallen*, pp. 419–21; Frame, 'Bruces in Ireland', p. 22.

41 *Ann. Clonmacnoise*, pp. 269–70.

42 *Ann. Inisfallen*, p. 419; *Ann. Connacht.*, pp. 233–34; *Ann. Loch Cé* i, 567.

43 Phillips, 'Documents', no.17, pp. 263–65.

44 Barbour, *The Bruce* XIV, 383–XV, 85; *Chart. St. Mary's Dublin* ii, 346; *Ann. Clonmacnoise*, pp. 271; *Ann. Inisfallen*, p. 421.

45 *Chart. St. Mary's Dublin* ii, 346; see above p. 78.

46 Phillips, 'Documents', no. 14, pp. 261–62.

47 Phillips, 'Documents', nos. 8, 14.

48 C260/60, no. 9 (dated to 1344).

49 *Chart. St. Mary's Dublin*, ii, 347.

50 The 'Rodel ship' may have been broadly representative of the vessels available to Thomas Dun, *Late Medieval Monumental Sculpture in the West Highlands*, K.A. Steer and J.M.W. Bannerman (Royal Commission on the Ancient and Historical Monuments of Scotland, 1977), pp. 180–84 and plates 16, 32 [Plate].

51 Phillips, 'Mission of John de Hothum', p. 67; *Rot. Scot.* i, 139, 144, 136.

52 *Rot. Scot.*, i, 146–48; *CPR 1313–17*, p. 333.

53 Connolly, 'Irish Entries on the Memoranda Rolls', pp. 196–97.The *Aliceot* of Bristol by 14th February 1316 had served half a year in Irish waters, NAI RC 8/10, pp. 532–33, 539–40.

54 *CCR 1313–18*, pp. 252–53.

55 *Rot. Scot.* i, 173

56 *CDS* iii, no. 451, p. 84; *CPR 1313–17*, p. 421.

57 Society of Antiquaries, MS 121, f. 29; *Clyn*, p. 13; Phillips, 'Documents', no. 20, p. 267.

58 Barbour, *The Bruce*, XIV, 381; *Chart. St. Mary's Dublin* ii, 346.

59 *CDS* iii, no. 450, p. 84.

60 *CDS* iii no. 912, p. 166.

61 Phillips, 'Documents', p. 267; Phillips, 'The Mission of John de Hothum to Ireland, 1315–16', p. 68. The term *satellite* often denotes native soldiery, in this case Welsh or Irish troops.

62 *Chart. St. Mary's Dublin* ii, 346; Phillips, 'Documents', no. 21, pp. 268–69.

63 Phillips, 'Documents', nos. 15, 16.

64 NAI KB2/8, p. 44; NAI KB2/7, p. 21.

65 Phillips, 'Mission of John de Hothum,' pp. 68, 71, 73.

66 *Chart. St. Mary's Dublin* ii, 347.

67 Phillips, 'Documents', pp. no. 7, pp. 255–57; 'Mission of John de Hothum,' pp. 69–70.

68 *Chart. St. Mary's Dublin* ii, 347; Frame, 'Bruces in Ireland', pp. 20–23; *Hist. Mun. Docs.* no. XCVII, pp. 456–62; Sayles, *Affairs of Ireland*, nos. 127 and 128.

69 SC8/004 (184), calendared in P. Connolly, 'Irish material in the Class of Ancient Petitions (SC8) in the Public Record Office London', *Analecta Hibernica* xxxiv (1987), pp. 7, 50; *Chart. St. Mary's Dublin* ii, 349; Duncan, *RRS* v no. 101, comment, p. 379.

70 *Chart. St. Mary's Dublin* ii, 349; P. Connolly, 'Irish material in the Class of Chancery Warrants Series (C81) in the Public Record Office London', *Analecta Hibernica* xxxvi (1995), p. 47.

71 Frame, 'Bruces in Ireland', p. 11, n. 35.

72 *Chart. St. Mary's Dublin* ii, 349.

73 NAI RC 8/10, pp. 552, 553–54, 570.

74 G.O. Sayles, 'The Siege of Carrickfergus Castle, 1315–16', *IHS* (1956–57), 94–100; NAI RC 8/10, pp. 651–52, 553–54, 581–82, 610; *Barbour, The Bruce* XV, 101–242; *Chart. St. Mary's Dublin* ii, 296–97, 350. Mandeville's body was the subject of a legal fracas between the Friars Minor of Carrickfergus and the Friars Preachers of Drogheda, *Calendar of Papal Letters, 1305–42*, p. 171. John MacNakill appears to have been a brother of Donald of Islay, *Rot. Scot.* i, 139.

75 *Chart. St. Mary's Dublin*, ii 297.

76 *Chart. St. Mary's Dublin*, ii 296; NAI RC 8/10, p. 570, 581–82.

77 Sayles, 'Siege of Carrickfergus', pp. 97–100.

78 Duncan, *RRS* v, no. 101, pp. 378–79.

79 E101/237/4; and E101/237/5 and /6. £4,000 had been assigned to Balscote by the Council of Lincoln, but the £578 was all that was forthcoming from the revenues of the colony, *NHI* ii, 290.

80 NAI RC 8/10, pp. 613, 651–52.

81 *CPR 1313–17*, p. 603; Fryde, 'Antonio Pessagno', p. 174.

82 Connolly, 'Irish Entries on the Memoranda Rolls', p. 189.

83 Duncan, *RRS* v, no. 101, pp. 378–79.

84 Frame, 'Bruces in Ireland', pp. 29–31; E372/166, m. 26.

85 *CPR 1313–17*, pp. 563, 574.

86 *Chart. St. Mary's Dublin*, ii 352–53; Barbour, *The Bruce* XVI, 63, places the start of this campaign in May probably for literary effect; O. Armstrong, *Edward Bruce's Invasion of Ireland* (London, 1923), pp. 101–2.

87 R. Frame, 'The Campaign against the Scots in Munster', *IHS* xxiv (1985), 361–72.

88 *Ann. Inisfallen*, pp. 425–7; *Clyn*, p. 13.

89 *CCW 1244–1326*, p. 461

90 *CPR 1313–17*, p. 632.

91 *Cathreim Thoirdhealbhaigh*, ed. S.H. O'Grady (Irish Texts Society, 1929), ii, 83–84. For discussion of this text and of the political situation in Thomond, see A. Nic Ghiollanhaith, 'Dynastic Warfare and Historical Writing in North Munster, 1276–1350', *Cambridge Medieval Celtic Studies* ii (1981), 73–90.

92 Duncan, *RRS* v, Introduction, p.140; *Rot. Scot.* i, 170.

93 Society of Antiquaries, MS 120, f.42; MS 121, ff. 25, 25d; *CPR 1313–17*, pp. 693–94.

94 C81/100(4219), calendared in *CDS* iii, no. 549, p. 106.

95 *Chart. St. Mary's Dublin* ii, 355; Society of Antiquaries, MS 121, f. 29.

96 Duncan, *RRS* v p. 379; *CDS* iii nos. 636, 637.

97 *Hist. Mun. Docs.*, pp. 352–53; *Chart. St. Mary's Dublin* ii, 357–58.

98 *Hist. Mun. Docs.*, pp. 442–43.

99 *Chart. St. Mary's Dublin* ii, 359.

100 Philip de Mowbray did not die at Fochart, Duncan, *RRS* v 'Introduction', p. 146; and John Stewart was reported to have died already at Connor

in September 1315, see p. 174 above. A full analysis of the lists of the 'fallen' is contained in the Duffy 'Continuation of Nicholas Trevet', pp. 309–12. See also Duffy, 'Bruce Brothers', pp. 73–74.

101 *Clyn*, p. 14; *Walsingham* i, 154; Connolly, 'Irish material in the Class of Ancient Petitions', pp. 29, 31, 33, 34, 37; *Reports of the Deputy Keeper of the Public Records of Ireland*, xlii, 13.

102 Barbour, *The Bruce* XVIII, 20–68.

103 *Ann. Clonmacnoise*, pp. 281–82.

104 *Lanercost*, pp. 225–6.

105 Duffy, 'Continuation of Nicholas Trevet', pp. 307–12; *Chart. St. Mary's Dublin* ii, 359–60; Sayles, *Affairs of Ireland* no. 143, p. 105.

106 Duffy, 'Bruce Brothers', p. 72.

107 *CPR 1317–21*, pp. 334–35.

108 BL MS Add. 9951, f. 17; *CPR 1317–21*, p. 313.

109 *CCR 1318–23*, p. 127, identified in K. Muhr, *Place Names of Northern Ireland (Vol. vi): North-West Co. Down from Rathfriland to Moira* (forthcoming), p. 10.

110 Sayles, *Affairs of Ireland* no. 144, pp. 105–6.

111 Connolly, 'Irish Entries on the Memoranda Rolls', p. 195.

112 *CPR 1321–24*, p. 126.

113 *CCR 1307–13*, p. 205; *CDS* iii nos. 95, 132, 157.

114 *CDS* iii no. 421, p. 80. The men of Bruce's garrison are all named. They included Henry le Welbe and John le Masoun of Carlingford, NAI KB2/7, pp. 31–32.

115 *CDS* iii no. 479, p. 92; E101/237/2, m. 2; E101/237/6.

116 *CDS* iii nos. 84.

117 E101/378/4, f.13d.

118 *CDS* iii nos. 423, 647, 649.

119 *CDS* iii no. 521, p. 99.

120 Barbour, *The Bruce* XV, 266–318, though the claim that 'John of Lorn' was captured on this expedition is untrue. Duncan, *RRS* v, Introduction, pp.136–7; Barrow, *Robert Bruce*, pp. 291–92.

121 Phillips, 'Documents', nos. 2, 3, 6, 19, draws attention to the persistent linkage in sources between affairs at Berwick and in Ireland.

122 *Vita Edwardi II*, pp. 61–62.

123 See above pp. 155–56.

124 E101/14/31, Schedule 2, 1.

125 E101/237/4, m. 1; Phillips, *Aymer de Valence*, p. 91, n. 4.

126 *Vita Edwardi II*, p. 60; *Chart. St. Mary's Dublin* ii, 346.

127 *CDS* iii no. 621, p. 117.

128 See Charts 5 and 6, p. 127.

129 J.F. Lydon, 'Ireland's Participation in the Military Activities of the English Kings in the Thirteenth and Fourteenth Century' (University of London Ph. D. thesis, 1955), pp. 281, 284, 290, 297.

Period	Quarters Wheat	Quarters Oats
1308–09	530	947
1310	642	428
1311	1377	
1312	400	
1314	702	360

It is however not a simple matter to reconcile dispatches from Irish ports with receipts at Carlisle. Periods of account differ, not all the supplies dispatched reached Carlisle, and it has not been possible to incorporate this information into Charts 5 and 6.

130 Lydon, 'Ireland's Participation', pp. 305–6.
131 *CDS* iii no. 479, p. 92; *Chart. St. Mary's Dublin* ii, 296; E101/237/2, m. 4; E101/237/4, /5.
132 *Vita Edwardi II*, p. 61.
133 *CCR 1313–18*, pp. 147, 148.
134 Beverley Smith, 'Gruffydd Llwyd and the Celtic Alliance', pp. 463–67.
135 *Calendar of Ancient Correspondence Concerning Wales*, ed. J.G. Edwards (Cardiff, 1935), no. LV.31, pp. 253–54.
136 SC6/1211/9, m3; Connolly, 'Irish material in the Class of Ancient Petitions', p. 58.
137 Beverley Smith, 'Gruffydd Llwyd and the Celtic Alliance', pp. 463–65.
138 SC6/1211/9; *Foedera* ii (I), 318–19. Beverley Smith considers that 'Bishop Enadens' might have been the Irish-speaking Bishop of Annaghdown, 'Edward II and the Allegiance of Wales', *Welsh Historical Review* viii (1976–77), 152.
139 *RRS* v, 695, no. 571, pp. 700–1, and J. Beverley Smith, 'Gryffyd Llwyd and the Celtic Alliance' 1315–18, *Bulletin of the British Board of Celtic Studies* xxvi (1976), 477–78, where the reply is also printed.
140 An extract from the letter printed in full by Beverley Smith, 'Gruffydd Llwyd and the Celtic Alliance, 1315–18', p. 478 and by Duncan, *RRS* v no. 571, pp. 700–1.
141 Duffy, 'Bruce Brothers', pp. 68–69, 79; Lydon, 'A Land of War', *NHI* ii, 241–43.
142 Frame, 'The Bruces in Ireland', pp. 16–25 is still the best treatment of the Gaelic reaction, but it contains references to sources now considered to be forgeries.
143 R.A. Griffiths, *Conquerors and Conquered in Medieval Wales* (Stroud, 1994), pp. 84–91; R.R. Davies, *Conquest, Coexistence and Change* (Oxford, 1987), pp. 387–88, 435. *Trokelowe*, p. 92, considers that the Welsh revolt was sparked off by the Scottish success at Bannockburn.
144 Beverley Smith, 'Gruffydd Llwyd and the Celtic Alliance', pp. 463–67 and 477–78.
145 Duncan's comment on the letter in Beverley Smith, 'Gruffydd Llwyd and the Celtic Alliance', p. 474, n. 2.
146 Barbour *The Bruce* IX, 666–76; *Fordun* ii, 340.
147 Duffy, 'Continuation of Trevet,' pp. 308, 314.
148 Duncan, *RRS* v no. 101, pp. 378–79.
149 *CPR 1313–17*, p. 536.
150 *Ann. Connacht*, p. 231. Compare *Ann. Loch Cé*, p. 565, *Ann. Clonmacnoise*, p. 276.
151 *Chart. St. Mary's Dublin* ii, 345.
152 Duncan, 'Scots' Invasion', p. 109.
153 Duncan, 'Scots' Invasion', p. 113.
154 Barbour, *The Bruce*, IX, 480–95, 661–71; Barrow, *Robert Bruce*, pp. 293–94.
155 *Ann. Inisfallen*, p. 416.

156 PRONI DIO 4/2/2, f. 39, dated to this period by K. Simms, 'The Archbishops of Armagh and the Ó Néills, 1347–1471', *IHS* xix (1974), 38–55.
157 F.X. Martin, 'Overlord becomes feudal lord', *NHI* ii, 89–91.
158 Phillips, 'Documents', no. 14, pp. 261–62, Appendix, pp. 269–70
159 *Bower* vi, 385–403. See J.R.S. Phillips, 'The Irish Remonstrance of 1317: an International Perspective', *IHS* xxvii (1990), 112–29. *Bower* vi, Introduction, pp. xxi-xxiv contains another valuable discussion of the Remonstrance. Michael MacLochlainn, Franciscan friar and unsuccessful candidate for the see of Armagh in 1307 is the putative author.

CHAPTER SIX

The North Sea Theatre of War and the Towns

'And now lately many are leaving the town, and those who stay die in anguish from starvation on the walls . . .'
'. . . scarcely anyone dared to stay in Northumbria, unless by a castle or a walled town'

Though insignificant by today's standards in terms of population, towns played a crucial role in determining the course and nature of the Wars of the Bruces. They were concentrations of wealth, foodstuffs and materials and often of shipping, invaluable to either side for the conduct of war on any scale. Many of the towns of Britain had originated as strongholds of strategic significance.[1] Berwick and Carlisle had long been recognised as important strategic positions, controlling coastal routes to and from Scotland. But by 1306 their economic importance had grown appreciably. Carlisle functioned as the chief market town of river valleys leading to the Solway, Berwick as a thriving outlet for the wool and hide exports of south-east Scotland. Newcastle upon Tyne was an even larger population centre and a busy port; and York was now a city of 10,000 souls, a regional centre of secular and ecclesiastical authority. While it had remained in distant parts of Scotland, the war may have stimulated urban economies, but as the war zone crept closer, the hinterlands upon which these towns depended suffered from flight of tenantry or war damage, and commercial activity declined. Only marginal benefits such as weapons manufacture remained; supply of magnate households and garrisons which could not be relied upon to pay brought only ruin. All of the towns mentioned had to endure threats to security; all had to construct or maintain defences. Many experienced friction between townsfolk and the garrisons employed to defend them. Many, too, harboured fears of betrayal, which exacerbated internal jealousies and divisions. The ports on the east coast of Britain were perhaps in the most difficult position of all; besides experiencing all the traumas described above, they were also menaced by the war at sea, which destabilised the wool and hide export trades upon which they depended.

THE NORTH SEA FROM 1307

England and Scotland alike relied upon the North Sea traffic to carry exports, especially wool to the cloth manufacturing towns of Flanders. For Robert I, Aberdeen, Perth, Dundee and later Berwick were vital harbours for the receipt of weaponry and foodstuffs from Flanders; while English east-coast ports such as Hartlepool, Scarborough, Whitby, Hull, Newcastle and Berwick were equally vital for the provision of munitions and victuals. Export duties on wool and hides were used by both sides to help pay for the war, and the English king awarded assignments on customs revenues as a means of repaying financiers who equipped and victualled his armies. Local merchants based in these ports were expected to provide credit. Walter de Gosewyk of Berwick and Richard de Emeldon of Newcastle played a vital part in financing the English war effort; later their efforts were eclipsed by those of William de la Pole of Hull who was able to advance £4,000 towards the Scottish War in 1327.[2] From about 1307, however, some Flemish and German seamen of the Hanseatic towns made common cause with the Scots in attacking English and Gascon vessels at sea.[3] The consequent disruption of the English wool export trade affected growers, merchants and urban communities far to the south of the war zone.

By contrast with the vessels of the Irish Sea, shipping on the North Sea generally took the form of round-hulled, clinker-built ships, or flat-bottomed plank-built 'cogs'. In either case the vessels tended to be higher-sided, deeper-draughted, dependent upon a sail for propulsion, and fitted with 'castles' fore and aft for protection against boarders.[4]

A considerable drain on the resources of the ports was the requisition of shipping for naval operations. Although the Cinque Ports of the English Channel provided the English king with the makings of a navy, even the small ports of Blyth, Newbiggin and Holy Island stored goods and were asked to provide ships.[5] This was a significant expenditure; maintenance of a ship for the king in 1322 cost the town of Hull £36, the largest expense item on the Chamberlain's account of that year apart from the fortifications.[6] Edward I had encountered opposition to and resentment of his demands from the ports of Durham in 1302; Edward II continued the exploitation of shipping and failed to return on time the vessels loaned to him.[7]

England provided the vast bulk of the raw material for the Flemish wool industry. It is thought that Scotland's wool exports amounted to only one fifth of England's; nevertheless Scotland was Flanders' second most important supplier and Scoto-Flemish trade was well established. It is reported that at Edward I's storming of Berwick in 1296, the Flemish community in the town were foremost in the resistance to the English.[8] For their part the Scots maintained a significant trading colony in

Bruges.[9] The German cities of the Baltic had also an established history of trading with Scotland; when Wallace briefly recaptured Berwick from the English in 1297, he lost no time in announcing to Hamburg and Lübeck that Scotland was once again open for business.[10] The network of North Sea shipping lanes also sustained a great number of pirate and robber-crews, especially in the estuaries and islands of the Low Countries. This persisted to the sixteenth century, when the Sea Beggars of Elizabeth's reign acted as a catalyst during England's struggle with Spain. This same presence, predatory and unpredictable, was active from an early stage in the Anglo-Scottish war. In July 1296 the King of England's Treasurer reported that a thousand Flemings, disguised as fishermen (and presumably in the pay of King Philip of France), were preparing to attack Yarmouth.[11]

Dr. Stevenson points out that the periods of firm French control of Flanders coincide with successful Scottish resistance from 1297 to 1302, while periods of rebellion in Flanders coincide with collapse of resistance in Scotland after 1303. In the long term it may be true that Flanders was used by French kings to maintain the 'auld alliance'; and certainly while Edward I reigned in England, the support which independent Scotland received from Flemish merchants was largely inspired by the French monarch and was effectively a manifestation of the 'auld alliance' between Scotland and France.[12] The years from 1303 to 1322, however, were characterised by Anglo-French détente culminating in the Peace of Paris, sealed in May 1303, which specified that neither England nor France was to succour the enemies of the other. This stand-off between the two great powers left each free to crush its smaller neighbours. Thus Edward I was enabled to organise his invasion of Scotland in 1303, and Philip the Fair to move against Flanders. Edward II was Philip IV's son-in-law, and posed a much less intimidating figure to Philip and his successors. Other characteristics of the period are growing animosity between Flanders and England which for a short time actually overcame the economic interests both had in the wool trade. This was partly the result of traditional and long-standing rivalries; and partly of Edward I's cynical abandonment of his allies, the Flemish towns, during his war with France from 1294 to 1298. When it had suited him, Edward had dropped the expensive Flemish alliance with alacrity, leaving Flanders exposed to French attack.[13] There is no evidence that Robert I received any aid (other than diplomatic support) from France prior to 1322; but no doubt that he was supported by the Flemish traders. For Scotland the continuation of support from Flanders was not in this period an aspect of the 'auld alliance' with France but an alternative to it.

Privateering in the North Sea became firmly bound up with the Anglo-Scottish war from 1308. In July of that year Edward II became sufficiently concerned at threats to naval security to appoint a Hartlepool shipowner and trader, William le Jettour, to take charge of all shipping between Aberdeen and Hartlepool. Jettour was made captain of ships and sailors within this zone, and ordered to assist in alleviating the siege of Aberdeen, and to enforce a blockade of independent Scotland.[14] But the fall of Aberdeen to Bruce's supporters occurred soon afterwards; and significantly, a Dortmund merchant, Herman Clipping, had helped the Scots to capture the castle.[15] Henceforth Aberdeen was to become a base for the operation of Scottish, Flemish and German privateers, and the pattern for conflict in the North Sea was set. Privateer crews running the gauntlet of blockade would prey upon ships carrying English wool to Flanders. English seamen inevitably took defence into their own hands, attacking Flemish vessels and exacerbating mutual distrust into an open war. Scottish privateers sometimes operated under formal letters of marque issued by Robert I. This is reported by the Count of Hainhault, who reported to Edward II that he had captured Scots with letters testifying that they were men of the king of Scotland, and that that king had sent them to sea to attack his enemies.[16] Aberdeen remained the favourite port of privateers, both as a base for attacks on English shipping and as a market for disposal of captured English cargoes. German privateers from Lübeck, Stralsund, Hamburg and other towns of the Hanseatic League were active from an early stage.[17] In March 1309 Edward II wrote to the city of Bruges and to Count Robert of Flanders requesting an end to trade with *Esterlings* (as the Baltic Germans were known) who were assisting the Scots. Again in October he complained of the activities of Scots and Germans, demanding that they be prohibited from entering Flemish ports.[18] As Robert succeeded in capturing Dundee (1312), Perth (1313), Edinburgh (1314) and eventually Berwick (1318), these more southerly bases became available to the privateers, stretching the English blockade to the point where it was beyond enforcement.

Piracy became a diplomatic issue for governments, and a way of life for seamen. In December 1310 relations between England and the Count of Flanders deteriorated as a result of an incident off the coast of Brittany, when English vessels attacked and plundered seven Flemish ships riding at anchor in Graunzon Bay. Though not directly related to the Scottish war, the incident brought about a sudden worsening of relations between king and count, encouraged co-operation between Flemish and Scottish seafarers and soured Anglo-Flemish relations for a generation.[19] Violence on the North Sea began to spiral beyond the control of the authorities. The most active of the Flemish privateers was John Crabbe, and in his lifetime he acquired the stature and reputation of a folk-hero among the North Sea communities.[20] His career as a pirate began in 1305 or 1306 when off La Rochelle he plundered a ship known as the *Waardebourc* which belonged to Flemish merchant John de Warde. In the spring of 1310 he was involved in an attack on the ship of Alice Countess Marshall, the cargo of which was said to be worth £2,000. Crabbe was actually captured by the English and imprisoned in Scarborough in 1309; he was however set at liberty by one of the contending factions in the town.[21]

The Flemish privateers were of course primarily interested in capturing English wool ships. Typically privateers would take the stolen cargo to Aberdeen where they would remove the cocket (the seal of the English customs and proof that duty had been paid) and exchange it for either the Scottish cocket, or for the seal of a Flemish trader operating in England. This enabled them to sell stolen English wool as legitimate in the markets of Flanders. Early in 1311 John Crabbe's privateers fell upon two ships leaving Newcastle and captured 89 sacks of wool and disposed of them in exactly this way.[22] A German merchant, John Witte of Lübeck, who operated as a legitimate merchant in England but whose company in Scotland allegedly handled stolen merchandise bought from privateers.[23] But attacks on convoys carrying victuals to the increasingly beleaguered English garrisons in Scotland were of more immediate assistance to the Scots, and occasionally these too were intercepted. A ship belonging to Adam le Clerk of Lynn was captured by privateers of unknown origin while on its way to victual the garrison of Perth. The cargo was sold at Aberdeen, the hull at Stralsund.[24] Another supply vessel, destined for Stirling Castle, was intercepted at sea by the Scots under cover of darkness.[25]

Tension between England and Flanders increased. In 1311 the English captured three Flemish-owned ships from Newport 'taken near Aberdeen in Scotland, amongst the king's enemies of Scotland, as aiding the king's enemies'. As a reprisal English merchants were arrested in Flanders, which provoked counter-measures against Flemish merchants in London.[26] Edward II tried to force Count Robert into prohibiting all trade with the Scots; Count Robert's position was that while he did not condone piracy, he would not prevent lawful trade with Scottish merchants. Neither side could afford to go to war on this issue: England was a more valuable trading partner to Flanders than Scotland could ever be,[27] and for their part the English had no wish to lose the Flemish market. From 1311 to 1313, therefore, a serious attempt was made to repair diplomatic relations. The talks were long and drawn out.[28] A mission was sent from Flanders, and negotiations commenced at the English parliament of August 1311. There was much wrangling over compensation regarding particular incidents at sea, and the English demanded that the Flemish should cease trading with the Scots and expel Scottish merchants. In the meantime English bases on the Tay, at Perth and Dundee, were threatened from the sea. Jettour and others were ordered to assemble barges and ships for their defence, but Dundee fell to the Scots early in 1312 and Perth in January 1313.[29] Talks between the Flemish and English broke down in 1313; and immediately there was an attack in the Scheldt on three (Flemish-owned) ships sailing from Hull to Flanders. Merchants of Malton, Scarborough and Beverley lost their cargoes in this shipment to a Flemish pirate whom they named as John le Sagher. The cargo (wool, woolfells, cash and other commodities) was said to exceed £4,000 in value. Even allowing for the inevitable exaggeration, this appears to have been a very large seizure. Five English merchants travelling with the convoy were taken captive to Aberdeen and sold to the Scots.[30]

On 1st May 1313 Edward II wrote to Count Robert complaining of the activities of John Crabbe, and alleging that a convoy of 13 Flemish ships 'laden with arms and victuals lately went from the port of Zwyn' and sailed to Scotland, despite his request that the Count should not permit the transport of aid in arms or victuals to Scotland.[31] Delivery of this consignment precipitated Edward's issue of the Staple Ordinance of 20th May 1313.[32] This decreed that all merchants exporting wool from England to Brabant, Flanders and Artois were henceforth to send their goods to a common destination and market on the Continent. The location chosen for this market was St. Omer, in Artois, outside Flanders and within the French sphere of influence. Privateering exploits of the Flemish and Scots may have been the last straw which brought about creation of this staple; nevertheless it had been in the offing for some time and not necessarily for reasons associated with the war. For some time previously English wool merchants had been co-operating as a 'staple association'; and the location of the staple at Artois was a concession to the French alliance (Edward II had visited France that Easter). It was also designed to facilitate royal supervision and taxation of the English wool trade and to cut out opportunities for corruption among customs officials. But denial of direct access to English wool was also a rebuke to Flanders, a biting retaliation for connivance with the privateers. Finally it meant that English wool could be transported across the North Sea in convoy to the staple port, under escort and in relative safety.

In anticipation of the establishment of the staple, the Count had protested that it was impossible for him to prevent commerce with legitimate Scottish traders.[33] He wrote to Edward II in July 1314, asking for safe conducts for his merchants and suggesting that the staple be moved to Bruges, and protested that he was powerless to prevent privateers from operating off his coasts. To his embarrassment, however, the privateers captured another ship at Michaelmas 1314, seizing the cargo and abducting a wool merchant of Beverley and his son.[34] Early in 1315 Edward II remonstrated once more about the growing incidence of piracy, directing letters not just to Flanders, but also to various other states of the Low Countries.[35]

England had flexed diplomatic and economic muscle; and it looked as though the Count was preparing to return to obedience. There were signs that the authorities in both countries might reconcile their differences; safe conduct until Christmas was granted to Flemish merchants in England, and a diplomatic mission was sent by the Flemish towns.[36]Yet on the high seas co-operation between Scottish and continental privateers went on regardless. Early in 1315 German merchants were arrested as they loaded the vessel *Le Paschday* with armour and victuals in Boston harbour, with the obvious intention of taking them to Scotland.[37] In the spring of 1315, to enforce the blockade of Scotland and deter privateers, Edward appointed his trusted household knight John Botetourt as captain of a North Sea task force based at Harwich. Botetourt was commanded to arrest 'thirteen great cogs of the Scottish rebels and their adherents now in the port of Sluys' which were preparing to take armour, victuals and other goods to Scotland.[38] This fleet in Sluys must have been composed of many of the same ships which had been preparing to break the English embargo in May 1313, apparently supplying Scotland regularly and on a large scale. Botetourt undertook to serve until Michaelmas with 20 ships and two smaller vessels of Yarmouth, and with 40 men-at-arms on board, in return for 500 marks. Furthermore, 300 archers were ordered to Harwich to serve with the fleet.[39] He experienced difficulties in manning his fleet; but towards the end of May he had 17 'great ships' at Hull and Boston and sought powers to requisition more ships on the voyage.[40]

Whatever edge the Staple Ordinance might have given the English was lost in the early summer of 1315, when Flanders rose in rebellion against France, causing a dramatic escalation in the war at sea. King Louis X of France called upon England to honour the Anglo-French alliance, not only by expelling Flemish merchants but also by sending ships in support of the French army.[41] Edward fell in with the first demand but stalled on the second, protesting that he needed his ships to fight off the Scottish invasion of Ireland. This was true: the Cinque Ports fleet under William de Creye was destined for a rendezvous with John of Argyll's fleet at Dublin; but this was currently in port, immobilised by contrary winds. However, an order was given that English vessels not yet on their way to Ireland should harass the Flemings in the North Sea.[42] Botetourt set sail with six ships on 8th July to assist the French. His role of blockading Scotland was to be taken by John de Sturmy and Humphery de Littlebury, commanding a squadron of 12 ships against the Scots from 14th July to 7th October. But with the onset of winter the number of their ships diminished, perhaps because it became more difficult to obtain crews.[43]

The royal ban on Flemish merchants in England greatly exacerbated the problem of privateering in the North Sea. Flemish crews, deprived of legitimate employment, had no option but to trade with and consequently fight alongside the Scots. The blockade of Scotland was enormously unpopular among English merchant communities and it was frequently flouted by English merchants keen to take advantage of the high prices in Scotland.[44] The Scots took advantage of the breach in Anglo-Flemish relations to step up pressure on Berwick, which had been under virtual siege and blockade since shortly after the English retreat from Bannockburn. At Michaelmas 1315 Botetourt's term of service expired, and almost at once the situation at Berwick became critical. In November William le Jettour and John Sturmy were appointed joint captains on the North Sea. They were given six ships to protect access to Berwick.[45] In February 1316 Berwick was again reported as starving. Sturmy and Jettour were ineffectual or worse; the king wrote to them in March, complaining that they had sat at anchor in Kirklee and other ports, and pillaged the countryside.[46] Attacks on English shipping increased. Peter de Wellewyk and his son William were attacked by pirates of Zeeland while returning from Denmark to Raveneserodd. Famine in Flanders may have exacerbated the war in the North Sea; the men of Great Yarmouth believed that in February Count Robert sent out a fleet under John Crabbe to seize by whatever means foodstuffs for the starving people of Flanders. Crabbe captured two ships from Great Yarmouth on 1st March 1316, and later, off the Isle of Thanet, seized an English wine ship returning from Gascony.[47] The victual convoys were obvious targets for the Flemings, and in May it was reported from Berwick that enemy cruisers had cut off the possibility of supply by sea, and that the town had provisions left for only one month.[48] Genoese merchants with galleys for hire were touting for business. Lambinus Doria tried to interest Edward II in hiring from him galleys and men-at-arms on horse and on foot. Edward appears to have declined this offer;[49] what changed his mind is revealed in his letter of July 1316 to the authorities in Genoa, complaining that letters had been found on a Scottish agent showing that two Genoese merchants were negotiating to supply Robert I with 'a service of galleys and divers sorts of arms'.[50] Six months later Edward II dispatched Leonardo Pessagno to Genoa to hire five galleys for his own Irish Sea fleet.[51]

It must have been with immense relief that English merchants learned that peace had been patched up between France and Flanders. Edward II raised the ban on the presence of Flemish merchants in England on 7th December 1316.[52] For a short time the situation in the North Sea improved for the English. The blockade of Berwick came to an end; the Scots gave up trying to take Berwick for the time being and seem to have agreed to a truce until Midsummer 1317.[53] Edward II's Genoese banker, Antonio Pessagno, began to amass vast quantities of victuals to be used in a campaign which was to follow.[54] Towards the end of the truce, the English earl of Arundel, *chevetaigne* in the north, sent a squadron of five ships from the Humber estuary with 323 armed sailors to raid 'Dundee and Aberdeen and other places on the coast of Scotland' in May and

June 1317; an attempted landing at Inverkeithing was beaten off by the bishop of Dunkeld. The incident is recounted in Barbour's *Bruce*.[55] English seamen of Newcastle and Hartlepool needed no encouragement to take on the Scots and Flemings at sea. Hartlepool had only lately commenced the process of building town walls, and was singled out for attack in 1315 and again in 1322 by Scottish raiders, apparently in retaliation for the attacks of its seamen on Scottish privateers.[56] Edward II started to mend his fences with the Count of Flanders by permitting the trial of the English sailors involved in the 'battle of Graunzon'. Other gestures of goodwill were made. Edward ordered the release of a privateer ship of 'Zierikzee' intercepted by the English and found to have been freighted at Aberdeen by Flemings with what was surely stolen English wool.[57] However, the English wool staple remained on French territory.

On 1st–2nd April 1318 Berwick was betrayed to the Scots, an event of enormous significance for the war at sea as for that on land.[58] When the following year a Scottish attack on Yorkshire forced Edward II to abandon the siege, he protested bitterly to the Count of Flanders that ships had sailed from Zwyn carrying arms and provisions for the Scots.[59] To this on 14th November the Count replied that Crabbe was wanted for murder and would be punished on the wheel if captured. The shipping of military aid to the Scots he had already prohibited. Of the convoy to Scotland the Count said that he knew nothing and believed that ships had gone to Scotland and to Ireland only to trade.[60] The existence of the staple had obviously mollifed the Count's stance; but Edward's demands for a Flemish embargo against Scotland was rejected by the citizens of Bruges who refused to prohibit trade with honest Scottish merchants.[61] With the truce of 1319 to 1321 Scotland was able to resume commerce with the Continent, and during this stage King Robert granted safe conducts to continental merchants on a regular basis. Negotiations and assemblies were set in train at which the English tried to detach the Flemish from trade with Scotland, and these talks seem to have had the effect of reducing attacks on English vessels.[62] But the habit of piracy died hard among privateers on all sides, and the English seamen of Hartlepool and Newcastle occasionally disrupted North Sea shipping, preying even upon English vessels.[63]

Following the renewal of war in December 1321, Edward II offered a treaty to the Count in the hope of having Flanders quiescent for the duration of hostilities; but already Flemish seamen were once more assisting the Scots with attacks on English shipping.[64] For his invasion of Scotland in 1322 Edward II relied heavily on provisioning his army from an accompanying fleet of supply vessels. Although half the size of the fleet of 1319 and consequently less expensive, the fleet of 1322 was nevertheless a vital logistical support.[65] As it turned out, the English army was forced to turn back on 20th August, precisely because the supply vessels did not turn up. Storms clearly played a part in the disruption of supplies to the invading army. One ship, *La Charitie* of Colchester, was wrecked at Leith, and the owner was compensated with a gift from the King of 100s.[66] Flemish activity also appears to have been the main reason why the English supply fleet failed to turn up:

> The Flemings had come to the aid of our enemies the Scots, and put to sea with the navy, just when our fleet was nearing Scotland, took ships with goods on them so that none dared to come to us.[66]

The actions of Flemish seamen, therefore, were responsible in large part for the ruin of Edward II's last and most threatening invasion of Scotland.

From this point, however, dynastic accident and a change in English priorities conspired to end the co-operation between Flemish and Scottish seamen. Two deaths transformed the alignment of England with France, and Scotland with Flanders. The death of Philip V of France in January 1322 and the accession of Charles IV (under the sway of a notoriously anti-English adviser, Charles of Valois) rocked Anglo-French *détente* to its shallow foundations. Mutual antagonisms increased, and this marks the beginning of the drift into the Anglo-French War of St Sardos.[67] Secondly, Count Robert III of Flanders died in September 1322, and his successor Count Louis II de Nevers initiated negotiations with England.[68] During spring 1323 the English were negotiating in Newcastle with the Scots and in London with the Flemings, and war with France was a definite prospect. Count Louis at first resisted the demand that all trade between Flanders and Scotland should cease, but in April 1323 he finally conceded the point and Scottish merchants were expelled from Flanders. A truce was proclaimed on 5th April between England and Flanders and each country released those merchants whom it had taken hostage.[69] Anglo-Flemish *rapprochement* was surely a factor in persuading Robert I to accept the 13-year truce with England, agreed at the end of May. Flemish naval support had been invaluable to him both in harassing English trade and stopping the flow of supplies to English forces, and in facilitating the import of vital stores and war material to Scotland. In return Scotland (and Aberdeen in particular) had provided an *entrepot* for contraband wool. By virtue of the Scots' control of parts of northern England, it is possible that Scotland had access to larger quantities of wool and hides for export than ever before.[70] War with England appears to have had the effect of increasing Scotland's commercial dependence on the Continent. Scotland's internal economy must have been devastated by war; but her seaborne export trade seems to have been preserved by the link with Flanders.[71] After the expulsion of Scottish merchants from Flanders the Scots seem to have turned to Zeeland as an alternative trading partner, since reciprocal trading privileges were granted to each other's merchants by William Count of Holland and Robert I in August 1323.[72]

SIEGE AND BLOCKADE AT BERWICK

One aspect of this war in the North Sea was the struggle for Berwick which, besides being a vital port for wool exports, commanded the landward approaches to Scotland on the eastern march. On taking the town in 1296, Edward I had planted a colony of English merchants there. Municipal government was controlled by these newcomers in the period immediately following Edward I's reconstitution;[73] but the indigenous families gradually reasserted themselves. Walter de Gosewyk, burgess in 1291, was able to become mayor by 1304.[74] Four of the nine leading burghal families which gave hostages to Edward II in 1318 were established in the town prior to 1291.[75] If anything, it was Robert I who most changed the character of the town by expelling in 1318 members of old Berwick families who had co-operated with the English authorities during the 20-year occupation.[76]

King Robert's first attempt to take Berwick came in December 1312, when his men tried to scale the walls using rope ladders by night, and the town was alerted only by the barking of a dog.[77] Shortly afterwards the burgesses asked for procedures to be established to settle disputes between the civil and military population.[78] Appalling garrison misbehaviour was reported in 1313; and a picture emerges of a garrison plundering the countryside, countering Robert's rural terrorism with a terrorism of their own, but impoverishing the hinterland upon which Berwick's commerce depended. The troops stole the livestock of country people, and killed or held them to ransom when they came to market.[79] Townsfolk complained of being driven out of their homes by the troops to dwell in tents.[80] Tension between the townsfolk and the garrison intensified as the external threat grew ever more menacing. Accusations of corruption were levelled at the king's receiver of victuals, and at John de Weston, the head of Edward II's Scottish administration.[81] After 1314 the royal stores in the town were run down; by 1316 the depot had been removed to Newcastle, probably due to the activities of Flemish and Scottish privateers. Supply of local grain to the royal stores was now impossible; and there was never enough money or food for the garrison. Financial demands on the townsfolk increased; in November 1313 the mayor and burgesses were asked to lend Weston money or food when asked; in March 1315 the king asked them to deliver victuals to Weston for the men-at-arms, as there was not enough in the royal stores.[82] After Bannockburn the burgesses had been forced to spend £270 on emergency defences, including a new wall outside Marygate, a new ditch, and a barbican; but even in January

1316 the enclosure of the town had not been completed, for Douglas launched an amphibious attack at a place between the Brighouse and the Castle where the wall was not yet built.[83] The town walls were still dangerously low even when Robert I had occupied Berwick 1318.[84]

From autumn 1315 to spring 1316 the situation became increasingly desperate. The garrison was starving, actually living off horse flesh according to one report, and the burgesses were deep in debt. In October 1315 the mayor had to promise food and winter clothing to prevent the garrison from walking out.[85] Letters dated at Berwick in that same month state that men were dying of hunger, and that the desertion of the garrison was imminent. Another, of 3rd November, tells how enemy cruisers forced a supply ship to jettison most of its cargo. Jettour and John Sturmy were then given seven ships with which to break the blockade.[86] It was a hard winter; yet the townsfolk had constantly to be vigilant, and succeeded in beating off the night attack of 7th January 1316.[87] Determined to fight rather than starve, part of the garrison disobeyed the keeper and on 14th February 1316 sallied out into the countryside to forage for provisions. Returning from Teviotdale, they were attacked, eight miles from Berwick, by Douglas and Soules. Twenty men-at-arms and 60 foot were lost. The episode is recounted in Barbour's *Bruce*.[88] By 2nd March 1316 the tone of the warden's letters to the king had changed from pleading to bitter resentment:

> Assuredly Sire, your people are dying of hunger and I have nothing but fine words for them . . . And now lately many are leaving the town and those who stay die in anguish from starvation on the walls . . . you know that no more than £4,000 in money and in every kind of victual has come here since I arrived and that there are still ten weeks to go in the year; and we have 300 men-at-arms enrolled of which we have only 50 mounted and armed, whose horses are not dead and whose arms are not pawned for food . . . For which reason we ask you, most honourable lord, that you should attend to this situation, and even if you think nothing of us or of those here, think of your town, which you hold so dear; because if you lose it, you will lose all the rest of the north; and not only that Sire, if you lose the town which God defend, we lose our lives and from that Sire, you will gain little. For which reason, Sire, ask, if you please, to ordain another Guardian in my place [89]

There was no let-up in the naval blockade; on 10th May 1316 the mayor reported that two vessels had recently been captured trying to enter the town.[90] As their exclusion from England did not cease until December 1316, the Flemish privateers continued to assist the Scots in blockading the town. A letter from John de Weston to the king, dated 3rd January 1317, claimed that there were supplies for only 15 days.

This emergency abated while Arundel occupied northern England and the Scots turned their attention to Ireland. But in October 1317 Berwick is again described as being under siege, and reinforcements were rushed there from Yorkshire. Bruce was by this stage refusing to countenance the two-year truce imposed by the pope because it would deprive him of the town; a Franciscan friar who conveyed to him the terms of the papal truce reported him as having vowed that 'he would have Berwick'.[91]

It is scarcely surprising that the intense psychological pressure of intermittent siege generated paranoia and bloodletting within the defences. The town's population was still largely Scottish, and the English warden and garrison were very much afraid of betrayal. Barbour relates that ill-feeling in the town was rife against the warden, who hated and abused all Scots, whatever their loyalties. In November 1313 Ralph Fitz William had reported the town 'grievously menaced by treason', and a commission was established to investigate suspects among the townspeople and to remove undesirables. Traitors were hanged in a treason trial in the summer of 1314, and it appears that their conspiracy had assistance from parties in Northumberland and Newcastle. Subsequently an attempt was made on the life of the judge.[92] In May 1316 the efforts of Richard fitzMarmaduke to parley with the enemy were reportedly bedevilled by 'treason and envy'.[93] Similar reactions to external threat are apparent at Carlisle and at Dublin. But the response of the Berwick merchant community to the threat of their own extinction was to try to turn it to their own profit. In 1317 the burgesses contracted with Edward II to defend Berwick in return for 6,000 marks yearly (£4,000). The townsmen could be expected to be zealous, and could not walk out on their responsibility; but the arrangement was criticised on the grounds that the burgesses were inexperienced and mean with money.[94] Their loyalty was not in question; but it had cost £4,993 to garrison Berwick in 1315–16,[95] during which time the men were often starving, and if the burgesses were to make a saving out of £4,000 – as presumably they hoped – some reduction in the level of security might be expected. Ultimately this was not a factor; Berwick was betrayed to Robert I on the night of 1st to 2nd April 1318.[96]

Aware that the English were bound to try to retake the town, Robert set about heightening the walls. The siege of Berwick by the English is best read in Barbour's inimitable verse.[97] Before the end of April, Jettour was supervising naval efforts to recapture the town for the English.[98] Ferocious fighting at sea preceded the assault on land. A huge English naval force was deployed; 77 ships vessels were involved, led by Simon Driby with a marine force of 11 men-at-arms and 17 crossbowmen, besides sailors, at a cost of £1,725.[99] Defence of the town was conducted by John Crabbe (the privateer captain), who constructed siege engines to counter the English assault. As five of Driby's men-at-arms were killed on 1st September, it would seem that a naval action of some sort took place on that date. The assault by land followed. Like Robert I's siege of Carlisle, it was a brief affair, lasting from 8th or 9th September to the 16th or 17th only. Barbour claims that within this period there was a five-day truce. The English may not have had sufficient opportunity to bring to bear all their enormous superiority in numbers and resources. Their army of 14,000 foot was adequate; and their naval force had confronted the Flemings in an action fought on 1st September, when five of Simon Driby's men-at-arms had been killed.[100] But there may have been a shortage of siege engines, for Edward II had to order them up from York.[101] In the meantime they resorted to primitive stratagems. On the seaward side, a ship was brought alongside the walls, and a small boat filled with soldiers hauled to halfway up the mast. The soldiers then tried to land a bridge from their boat onto the walls. The first ship attempting this manoeuvre ran aground, and the Scots sallied out, and attacked and burnt it. In another stratagem, a mobile shelter known as a 'sow' was made, and placed under the walls to enable sappers to undermine the foundations. This was an easy target for missiles, and the Scots succeeded in smashing it. Then, using a crane, they landed on it a flaming bale of combustible material. However, Berwick was not saved by its valiant defenders, or by the ingenuity of John Crabbe (said to have hit upon the idea of the crane), but by the diversionary raid on Yorkshire, which so discomfited the northern English that they turned back to protect their estates.

WAR AND TOWNS GENERALLY

The urban communities worst affected by the Scottish war were those without walls, generally the smaller towns which could not afford them. For them, destruction could be avoided only by payment of ransoms. A visitation of the Scots always entailed severe damage, for most buildings (except churches and castles) were of wood. Penrith and Lancaster had to appeal to the king for timber to rebuild houses after Scottish attacks. At Northallerton the church was destroyed in 1318; and at Lancaster in 1322 even the castle was burned down by the raiders.[102] The lords of boroughs or those leasing their profits suffered severe financial losses as tenants fled or were impoverished by raiding. At Felton in Northumberland burgage rents had brought in 46s. annually in peacetime, but in 1323 they were worth only 8s;[103] at Hexham burgage rents had been worth £15 a year before the war, but nothing was paid between 1315 and 1317; and at Wark-on-Tweed, 62 burgages had each paid 12d. before the war, a total of over £3, but no rent was forthcoming in 1323. The decline in burgage revenues was far from uniform, however: at Alnwick the farm of the town was paid up in full right until the summer of 1318, when it fell by 25 percent.[104] Some of the smallest settlements in the border counties may have been temporarily abandoned due to repeated burnings. Mason in Northumberland seems to have disappeared some time between 1303 and 1335. East and West Backworth, also in Northumberland, are thought to have merged; and reference has already been made to the fate of Mortham in Yorkshire. But settlement patterns in Northumberland have been shown to be remarkably resilient, remaining practically unaltered from Anglian times until the plagues. Villages may have shrunk in size, but no significant settlement disappeared. Even so recent a borough as Warnmouth (founded in 1247) survived at least this phase of the Scottish wars.[105]

More southerly towns suffered fewer visitations. Durham certainly suffered some burning when the Scots arrived on market day in 1312. Rent rolls of the Almoner's estate in the city dated 1313 and 1325 reveal a decline in rents from outlying areas, but there is no evidence of any further attacks on the city.[106] Northallerton must have sustained severe damage from the raids of 1318, 1319 and 1322, but no details have survived. Boroughbridge was burnt and wasted by the Scots in 1318, with the result that profits of mills and revenue from fairs and markets were both severely reduced. Tolls worth £8 were lost; so were customs dues worth £11 because ships no longer landed there. Furthermore, the men of Boroughbridge complained that they were losing £4 per annum 'as a result of defensive precautions adopted by the City of York'. At Knaresborough it was reported in 1318 that the Scots burnt down 140 houses out of 160.[107] At Lancaster, though five burgages, four tofts and a forge and the castle were destroyed, the Scots are said to have spared two religious houses in the town. At Preston a rent roll of tenants in 1324 shows only one tenement out of eight failing to pay on account of burning, so here recovery from the raid of 1322 seems to have been swift.[108] The option of buying off the Scots was not always on offer; by the time Richmond had negotiated a ransom in 1316, a portion of the town had already been laid waste. The burgesses of Ripon gave six hostages to the enemy in 1318 as security for payment of a 1,000-mark ransom. They tried to avoid paying by the simple expedient of neglecting to redeem their hostages, whose womenfolk complained bitterly to the king.[109] As both Richmond and Ripon discovered, when they had been bought off once, the Scots tended to come back for more.

Small communities turned for protection to nearby castles and peels. The people of Bamburgh were said to fold up their wooden houses and carry them into the castle. But, as has been pointed out, at Bamburgh they learned that they could not rely upon the goodwill of the castellan.[110] If a town was large enough, it might build fortifications of its own; but fortifications brought other problems. Walls were expensive to maintain, and had to be patrolled. Ten northern English towns put their trust in bricks and mortar. Carlisle and Scarborough had walls already; York, Berwick and Newcastle reinforced or completed theirs; and Durham, Hull, Hartlepool, Lancaster, Richmond and Beverley applied for licences to collect 'murage'.[111] This was a toll levied on goods entering a town and used to finance the building of walls, which may have been good at raising funds but inevitably discouraged trade. A spur was given to Hartlepool's efforts by the pointed exclusion of the town from a truce granted to the community of the Bishopric of Durham.[112] But the expense of building walls must have discouraged many towns; and the Hull Chamberlain's account roll for 1321–24 gives an idea of the sort of sums involved.[113] The cost of digging a great foss and other defensive ditches came to £110. Stone, bricks, lime and sand for building the north gate cost £40. Iron for making nails for the palisade cost £14 and timber, including the cost of its transport to Hull, came to £142. Another £41 paid in wages to the men working on the palisade and gate brought the cost of the defences to £347. To this had to be added £11 for gifts and costs incurred in London while procuring the licence to collect murage and compensation paid for damage to property. The burgesses struggled to raise the cash; they could manage only £140 by tallaging themselves and a further £61 from murage. At Carlisle additional defences were necessary as the siege of 1315 became imminent. Andrew Harclay destroyed buildings outside the walls to deprive the enemy of cover, bricked up the city gates and drove a ditch around the city, which subsequently drew a complaint from the Prior of Carlisle.[114]

The decision as to which areas should lie within the defensive ring was a difficult and potentially acrimonious issue. At Newcastle the building plan of the city walls was radically altered by the onset of the Scottish raids. It had been intended to incorporate the castle into the defensive circuit; but after the approach by Wallace in 1297 the riverbank suburbs had demanded to be included within the walls. This necessitated the building of walls to the riverside, enclosing the castle completely. The course of the east wall was altered to include Pandon, a manor which had been granted to Newcastle in 1298; and when the Scottish raids intensified in 1311, it was decided to continue the west wall to the river. The plan of the Newcastle walls shows re-entrants on either side, indicating the stages at which the original plan was abandoned. The digging of a foss and simultaneous construction of a wall were in progress by 1311, the work paid for by grants of murage. The commonalty petitioned for royal aid to complete the fortifications in 1317, stating that they had 'enclosed part of the town with a wall and all of it with a ditch', so the circuit of the ditch must then have been complete.[115] Suburbs excluded from the defensive ring could be a security hazard, in that they might provide shelter for approaching enemies. For this reason, suburbs were destroyed at Tynemouth.[116] At

Dublin in February 1317 the citizens burned down the suburb of St. Thomas, a standard precaution to deny shelter to the besiegers; but the fire spread wildly through the city, destroying churches and the royal courts of justice and the exchequer, and encouraging the mob to loot. Other measures at Dublin included demolition of the church of St. Saviour to provide material for barricading the streets; and the belfry of St. Mary del Dam was pulled down and its stones used in the repair of nearby Dublin Castle.[117]

In addition to paying for material defences, townsfolk often had to contribute to defence by undertaking onerous watch duties. In answer to a summons of burgesses of Newcastle to parliament in January 1316, the sheriff of Northumberland replied that 'all the burgesses of the town were scarcely equal to defence of the town and therefore it was impossible to put the writ into force'. In 1322 the bailiffs did not dare to send any burgess to an assembly of wool merchants because many of the men-at-arms were at sea on the king's service and Scottish invasion was imminent; in 1327 they refused to send burgesses to parliament on similar grounds.[118] Details of the manning of the walls and provision for internal security are available at York and Dublin. The York 'Custody' of 1315 assigns defence of specific sectors to men of particular city parishes. It also provides for a check on comings and goings at the city gates; for the expulsion of 'Scots and rascals'; for nightly patrols; custody of keys; and penalties for contravention of security regulations.[119] Unlike those of English towns, the citizens of Dublin had long anticipated direct attack. An undated petition from the 'common folk of Dublin' to the mayor and commonalty includes requests for security measures similar to those listed in the 'Custody' of York: a general muster at the toll of the city bell, by day or night; sallies from the city to be made only by command of the mayor; and general contribution to the watch of the city.[120]

The costs of defence are illustrated by a view of account of Carlisle in 1319. In this, Andrew Harclay queried on the king's behalf whether the farm of 1318/19, pardoned in November 1318, had actually been spent on the defence of the city as the king had stipulated. The citizens maintained that they were unable to pay for defence from their own resources, and that the foss dug around the city in 1315 had cost them £80 at least in wages paid to the ditchers. They said that they had been supporting the whole cost of defence since 1315 and that the king was constantly in debt to them. Asked whether they had been impoverished by the keeping of the city, they replied that most of them had, but especially those holding lands and tenements outside the walls which were devastated by the enemy. Of those who held no such lands, some were worse off, some the same as they had been before the war. They did not complain of extra watching duties being imposed by the sheriff unnecessarily, nor of debts outstanding from their improvements to the defences; but they did say that they were not always recompensed for quartering of troops, and that mulcture was due to them for the garrison's use of their mills.[121]

The fear of betrayal seeped through the stoutest walls. As the Scots gained control of Northumberland, concern for internal security at Newcastle increased. In August 1314 Sir John de Halton was arrested on suspicion of friendship with the Scots. In June 1315 the burgesses arrested William Heryng on the word of a boy for plotting to betray the town. Heryng blamed commercial rivals for trying to ruin him by false accusations. In 1316 a Scotsman carrying dispatches for the King of Scots was arrested; and during the Middleton rebellion the mayor and bailiffs were forbidden to allow any armed men to enter the town.[122] At Carlisle, too, there was a fear of treachery that bricks and mortar alone could never quite allay. The town was riven between factions, led by rival gentry commanders. Allegations were levelled at John Harclay in summer 1315, that he had colluded with *schavaldores* to warn the Scots of impending attack and had trafficked with them. An inquiry was conducted that same year by Ralph fitz William into suspicious persons amongst the citizens, though its outcome is unknown.[123]

Fears of betrayal were accentuated by the clamour of country people for refuge within the walls during time of danger. In spite of the serious decline in trade, Carlisle's population may have temporarily increased as the city became a haven for refugees. Many of them would have been destitute labourers and small farmers, but only the presence of well-to-do refugees is borne out by the records. Many leading gentry and ecclesiastics already owned property in Carlisle, and such bolt-holes became very valuable.[124] Bishop Halton and the Prior of Lanercost sought further property in Carlisle in the 1310s; and when Joan de Boyvil sold her town house to her son John, she reserved for herself the right to stay there when it was too dangerous to remain at Thursby 'on account of the war of the Scots'.[125] At York in the later stages of the war there are signs that the deteriorating military situation encouraged immigration into the city; in particular the rents of urban properties of the Vicars Choral rose slightly from 1311 to 1325, and more markedly from 1321 to 1336.[126]

Garrisons were a necessary evil. A large garrison was to some extent a guarantee of safety, but there was a financial cost and a cost to public order. At Berwick where garrison misbehaviour was particularly rife, numbers had increased steadily from 1307 until, in June 1313, 239 cavalry were stationed there with perhaps a thousand infantry.[127] Carlisle became host to a large permanent garrison from 1311. From then on there were 50 to 120 cavalry and as many foot based in the city. On one occasion there were 150 cavalry and 420 archers; on another, 800 cavalry – in a city which could hardly have boasted 3,000 inhabitants.[128] Supplying the swollen garrison became difficult as access by sea from Ireland and by land from the rest of England was impeded by the Scots.[129] Occasionally the citizens had to pay for the quartering of the troops. One of the king's receivers was said to have sold bad rations at extravagant prices and to have avoided settling accounts. The garrison, for their part, complained of hunger and of lack of pay, forcing them to pawn horses and equipment. An order to John de Castre in February 1316 to buy stores in the town resulted in ruinous prises and elicited complaints of seizures of goods.[130] Around 1316 the king was implored to send money and victuals to both city and castle, 'for the householders are in such straits that they can scarcely abide there'.[131] Garrisons at Newcastle were much smaller than at Berwick and Carlisle, because the castle was not built into the town walls, and security of the town walls was the responsibility of the citizens. Cases of friction between citizens and soldiers were then relatively few.[132] But at Newcastle a greatly increased military presence led to a riot in 1322, when during the muster for the invasion of Scotland, a fight broke out between English and Welsh troops, leaving seven Welsh injured.[133] The garrison at York was usually small – 12 men-at-arms and 40 archers in 1312–13 – but it rose during the Scottish invasion of 1322 to three bannerets, eight knights and 38 other men-at-arms.[134] There is no evidence at York of repeated friction between garrison and citizens of the sort that characterised Berwick and Carlisle, but concentrations of troops in the city threatened law and order. During a muster in 1318 a 'tumult' occurred among the soldiers; and in 1322 a clash between Hainaulter mercenaries and the English infantry was witnessed by Jehan le Bel in which 527 Hainaulters and 241 Englishmen died and almost a whole suburban parish was burnt down.[135]

The presence of magnates and royalty can be seen to have benefited the local economy of Carlisle in 1307; but the benefits of the royal sojourn at Berwick in 1310–11 are less evident.[136] Only York seems to have prospered from aristocratic expenditure connected with the war. A steep rise in food prices precipitated enactment of the Civic Ordinances in 1301, and this seems to have been caused by the city's temporary status as seat of government.[137] York's spell as a capital did not end abruptly in 1304. The exchequer returned in 1319–20, 1322–23 and October to December 1327; and chancery returned briefly to York in 1312 and again in 1316. No fewer than six parliaments were held there between 1314 and 1327; and it was the venue for other assemblies to discuss Scottish and northern affairs.[138] The armorial bearings of the magnates attending the 'parliament' of 1309 and the muster in 1314 decorate the walls and windows of York Minster and testify to the magnates' contributions to the building fund.[139] But the presence of magnates was never wholly beneficial for trade; in 1327 merchants complained about seizures of provisions for royal and magnate households and as a result were reluctant to enter York to sell goods.[140]

The war entailed profound disruption to commerce. Scottish towns may have prospered in the short term from the robber economy which functioned under Robert I, and in particular the Scottish raids into and presence in northern England may have brought Berwick wider access to wool. Figures for wool exports from Berwick from 1326 survive in the *Exchequer Rolls of Scotland*, and it has been calculated that Berwick's annual average wool export from 1327 to 1333 amounted to an enormous 1,800 sacks.[141] Newcastle, a much larger port, exported only a thousand sacks in the same period, and it seems as though Berwick had eaten into Newcastle's share of the local wool supply in the 1320s, exporting more wool in six months of 1328 than did Newcastle in the whole year.[142] Even so, Berwick's trade had undoubtedly suffered as a result of the long years of siege and blockade. Stevenson suggests that wool exporters may have used Berwick simply as an *entrepot*, without making any significant investment in the town, and points out that Robert I set the 'feu farm' of Berwick (annual payment to the king) at £266. 13s. 4d., a figure which was 20 percent lower than the corresponding sum demanded by Scottish kings before 1296.[143]

The disastrous war in Northumberland had a readily discernible and wholly adverse impact on the economy of Newcastle, as is borne out by the text of a petition of 1317:

Those of the town who have lands outside it are ruined by the enemy. Merchants in the town have so given themselves to defence that they cannot trade. Their goods are stolen on the sea by the enemy and by Flemings. Tradesmen of the town can find no work because the country round about is destroyed and their possessions have been spent in the defence of the town. The Commonalty are unable to sustain this responsibility without royal aid.[144]

This petition highlights a factor which was also significant at Carlisle, separation of the town from the economic hinterland upon which it depended, and the vulnerability of that hinterland to destruction by Scottish raiders. The graph of wool exports shows a deep trough between the high points of 1309 and 1329 which corresponds broadly with the years of the worst border warfare; as does that of animal hides. Wool exports are seriously depressed from 1314, hides from 1311; and the troughs in each graph at 1319, 1322 and 1326–28 undoubtedly reflect the evacuation of flocks and herds in response to Scottish raids. Warfare was however only one of a host of variables affecting exports: the level of smuggling; fluctuations in demand for wool in the towns of Flanders; the introduction of the wool staple in 1313; the sheep murrain of 1315–16; and, most powerfully, the threat of privateering on the North Sea. Dr.

Chart 7

Newcastle and Hartlepool Wool Exports
(Source: E. M. Carus Wilson and O. Coleman, *England's Export Trade, 1275-1547* (Oxford, 1963) pp. 38-45)

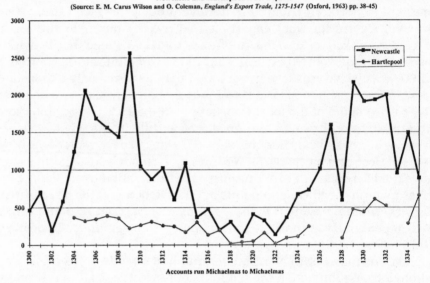

Accounts run Michaelmas to Michaelmas

Chart 8

Exports of Hides from Newcastle 1304/5 to 1332/33
(Source: J. B. Blake, Some Aspects of the Trade of Newcastle upon Tyne in the Fourteenth Century (M.A. Thesis, Bristol University, 1962) p. 120)

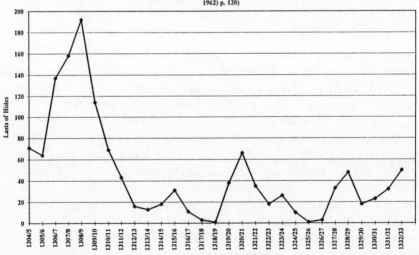

Accounts run Michaelmas to Michaelmas

Fraser has drawn attention to the fall in the number of Newcastle wool exporters, from 118 in 1308 to only 44 in 1326: '. . . it now paid only the substantial merchants to face the risks of the sea crossing to the great wool markets in Flanders'.[145] As wool exports failed, Newcastle merchants may have turned to coal as a substitute export commodity; occasionally ransoms were paid to the Scots in coal.[146] In the immediate aftermath of war, commercial activity at Newcastle seems to have recovered. By 1329 her wool exports had exceeded even the level of 1305, and they continued at a high level until the next outbreak of border violence. Assessments for lay subsidies provide another broad indicator of general prosperity in Newcastle. In 1296 Newcastle's total taxable wealth was given as £948, but in 1336 the town paid a fine of 200 marks for exemption from a tenth, suggesting that total taxable wealth had increased to something in excess of £1,333.[147] As to population, an influx of refugees from war-torn Northumberland, seeking safety behind the town walls, may have swollen the population of the town, increasing the prices of foodstuffs and property. Signs of building on the castle mound and along the Tyne bridge have been detected, and indications of land reclamation from the river may date from this period.[148] It is noticeable however that hide exports did not recover to the same degree as wool exports; and, if there was a rise in population giving rise to prosperity for merchants and property holders, this too was short-lived. As early as 1327 Newcastle claimed to have been impoverished and depopulated by costs of defence and enclosing the town; that the huge costs of defence and all the inconveniences of war were driving common people away from the town, and impoverishing the community.[149] In 1348 the men of Newcastle asked for a 20-year grant of murage on grounds that the town was suffering greatly from shortage of population.[150] Any growth was therefore succeeded by a long-term decline, caused most probably by war damage to the hinterland on which Newcastle depended.

CONCLUSION

It is difficult to underestimate the role of the towns and North Sea commerce during the Wars of the Bruces. Flemish imports compensated the Scots to some extent for the lack of a large town in the early stages of the war; and the support of Flemish seamen allowed Robert I to survive in the face of Anglo-French détente. As concentrations of wealth, manpower, materials and shipping, the large towns bestowed enormous advantages on their controller, such as could never come from possession of a mere castle. If walled, they were defensible against all but the most powerful assailants. The capture of a major English or Irish town may have brought the Bruces much closer to their political aims than a decade of raiding the English countryside. Had they been able to attain such a prize and hold it, Edward II might have been compelled to negotiate, and perhaps moved to compromise on the issue of Scottish sovereignty. The capture and defence of Berwick forced Edward to agree to a two-year truce, and must have played a large part in persuading him to approve the Truce of Bishopthorpe. How much more would Edward have given for the return of Carlisle, Newcastle or even Dublin? Had the Bruces captured such a town and not bartered it away in return for theoretical concessions, they might have permanently altered the political map of the British Isles – enlarged the boundaries of Scotland or occupied or partitioned Ireland. Their failure to do so can be attributed largely to their shortage of engineering skills and technological expertise in siege warfare, apparent at the siege of Carlisle and in their shying away from Dublin and Newcastle.

NOTES

1 Discussed in R. Dobson, 'Cathedral Chapters and Cathedral Cities: York, Durham and Carlisle in the Fifteenth Century', *NH* xix (1983), 15–44 ; *The Scottish Medieval Town*, ed. M. Lynch , M. Spearman, G. Stell (Edinburgh, 1988). H. Summerson, *Medieval Carlisle* (CWAAS Extra Series xxxv, 1993) treats extensively of Carlisle in this period.

2 E.B. Fryde, *William de la Pole* (London, 1988), p. 18; R. Horrox, *The De La Poles of Hull* (East Yorkshire Local Record Society xxxviii, 1983), p. 10.

3 A trio of articles by W.S. Reid forms the basis of discussion: 'Trade, Traders and Scottish Independence', *Speculum* xxix (1954), 210–22; 'The Scots and the Staple Ordinance of 1313', *Speculum* xxxiv (1959), 598–610; 'Sea Power and the Anglo-Scottish War', *The Mariners' Mirror* xlvi (1960), 7–23. Chapters in *The Scottish Medieval Town* are especially relevant: D. Ditchburn, 'Trade with Northern Europe, 1297–1540', pp. 161–63 and A. Stevenson, 'Trade with the South, 1070–1513', pp. 185–89.

4 B. Greenwood, *Archaeology of the Boat* (London, 1976), pp. 250–65.

5 *Rot. Scot.* i, 83, 129, 178; Bodleian Library MS Tanner 197, f. 40d.

6 R. Horrox, *Selected Records and Accounts of Medieval Hull 1293–1528* (Yorkshire Archaeological Society, Record Series, cxli, 1983), pp. 57–58.

7 M. Prestwich, *War, Politics and Finance under Edward I* (London, 1972), pp. 141–47; Reid, 'Sea Power', pp. 11–12.

8 A. Stevenson, 'The Flemish Dimension of the Auld Alliance', *Scotland and the Low Countries 1124–1994*, ed. G.G. Simpson (East Linton, 1996), pp. 30–31; *Guisborough*, p. 275.

9 A. Stevenson, 'Trade between Scotland and the Low Countries in the Middle Ages' (Aberdeen University Ph.D., 1982), p. 11.

10 Full text and facsimile in *Documents Illustrative of Sir William Wallace, his Life and Times*, ed. J. Stevenson (Edinburgh, 1870), p. 159 and frontispiece. *Lanercost*, pp. 164–65 and *Scalachronica*, pp. 19–21 agree that Wallace had brief possession of Berwick.

11 T.H. Lloyd, *The English Wool Trade in the Middle Ages* (Cambridge, 1977), p. 324, n. 46.

12 Barrow, *Robert Bruce*, p. 199. Edward I suspected the Flemings of sustaining Scottish revolt in April 1305, *CDS* v, no. 411, p. 189.
13 Prestwich, *Edward I*, pp. 394–98.
14 *Rot. Scot.* i, 55 where his name is written 'le Betour'.
15 Ditchburn, 'Trade with Northern Europe, 1297–1540', p. 164.
16 *RRS* v no. 425, p. 665.
17 J.W. Dilley, 'German Merchants in Scotland', *SHR* xxvii (1948), 142–55.
18 *Rot. Scot.* i, 78.
19 Lloyd, *English Wool Trade*, pp. 104–5.
20 H.S. Lucas, 'John Crabbe, Flemish Pirate, Merchant and Adventurer', *Speculum* xx (1945), 334–50; E.W.M. Balfour-Melville, 'Two John Crabbs', *SHR* xxxix (1960), 31–34.
21 JUST 1/1146/4, m. 1d. The bitter municipal rivalries are examined in *The History of Scarborough*, ed. A. Rowntree (London, 1931), pp. 111–16; *VCH of Yorkshire (North Riding)* ii, 550.
22 Reid, 'Trade, Traders and Scottish Independence', p. 221; *CCR 1307–13*, p. 436.
23 Dilley, 'German Merchants in Scotland', pp. 142–55. But as Reid points out, such accusations may have been spurious, levelled against the Germans by their English competitors: 'Trade, Traders and Scottish Independence', p. 219, n. 70.
24 *CDS* iii no. 679, p. 129.
25 BL MS Cotton Nero C viij, ff. 67d, 71.
26 *CCR 1307–13*, p. 432; Lloyd, *English Wool Trade*, p. 104.
27 Stevenson, 'Trade between Scotland and the Low Countries', p. 18.
28 Lloyd, *English Wool Trade*, pp. 105–6.
29 *Fordun* ii, 339; *Rot. Scot.* i, 108–9.
30 SC1/33/34, 36; SC1/34/126, 178; SC1/35/85.
31 *CCR 1307–13*, pp. 570–71.
32 *CPR 1307–13*, p. 591; Lloyd, *English Wool Trade*, pp. 106–7.
33 *CCR 1307–13*, pp. 570–71; Lloyd, *English Wool Trade*, p. 106.
34 SC1/33/35.
35 *Rot. Scot.* i, 136.
36 Lloyd, *English Wool Trade*, p. 107.
37 Dilley, 'German Merchants in Scotland', pp. 146–47.
38 *Rot. Scot.* i, 139, 141; *CCR 1313–18*, p. 218.
39 E101/376/7, f. 19d; *Rot. Scot.* i, 141.
40 *British Naval Documents 1204–1960*, ed. J.B. Hattendorf *et al* (Naval Records Society cxxxi, 1993), no. 35, p. 46.
41 Lloyd, *English Wool Trade*, pp. 107–8.
42 *CDS* iii no. 448, p. 84.
43 E101/376/7, ff. 67d-69; *CCW 1244–1326*, p. 432.
44 Reid, 'Trade, Traders and Scottish Independence', pp. 214–15.
45 *Rot. Scot.* i, 151.
46 *CDS* iii no. 486, p. 93; *Rot. Scot.* i, 154.
47 SC1/34/162; *CIM* ii no. 358, p. 89; *CCR 1313–18*, pp. 387–88.
48 *CDS* iii no. 486, p. 93.
49 *CCR 1313–18*, p. 310. In the next reign the Dorias supplied Genoese galleys to Edward III for use against the Scots in the North Sea, *British Naval Documents*, no. 13, p. 21.

50 *CCR 1313–18*, p. 422.
51 See above, p. 181.
52 *CCR 1313–18*, p. 444.
53 See pp. 84, 181.
54 *CPR 1313–17*, p. 603 ; SC1/36/173.
55 Society of Antiquaries, MS 120, f. 29d; Barbour, *The Bruce* XVI, 543–666.
56 Fraser, *Northern Petitions* no. 131, pp. 177–78; Scammell, 'Robert I', pp. 393–94; SC1/19/142.
57 Lloyd, *English Wool Trade*, p. 109; *RRS* v no. 126, p. 397.
58 *Lanercost*, pp. 219–20.
59 This is inferred from the Count's reply.
60 *CDS* iii no. 673, p. 126.
61 *CDS* iii no. 683, p. 130. Stevenson suggests that Robert I had established a staple of his own at Bruges at this time or shortly afterwards, 'Trade between Scotland and the Low Countries', p. 233 n. 80.
62 Lloyd, *English Wool Trade*, pp. 109–114.
63 Fraser, *Northern Petitions*, no. 131, pp. 177–78 ; SC1/36/12, 13.
64 Lloyd, *English Wool Trade*, p. 113.
65 BL MS Stowe 553, ff. 51, 77–78. The fleet numbered either 36 or 25 vessels; but it is unclear which ships were involved in the Scottish expedition and which in other royal service. The total pay of sailors was £1,201; but this includes the pay of the crews of the western fleet of 14 vessels.
66 BL MS Stowe 553, f. 67v. Dr Fryde states that 14 ships were wrecked by storm. I have been unable to find the reference to this in the Wardrobe Book, BL MS Stowe 553.
67 Fryde, *Tyranny and Fall*, pp. 134–41.
68 *Foedera*, ii (I), 499, 500, 508. Prior to March 1323 the new Count was able to act independently of France, but after that date he became a tool of the French monarchy, D. Nicholas, *Medieval Flanders* (London, 1992), pp. 209–11. I am grateful to Dr. Ditchburn for pointing this out to me.
69 Lloyd, *English Wool Trade*, p. 114.
70 See below, pp. 224–25.
71 Stevenson, 'Trade with the South, 1070–1513', pp. 187–88.
72 *Bronnen tot de Geschiedenis van den Handel met Engeland, Schotland en Ierland, 1150–1485*, ed. H.J. Smit(s'Gravenhage, 1928), nos. 310, 311. I owe this reference to Dr. Ditchburn.
73 Fraser, *Northern Petitions* no. 13, p. 28.
74 *CDS* v no. 358, p. 183; BL MS Cotton Nero C viij, f. 5d; J. Scott, *Berwick Upon Tweed* (London, 1888), Appendix I, p. 445.
75 Comparing *CPR 1313–17*, p. 671 with Scott, *Berwick*, Appendix I, p. 445.
76 Fraser, *Northern Petitions*, no. 38, pp. 68–70 which lists the names of 27 exiles; *Ibid.*, nos. 3, 5; *Rot. Scot.* i, 264–75.
77 *Lanercost*, pp. 200–1.
78 Fraser, *Northern Petitions*, no. 14, pp. 28–34.
79 *CDS* iii nos. 186, 337.
80 *Rot. Scot.* i, 132.

81 *CDS* iii nos. 427, 553; Fraser, *Northern Petitions*, no. 30, pp. 59–61.
82 *CCR 1313–18*, p. 32
83 *CDS* v nos. 591, 596; *Lanercost*, p. 232.
84 Barbour, *The Bruce* XVII, 377–81.
85 *CDS* iii nos. 452, 470, 477.
86 *Rot. Scot.* i, 151.
87 *Lanercost*, p. 232; confirmed by E101/376/7, f. 41.
88 *CDS* iii no. 477, p. 91; Barbour, *The Bruce* XV, 315–85.
89 Text in *CCW 1244–1326*, pp. 438–39, calendared in *CDS* iii no. 477, p. 91.
90 *CDS* iii no. 486, p. 93.
91 *CCW 1244–1326*, p. 458; Duncan, *RRS* v Introduction, pp. 142–45.
92 *CDS* iii nos. 333, 384; *Rot. Scot.*i, 113, 149–50; Fraser, *Ancient Petitions*, no. 48, p. 63.
93 *CDS* iii no. 486, p. 93.
94 E159/90, m. 117; Fraser, *Northern Petitions*, no. 34, pp. 65–66.
95 E101/367/7, ff. 111d–113d.
96 *Lanercost*, pp. 219–20; Barbour, *The Bruce*, XVII, 16–170.
97 Barbour, *The Bruce*, XVII, 327–504, 589–862 ; Maddicott, *Lancaster*, pp. 244–49.
98 *Rot. Scot.*, i, 178, 181; *CDS* iii no. 602, p. 114.
99 BL MS Add 17362, ff. 25, 28.
100 Phillips *Aymer de Valance*; BL Add MS 17362, ff. 25, 28.
101 *CDS* iii no. 663, p. 124.
102 Fraser, *Northern Petitions* no. 71, pp. 105–6; *Reg. Melton* i, no. 394, p. 120 and *Lanercost*, p. 238; Farrer, *Lancashire Inquests* ii, 168.
103 M. Beresford, *The New Towns of the Middle Ages* (London, 1967), pp. 471–725) and 475.
104 SC6/1144/3; SC6/952/12, 13; SC6/950/1; Fraser, *Northern Petitions*, no. 131, pp. 181–82.
105 C.P.M. Olsen, 'The Older Settlements of North Northumberland' (London University MA thesis, 1947), pp. 139, 241–42, 244–45; S. Wrathmell, 'Deserted and Shrunken Villages in Southern Northumberland from the Twelfth to the Twentieth Centuries' (Cardiff University Ph.D thesis, 1976) i, 14–15; Beresford, *New Towns*, p. 475, citing SC6/950/3 and SC6/950/2; Fraser, *Ancient Petitions*, no. 215, pp. 242–43; R.A. Lomas, *North-East England in the Middle Ages* (Edinburgh, 1992), pp. 161–62.
106 See p. 69 n. 106; DCD Almoner's Rent Rolls 1313, 1325.
107 *CIM* ii no. 385, 392, 489.
108 Farrer, *Lancashire Inquests*, pp. 107, 116, 168, 172; J.F. Willard, 'The Scotch Raids and the fourteenth century taxation of northern England', *University of Colorado Studies* v, No. 4 (1908), p. 239; *Lanercost*, p. 246; E159/102, m. 177d.
109 *Lanercost*, p. 233; KB27/250, m. 88d; *CIM* ii no. 452, pp. 111–12; *CDS* iii nos. 707, 858.
110 See above p. 144.
111 H.L. Turner, *Town Defences in England and Wales* (London, 1970), pp. 97–117.
112 Fraser, *Northern Petitions*, no. 131, pp. 177–78.

113 R. Horrox, *Selected Records and Accounts of Medieval Hull 1293–1528* (Yorkshire Archaeological Society, Record Series, cxli, 1983), pp. 53–58.

114 *CDS* iii nos. 524, 621.

115 B. Harbottle, 'The Town Wall of Newcastle Upon Tyne: Consolidation and Excavation in 1968', *AA* 4th series, xlvii (1969), 72; C.M. Fraser, 'The Town Ditch of Newcastle Upon Tyne' *AA* 4th series xxxix (1961), 381–3; Turner, *Town Defences*, p. 104.

116 *NCH* viii, 83–92, 146, 150–204.

117 *Chart. St. Mary's Dublin* ii, 353; *Hist. Mun. Docs.*, pp. 392–93, 402–12.

118 C.M. Fraser, 'The Life and Death of John Denton', *AA* 4th series xxxvii (1959), 304; J.C. Davies, 'An Assembly of Wool Merchants in 1322', *EHR* xxxi (1916), 600.

119 *An Inventory of the Historical Monuments of the City of York*, Vol.ii, *The Defences* (Royal Commission on Historical Monuments, 1972), p. 36.

120 *Hist. Mun. Docs.*, pp. 359–66.

121 E159/93, mm. 126d-127. Elsewhere the citizens did complain about 'constant watchings', *CDS* iii no. 616, p. 117.

122 *CCR 1313–18*, pp. 182, 422; Welford, *Newcastle*, i, 42–43.

123 *CDS* iii no. 675, pp. 127–28. These indictments are fully discussed in I. Hall, 'The Lords and Lordships of the English West March: Cumberland and Westmoreland from circa 1250 to circa 1350' (Durham University Ph.D thesis, 1986), pp. 306–10.

124 B.C. Jones, 'The Topography of Medieval Carlisle', *CWAAS* 2nd series lxxvi (1976), 77–78.

125 *Rot. Parl.*, i, 195; *CPR 1313–17*, p. 632; Cumberland Record Office Lonsdale Deeds D/Lons/L c. 20, dated by Jones to c. 1311, 'Topography of Medieval Carlisle', p. 78.

126 York Minster Library, VC6/2/3, 9; *VCH Yorkshire (City of York)*, pp. 55–56.

127 E101/7/8; E101/11/1; E101/374/16, f. 5d.

128 *CDS* iii no. 514, p. 98; Society of Antiquaries MS 120, f. 45d; Society of Antiquaries MS 121, f. 21d; E101/14/31 (1314); BL MS Stowe 553, f. 61d (1322). R. B. Dobson estimates the city's population to have been around 2,000 in 1400, 'Cathedral Chapters and Cathedral Cities', p. 30.

129 See above, p. 189.

130 *Rot. Scot.* i, 154; E159/93, m. 127; Fraser, *Northern Petitions*, no. 81, pp. 114–15; *CDS* iii no. 674, pp. 126–27; *CCR 1313–18*, pp. 127–28.

131 *CCR 1313–17*, pp. 127–28; Fraser, *Northern Petitions* no. 79, p. 113.

132 Garrison strength was a mere 10 men-at-arms on 16th May 1315, *CCR 1313–18*, p. 173.

133 BL MS Stowe 553, f. 23d, and *Scalacronica*, p. 68. There are other instances of disorder among the troops, *CIM* i no. 2376, p. 632.

134 E101/375/8, f. 25; BL MS Stowe 553, f. 63.

135 *Trokelowe*, p. 101; *Walsingham* i, 154; *Le Bel*, pp. 39–42; an English source claims that the riot was between citizens and the foreigners, see *Eulogium Historiarum* iii, 199.

136 Summerson, *Medieval Carlisle*, pp. 205–11.

137 M. Prestwich, *York Civic Ordinances, 1301*, (Borthwick Papers 49, 1976), p. 1.

138 *Handbook of British Chronology*, ed. F.M. Powicke and E.B. Fryde (Royal

Historical Society, 1961), pp. 515–17; *CCR 1296–1302*, pp. 259–60; *Reg. Greenfield* ii, no. 1092, p. 196.

139 *A History of York Minster*, ed. G.E. Aylmer and R. Cant (Oxford, 1977), pp. 341–50.

140 *Rot. Scot.* i, 216.

141 J. Campbell, 'England, Scotland and the Hundred Years War', in *Europe in the Late Middle Ages*, ed. J.R. Hale, J.R.L. Highfield and B. Smalley (London, 1965), p. 185.

142 Figures for Berwick from *The Exchequer Rolls of Scotland*, ed. J. Stuart and G. Burnett (Edinburgh, 1878), i, 79–81, 97, 173, 278, 370, 419–20, 428–29; figures for England from E. Carus-Wilson and O. Coleman, *England's Export Trade, 1275–1547* (Oxford, 1963), pp. 43–44. Differences between English and Scottish customs rates are insignificant at this stage, and are unlikely to have affected trade, *Exchequer Rolls of Scotland* i, p. xcix and n. 2; D.W.H. Marshall, 'The Organisation of the English Occupation of Scotland, 1296–1461' (Oxford University B. Litt. thesis, 1925), pp. 58–59.

143 Stevenson, 'Trade between Scotland and the Low Countries', pp. 249–50.

144 Fraser, 'Town Ditch', pp. 382–83.

145 Fraser, 'John Denton', p. 305.

146 *CDS* iii nos. 698, 813; Welford, *Newcastle*, i, 63, 72; J. Blake, 'Some aspects of the Trade of Newcastle upon Tyne in the Fourteenth Century' (Bristol University MA thesis, 1962), pp. 45–81.

147 C.M. Fraser, *The Northumberland Lay Subsidy of 1296* (Society of Antiquaries of Newcastle Upon Tyne, 1968), p. xiv; R. Glascock, *The Lay Subsidy of 1334* (London, 1975), p. 219.

148 *Trokelowe*, p. 91; *Archaeology in the North*, Appendix I, p. 118; J. Brand, *The History and Antiquities of the County and Town of Newcastle Upon Tyne* (London, 1789) ii, 10–11, note 'y'; C.M. Fraser and K. Emsley, *Tyneside* (1973), p. 26.

149 C47/2/63 (7).

150 Fraser, *Northern Petitions* no. 13, p. 12.

Conclusion: The Climax and Collapse of the Scottish Hegemony in the British Isles, 1322–1330

Someone hereafter may perhaps wonder how the Scottish people had the boldness to resist, and why the courage of the English should so suddenly have failed them

The Scottish military supremacy in the British Isles which lasted from 1311 to 1333 was made possible principally by the coincidence of two special circumstances. These were: an economic catastrophe that seems to have affected England, the more populous, more corn-dependent country, much more severely than Scotland; and the absorption of England's aristocracy in domestic disputes of peculiar bitterness. The Scots however encountered enormous difficulty in translating their temporary military supremacy into political and diplomatic triumph. Forcing the English to the negotiating table involved a further five years of diplomatic manoeuvring and processes at the papal court; a fresh wave of Scottish invasions of northern England including another attempt to capture the English king; revival of the plan to involve the Irish and the Welsh in containing England; and a final assault on the castles of Northumberland. Even then it took one further special circumstance to give to Scotland even the illusion of victory: the emergence in England of a new regime, unstable enough to need peace at any price.

MANOEUVRING FOR SECURITY:
ENGLAND, SCOTLAND AND FRANCE, 1322–27

In war English armies had been unable to bring the Scottish hobelars to battle, but in diplomacy, the Scottish king could not bring the English to admit defeat. During the winter of 1322–23 truces were extended to allow for prolonged negotiations,[1] but it was not at all certain that a lasting peace was yet on the horizon. Aspects of the Middleton rebellion and the Harclay episode are suggestive of a groundswell for peace among the northern English gentry; but although the north of England was exhausted, devastated and largely disaffected, the English king and aristocracy were determined to fight on. English magnates who stood to lose forever titles to land in Scotland included Henry Beaumont, Henry Percy, Thomas Wake and David de Strabogie, Earl of Atholl. English preparations for a fresh campaign had been interrupted early in 1323 by the Harclay incident; afterwards, they recommenced against a background of uneasy truces with the Scots and alarms of imminent raids. The Scots were thought to be preparing to raid in March of that year and again on the lapse of a truce in May. On this last occasion it was ordered that cattle on the west march should be evacuated to Yorkshire and that civilians should take shelter in walled towns and castles 'so that the enemy if they invade the county, may not have any sustenance'. Almost 10,000 Welsh infantry were summoned in April to appear at Newcastle on 1st July 1323; other infantry were to arrive equipped with heavy armour, aketons, bascinets and *palettis*.[2] Although negotiations were conducted through the French knight Henry de Sully (who had been captured at Bylands), Edward II still refused to address Robert as king, and addressed his remarks only to the Scottish people.[3] In April he was assessing the cost of raising troops in Gascony for a new Scottish campaign.[4]

Robert claimed with considerable justification that he had consistently desired 'always to negotiate with the king of England ... in the form of a final peace'.[5] As time wore on, his anxiety to secure lasting peace increased. Though he was still only 48 years old, he must have been aware that Scotland's safety depended upon his own personal leadership. His health may already have been declining and he had as yet no direct heir. More pressing than either of these considerations however was the re-emergence of a dormant threat to the Bruce monarchy. Although all indications of an alternative to Robert I's kingship have been expunged from the narrative sources, Professor Duncan has shown that sections of the Scottish aristocracy remained sympathetic to the idea of a Balliol revival. It seems to have been this potential for instability more than any other factor that prompted Robert to make peace. At the Scottish parliament of 1318 it was ordered that conspirators and spreaders of discontent be imprisoned, suggesting a degree of domestic dissatisfaction.[6] Then in 1320 a shadowy conspiracy came to light.

The occasion for this conspiracy was the making of the Declaration of Arbroath, the famous letter from the people of Scotland to Pope John XXII, which sought papal intervention to persuade Edward II to make a final peace with Scotland. A masterpiece of nationalist rhetoric, it was intended to be interpreted by the pope as a spontaneous expression of outrage from the community of the realm at English machinations against Robert at the papal curia. The letter was of course concocted by Robert's chancery. Seals were collected from individual magnates named in the prologue (and from others besides), and appended to the document.[7] The process of collecting personal seals and their use on such a spirited justification of Bruce kingship seems to have aroused the rancour of magnates and stirred up latent Balliol sentiment. Robert's diplomats, carrying the Declaration to the curia by way of the French court, discovered contacts between French magnates and pro-Balliol elements in Scotland. The leader of the mission, Patrick Earl of Dunbar, hurried back to Scotland to warn Robert;[8] and his warning resulted in the trials of conspirators at the Black Parliament of 1320. One of the plotters, the Countess of Strathearn, turned king's evidence. David Brechin and William Soules were convicted of treason; and the same verdict was pronounced on the corpse of Roger Mowbray, a conspirator who had died before the trial. Brechin was hanged as a traitor; Soules and Strathearn were imprisoned for life. According to the chronicles, the object of the conspiracy had been to install Soules as king; but this is most unlikely, as he had no claim to the throne and his life was spared by Robert.[9] The plot can only have made sense if it supported the Balliol alternative.

The Soules conspiracy and the executions following the Black Parliament were profoundly unsettling, and explain why long-term security became Robert's priority. In negotiations at Bamburgh in 1321 a truce of 26 years had already been suggested by the Scots.[10] By 1323 Flemish support for the Scots had evaporated, making it yet more desirable for Scotland's security to be guaranteed. But a major obstacle to peace with England was those English magnates who had been granted lands and titles in Scotland and who refused to contemplate any settlement that would make permanent their loss. They were to become 'the disinherited', lords who felt cheated of rights in Scotland and a powerful force for war with Scotland. In April, when the earl of Moray was granted safe conduct to come to Newcastle to continue negotiations, Henry Beaumont, Thomas Wake, William Ros of Hamelak and Ralph Graystoke, who were among the most prominent intransigents, were selected to go to Scotland as hostages for Moray's safety.[11] Whoever made this selection recognised the threat that they posed to a settlement and hit upon this device to sideline them for the duration of negotiations.

On 30th May 1323 Edward II agreed to the Truce of Bishopthorpe with Scotland.[12] This temporary settlement saved Edward's blushes by shelving the issue of the title to the Scottish throne and providing for a 13-year truce, binding on the successors of each king. Occupied territory was to be surrendered by 12th June 1323, a provision probably intended to apply to the Scottish presence in Tynedale. No fortifications were to be built between the border and the line of the Tyne and South Tyne, or in the sheriffdoms of Berwick, Roxburgh and Dumfries, but those in the making (for example, the new castle at Dunstanburgh which Edward II had garrisoned) were allowed to remain. Subjects of either king were forbidden to have any dealings with those of the other, and neither king was to receive the enemies of the other. Finally, Edward II undertook not to prevent the Scots from obtaining absolution and an end to the excommunication from the papal curia, a promise he flagrantly breached.

This agreement was fair, balanced and ought to have provided a basis for a permanent peace. Yet it was only just sufficient to win acceptance in England. At a royal council in 1323 Henry Beaumont showed the depth of his disgust at the agreement to suspend hostilities with Scotland, as an account of council debate on the truce reveals:

> And when the king enjoined each of those present, singly, including Henry, to give their advice, the said Henry, with an excessive motion and irreverent mind, answered the king frequently that he would not counsel him in this behalf. The king being moved by such an answer ordered him to leave his council, and Henry in leaving the council said, as he had said before, that it would please him more to be absent from the council than to be present.[13]

Edward II then forced this sensible arrangement upon intransigent magnates, but he was compelling them to accept precisely what he himself was not prepared to stomach, loss of 'title' or 'right' in Scotland. Royal power in England was now at its height; the 'tyranny of Edward II' was in full swing. Harclay's defeat of Thomas of Lancaster and the king's cowing of opposition from the lords of the Welsh marches left no effective opposition.[14] Royal coffers were suddenly filled by the revenues of confiscated estates, and swollen further by a streamlining of exchequer procedures. The administration was controlled by a narrow, avaricious clique of royal favourites, led by the two Hugh Despensers (father and son), Robert Baldock (a clerk of Hugh the younger), the king's half-brother Thomas of Woodstock earl of Kent, and the earl of Arundel. 'Contrariants' were persecuted vindictively, and few were prepared to put their heads above the parapet. The leader of opposition on the Welsh marches, Roger Mortimer of Wigmore, was detained in the Tower of London. In a daring escape from the Tower in August 1323, he cheated the hangman and fled to France where he worked to undermine the regime.[15]

With respect to the peace, there may also have been considerable opposition in Scotland. For Scottish lairds war on England must have been infinitely more lucrative than agriculture, and it is not surprising to find that a report to Edward II of 29th April 1323 maintained that 'the nobles and commons desire war more than peace', and furthermore in a letter to Edward paraphrased in the *Vita Edwardi II* Robert protested his inability to 'withhold the fury of a raging throng'.[16] In spite of the lack of statistical evidence from Scotland, there are a few indications of enrichment as a result of the wartime robber-economy. Fordun asserts that the reign of King Robert was a time of prosperity; and the fact that Flemish, German and even English merchants defied Edward II's blockade to trade with the Scots might suggest that Scots could pay higher prices.[17] When Scottish commodity prices become available to the historian after 1327 they are high, suggesting a relatively large amount of bullion circulating in the country, fruits of a buoyant wool export trade and recent successful war.[18]

Nevertheless two factors arose the following year which might have paved the way for lasting peace between England and Scotland. The first was the birth of an heir to Robert I in March 1324. The arrival of David Bruce lent a new urgency to Robert's quest for lasting security; and negotiations commenced for a final settlement in July 1324 at Robert's instigation and carried on through the autumn.[19] The second factor, the collapse of the Anglo-French understanding, prodded Edward II in the same direction. Tension between France and England had escalated following Charles IV's succession to the French throne in January 1322. The eventual outbreak of the War of St. Sardos between England and France in the autumn of 1323 exerted pressure on Edward to come to some arrangement with the Scots. Edward may have been hoping for military service or assistance from Scotland, and there was talk of his leading an army of English and Welsh, Irish and Scots to save Gascony from French invasion.[20] But Scottish terms had been raised in order to take advantage of Edward's difficulty in Gascony, and now included a claim to 'perambulation of the Anglo-Scottish march'. Exactly what is meant by this is unclear; the only source is the *Vita Edwardi II* whose author is outraged at the suggestion, as though it amounted to a territorial claim over parts of northern England: 'they demanded by right of conquest and lordship that the whole land that they had perambulated should be free as far as the gates of York'.[21] Perhaps a 'buffer' or 'security zone' was envisaged; not a huge step from the restrictions under the current treaty on the building of castles in border areas. But ultimately the negotiations foundered on the question of Edward II's right in Scotland, on which the English had never contemplated concession.

The Truce of Bishopthorpe might have run its full course had not English domestic politics taken a dramatic turn, transforming relations with Scotland. The administration of Edward II began to look increasingly unstable, the price of a ruthless exploitation of the privileges of kingship, and woeful management of royal patronage. It dispatched an expedition to Gascony, but Edward dared not leave England to lead it for fear of a *coup* against his hated favourites the Despensers.[22] In March 1325 Queen Isabella left her husband's court for that of her brother's in Paris, the formal purpose of her visit being to conclude on Edward's behalf a peace to end conflict over Gascony. But having executed this task, Isabella refused to return to England while the Despensers were at court. She became a focus for discontented exiles in France; English dissidents collected around her and Roger Mortimer, the foremost of them, formed an open liaison with her. Although Isabella and her coterie of supporters moved to Hainault early in 1326, Edward II continued to expect further war with France.

There was much in Edward's behaviour over the period 1323 to 1326 to provoke the Scots; apart from his continued refusal to recognise Robert's title, he had sent a powerful delegation to Rome in an effort to bring further ecclesiastical sanctions to bear on Scotland.[23] His policies were responsible for driving Robert I into the arms of the French, and in April 1326 Robert concluded an alliance with France culminating in the Treaty of Corbeil. This treaty was designed to increase pressure on Edward II to come to a final agreement, but it specifically allowed for the Truce of Bishopthorpe to run its course. If there was to be an Anglo-French war, Scotland would join the side of France, but only when the Anglo-Scottish truce had ended.[24] Robert had not therefore despaired of wringing a final peace out of Edward II; but at about the same time he seems to have orchestrated surprise attacks on the key northern castles of Carlisle, Norham, Alnwick and Dunstanburgh.[25] The capture of just one of these strongholds might have given Robert sufficient leverage to wring a final settlement from the increasingly vulnerable Edward II. In the event Robert may have had to disown these attempts; at any rate the English chose to overlook these violations of the truce, a clear sign that Edward now needed the truce more than Robert. Thus by diplomatic and military means Robert hoped to force Edward to give priority to the issue of a final settlement with Scotland. Stubborn to the last and isolated at home and abroad, Edward decided to trust that the Scottish truce would hold, and to take on the French. By summer 1326 he was openly at war with France; and in September Isabella and Mortimer landed in England, their army spearheaded by 700 men-at-arms led by John of Hainault.[26] Significantly Isabella was joined by two northerners who had much to lose if a permanent peace were concluded with Scotland, Henry Percy and Thomas Wake. Edward's oppressive regime crumbled; and he fled London on 2nd October, making for Wales.

There was no sympathy among the English lords of the Welsh march for Edward II , who had oppressed them since their abortive rising of 1321–22. Mortimer's tenants and retainers would have been particularly hostile. But Edward could rely upon the loyalty of the native Welsh, particularly upon Gruffydd Llwyd in North Wales and Rhys ap Gruffydd in the South. Both had assisted him against the marcher lords in 1321, and both had led infantry contingents during the invasion of Scotland in the following year.[27] But aware that he would need greater military assistance to effect a restoration, Edward may at last have contemplated the surrender of his claim to Scotland. In its last months his regime had softened towards the Scots.[28] Robert preferred to deal with Edward II (with whom he had a truce and perhaps now something of an understanding) rather than the new regime supported by the warlike disinherited lords. Contact with Edward was maintained through Donald Earl of Mar, a nephew of Robert I who had been brought up at the English court, and who had shown great personal attachment to Edward, refusing to return to Scotland after Bannockburn.[29] Lanercost alleges that Edward wrote to Robert I surrendering his right in Scotland and ceding to him a part of northern England, but there is no evidence to substantiate this.[30]

In England meanwhile, Mar assisted in the elder Despenser's desperate defence of Bristol against the army of Isabella and Mortimer. When the city fell, he escaped (or was spared) and, accompanied by Rhys ap Gruffydd, returned to Scotland, from where he continued to plot for Edward's restoration.[31] Edward and his dwindling band of courtiers meanwhile continued to flee westwards. They were pursued by Mortimer and John of Hainault who feared

> that if the king could reach Ireland he might collect an army there and cross over into Scotland, and by the help of the Scots and Irish together he might attack England.[32]

Thus Ireland was seen as a locale for a reserve royalist army, as it was to be centuries later in the 1640s. But Edward II was captured on or about 16th November 1326, and in January 1327 he was tried before an assembly, representative of the realm but of dubious legality and summoned in the name of Edward Prince of Wales. By this assembly Edward II was deposed. The articles of his deposition are chiefly taken up with the king's domestic misrule. They include the allegation that he had been personally responsible for the loss of Scotland; but no particular stress is put on the old king's failures in Scotland and in the same breath he is accused of diminishing the lands of the crown in Ireland and Gascony.[33] The Prince of Wales was crowned as Edward III on 2nd February and the old king remained in prison, an embarrassment and a challenge to the new regime. But Donald of Mar did not despair of Edward II's restoration. Returning in July and August 1327 to the Welsh marches (perhaps to the vicinity of Edward II's prison at Berkley), Donald began rousing the people to resist the new regime.[34]

THE WEARDALE CAMPAIGN OF 1327

Robert I continued his attacks on border castles, warning the new regime in England that he expected his demands for a final settlement to be met. A Scottish attack on Norham Castle occurred on the very day the young Edward III was crowned.[35] Isabella and Mortimer, now firmly in control of the English administration, did not retaliate but instead ordered strict observation of the truce. They also took a number of defensive measures, chief of which were commissions to Antony Lucy to keep Carlisle, and to Henry Percy to serve as *chevetaigne* in the north with 100 men-at-arms, 100 hobelars and as many of his own men as he wished. Both commissions were to run until Whitsun (31st May).[36]

In the meantime both sides negotiated at York for peace and both prepared for war. It was not until after 10th June that the English administration had decided definitely for war, for on that date letters for the use of envoys were drawn up.[37] The first Scottish raid occurred on the English west march on 15th June, in response to which the militias of Lancashire and Yorkshire were summoned to York. Edward III left York for the north on 1st July with a large English army and accompanied by Hainaulter mercenaries. While the English prepared to invade Scotland *en masse* by the eastern march, the Scots raided the west. By 3rd July they were marauding in the vicinity of Appleby and Kirkby Stephen. Antony Lucy wrote on 12th July to warn Edward III that they would invade on the following Tuesday 14th; they would either attack Carlisle or make straight for the new king wherever he should be.[38] There may be an implication here that they intended to capture him; previous encounters suggest that the Scots' best hope of winning the war rapidly was to capture a prisoner whose ransom might add to their leverage in extracting a permanent settlement. Lanercost states that the Scots entered England in three columns (commanded by Moray, Douglas and Mar),[39] and this may mean that they entered England at three separate locations. Some of the Scots crossed into England on Tuesday 14th (as Lucy had predicted) and made for the Bishop of Carlisle's manor of Rose. This same force may have traversed the Pennines. Following the account in Fordun, Barrow suggests that Moray came by the Kielder Gap and down the valley of the North Tyne. Either way, the Scots were riding towards the English in order to divert them from invading Scotland. A great deal of risk was involved in this tactic, for King Robert was in Ulster at the time and thus unable to defend Scotland should the English invade.[40]

On 18th July the Hainaulters at Durham could see smoke from smouldering fields and buildings, and the chase was on.[41] Jehan le Bel provides an eyewitness account of how the cavalry pursued the raiders.[42] With the painful remembrance of a participant he describes how the heavily encumbered English knights and men-at-arms hopelessly pursued Moray's lightly armed hobelars at breakneck speed for two days across moors and bogland, vainly attempting to bring them to battle. But they lost contact. It seems that the Scots evaded pursuit by lying low for a time in the valley of the River Gaunless.[43] Then the English resolved to cut off the Scots' retreat, and waited for eight miserable, hungry, rain-sodden days at Haydonbridge on the Tyne. They had no idea where the Scots might be; and a proclamation was made promising a knighthood and a hundred pounds of land to whoever could lead the host to the Scots. At last one Thomas de Rokeby located them in Stanhope Park on the south bank of the Wear.[44] On 30th July the English moved to confront them; but the Scots refused to fight, moving twice under cover of night from one position of natural strength to another. On a night raid into the English camp James Douglas, now a living legend of chivalric daring-do, almost captured the young king. But having failed in this, the Scots withdrew through mosses and rough country where the English could not follow. It was a humiliating failure for the English host, superior in numbers and in all the paraphernalia of war. The young Edward III 'wept tears of vexation' at the defeat; so too might Isabella and Mortimer have wept at the cost of the campaign. Their Hainaulter mercenaries had to be paid both for this expedition and for that of 1326, and the bill came to £55,000, leaving their government desperate for money.

ROBERT I IN ULSTER, 1327

In 1326 the Red Earl of Ulster breathed his last.[45] One may doubt that he had ever fully regained control of his extensive territories in Ulster, and the Scots maintained their influence, and perhaps some military presence there, at least until 1322.[46] A letter from her council in Ireland to Elizabeth de Burgh, mother of the heir, reveals the damage that decades of war had wrought in the earldom.[47] During his last years the Red Earl's control of the lordship had been lax, and comital authority in Ulster was on the point of collapse. The lands of the earldom lay burnt and destroyed; the tenants had mostly fled. The suggestion was made (but apparently rejected) that settlers from England and Wales should be encouraged to settle in Ulster, and it was alleged that 3,000 immigrants could find sufficient lands there. Unless the heir arrived soon with sufficient force to restore his authority, the men of Ulster would 'choose some other lord'.[48]

Robert I was already moving into the power-vacuum. His arrival in Ulster in 1327 was anticipated; at a date unspecified Brother Roger Outlaw was paid £10 'towards expenses which he incurred in going to Ulster to treat with the men of Ulster and to scrutinise their hearts on resistance to the Scots, enemies, and rebels of the said lord king, and on curbing their malice, if it should happen that they land there'. But Scottish intervention in Ireland may not have been unwelcome to sections of the Dublin administration, for the justiciar was in communication with the Scots. In February 1327 the justiciar, John Darcy, sent the Franciscan clerk Henry Cogery as special messenger to Scotland 'to further certain confidential business touching the lord king'.[49] The objective of his mission is unknown; but the administration in Ireland was still loyal to Edward II at this time, and with the about-turn in policy towards Scotland in the last desperate days of Edward II's reign, Cogery may have sought some Scottish intervention, in Britain or Ireland, on that king's behalf.[50] Speculating further, it is even possible that Robert was offered the earldom of Ulster as a *quid pro quo*.

At any rate, Robert is said to have made the crossing to Ulster at Eastertide (12th April) and may therefore have been in Ulster for some considerable time before 12th July 1327, when he made an indenture with Henry Mandeville, steward of the Earldom of Ulster. Threatened by the Scots on the one hand (recently a Scottish attack on Rathlin had been beaten off) and the Gaelic Irish on the other, the men of the earldom bought off the Scottish king.[51] A copy of this document was sent to Elizabeth de Burgh; and according to this the people of Ulster bought from Robert a truce to last for one year from 1st August 1327, in return for a hundred chaldrons of wheat, and a hundred of barley, payable at Larne.[52] This was not a punitive peace; Robert allowed for deductions in the payment as compensation for damage caused to Rathlin. As already stated, none of the sources actually justifies the conclusion that Robert claimed the earldom as his own; but besides making logistical provision for the coming war, Robert was marking out his very personal interest in the earldom as husband of the last earl's eldest daughter. The one glimmer of hope reported to Elizabeth de Burgh was that the health of the King of Scots was deteriorating. He was at this stage virtually paralysed, and described as

> so feeble and so weak that he will not last much longer from this time, with the help of God, because he cannot move anything except his tongue.[53]

While Isabella and Mortimer had enjoyed effective control of the English administration from January, they gained unchallenged control of Ireland only when Edward II's justiciar, John Darcy, fled the country in May 1327. Thomas fitz John, earl of Kildare, took over on 12th May, and the reign of Edward III was not proclaimed in the lordship until the following day. Throughout Ireland the summer of 1327 seems to have witnessed an escalation of the 'low-intensity' war between the Gaelic Irish and the Anglo-Irish colony. In July the English government ordered that funds in the Irish exchequer be conserved for defence, and that justiciar, chancellor and chief justice of the colony confer as to how the Irish might be repulsed.[54] Whether Robert was behind this general revolt is impossible to tell; but in the same month, he tested in a much more direct fashion the loyalty of the new administration in Dublin to Isabella and Mortimer. An inquisition (ordered in 1333) into the good services of John son of William Jordan in 1327 reveals that letters passed between the King of Scots and the justiciar of Ireland, the earl of Kildare.[55] The return states that Robert had come to Ulster to gather support for the landing of an army in Wales with the ultimate aim of invading England. The justiciar's response to this was to send a message to Robert through John Jordan; and as a result of this message Robert returned to Scotland. John Jordan's mission is confirmed in the account of Robert de Cogan, treasurer of Ireland, in which Robert Cruys and John Jordan were both paid 100s. by the justiciar and council 'for going to Ulster to expedite certain matters touching the business of the King and his land of Ireland', and John Jordan is paid £4. 6s. 8d. for 'good and praiseworthy action'.[56] John Jordan's 'praiseworthy action' appears to have been delivery of the justiciar and council's rejection of Robert's overtures to join him in resisting the new regime in England. Events described in the Laud Annals and associated with Robert's final visit to Ireland with the heir to Ulster in 1328 seem to be mistakenly attributed to that year, and to relate instead to the mission of John Jordan. The entry states that Robert

> sent to the Justiciar of Ireland and to the Council that they should come to Greencastle to draw up a peace between Scotland and Ireland, and because the said Justiciar and Council did not come as he wished . . . he returned to his native land after the feast of the Assumption of the Blessed Virgin (15th August).[57]

This exchange is more likely to relate to Robert's visit of 1327 than to that of 1328. In 1328, when he had just succeeded in making the English come to terms, and promised not to intervene in Ireland, Robert would not have risked the destruction of that peace by making such an overt attempt to detach Ireland from its allegiance to the crown of England. Equally remarkable events were happening in England. At some time in the summer of 1327 (though it is not certain precisely when) Edward II was rescued by his supporters for a short time from his prison in Berkeley Castle.[58] News of the old king's escape (or equally, news of his recapture) may have had a bearing on the decision of Kildare's Irish administration to reject Robert's overtures, and things in Ireland might have turned out very differently. As it was, Robert could only return to Scotland, relinquishing for the last time the idea of a western alliance against England. It is interesting that during his interventions of 1327 and 1328 Robert seems to have sought co-operation from Anglo-Irish magnates much more actively than between 1315 and 1318. This impression may be created by dependence on Anglo-Irish sources; by the text of his agreement with Mandeville Robert demanded that they be included in the treaty; and Robert may have been behind general Gaelic revolt. But the fact that Gaelic sources are silent on his visit, and that he strove to woo the Dublin government tends to support the view that he now considered the Anglo-Irish colonists more useful allies.

Robert was back in Scotland probably by mid-August.[59] After the English army had disbanded, and in spite of debilitating illness, he entered the field on a final *chevauchée* into the English east march, accompanied by Moray and Douglas, in a striking demonstration of Scottish power. So confident were the Scots that they now concentrated on besieging major castles, entirely abandoning their former hit-and-run tactics. Robert besieged Norham with engines, assisted once again by the Flemish engineer John Crabbe; Moray and Douglas attacked first Alnwick, then Warkworth, then rejoined the king for a determined attempt to capture Norham.[60] Fortalices were built in England and lands were granted out.[61] Professor Nicholson interpreted these activities as a new departure in Scottish policy, a threat to annex Northumberland. In fact Robert had previously granted out lands of living English lords and constructed peels in Northumberland and Cumberland.[62] Much more threatening were his attacks on border castles, which, as a means of forcing the English to negotiate, had been tried successfully in 1322 and 1326. Nicholson is surely correct in detecting a terrifying escalation of the war which must have panicked the English administration. The area taken into Scottish *suffrance* was enlarged to include not only Durham, Cumberland and Westmorland, but also Richmondshire and Cleveland (which amounted to the whole of the North Riding of Yorkshire); and the border castles which had withstood the Scots for centuries seemed on the point of falling. The threat to dismember the English kingdom had never seemed so real, and the unstable regime of Isabella and Mortimer was in no position to sustain further military catastrophes.

THE TREATY OF EDINBURGH/NORTHAMPTON

On 9th October 1327 Henry Percy and William de Denum were appointed to treat of a final peace with the Scots.[63] As Professor Stones observed, both sides show desperation to achieve a settlement in 1327–28: the English selling their rights even though Robert I was on his deathbed and a four-year-old child was shortly to ascend the Scottish throne; the Scots prepared to pay cash for paper recognition of a victory they had already won in the field.[64] By 30th October the basis for a peace was outlined. Edward III (under the influence of his mother and Roger Mortimer) was prepared to surrender to Robert I all his right in Scotland. Robert, for his part, had committed himself to pay £20,000 for the peace, and to a marriage settlement which would bind together the royal families of Scotland and England. It would appear that the £20,000 was to indemnify the Kings of England for the loss of legal title in Scotland, but the official documents describe the payment simply as 'for the good of the peace and concord of the kings and of the kingdom of Scotland'. This then was the measure of Robert's anxiety to secure a permanent peace for his infant son. The English, for their part, seem to have been most anxious to secure the royal marriage, between Joan, sister of Edward III, and Robert's son David, the future David II. If the marriage project were to fail, Scotland undertook to pay further the impossible sum of £100,000 when David reached the age of 14, the legal age of consent.

In October 1327 Robert I seems to have been determined to resist claims to restoration by the disinherited, and there is no indication that provision for restoration of their titles was discussed as part of the treaty negotiations. Certainly there could be no question of 'restoring' to English magnates the grandiose Scottish titles (including earldoms) granted them by Edward I and Edward II. But Queen Isabella was authorised to renew discussions on this point and she seems to have prevailed upon Robert to allow a partial restoration, lifting forfeitures of war and giving these lords leave to pursue claims in the Scottish courts. In 1330 Henry Percy is reported to have had his claims satisfied; and there is record of letters patent by Robert, granting 'relief from forfeiture of war' to Thomas Wake, Henry Beaumont and William de la Zouche. The English for their part made some restoration to 'disinherited' Scots, including James Douglas and Henry Prendergast.[65] Another stipulation of the treaty was that the English should renounce any claim over the Isle of Man, and undertake to cease their interference in the isles of Scotland; in return for which Robert undertook not to assist enemies of the English king in Ireland. Narrative sources specify certain other conditions which do not appear in the official texts.[66] The Stone of Scone was to be returned to Scotland according to one report, but there is no evidence that this was agreed, and the Stone was definitely not delivered. There was no agreement either to return that most sacred of relics stolen by Edward I, the Black Rood; but the Rood was returned to Scotland at some time before 1346, for in that year the Scots lost it once more to the English at the Battle of Neville's Cross.

THE LEGACIES OF THE WARS OF THE BRUCES

I have taken the Treaty of Northampton–Edinburgh to mark the end of the Wars of the Bruces, but in history a clean break is a rare occurrence. The Treaty marks no fundamental change in relations between Scotland and England; and as pointed out previously, the Bruce monarchy survived for a generation yet under David II. The Anglo-Scottish war was renewed in July 1332 when Edward Balliol son of King John, enjoying the tacit support of Edward III and the active support of the 'Disinherited', invaded Scotland in quest of his father's throne. With the Battle of Halidon Hill in July 1333, Berwick fell once more to the English; and changed hands four times in the two centuries following. The north of England suffered Scottish incursions in 1333, 1342, 1346, 1388, and intermittently throughout the fifteenth century as the war continued, a 'weary cycle of desultory warfare and uneasy peace'. For the next three centuries, England and Scotland were locked into a war which neither could win. The principal factor driving this cycle was the threat posed to England by alliance between Scotland and France, and the Anglo-Scottish wars became inextricable from the Hundred Years War, grinding painfully on, sporadic, destructive and enduring, each side endowed with the potential to inflict enormous damage on the other, but neither able to win decisive victory, to conquer or occupy the other permanently. England's superiority over Scotland in terms of population, wealth and resources allowed her the upper hand; yet she was unable finally to defeat the Scots, who could retreat into an infinite wilderness of moors, mountains and islands. Each time either country was weakened by royal minority or rebellion, the other seized the opportunity to attack.

Nevertheless the Treaty, or 'Shameful Peace' as it was termed by the English, does at least mark the end of a supremacy which the Scots had enjoyed from 1307 to 1327 and which had no subsequent parallel. The two circumstances which enabled the Bruces to dominate the British Isles during this comparatively brief period would never again occur simultaneously: an English king with a gift for alienating his magnates to the extent of provoking civil war; and crop failure and animal pestilence that paralysed the movement of large armies, annihilating the advantage of the larger kingdom. The treaty also marked the passing of a generation. The main players of this drama had all died by 1328. The ambivalent and brooding figure of Thomas, Earl of Lancaster had been removed by his execution following revolt in 1322; Richard de Burgh, Red Earl of Ulster died a broken man in 1326; King Robert did not live long to enjoy his triumph, and died in his house in Cardross, in June 1329, of 'leprosy'.[67] His faithful lieutenant James Douglas was cut down in Spain in 1330, carrying Robert's heart in a silver casket in battle against the infidel. Doubt lingers over the fate of Edward of Caernarfon, but the chances are that he died a brutal and degrading death in 1327 at the hands of his captors; and soon afterwards, in October 1330, the regime of Isabella and Mortimer was toppled in a *coup d'état* by the young Edward III, after which Mortimer was executed. The generation which had waged this particular phase of the Anglo-Scottish wars was passing; and the compromise which it hammered out did not long survive it.

FROM BORDER TO FRONTIER: THE TRANSFORMATION OF NORTHERN ENGLAND

Even for the victors the Wars of the Bruces appear to have produced little in the way of lasting economic benefit. The temporary enrichment of Scotland in cattle and in coin was short-lived. Robert I was prepared to repatriate large quantities of bullion to England in return for the peace; and war had seriously damaged the mainstay of the Scottish economy, which was not wool export, but agriculture. Furthermore it is now considered that the war had increased Scotland's dependence upon imported manufactures, and eroded the skills-base upon which many sectors of the economy depended.[68]

The main legacy of the Wars of the Bruces to Britain was the transformation of the Anglo-Scottish border from boundary line into frontier zone. War had fundamentally altered life in the border regions. It had broken out at the climax of medieval economic activity in the north of England; and the Scottish raids certainly contributed to the long-term decline in arable productivity, the growing emphasis on pastoralism and perhaps also the retreat of human settlement. But just how far warfare actually caused the long-term economic decline of northern England, and how far its effects were reversible, is a difficult question. Evidence that the Scottish raids of the period had a significant long-term impact is presented in the 'Inquisitions of the Ninth' compiled in 1341, an assessment of agrarian incomes for taxation. In this source exemption from or reduction of taxation is sought on a variety of grounds. In Yorkshire land is said to have reverted to waste on account of 'sterility of the ground', 'default of tenants', 'the impoverishment of parishioners' and 'the drought'.[69] Raids of the Scots are blamed for the declines in four parishes of north-western Yorkshire, which allege that arable acreage had receded dramatically since 1291; 355 carucates were said to have been lost in the archdeaconry of Richmond alone.[70] In the returns for Lancashire Scottish raids are blamed for declines in arable acreage in Lonsdale, Amounderness and part of Blackburnshire.[71] These indications of the lingering effects of war damage are corroborated by two documents. The first is a complaint to the Prior of Durham in 1337 by Robert de Herrington, Vicar of Dalton, that his parish was wasted and depopulated by the Scottish War; that in Dalton there used to be 15 husbandmen who had draught animals, but now there were only five poor men who had no stock; and that the parishes of Morton and Hesilden were in a similar condition.[72] The second is a licence granted by Fountains Abbey in 1336 to convert nine of their granges into vills and to demise them to lay persons. The Scottish raids were cited as one of four reasons why they had fallen into decline, pestilence of animals and the weather being among the others.[73]

However, one might expect the returns to the Inquisitions, as assessments for taxation, to have painted as bleak a picture as possible; and in any case the Inquisitions and the other sources mentioned all offer other explanations besides warfare: animal pestilence, climatic fluctuation, soil exhaustion and plague. Dr. Lomas demonstrated that the pattern was not one of unremitting economic descent as a result of constant warfare, but rather of decline and partial recovery. Examining the sale of tithe corn from the border parishes of Norham and Islandshire and Ellingham, he concluded that the effect of warfare to 1328 was that grain production in this area was permanently reduced by not much more than 20 per cent of what it had been prior to 1314.[74] Lomas also showed that a decade after 1328 the corn tithe sales of townships in these border parishes had made a stronger recovery than townships 80 miles to the south in the Bishopric of Durham, an area which was protected from Scottish raids for much of the period by payments for *suffrance*.[75] For those who would use the evidence of the Yorkshire and Lancashire Inquisitions of 1341 as a measure of the impact of the Scottish raids, the lesson of the Durham evidence is surely that much of the decline had nothing to do with warfare. Further evidence for a swift recovery of agrarian incomes from the effects of raiding may be garnered from the records of the keeper of the Honour of Penrith, where raids in 1322 and 1327 failed to prevent a steady rise in rental income.[76] Given the simplicity of the medieval economy, it may have been relatively easy, after an isolated raid, to start over again. Even in Ireland, it is surely significant that large quantities of grain could be purveyed for dispatch to Carlisle within five years of the end of Edward Bruce's attempted conquest.[77] It would therefore appear that animal pestilence, climatic fluctuation and soil exhaustion had a more permanent impact than warfare in the long-term economic decline of northern England.

It is however probably true to say that the Wars of the Bruces assisted a trend towards pastoralism in the northern economy. Here again, Lomas has shown that income from lamb and wool tithes of Norhamshire grew from around £30 before 1314 to about £50 in the 1330s. There is no body of evidence comparable to the Norhamshire and Islandshire tithe records for the western march; but it is accepted that warfare and more casual raiding accentuated the trend towards pastoralism.[78] The reasons for this are fairly clear: fields of standing crops, barns and mills presented permanent fixed targets for raiders, whereas cattle and sheep could be driven off to safety.

But although their economic impact was less permanent than natural forces simultaneously at work, the wars brought about lasting developments in northern English society. This phase of Anglo-Scottish warfare created the conditions for that deterioration in law and order which became characteristic of border areas until the seventeenth century. Border unrest was not a new phenomenon; Tynedale and Redesdale had long been the haunt of bandits taking advantage of the refuge offered by the wilderness, and the prospect of escape to separate jurisdictions.[79] Yet by 1328, with widespread purveyancing, demands for military service, the *chevauchées* of hobelar warfare, and allegations and counter-allegations of treachery, the Wars of the Bruces had multiplied the opportunities and pretexts for lawlessness and local terrorism on the borders. Both Antony Bek and Edward II had utilised the military potential of the outlaws of the marches.[80] In obvious ways the *schavaldores* of the 1310s, products of the

Wars of the Bruces, anticipate the 'riders' and 'reivers' of the early modern era. Many features associated with the border reivers of the sixteenth century had still to appear by 1328. The 'riding surnames' used by later reivers were unknown until at least 1400; there is no evidence of feuding between kinship groups at this stage; and the oldest of the border ballads commemorates no events prior to the Battle of Otterburn in 1388.

Twenty years of intermittent warfare had an important psychological impact on the North of England. By 1330 there is a sense that war had become endemic in the region. This can be inferred from the number of minor fortifications springing up either side of the border during the first quarter of the fourteenth century, each peel or tower representing a considerable investment by local families or communities.[81] In 1328 the northerners were already 'dug in' for continuous conflict. A mentality of permanent, low-intensity warfare had taken over. It appears from a petition of the prior and convent of Durham dating from 1344 that a custom, whereby the armour of the deceased was given in mortuary to the vicar, had been prohibited for some considerable time to facilitate defence.[82] Provision for war damage began to be written into property transactions. In a Cumberland lease of 1317 the tenant undertook to keep a messuage (or building-plot) in good condition, though with due allowance made for 'burning and destruction by the Scots'. Similar provisions can be found in Yorkshire deeds. In the 1320s when the Chapter of Ripon leased the tithes of the chapel of Nidd, they conceded that whatever losses the tenant might incur through the agency of the king or 'the coming of the Scots' might be assessed and allowance made to him. Another Cumberland lease, this time of 1334, also reveals an expectation of permanent war: the abbot of St. Mary's leased his manor and tithes of Bromfield for six years, but allowed indemnification for war damage only if war had been publicly proclaimed, or if the manor house was destroyed and burnt down. The tenant was therefore to expect occasional 'peacetime' raids and to cover these losses himself, and the abbot would consider his claims only in the case of declared war or serious damage.[83]

Warfare also helped to bring about drastic changes in lordship and the pattern of landholding.[84] The rift with Scotland and the war brought about the removal of several leading northern English families: Clavering, Ros, Umfraville and Clifford. The extinction of these families coincided with the natural extinction of others, notably Vesci of Alnwick and Multon of Gilsland. During the rest of the fourteenth century the Percy and Neville families rose to positions of dominance in the north through service to the crown, and their fortunes depended upon the successful prosecution of war with Scotland. Percy and Neville lords were a new kind of over-mighty subject, warlords with absolute control over a wide region. These regional dynasts became indispensable as buffers against

Scotland; and in the future they were to exercise immense power in the politics of the realm. By the late fourteenth century, the marcher lords on either side of the border had become powerful advocates of war.

THE LESSONS OF WARFARE

Other legacies of the Wars of the Bruces lie in the military sphere. In twenty years of warfare the Scots had refined a survival strategy for small and relatively weak lordships faced with aggressive and powerful neighbours. Few if any of the elements in this strategy were novel. There is one aspect of Robert's strategy which may have been completely innovative: there appears to be no exact precedent for Robert I's systematic slighting of castles to render a territory invulnerable to occupation and at the same time to ensure the susceptibility of magnates to royal discipline.

Mounted raids or *chevauchées* had been used by Edward I's commanders to destroy the agricultural capacity in areas of Scotland hostile to his occupation. Light cavalry, highly mobile and able to live off the land, must have predominated in disputed border territories throughout Europe; certainly they existed on the borders of Wales in the thirteenth century, in the shape of the *muntatores* of Oswestry. These were mounted raiders, equipped with iron helmet and hauberk, who had the capacity to inflict surprise raids on the Welsh. The similarity with the hobelars however cannot be carried too far, for *muntatores* held land by specified tenure on set terms of military service,[85] whereas the hobelars were simply turbulent mercenaries who often had no respect for property of any kind. Use of mounted infantry as raiders, with the capacity to strike deep into the heart of enemy territory and to fight a battle on foot there if necessary, was another refinement which can be credited to Moray, Douglas and Robert I, and this does appear to have been deliberately emulated by the English. Andrew Harclay, who employed Irish and local hobelars and organised mounted raids on Scotland, is said to have deployed a phalanx of infantry spearmen to defeat the earls of Lancaster and Hereford at Boroughbridge in 1322 'in the Scottish fashion'.[86] It has also been pointed out that Edward II recognised the value of mobility and the devastating capacity of the Scottish raiders but was diverted by the need (as he saw it) to occupy Scotland with large armies of heavily armoured infantry.

In a broader sense, the Scottish tactic of plundering raids deep into enemy territory formed the basis of English strategy in the first phase of the Hundred Years War. Faced with the task of defeating a country much larger and richer than their own, the English, led by the Black Prince, adopted the *chevauchée*.[87] In 1355 and again in 1356 he led great looting expeditions, cutting a great swathe of devastation across southern France. The analogy is far from exact, for England was protected by sea from France whereas Scotland was open to retaliation by land. There was also a difference of scale: the Black Prince had forces at his disposal far greater than those which might have been available to Moray and Douglas. On his first expedition the Black Prince is believed to have been accompanied by a thousand men at arms and a thousand horse-archers, besides a company of foot.[88] The *chevauchées* allowed the English to transform the Hundred Years War from a potentially disastrous clash with a stronger kingdom into an opportunity to plunder and enrich England at the expense of her enemy.

AULD ALLIANCES: THE 'CELTIC ALLIANCE' IN THE MIDDLE AGES

Throughout Scottish history, the 'auld alliance' between France and Scotland tended to have an effect more moral than practical. Its impact upon contemporary perceptions and motivations was often out of all proportion to its impact upon military and even diplomatic events. While it is clearly the case that France often used Flemish ports during the middle ages to bolster Scottish resistance to England, the Bruces enjoyed no such advantage. In the summer of 1315 when France actually dragged a reluctant England into confrontation with Flanders, it is clear that the two great kingdoms were in alliance against their troublesome smaller neighbours. Hence the bitter complaint (cited by Duncan (*Nation of Scots*, p. 36)) to Pope John XXII about the conduct of England and France:

> Then rouse the Christian Princes who for false reasons pretend that they cannot go to the Holy Land because of wars they have with their neighbours. The other reason that prevents them is that in warring on their smaller neighbours they anticipate a readier return and weaker resistance.

Until 1326 Robert I had to survive in the teeth of an Anglo-French understanding, which, though far from solid, was sufficient to keep France from intervening with energy in the affairs of the British Isles. As an alternative to alliance with France he could rely upon assistance from the traders of Flanders and Germany to the east; and to the west, he summoned into existence an understanding with certain principalities of the Gaeltacht. Using both these sources of support, informal and unreliable as they were, he succeeded in asserting the independence of Scotland.

When war loomed once more in 1326, Flanders and France were once more in harmony and Scotland was able effectively to enjoy alliance with both on its eastern flank. On the west, however, the situation was more complex. Robert's solicitude for the earldom of Ulster in 1328 appears to contrast with his aggression of the previous year. But this was a change of style, rather than of attitude, brought about by the conclusion of the peace. While his expedition of 1327 gained for him effective control of the earldom in the absence of the heir, that of 1328 was intended to prolong his influence in the earldom through the installation of the legally recognised earl. He was actually forbidden by the terms of the Treaty of Edinburgh/Northampton to interfere in the affairs of Ireland.[89] However, Robert appears to have been anxious, without endangering the peace, to establish the earldom of Ulster as a client-lordship of the Scottish crown. The earl's council in Ireland had been insistent that the heir, William de Burgh, grandson and heir of the Red Earl, should come in person to take charge of Ulster. Earl William had been granted custody of Ulster (including the castle of Carrickfergus) in February 1327; but after the Scottish invasion of that year, the English council reversed its decision and withheld the castle, apparently to ensure its safe keeping.[90] To regain his patrimony in Ireland, William accompanied Queen Isabella to Berwick to attend the marriage of David Bruce with Joan. After the royal wedding, in August 1328, Robert I, on his last journey out of Scotland and accompanied by Murdoch Earl of Menteith and other Scottish magnates, crossed 'in peace' to Ulster with Earl William. There the young earl was installed in his lordship.[91] This was not an infringement of the provisions of the peace, for Robert had undertaken not to assist the enemies of the English king in Ireland, and the 'Brown Earl' as he is known remained a liegeman of Edward III. The traditional alliance between de Burgh and Bruce was thus restored; and security on this flank was purchased for Robert's infant heir.

To a large extent the interests of the English and Scottish kings coincided in Ulster, where the strong earldom had kept at bay the Gaelic subjects of both. Robert's concerns for Ulster were justified by subsequent events. In 1333 Earl William was murdered, and the earldom of Ulster thereafter was held by absentees, ceasing, in effect, to exist as a lordship.[92] In memorable terms Edmund Curtis described the effect on the geo-politics of the North Channel:

> . . . the sea was thrown open, the northern chiefs could draw from the Scottish Isles unlimited galloglasses, and so was knitted again the old Gaelic world of Erin and Alba, severed for a time by the Anglo-Norman wedge driven in it by de Courcy and his successors in eastern Ulster.[93]

Although Scottish intervention in Ireland on the scale of the Bruce invasion was never repeated, Robert's preoccupation with Ireland and the western approaches proved to be well founded. Not long after Robert's death John MacDonald of Islay felt sufficiently confident to rebel against the government of David Bruce and began the process of founding the autonomous Lordship of the Isles. For the remainder of the middle ages kings of Scotland were obliged to intervene in Ulster, often as a check on the MacDonalds and other Scots-Gaelic lords, or simply to stir up trouble for the English government. In 1404 a force of Scots assisted Gaelic-Irish chieftains in devastating the Anglo-Irish colony in Ulster, burning Inch Abbey, Downpatrick and Coleraine; and in 1433 a large fleet from the Scottish isles arrived to assist Eoghan Ó Néill against Niall Ó Domhnaill. Following a long-standing tradition, Ireland continued to provide safe-haven for English and Scottish political exiles. In 1425 James Stewart fled to Ulster from the wrath of James I of Scotland and threatened to use it as a springboard for the recovery of his position in Scotland. There was every danger that James would find military support from disaffected elements in the Western Isles, just as Robert I had done a hundred years previously, and a Scottish fleet is said to have arrived to take him home 'that he might be king'.[94] Fear of 'celtic alliance' continued to haunt the dreams of the English royal officials and political classes. The Welsh leader Owain Glyn Dûr received material support by sea from the Scots and he appealed for military assistance to the Gaelic Irish in 1401;[95] and the *Libell of Englishe Policye* in 1436 gave lurid expression to the dread of pan-celticism, warning that England controlled a dwindling proportion of the land of Ireland 'which if be lost, as Christ Jesus forbid, farewell Wales'. It was stressed that if such a circumstance arose an alliance of Scotland, Spain and other powers could encircle England.[96] As late as 1522 the Anglo-Irish government in Dublin feared the possibility of a Scottish invasion.[97] But increasingly the English and Scottish governments ceased to consider the Gaeltacht as an arena where each sparred with the other through little wars fought by proxy; increasingly they began to envisage the Gaeltacht as a common problem, and one best addressed by co-operation.

CONCLUSION

From the early sixteenth century the development of common interests binding together England and Scotland, as Protestant kingdoms sharing the one island and menaced from the continent by the forces of counter-reformation, began to render less galling the old antipathies. After the union of the crowns in 1603, the fury and passion that had fed the Wars of the Bruces began to subside, and receded eventually into a past too remote, too obscure, to be taken seriously by any but antiquarians. In the whig interpretation of British history, the struggle for an independent Scottish kingdom appeared as a temporary and unfortunate deviation from the destiny of political unity for the British Isles first conceived by the perspicacious and far-sighted Edward I.

From a modern point of view, the most striking aspect of the episode is undoubtedly the potential that was briefly created for the development of alternative relationships between the peoples of these islands. Between

1307 and 1328 there were briefly thrown open possibilities for radical departures from the course of actual history. Seen in this light, the Wars of the Roses are a sharp reminder that nothing in history is inevitable. Had the Bruces met with wider co-operation in Ireland, for example, it is possible that Ireland, under a cadet line of the Bruce dynasty, might have achieved 'regnal solidarity', that 'match between people and polity' which was the magic ingredient of medieval state-building. Had events turned out differently again, it might have come to pass that the north–south partition which existed in Ireland from 1315 to 1318 might have been perpetuated, mirroring the partition which existed already in Britain and foreshadowing that of modern Ireland. It is even possible, had both the Gaelic Irish and the native Welsh accepted the overlordship of Edward Bruce, that there might have arisen a transmarine 'Irish Sea' kingdom.

Any such solution might have been entertained by the Bruces up until Edward's disaster at Fochart. It is difficult to regret the failure of Edward Bruce, in view of the comments of contemporaries. Irish annalists characterise Edward's three-and-a-half year reign as a time when 'falsehood and homicide filled the country'. Certainly the chroniclers were unanimous in their approval for the slaying of Edward Bruce:

> Never a better deed was done since the banishing of the Formorians than the killing of Edward Bruce, the common ruin of the Galls and the Gaels of Ireland in general . . .[98]

The disappearance of Edward Bruce from the scene, however, reduced the possible outcomes of the wars. For the Scots the conquest of Ireland ceased to be an end in itself. Interference in Ireland became purely a means of extorting from England recognition of the Bruce monarchy. Edward Bruce's regality depended upon a permanent separation of Ireland from England; similarly Robert's kingship depended upon separation of Scotland from England. Yet in both cases independence was only a means towards recognition of kingship. In both the settlements which Robert formulated, the Treaty of Edinburgh and the earlier abortive treaty with Andrew Harclay, provision was made for intermarriage between the royal families of England and Scotland. This intermarriage was intended to lead to, or at least to create the possibility of, dynastic union of the kingdoms. From this one can gather that Robert by no means ruled out the emergence of a pan-British kingdom in the future. In fact his vision for the British Isles may not have been so very far removed from that originally entertained by Edward I in the Treaty of Birgham of 1290. The preservation and recognition of his own royal title had been Robert's supreme objective; and despite the anti-English rhetoric to which he resorted on occasion, the preservation of Scottish independence only served this objective. As far back as 1304 it looks very much as though Robert had been prepared to compromise the independence of the Scottish monarchy to win from Edward I recognition even as a vassal king. Accident alone forced him to adopt a grander design.

But however the coup of 1306 is interpreted, no historian will deny that the brothers Bruce were driven, not so much by magnate self-interest as by a consuming ambition for kingship, born of a passionate belief in the regality of the blood they shared. The claim articulated on behalf of Scottish magnates in the Declaration of Arbroath that 'we fight not for glory, nor riches, nor honours, but for freedom' could hardly have been advanced with any sincerity by Robert and Edward. Robert was prepared to unleash a terrible war on the defenceless communities of northern England in order that his right be vindicated; Edward Bruce had such craving for royal dignity that he sought offers of kingship from the magnates of Ireland, Wales and even perhaps of the Western Isles as well. Both were manipulators of patriotism and xenophobic sentiment. Yet it is scarcely just to consider the Bruces more responsible for these wars than 'King Edward's covetousness'.

However much their actions were informed by self-interest, the brothers were upholders of rights and customs threatened by the Edwardian super-kingdom. Their claims to be protectors of threatened peoples and identities, articulated in the Declaration of the Clergy, the Remonstrance of the Irish Princes and the Declaration of Arbroath, were self-serving but far from hollow. Robert's seizure of the kingship, and the brothers' twenty years' resistance to a powerful enemy rescued the Scottish monarchy from oblivion. They preserved for Scotland an identity of king and community, and saved Scotland from endless wars between natives and colonists. In effect they saved her from the fate of Ireland and Wales. This was the great achievement of the Wars of the Bruces, and it is for this that they deserve to be remembered.

NOTES

1 *RRS* v nos. 222, 448.
2 *CPR 1321–24*, pp. 261, 264, 274, 288–89. The term *palettis* indicates plate armour of some sort.
3 *RRS* v no. 222, pp. 490–91, translated in Barrow, *Robert Bruce*, pp. 244–45.
4 *CPR 1321–24*, pp. 268, 271; *CDS* v no. 686, p. 253.
5 *RRS* v no. 222, pp. 490–91.
6 *RRS* v no. 139, p. 412, [xxi].
7 The text is translated in A.A.M. Duncan, *The Nation of Scots and the Declaration of Arbroath* (Historical Association, 1970), pp. 34–37.
8 Duncan, 'War of the Scots', pp. 129–31.
9 *Fordun* ii, 341; *Barbour* XIX, 1–72; *Scalacronica*, p. 59.

10 Stones, *Anglo-Scottish Relations*, no. 38(h), p. 152.
11 *CPR 1321-24*, p. 277.
12 *RRS* v no. 232, pp. 499–503.
13 *CCR 1318-23*, p. 717; Fryde, *Tyrrany and Fall*, p. 159.
14 Fryde, *Tyrrany and Fall*, pp. 49–57 and M. Buck, *Politics, Finance and the Church in the Reign of Edward II* (Cambridge, 1983), Chapter 7.
15 Fryde, *Tyrrany and Fall*, pp. 160–61.
16 *CDS* v no. 687, p. 254; *Vita Edwardi II*, pp. 131–32.
17 *Fordun* ii, 340; W.S. Reid, 'Trade, Traders and Scottish Independence', *Speculum* xxix (1954), 213–18.
18 E. Gemmill and N. Mayhew, *Changing values in medieval Scotland: A study of prices, money and weights and measures* (Cambridge, 1995), pp. 15–16, 147, 163, 181, 190, 222–23, 235, 251, 259, 268, 280, 286.
19 *CDS* iii nos. 845, 846, 848, 851, 852.
20 P. Chaplais, *The War of St. Sardos (1323–1325): Gascon Correspondence and Diplomatic Documents* (Camden 3rd Series lxxxvii, 1954), nos. 57, 79, 151. These are calendared in *CDS* v nos. 692, 694, 698.
21 *Vita Edwardi II*, p. 132.
22 Fryde, *Tyrrany and Fall*, pp. 145–6; *Vita Edwardi II*, pp. 138–39.
23 Barrow, *Robert Bruce*, pp. 251–52.
24 *RRS* v no. 299, pp. 556–59, sealed by Robert I on 12th July.
25 *CDS* iii nos. 882, 883; *CCR 1324-27*, p. 476.
26 Fryde, *Tyrrany and Fall*, pp. 185 - 92.
27 D. Walker, *Medieval Wales* (Cambridge, 1990), pp. 150–51; J.G. Edwards, 'Sir Gruffydd Llwyd', *EHR* xxx (1915), 589–601.
28 *CDS* iii nos. 888, 889.
29 Barrow, *Robert Bruce*, p. 274; R. Nicholson, 'The Last Campaign of Robert Bruce', *EHR* lxxvii (1962), 234.
30 *Lanercost*, p.253.
31 Nicholson, 'The Last Campaign of Robert Bruce', p. 234.
32 *Lanercost*, p. 253.
33 B. Wilkinson, *The Constitutional History of Medieval England, 1216–1399* (London, 1952), ii, 170–71.
34 *CCR 1327-30*, pp. 157, 212; *CPR 1327-30*, p. 139.
35 *Lanercost*, p. 256.
36 Nicholson, 'The Last Campaign of Robert Bruce', p. 234.
37 E.L.G. Stones, 'The Anglo-Scottish Negotiations of 1327', *SHR* xxx (1950), 29–30. Nicholson's account of this campaign, *Edward III and the Scots*, pp. 13–23 has recently been revised by Barrow, *Robert Bruce*, pp. 252–53.
38 Nicholson, *Edward III and the Scots*, p. 23; *CDS* iii nos. 920, 924.
39 *Lanercost*, pp. 356–57.
40 SC1/34/110 calendared in *CDS* v no. 606, p. 240; Barrow, *Robert Bruce*, pp. 252, 372. Places mentioned in the following paragraph are marked on Map 11, p. 150.
41 *Le Bel*, pp. 46, 49.
42 *Lanercost*, pp. 257–58; *Le Bel*, pp. 49–71.
43 Barrow, *Robert Bruce*, pp. 252–53.
44 *Foedera* ii (II), 717.
45 Date given by Sayles, *Affairs of Ireland*, p. 127 as 29th July 1326.
46 See above, p. 186.

47 Sayles, *Affairs of Ireland*, no. 155, pp. 126–29. Frame, *English Lordship in Ireland*, p. 137 states that the author was Thomas Chedworth, an official of the lady de Burgh.
48 R. Nicholson 'A Sequel to Edward Bruce's Invasion of Ireland', *SHR* xlii (1963–64), p. 34; Duncan, *RRS* v Introduction, p. 155.
49 E101/239/5.
50 R. Frame, *English Lordship in Ireland, 1318–1361* (Oxford, 1982), pp. 139–42.
51 Sayles, *Affairs of Ireland*, no. 155, pp. 126–29.
52 R. Nicholson, 'A Sequel pp. 40–41, Appendix II; *RRS* v no. 332, pp. 574–75; see above p. 131.
53 Sayles, *Affairs of Ireland*, no. 155, p. 128; Barrow, *Robert Bruce*, p. 323.
54 *CCR 1327–30*, p. 145.
55 Printed in Nicholson, 'A Sequel', Appendix II, pp. 39–40.
56 E101/239/5.
57 *Chart. St. Mary's Dublin* ii, 367.
58 Fryde, *Tyrrany and Fall*, p. 201.
59 Duncan, Introduction, *RRS* v, p. 155.
60 Nicholson, 'The Last Campaign of Robert Bruce', pp. 242–44.
61 Raine, *Northern Registers*, pp. 344–46; *Rot. Scot.* i, 221–22; Barbour, *The Bruce* XX, 1–26; *RRS* v no. 324, pp. 575–76 is a note of a grant of Belford in Northumberland to Nicholas Scrymgeour.
62 See above p. 79.
63 *Rot. Scot.* i, 223.
64 Three articles by E.L.G. Stones are vital to the understanding of the peace settlement: 'The English Mission to Edinburgh in 1328', *SHR* xxviii (1949), 97–118; 'The Anglo-Scottish Negotiations of 1327', *SHR* xxx (1951), 49–54; 'An Addition to the *Rotuli Scotiae*', *SHR* xxix (1950), 23–51.
65 *RRS* v nos. 353, 457; Nicholson, *Edward III and the Scots*, pp. 58–59.
66 Stones, 'An Addition to the *Rotuli Scotiae*' , 32–33.
67 Barrow, *Robert Bruce*, p. 322.
68 A. Stevenson, 'Trade between Scotland and the Low Countries in the Middle Ages', (Aberdeen Ph.D, 1982), pp. 219, 248–51.
69 *Nonarum Inquisitiones in Curia Scaccaria* ed. G. Vanderzee Record Commission, London, 1807, pp. 243, 224, 228. The Inquisitions are discussed by A.R.H. Baker, 'Evidence in the *Inquisitiones Nonarum* of contracting arable lands in England during the early fourteenth century', *EcHR* 2nd series xix (1966), 518–32.
70 *Ibid.*, 233–34
71 *Ibid.*, 35–40.
72 Surtees, *Durham*, i, II, 2–3.
73 *Memorials of the Abbey of St. Mary of Fountains*, ed. J.R. Walbran and J.T. Fowler (Surtees Society xlii, 1863), pp. 203–5. A similar combination of circumstances is recorded for the inquisition in the parish of Easingwold, E179/206/46b, m. 3.
74 R. Lomas, *North-East England in the Middle Ages* (Edinburgh, 1992), p. 59.
75 *Ibid*, pp. 60–61.
76 See Chart 2, p113.

77 See Charts 5 and 6, p. 127.

78 Lomas, *North-East England*, p. 59; H. Summerson, 'Crime and Society in Medieval Cumberland', *CWAAS* 2nd series, lxxxii (1982), 116.

79 Cattle rustling had always been common: JUST 3/10A, m. 1d; JUST 3/53/1, mm. 1, 5; JUST 3/53/2, mm. 3, 4. *NCH* xii, 312; *CDS* i, no. 1244, p. 227; Barrow, 'Northern English Society', pp. 13–14; Fraser, *Ancient Petitions*, no. 87, pp. 112–13.

80 C.M. Fraser *A History of Antony Bek* (Oxford 1957) p. 143; and see pp. 155–57 above.

81 Of 18 licences to crenellate granted in the North of England in the period 1296–1328, 16 were for minor fortifications, *CPR 1296–1327*.

82 Raine, *North Durham*, p. 268.

83 Cumbria Record Office D/Mus/Medieval Deeds/Edenhall, Bramery 19; *Memorials of the Church of SS Peter and Wilfred, Ripon*, ed. J.T. Fowler iv (Surtees Society cxv, 1908), p. 52; W. Dugdale, *Monasticon Angicanum* (London, 1846) iii, 567–68, Num. LXVII. Northumberland Record Office ZSW 4/77 contains a clause to the effect that if lands are destroyed in war with the Scots, the tenant will not be held for payment of rent (Northumberland, 1332).

84 J.A. Tuck, 'War and Society in the Medieval North', *NH* xxi (1985), pp. 33–52.

85 F. C. Suppe, *Military Institutions on the Welsh Marches: Shropshire, A.D. 1066–1300* (London, 1994), pp. 63–87.

86 *Lanercost*, p. 232.

87 H.J. Hewitt discussed the nature of the *chevauchée* in *The Black Prince's Expedition, 1355–57* (Manchester, 1958), pp. 46–49 and in *The Organisation of War under Edward III 1338–62* (Manchester, 1966), pp. 93–99.

88 Hewitt, *The Black Prince's Expedition*, p. 21.

89 *RRS* v no. 342, pp. 591–94.

90 Frame, *English Lordship in Ireland*, pp. 141–42 and note 19.

91 *Chart. St. Mary's Dublin* ii, 367; *Ann. Loch Cé*, ii, 607; Nicholson, 'A Sequel', p. 36.

92 Frame, *English Lordship in Ireland*, pp. 144–46; *Chart. St. Mary's Dublin*, ii, 378–79.

93 E. Curtis, *A History of Medieval Ireland*, (2nd edition, 1938), p. 211.

94 *NHI* ii, 574–76.

95 R.A. Griffiths, *Conquerors and Conquered in Medieval Wales* (Stroud, 1994), pp. 127–28.

96 *The Libell of Englishe Policye, 1436*, R. Pauli (Leipzig, 1878), p. 50.

97 B. Bradshaw, *The Irish Constitutional Revolution of the Sixteenth Century* (Cambridge, 1979), pp. 58–83.

98 *Annals of Connacht*, p. 253. See also *Annals of Ulster* iii, 433; and *Annals of Clonmacnoise*, pp. 281–82.

Bibliography

A. MANUSCRIPT SOURCES

i) Public Record Office

E101	Exchequer Miscellanea
E159	Memoranda Rolls
E179	Subsidies
E199	Sheriffs' Accounts
E372	Pipe Rolls
C47	Chancery Miscellanea
SC1	Ancient Correspondence
SC6	Ministers' Accounts
Just 1	Assize Rolls
Just 3	Gaol Delivery Rolls
KB27	King's Bench

ii) British Library

Additional MS 7965	Wardrobe Book 1296–97
Additional MS 7966A	Wardrobe Book 1300–1
Additional MS 8835	Wardrobe Book 1303–4
Additional MS 17362	Wardrobe Book 1319–20
Additional MS 9951	Wardrobe Book 1320–21
Cottonian MSS	
Cleopatra D III	Les Chroniques d'Engleterre
Domitian A XII	Anonymous Chronicle
Julius D IV	Anonymous Chronicle
Nero C viij	Wardrobe Book 1310–11
Stowe 553	Wardrobe Book 1322–23

iii) Society of Antiquaries

MS 120	Wardrobe Book 1316–17
MS 121	Wardrobe Book 1317–18

iv) Dean and Chapter of Durham

Enrolled Manorial Accounts	1319–20, 1322–23
Holy Island Status	1308, 1326, 1327, 1328, 1330, 1332
Livestock Accounts	1310, 1323
Locelli	XIII, XVIII, XIX, XXVII, XXVIII
Manorial Accounts	Ketton 1316–17

Pittington 1316–17

Miscellaneous Charters
Norham Proctor's Accounts   1330–1, 1314–15, 1315–16(A) and (B),
                             1317–21, 1327–28, 1328(A) and (B),
                             1329–30, 1330–31, 1335–36

Obedientaries Accounts
    Almoner's Rent Rolls   1290–1322
    Bursar's Account Rolls   1292–1331
    Cellarer's Account Rolls   1307–1322
    Hostillar's Account Rolls 1318–c.1331
    Sacristan's Account Rolls 1318–1322

v) Northumberland County Record Office
    Swinburne (Capheaton) MSS
    Ridley Charters
    Waterford Charters

vi) Cumbria County Record Office
    DRC 1/1 Episcopal Register
    Deeds: Lonsdale
                               Aglionby
                               Musgrave

vii) York Minster Library
    Vicars' Choral Chamberlain Accounts
    Vicars' Choral Cartulary

viii) Bodleian Library, Oxford
    MS Tanner 197

ix) Merton College MCR, Oxford
    Ponteland and Embleton, Accounts of Bailiffs, etc, receipts: 511,
5975,
    5976, 5978, 5983, 5984, 5985, 5986, 5987, 5988, 5992, 5995a,
    5995b, 6002.

x) National Archives of Ireland
    Ex2/1   Calendar of Memoranda Rolls
    KB1   Justiciary Rolls
    RC8   Record Commission calendar of memo-
                               randa rolls

xi) Public Record Office Northern Ireland
    Registers of the Archbishops of Armagh   DIO 4/2/2

B. PRINTED SOURCES

i Chronicles
Adae Murimuth Continuatio Chronicorum, ed. E.M. Thompson (R.S., 1889)
The Annals of Connacht, ed. A.M. Freeman (Dublin, 1944)
The Annals of Clonmacnoise, ed. D. Murphy (Dublin, 1896)
The Annals of Inisfallen, ed. S. Mac Airt (Dublin, 1951)
The Annals of Loch Cé, ed. W.M. Hennessy, i (R.S., 1871)
The Annals of Ireland by Friar John Clyn and Thady Dowling, ed. R. Butler (Dublin, 1849)
Barbour's Bruce, ed. M.P. McDiarmid and J.A.C. Stevenson (3 vols.) (Scottish Text Society, 4th series, 1980–85)
Jehan le Bel: Les Vrayes Chroniques, ed. M.L. Polain, i (Brussels, 1863)
The Book of Pluscarden, ed. F.J.H. Skene (*The Historians of Scotland*, Vol. X, Edinburgh, 1880)
The Brut, or the Chronicles of England, ed. F.W.D. Brie, i (Early English Text Society, original series, cxxxi, 1906)
Chartulary of St. Mary's Abbey, Dublin, ed. J.T. Gilbert, ii (R.S., 1886)
Chronica Regum Manniae et Insularum, Facsimile of BL MS Julius A VII (Douglas, 1924)
Chronica Monasterii de Melsa, ed. E.A. Bond, ii (R.S., 1867)
Chronicles of the Reigns of Edward I and Edward II, ed. W. Stubbs, ii, Gesta Edwardi de Carnarvon Auctore Canonico Bridlingtoniensi (R.S., 1882–83)
The Chronicle of Walter of Guisborough, ed. H. Rothwell (Camden 3rd series lxxxix, 1957)
The Chronicle of Pierre de Langtoft, ed. T. Wright, ii (R.S., 1868)
Chronicon Galfridi le Baker de Swynebroke, ed. E.M. Thompson (Oxford, 1881)
Chronicon de Lanercost, ed. J. Stevenson (Maitland Club, Edinburgh, 1839)
The Chronicle of Lanercost, ed. and translated H. Maxwell (Glasgow, 1913)
The Chronicle of St. Mary's Abbey, York, ed. H.H.E. Craster and M.E. Thornton (Surtees Society cxlviii, 1933 for 1934)
Eulogium Historiarum, ed. F.S. Haydon, iii (R.S., 1836)
'Extracts from the Historia Aurea and a French "Brut"', ed. V.H. Galbraith, *EHR* xliii (1928), 203–17
Flores Historiarum, ed. H.R. Luard, iii (R.S., 1890)
John of Fordun's Chronicle of the Scottish Nation, ed. W.F. Skene (*The Historians of Scotland* Vol. IV, Edinburgh, 1872)
Jacobi Grace, Kilkenniensis, Annales Hiberniae, ed. R. Butler (Irish Archaeological Society, 1842)
Historiae Dunelmensis Scriptores Tres, ed. J. Raine (Surtees Society viii, 1839)
Le Livere de reis de Brittanie, ed. J. Glover (R.S., 1865)
Scalacronica by Sir Thomas Grey of Heton Knight, ed. J. Stevenson (Maitland Club, Edinburgh, 1836)
Scalacronica, by Sir Thomas Grey of Heton, Knight, ed. and transl. H. Maxwell (Glasgow, 1907)

Scotichronicon by Walter Bower, ed. D.E.R. Watt, vi (Aberdeen, 1991)
Johannis de Trokelowe et Henrici de Blaneforde Chronica et Annales, ed. H.T. Riley (R.S., 1866)
Vita Edwardi Secundi, ed. N. Denholm-Young (London, 1957)
Thomae Walsingham Historia Anglicana, ed. H.T. Riley, i (R.S., 1863)

ii Other Printed Sources

Acts of the Parliaments of Scotland, ed. C. Innes, i (London, 1844)
Ancient Petitions Relating to Northumberland, ed. C.M. Fraser (Surtees Society, clxxvi, 1966)
Anglo-Scottish Relations 1174–1328, Some Selected Documents, ed. E.L.G. Stones (London, 1965)
Bishop Hatfield's Survey, ed. W. Greenwell, (Surtees Society xxxii, 1857)
British Naval Documents 1204–1960, ed. J.B. Hattendorf, *et al* (Naval Records Society cxxxi, 1993)
Calendar of Documents Relating to Ireland, ed. H.S. Sweetman, v 1302–1307 (London, 1875)
Calendar of Documents Relating to Scotland (5 vols.): i–iv, ed. J. Bain (1881–88); v (Supplementary), ed. G.G. Simpson and J.D. Galbraith (Scottish Record Office, 1988)
Calendar of Chancery Warrants (HMSO, London, 1927), vol. i, *1244–1326*
Calendar of Close Rolls (HMSO, London, 1892–1907), *1302–30*
Calendar of Inquisitions Miscellaneous (Chancery) (HMSO, London, 1916), vol. ii, *1308–48*
Calendar of Inquisitions Post Mortem (HMSO, London, 1908–10), vols v–vii, *1307–36*
Calendar of the Justiciary Rolls of Ireland (3 vols.), vols. i and ii ed. J. Mills (HMSO, Dublin, 1905, 1914); vol. iii ed. H. Wood and A.E. Lanagan, revised M.C. Griffith (Dublin, 1956), *1305–7*
Calendar of Papal Letters (HMSO, London, 1895), vol. ii, *1305–42*
Calendar of Patent Rolls (HMSO, London, 1894–1904), *1301–30*
Cartularium Abbathiae de Rievaulx, ed. J.C. Atkinson (Surtees Society lxxxiii, 1889 for 1887)
Cathreim Thoirdhealbhaigh, ed. S.H. O'Grady, ii (Irish Texts Society, 1929)
Chartularies of St. Mary's Abbey, Dublin, ed. J.T. Gilbert, ii (R.S., 1884)
Connolly, P., 'Irish material in the Class of Ancient Petitions (SC8) in the Public Record Office London', *Analecta Hibernica* xxxiv (1987), 3–106
'Irish material in the Class of Chancery Warrants Series (C81) in the Public Record Office London', *Analecta Hibernica* xxxvi (1995), pp. 135–61
'List of Irish Entries on the Memoranda Rolls of the English Exchequer, 1307–27', *Analecta Hibernica* xxxvi (1995), pp. 103–218
Correspondence, Inventories, Account Rolls and Law Proceedings of the Priory of Coldingham, ed. J. Raine (Surtees Society xii, 1841)
The Coucher Book of Furness Abbey, ed. J.C. Atkinson, iii (Chetham Society, new series xiv, 1887).
Documents Illustrative of the History of Scotland, ed. J. Stevenson (2 vols.) (Edinburgh, 1870).
Documents on the Affairs of Ireland before the King's Council, ed. G.O. Sayles (Irish Manuscripts Commission, Dublin, 1979)

Dugdale, W., *Monasticon Anglicanum*, vi, Part I (London, 1846)

Edward I and the Throne of Scotland, 1290–1296, ed. E.L.G. Stones and G.G. Simpson (Oxford, 1978) (2 vols.)

The Exchequer Rolls of Scotland, ed. J. Stuart and G. Burnett, i (Edinburgh, 1878)

Extracts from the Account Rolls of the Abbey of Durham, ed. J.T. Fowler (3 vols.) (Surtees Society 1898–1901)

Foedera Conventiones, Litterae, et Acta Publica, ed. T. Rymer, Part II, vol. i (Record Commission, 1816)

Historical and Municipal Documents of Ireland A.D. 1172–1320, ed. J.T. Gilbert (RS, 1870)

Historical Papers and Letters from Northern Registers, ed. J. Raine (R.S., 1873)

The Inventories and Account Rolls of Jarrow and Monkwearmouth, ed. J. Raine (Surtees Society xxix, 1854)

The Libell of Englishe Policye, 1436, R. Pauli (Leipzig, 1878)

Liber Quotidianus Contrarotulatoris Garderobiae, ed. J. Nichols (Society of Antiquaries, 1787)

Memorials of the Abbey of St. Mary of Fountains, ed. J.R. Walbran and J.T. Fowler (Surtees Society xlii, 1863)

Memorials of Beverley Minster, ed. A.F. Leach, ii (Surtees Society cviii, 1903).

Memorials of the Church of SS Peter and Wilfrid, Ripon, ed. J.T. Fowler (3 vols.) (Surtees Society, 1882–86)

Nonarum Inquisitiones in Curia Scaccaria, ed. G. Vanderzee (Record Commission, London, 1807)

Northern Petitions, ed. C.M. Fraser (Surtees Society cxciv, 1981)

Northumberland and Durham Deeds from the Dodsworth MSS, ed. A.M. Oliver (Newcastle upon Tyne Record Commission, 1929)

Parliamentary Writs and Writs of Military Summons, ed. F. Palgrave (Record Commission, London, 1827–34)

Political Songs of England, from the Reign of John to that of Edward II, ed. T. Wright (Camden Society, 1839)

The Priory of Hexham, ed. J. Raine (2 vols.) (Surtees Society xlvi, 1865)

Raimes, F., *Proceedings of the Society of Antiquaries of Newcastle upon Tyne*, 3rd. series, iv (1909–10), 20–25

Regesta Regum Scottorum Vol. v, *Robert I*, ed. A.A.M. Duncan (Edinburgh, 1988)

The Register and Records of Holm Cultram, ed. F. Grainger and W.G. Collingwood (CWAAS Record Series vii, Kendal, 1929)

The Register of John de Halton, Bishop of Carlisle, 1292–1324, ed. W.N. Thompson (2 vols.) (Canterbury and York Society, 1913)

The Register of William Greenfield, Lord Archbishop of York, 1306–1315, ed. A.H. Hamilton Thompson and W. Brown (5 vols.) (Surtees Society, 1931–40)

The Register of William Melton, 1317–40, ed. R.M. Hill and D. Robinson (3 vols.) (Canterbury and York Society, 1977–88)

Registrum Palatinum Dunelmense, The Register of Richard de Kellawe, ed. T.D. Hardy (4 vols.) (R.S., 1873–78)

Rotuli Parliamentorum, 1272–1326, ed. J. Strachey et al. (London, 1767)

Rotuli Scotiae, ed. D. Macpherson, i (Record Commission, London, 1814–19)

The Royal Charters of Carlisle, ed. R.S. Ferguson (CWAAS Extra series x, 1894)

South Lancashire in the Reign of Edward II, ed. G.H. Tupling (Chetham Society, 3rd. series i, 1949)
Scotland in 1298, ed. H. Gough (London, 1888)
The Siege of Carlaverock, ed. N.H. Nicholas (1828)
Taxatio Ecclesiastica Angliae et Walliae Auctoritate P. Nicholai IV circa A.D. 1291, ed. J. Topham (Record Commission, London, 1802)
The War of St. Sardos (1323–1325): Gascon Correspondence and Diplomatic Documents, P. Chaplais (Camden 3rd series lxxxvii, 1954)
Year Book of 12 Edward II, ed. J.P. Collas (Selden Society, lxxxi, 1964)

C. SECONDARY WORKS

The Agrarian History of England, Vol ii, *1042–1350*, ed. H.E. Hallam (Cambridge, 1988)
Armstrong, O., *Edward Bruce's Invasion of Ireland* (London, 1923)
Baker, A.R.H., 'Evidence in the *Inquisitiones Nonarum* of contracting arable lands in England during the early fourteenth century', *EcHR* 2nd series xix (1966), 518–32
Baker, R.L., 'The Establishment of the English Wool Staple in 1313', *Speculum* xxxi (1956), 444–53
Balfour-Melville, E.W.M., 'Two John Crabbs', *SHR* xxix (1950), 31–34
Barron, E.M., *The Scottish War of Independence* (2nd edition, Inverness, 1934)
Barrow, G.W.S., 'The Anglo-Scottish Border', *NH* i (1966), 21–42
'Northern English Society in the Twelfth and Thirteenth Centuries', *NH* iv (1969), 1–28
The Kingdom of the Scots (London, 1973)
'Lothian in the War of Independence' *SHR* lv (1976), 151–71
'The Aftermath of War: Scotland and England in the Late Thirteenth and Early Fourteenth Centuries', *TRHS* xxvii 5th series (1978), 103–26
Robert Bruce and the Community of the Realm of Scotland (third edition, Edinburgh, 1988)
'A note on Falstone', *AA* 5th series ii (1974), 149–52
Barrow, G.W.S., and Royan, A., 'James Fifth Stewart of Scotland', in *Essays on the Nobility of Medieval Scotland*, ed. K.J. Stringer (Edinburgh, 1985), pp. 166–87
Bean, J.M.W., 'The Percy Acquisition of Alnwick', *AA* 4th series xxxii (1954), 309–19
'The Percies and their Estates in Scotland', *AA* 4th series xxxv (1957), 91–99
Before the Black Death: Studies in the Crisis of the Early Fourteenth Century, ed. B.M. Campbell (Manchester, 1991)
Beresford, M., *The New Towns of the Middle Ages* (London, 1967)
'The Lost Villages of Yorkshire, Part II', *Yorkshire Archaeological Journal* xxxviii (1952–55), 44–70
Blair, C.H., 'The Knights of Northumberland in 1278 and 1324', *AA* 4th series xxvii (1949), 122–76
'Members of Parliament for Northumberland (October 1258–January 1327)', *AA* 4th series x (1933), 140–77

'Northern Knights at Falkirk, 1298', *AA* 4th series xxv (1947), 68–114

'The Sheriffs of Northumberland, Part I (1076–1602)', *AA* xx, 4th series (1942), 11–90

Bradbury, J. *The Medieval Archer* (London, 1985)

Bradshaw, B., *The Irish Constitutional Revolution of the Sixteenth Century* (Cambridge, 1979), pp. 58–83

Brand, J., *The History and Antiquities of the County and Town of Newcastle Upon Tyne* (2 vols.) (London, 1789)

Britnell, R.H., 'The Proliferation of Markets in England, 1200–1349', *EcHR* 2nd series xxxiv (1981), 209–21

Broome, D.M., 'Exchequer Migrations to York in the Thirteenth and Fourteenth Centuries', in *Essays in Medieval History Presented to Thomas Frederick Tout*, ed. A.G. Little and F. M. Powicke (Manchester, 1925), pp. 291–300

Brown, R.A., Colvin, H.M., and Taylor, A.J., *The History of the King's Works* vol. i, *The Middle Ages* (HMSO, 1963)

Buck, M., *Politics, Finance and the Church in the Reign of Edward II: Walter Stapledon, Treasurer of England* (Cambridge, 1983)

Bulman, G.C., 'Carlisle Cathedral and its Development in the Thirteenth and Fourteenth Centuries', *CWAAS* new series xlix (1950), 87–117

Campbell, J., 'England, Scotland and the Hundred Years War', in *Europe in the Late Middle Ages*, ed. J.R. Hale, J.R.L. Highfield and B. Smalley (London, 1965), pp. 184–216

Carus-Wilson, E.M. and Coleman, O., *England's Export Trade, 1275–1547* (Oxford, 1963)

Chaplais, P., *The War of Saint-Sardos (1323–1325)* (Camden 3rd Series, lxxxvii, 1954)

Piers Gaveston, Edward II's Adoptive Brother (Oxford, 1994)

Childs, W., 'Finance and Trade under Edward II', in *Politics and Crisis in Fourteenth Century England*, ed. J.Taylor and W. Childs (Gloucester, 1990), pp. 19–37

Clack, P.A.G. and Gosling, P.F., *Archaeology in the North* (HMSO, 1976)

Cosgrove, A., *Late Medieval Ireland* (Dublin, 1981)

Coss, P.R., *The Knight in Medieval England, 1000–1400* (Stroud, 1993)

Cowling, G.C., *The History of Easingwold and the Forest of Galtres* (Huddersfield, 1967)

Curtis, E., *A History of Medieval Ireland from 1086 to 1513* (2nd edition, London, 1938)

Curwen, J.F., *Castles and Towers* (*CWAAS*, Extra series xiii, Kendal 1913)

Davies, J.C., 'An Assembly of Wool Merchants in 1322', *EHR* xxxi (1916), 596–606

The Baronial Opposition to Edward II (Cambridge, 1918)

'Shipping and Trade in Newcastle Upon Tyne, 1294–96', *AA* 4th series xxxi (1953), 175–204.

Davies, R.R., *Conquest, Coexistence and Change: Wales 1063–1415* (Oxford, 1987)

Domination and Conquest: The Experience of Ireland, Scotland and Wales 1100–1300 (Cambridge, 1990)

'The Peoples of Britain and Ireland, 1100–1400, i Identities', *TRHS* 6th series iv (1994), 1–20

'The Peoples of Britain and Ireland, 1100–1400, ii Names, Boundaries and Regnal Solidarities', *TRHS* 6th series v (1995), 1–20

Davis, I.M., *The Black Douglas* (London, 1974)

Davis, R.H.C., *The Medieval Warhorse: Origin, Development and Redevelopment* (London, 1989)

Dendy, F.W., 'Purchases at Corbridge Fair in 1298', *AA* 2nd series, ii (1906), 1–8

Denton, J.H., *Robert Winchelsea and the Crown, 1294–1313* (Cambridge, 1980)

Dickinson, J.C., *The Land of Cartmel: A History* (Kendal, 1980)

Dilley, 'German Merchants in Scotland 1297–1327', *SHR* xxvii (1948), 142–55

Dobson, R., 'Cathedral Chapters and Cathedral Cities: York, Durham and Carlisle in the Fifteenth Century', *NH* xix (1983), 15–44

Donnelly, J., 'Thomas of Coldingham, merchant and burgess of Berwick upon Tweed', *SHR* lix (1981), 105–25

Duffy, S., 'The Gaelic Account of The Bruce Invasion, *Cath Fhochairte Brighite*: Medieval Romance or Modern Forgery?', *Seanchas Ard Macha* xiii (1988), 59–121

'The 'Continuation' of Nicholas Trevet: A New Source for the Bruce Invasion', *PRIA* xci C (1991), 303–15

'The Bruce Brothers and the Irish Sea World, 1306–29', *Cambridge Medieval Celtic Studies* xxi (1991), 55–86

Duncan, A.A.M., 'The Community of the Realm of Scotland and Robert Bruce', *SHR* xlv (1966), 184–201

The Nation of Scots and the Declaration of Arbroath (Historical Association, 1970)

Scotland: The Making of the Kingdom (Edinburgh, 1975)

'The Scots Invasion of Ireland, 1315', in *The British Isles 1100–1500, Comparisons Contrasts and Connections*, ed. R.R. Davies, (Edinburgh, 1988), pp. 100–17

'The War of the Scots, 1306–23', *TRHS* 6th series, ii (1992), 125–51

'The Bruces of Annandale, 1100–1304', *TDGNHAS* lxix (1994), 89–102

Edwards, J.G., 'Sir Gruffydd Llwyd', *EHR* xxx (1915), 589–601

Calendar of Ancient Correspondence Concerning Wales, ed. J.G. Edwards (Cardiff, 1935)

The English Government at Work, 1327–1336, eds. J.F. Willard, J.R.Strayer and W.H. Dunham (3 vols.) (Cambridge, Mass., 1940–50)

Farrer, W., *Lancashire Inquests, Extents and Feudal Aids (1205–1355)*, ii (Lancashire and Cheshire Record Society, liv, 1907)

Fletcher, I., 'Brigham Church', *CWAAS* 1st series iv (1878–79), 149–73

Frame, R.,'The Bruces in Ireland, 1315–18', *IHS* xix (1974), 3–37

'Power and Society in the Lordship of Ireland 1272–1377', *P&P* lxxvi (1977), 3–33

English Lordship in Ireland, 1318–1361 (Oxford, 1982)

'The Campaign against the Scots in Munster', *IHS* xxiv (1985), 361–72

The Political Development of the British Isles 1100–1400 (Oxford, 1990)

Fraser, C.M., 'Edward I of England and the Regalian Franchise of Durham', *Speculum* xxxi (1956), 329–42

A History of Antony Bek, Bishop of Durham 1283–1311 (Oxford, 1957)

'The Life and Death of John Denton', *AA* 4th series xxxvii (1959)

'The Town Ditch of Newcastle Upon Tyne', *AA* 4th series xxxix (1961), 381–83

The Northumberland Lay Subsidy of 1296 (Society of Antiquaries of Newcastle Upon Tyne, 1968)

'The Pattern of Trade in the North-East of England, 1265–1350', *NH* iv (1969), 44–66

Fraser, C.M., and Emsley, K., 'Law and Society in Northumberland and Durham, 1290–1350', *AA* 4th series xlvii (1969), 47–70

Fryde, E.B., *William de la Pole* (London, 1988)

Fryde, N., 'Antonio Pessagno of Genoa, King's Merchant of Edward II of England', *Studi in Memoria di Federigo Melis* ii, (Rome 1978), 159–78

The Tyranny and Fall of Edward II (Cambridge, 1979)

Gemmill, E. and Mayhew, N., *Changing values in medieval Scotland: A study of prices, money and weights and measures* (Cambridge, 1995)

Greenwood, B., *Archaeology of the Boat* (London, 1976)

Greenwood, W., *The Redmans of Levens and Harewood* (Kendal, 1905)

Greeves, J.R.,'Robert I and the De Mandevilles of Ulster', *TDGNHAS* (3rd series) xxxiv (1955–56), 59–73

Griffiths, R.A. *Conquerors and Conquered in Medieval Wales* (Stroud, 1994)

Hallam, E., 'The Climate of Eastern England, 1250–1350', *Agricultural History Review* xxxii (1984), 124–32

Hamilton, J.S., *Piers Gaveston Earl of Cornwall, 1307–1312: Politics and Patronage in the Reign of Edward II* (Detroit, 1988)

Handbook of British Chronology, ed. F.M. Powicke and E.B. Fryde (Royal Historical Society, 2nd edition, 1961)

Harbottle, B., 'The Town Wall of Newcastle Upon Tyne: Consolidation and Excavation in 1968', *AA* 4th series, xlvii (1969), 71–95

Hartshorne, C.H.H., *Feudal and Military Antiquities of Northumberland and the Scottish Border* (London, 1858)

Harvey, B., 'The Population Trend in England between 1300 and 1348', *TRHS* 5th series xvi (1966), 23–42

Hay, D., 'Booty and Border Warfare', *TDGNHAS* 3rd series xxxi (1954), 145–66

Hedley, C.P., *Northumberland Families* (2 vols., Newcastle, 1968, 1970)

Hewitt, H.J., *The Black Prince's Expedition, 1355–57* (Manchester, 1958)

The Organisation of War under Edward III 1338–62 (Manchester, 1966)

Hill, R., 'An English Archbishop and the Scottish War of Independence', *Innes Review* xxii (1971), 59–71

The Labourer in the Vineyard (Borthwick Papers No. 35, 1968)

A History of York Minster, ed. G.E. Aylmer, and R. Cant (Oxford, 1977)

A History of Northumberland (15 vols.) (Northumberland County History Committee, Newcastle upon Tyne, 1893–1940)

The History of Scarborough, ed. A. Rowntree (London, 1931)

Holmes, G.A., *The Estates of the Higher Nobility in 14th Century England* (Cambridge, 1957)

Holt, J.C., *The Northerners* (Oxford, 1961)

Horrox, R., *The De La Poles of Hull* (East Yorkshire Local Record Society xxxviii, 1983)

Selected Records and Accounts of Medieval Hull 1293–1528 (Yorkshire Archaeological Society, Record Series, cxli, 1983)

Hunter, J.R., 'Medieval Berwick upon Tweed', *AA* 5th series x (1982), 67–124

An Inventory of the Historical Monuments of the City of York, Vol. ii, *The Defences* (RCHM, 1972)

Itinerary of Edward I Part II 1291–1307 (List and Index Society cxxxii, 1976)

The Itinerary of Edward II and His Household, 1307–1328, ed. E.M. Hallam (Lists and Index Society ccxi, 1984)

Jewel, H.M., 'North and South: the Antiquity of the Great Divide', *NH* xxvii (1991), 1–25

Jones, B.C., 'Notes on Caldewgate', appendix to D.R. Perriam, 'An Unrecorded Carlisle Church', *CWAAS* new series lxxix (1979), 51–55

'The Topography of Medieval Carlisle', *CWAAS* 2nd series lxxvi (1976), 77– 96

Keen, M., *Chivalry* (New Haven and London, 1984)

Keeney, B.C., 'Military Service and the Development of Nationalism in England, 1272–1327', *Speculum* xxii (1947), 534–49

Kershaw, I., 'The Great Famine and Agrarian Crisis in England', *P&P* lix (1973), 3–50, reprinted in Peasants, Knights and Heretics, ed. R.H. Hilton (Cambridge, 1976), pp. 85–132

Bolton Priory: the Economy of a Northern Monastery (Oxford, 1973)

'The Scots in the West Riding, 1318–19', *NH* xvii (1981), 231–39

King, D.J.C., *Castellarium Anglicanum, an Index and Bibliography of the Castles in England, Wales and the Islands* (2 vols.) (Millwood New York and London, 1983)

Kosminsky, E.A., *Studies in the Agrarian History of England in the Thirteenth Century* (Oxford, 1956)

Lapsley, G.T., *The County Palatine of Durham* (Cambridge Mass., 1900)

Leadman, A.D.H., 'The Battle of Bylands Abbey', *YAJ* viii (1884), 475–80

Little, A.G., 'The Authorship of the Lanercost Chronicle', *EHR* xxxi (1916), 269–79

Lomas, R.A., 'Developments in Land Tenure on the Prior of Durham's Estate in the Later Middle Ages', *NH* xiii (1977), 27–43

North-East England in the Middle Ages (Edinburgh, 1992)

Longley, K.M., 'The Scottish Invasion of 1327: A Glimpse of the Aftermath (Wigton Church Accounts, 1328-9), *CWAAS* 2nd series lxxxiii (1983), 63–72

Lloyd, T.H., *The English Wool Trade in the Middle Ages* (Cambridge, 1977)

The Movement of Wool Prices in Medieval England (*EcHR* Supplement 6, 1973)

Lucas, H.S., 'John Crabbe, Flemish Pirate, Merchant and Adventurer', *Speculum* xx (1945), 334–50

Lydon, J.F., 'Edward I, Ireland and the War in Scotland, 1303–1304', in *England and Ireland in the Later Middle Ages: Essays to Jocelyn Otway-Ruthven,* ed. J. Lydon (Dublin, 1981), pp. 43–59

'An Irish Army in Scotland, 1296', *Irish Sword* v (1961–62), 184–89

'The Hobelar: An Irish Contribution to Mediaeval Warfare', *Irish Sword* ii (1954–56), 12–16

'Irish Levies in the Scottish Wars, 1296–1302', *Irish Sword* v (1963), 207–17

'Edward II and the Revenues of Ireland in 1311–12', *IHS* xiv (1964), 39–57

'The Dublin Purveyors and the Wars in Scotland, 1296–1324', *Keimelia: Studies in Medieval Archaeology and History in Memory of Tom Delaney*, ed. Gearoíd Mac Niocoill and Patrick F. Wallace (Galway, 1988), pp 435–48

Lynch, M., *Scotland: A New History* (London, 1991)

McDonnell, J., 'The Role of Transhumance in Northern England', *NH* xxiv (1988), 1–17

MacIomhair, D., 'Bruce's Invasion and the First Campaign in County Louth', *Irish Sword* x (1971–72), 188–212

MacIvor, D., 'Estate of Benedict Pippard of Pippardeston, A.D. 1316', *Louth Archaeological Journal* xiv (1957–60), 165–69

McNamee, C.J., 'William Wallace's Invasion of Northern England, 1297', *NH* xxvi (1990), 40–58

'Buying off Robert Bruce: An Account of Monies Paid to the Scots by Cumberland Communities in 1313–14', *CWAAS* new series xcii (1992), 77–89

McNeill, T.E., *Anglo-Norman Ulster: The History and Archaeology of an Irish Barony, 1177–1400* (Edinburgh, 1980)

Maddicott, J.R., *Thomas of Lancaster* (Oxford, 1970)

The English Peasantry and the Demands of the Crown 1294–1341 (P&P Supplement 1, 1975), reprinted in *Landlords, Peasants and Politics in Medieval England*, ed. T.H. Aston (Cambridge, 1987), pp. 285–359

Middleton, A.E., *Sir Gilbert de Middleton* (Newcastle, 1918)

Miller, E., *War in the North* (University of Hull Publications, 1960)

'Farming in Northern England During the Twelfth and Thirteenth Centuries', *NH* xi (1976 for 1975), 1–16

War, Taxation and the English Economy in the late Thirteenth and early Fourteenth Centuries', in *War and Economic Development: Essays in Memory of David Joslin*, ed. J.M. Winter (Cambridge, 1975), pp. 11–31

Morris, J.E., *The Welsh Wars of Edward I* (Oxford, 1901)

'Cumberland and Westmorland Levies in the time of Edward I and Edward II', *CWAAS*, new series iii (1903), 307–27

'Mounted Infantry in Medieval Warfare', *TRHS* 3rd series viii (1914), 77–102

NicGhiollanhaith, A., 'Dynastic Warfare and Historical Writing in North Munster, 1276–1350', *Cambridge Medieval Celtic Studies* ii (1981), 73–89

Nicholson, R., 'The Last Campaign of Robert Bruce', *EHR* lxxvii (1962), 233–246

'A Sequel to Edward Bruce's Invasion of Ireland', *SHR* xlii (1963–64), 30–40

Edward III and the Scots (Oxford, 1965)

Scotland: The Later Middle Ages (Edinburgh, 1974)

Neilson, G., *Peel: Its Meaning and Derivation* (Glasgow, 1893)

A New History of Ireland, Vol. ii *Medieval Ireland, 1169–1534*, ed. A. Cosgrove (Oxford, 1987)

Offler, H.S., 'Murder on Framwellgate Bridge', *AA* 5th series xvi (1988), 193–211

Ó'Murchadha, D., 'Is the O'Neill–MacCarthy Letter of 1317 a Forgery?', *IHS* xxiii (1982–83), 61–67

Otway-Ruthven, A.J., *A History of Medieval Ireland* (London, 1968)

Phillips, J.R.S., *Aymer de Valence, Earl of Pembroke, 1307–1324* (Oxford, 1972)

'Documents on the Early Stages of the Bruce Invasion of Ireland, 1315–1316', *PRIA*, lxxix, C (1979), 247–70

'The Mission of John de Hothum to Ireland, 1315–16', in *England and Ireland in the Later Middle Ages: Essays in honour of Jocelyn Otway-Ruthven*, ed. J.F. Lydon (Dublin, 1981), pp. 62–85

'The Irish Remonstrance of 1317: an International Perspective', *IHS* xxvii (1990), 112–29

Powicke, M., 'Edward II and Military Obligation', *Speculum* xxxi (1956), 92–119

Military Obligation in Medieval England (Oxford, 1962)

'The English Commons in Scotland in 1322 and the Deposition of Edward II', *Speculum* xxxv (1960), 556–62

Prestwich, M.C., 'Victualling Estimates for English Garrisons in Scotland during the Early Fourteenth Century', *EHR* lxxxii (1967), 536–43

'Isabella de Vescy and the Custody of Bamburgh Castle', *Bulletin of the Institute of Historical Research* xliv (1971), 148–52

War, Politics and Finance under Edward I (London, 1972)

York Civic Ordinances, 1301 (Borthwick Papers 49, 1976)

The Three Edwards: War and State in England 1272–1377 (London, 1980)

'English Castles in the Reign of Edward II', *Journal of Medieval History* viii (1982), 159–78

'Cavalry Service in Early Fourteenth Century England', in *War and Government in the Middle Ages,* ed. J.B. Gillingham and J.C. Holt (Woodbridge, 1984), pp. 147–58

Edward I (London, 1988)

'Gilbert de Middleton and the Attack on the Cardinals, 1317', in *Warriors and Churchmen in the High Middle Ages: Essays to Karl Leyser*, ed. T. Reuter (London, 1992), pp. 179–194

Raine, J., *The History and Antiquities of North Durham* (London, 1852)

Ramm, H.G., McDowall, R.W., Mercer, E., *Sheilings and Bastles* (RCHM, London, 1970)

Reid, W.S., 'Trade, Traders and Scottish Independence', *Speculum* xxix (1954), 210– 22

'The Scots and the Staple Ordinance of 1313', *Speculum* xxxiv (1959), 598– 610

'Sea Power and the Anglo-Scottish War 1296–1328', *The Mariners' Mirror* xlvi (1960), 7–23

Reynolds, S., *Kingdoms and Communities in Western Europe, 900–1300* (Oxford, 1984)

Robinson, D., *Beneficed Clergy in Cleveland and the East Riding, 1306–1340* (Borthwick Papers no. 37, 1969)

Sayles, G.O., 'The Siege of Carrickfergus Castle, 1315–16', *IHS* (1956–57), 94–100

Scammell, J., 'Robert I and the North of England', *EHR* lxxiii (1958), 385–403

'Some Aspects of Medieval English Monastic Government: The Case of Geoffrey de Burdon, Prior of Durham (1313–1321)', *Revue Bénédictine* lxviii (1958), 226–50

Scott, J., *Berwick Upon Tweed* (London, 1888)

Scott, Sir W., *The Border Antiquities of England and Scotland* (London, 1817)

The Scottish Medieval Town, eds. M. Lynch, M. Spearman, G. Stell (Edinburgh, 1988)

Simpson, W.D., 'Dunstanburgh Castle', *AA* 4th series xvi (1939), 31–48

    'Further Notes on Dunstanburgh Castle', *AA* 4th series xxvii (1949), 1–28

    'Brough-under-Stainmore: The Castle and the Church', *CWAAS* 2nd series xlvi (1946), 223–95

    'Warkworth: A Castle of Livery and Maintenance', *AA* 4th series xv (1938), 115–36

Smallwood, T.M., 'An unpublished early account of Bruce's murder of Comyn', *SHR* liv (1975), 1–10

Smith, B., 'A County Community in Fourteenth Century Ireland: The Case of Louth', *EHR* cviii (1993), 561–88

Smith, J. Beverley, 'Gruffydd Llwyd and the Celtic Alliance', *Bulletin of the British Board of Celtic Studies* xxvi (1976), 463–78

    'Edward II and the Allegiance of Wales', *Welsh Historical Review* viii (1976–77), 139–71

Steer K.A., and Bannerman, J.M.W., *Late Medieval Monumental Sculpture in the West Highlands* (Royal Commission on the Ancient and Historical Monuments of Scotland, 1977)

Stevenson, A., 'The Flemish Dimension of the Auld Alliance' in *Scotland and the Low Countries 1124–1994*, ed. G.G. Simpson (East Linton, 1996)

Stones, E.L.G., 'The English Mission to Edinburgh in 1328', *SHR* xxviii (1949), 97–118

    'The Anglo-Scottish Negotiations of 1327', *SHR* xxx (1951), 49–54

    'An Addition to the *Rotuli Scotiae*', *SHR* xxix (1950), 23–51

Studies of Field Systems of the British Isles, ed. R.A. Butlin and A.H.R. Baker (Cambridge, 1973)

Summerson, H., *Medieval Carlisle: the city and the borders from the late eleventh to the mid sixteenth century,* i (CWAAS Extra series xxv, 1993)

    'The Place of Carlisle in the Commerce of Northern England in the Thirteenth Century', *Thirteenth Century England: Proceedings of the Newcastle Upon Tyne Conference, 1985*, ed. P.R. Coss and S.D. Lloyd (Newcastle, 1985), pp. 142–49

Suppe, F. C., *Military Institutions on the Welsh Marches: Shropshire, A.D. 1066–1300* (London, 1994)

Surtees, R., *The History and Antiquities of the County Palatinate of Durham* (London, 1816–40)

Tate, G., *History of the Borough, Castle and Barony of Alnwick* (Alnwick, 1866)

Tuck, J.A., 'Northumbrian Society in the Fourteenth Century', *NH* vi (1971), 22–39

    'War and Society in the Medieval North', *NH* xxi (1985), 33–52

    'The Emergence of a Northern Nobility', *NH* xxii (1986), 1–17

Tupling, G.H., *An Economic History of Rossendale* (Chetham Society, 1927).

    South Lancashire in the Reign of Edward II (Chetham Society I, 3rd series, 1949)

Turner, H.L., *Town Defences in England and Wales* (London, 1970)

Victoria County History of Yorkshire North Riding (2 vols.) (London, 1914)

East Riding (5 vols.) (Oxford, 1969–84)

City of York (Oxford, 1961)

Waites, B., *Moorland and Vale Farming in North-East Yorkshire: The Monastic Contribution in the Thirteenth and Fourteenth Centuries* (Borthwick Papers No. 32, 1967)

Walker, D. *Medieval Wales* (Cambridge, 1990)

Watt, J.A., 'Negotiations between Edward II and John XXII concerning Ireland', *IHS* x (1956), 1–15

Webster, B., 'Anglo-Scottish Relations, 1296–1389: Some Recent Essays', *SHR* lxxiv (1995), 97–108

West Yorkshire: An Archaeological Survey to 1500 (3 vols.) (West Yorkshire Metropolitan County Council, Wakefield, 1981)

Whitewell, R.J., and Johnson, C., 'The Newcastle Galley', *AA* 4th series ii (1926)

Wilkinson, B., *The Constitutional History of Medieval England, 1216–1399* (3 vols.) (London, 1948–58)

Willard, J.F., 'The Scotch Raids and the Fourteenth Century Taxation of Northern England', *University of Colorado Studies* v, No. 4 (1908), 240–42

Wright, T., *Political Songs* (Camden Society, 1839)

D. UNPRINTED THESES

Blake, J.B., 'Some aspects of the Trade of Newcastle upon Tyne in the Fourteenth Century' (Bristol University M.A., 1962)

Boyle, M.L., 'The Early History of the Wardens of the Marches of England towards Scotland, 1296–1377' (Hull University M.A., 1980)

Camsell, M.,'The Development of a Northern Town in the Later Middle Ages: The City of Durham, c. 1250–1540' (York University D. Phil., 1985)

Halcrow, E.M., 'The Administration and Agrarian Policy of the Manors of the Cathedral Priory of Durham' (Oxford University B. Litt., 1949)

Hall, I., 'The Lords and Lordships of the English West March: Cumberland and Westmorland from circa 1250 to circa 1350' (Durham University Ph.D., 1986)

Lomas, R.A., 'Durham Cathedral Priory as a Landowner and Landlord, 1290–1540' (Durham University Ph.D., 1973)

Lydon, J.F., 'Ireland's Participation in the Military Activities of the English Kings in the Thirteenth and Fourteenth Century' (London University Ph.D., 1955)

Marshall, D.W.H., 'The Organisation of the English Occupation of Scotland, 1296–1461' (Oxford University B. Litt., 1925)

Olsen, C.P.M., 'The Older Settlements of North Northumberland' (London University M.A., 1947)

Stevenson, A., 'Trade between Scotland and the Low Countries in the Middle Ages' (Aberdeen University Ph.D., 1982)

Wrathmell, S.,'Deserted and Shrunken Villages in Southern Northumberland from the Twelfth to the Twentieth Centuries' (Cardiff University Ph.D., 1976)

Index

Abbreviations